ENDORSEMENTS FOR CALL

In *Called to Worship*, Dr. Vernon Whaley systematically shows us, from Genesis to Revelation, how biblical worship has always been and always will be man's obedient response to God's revelation of Himself. This presentation of truth transcends much of the modern discussion of worship, and puts worship in its rightful place. Whaley shows us how worship is from God, through God and back to God! *Called to Worship* serves as a powerfully practical resource for church leaders, teachers, students and all who consider themselves worshipers of the Living God.

—**Alicia Williamson Garcia**
Artist, Conference Speaker, Worship Leader, Author
President, In-Worship Inc.

Too many courses, conferences, and publications about worship remain focused primarily on techniques. What the church needs is not primarily a better sound system or more seamless flow of worship songs. Instead, we need the ongoing renovation of our theological imagination. We need to set aside the distorted notions of God that thrive even inside the church and its worship life. The only way to do that is to open our Bibles and to constantly chisel away the idols of our own making. *Called to Worship* is an accessible invitation to this crucial and life-giving project. It will not only teach readers about worship; it will also equip readers to teach others.

—**Rev. Dr. John D. Witvliet**
Director, Calvin Institute of Christian Worship
Professor of Music and Worship, Calvin College and Calvin Theological Seminary

Vernon M. Whaley has accomplished the near impossible. He's given us a biblical tour of worship that covers the Bible coast to coast without getting bogged down on side streets or back allies. It's a terrific study—simple enough for teens, deep enough for pastors. Informal, yet informative. A fresh resource for a new generation, a rich treat for mature believers. Read it and you'll feel called to worship!

—**Robert J. Morgan**
Pastor and Author

Called to Worship is an amazing and engaging read. I simply could not put it down! Dr. Whaley takes the reader on a journey through God's Word, beginning in Genesis with lessons on worship from creation and climaxing with the heavenly worship of Revelation. I've read many books on worship, but I've not seen one that so effectively teaches the history and doctrines of worship in simple and relevant terms. Dr. Whaley brings fresh and brilliant application of age-old truths to our daily, modern lives. This book should be read by every believer who longs to offer authentic and acceptable worship to God.

—Dwayne Moore
President, *Next Level Worship*
Author of *Pure Praise: A Heart-Focused Bible Study on Worship*

As you read Vernon Whaley's new book entitled *Called to Worship: from the Dawn of Creation to the Final Amen*, may you get insight into worship that you have never had before. But more importantly as you read this book, may God stir your heart to reach out and touch Him. And, may God touch you in return.

—Elmer L. Towns
Dean, School of Religion
Liberty Baptist Theological Seminary
Lynchburg, Virginia

I am impressed with Vernon Whaley's book on worship. It reads like a continuing story or an unfolding of history. You can't do better than that. Also, the text reads like the observations of one who has been there, rather than one who talks about something he's never experienced. And, it will bless those who study its pages.

—Dr. John Baker Thomas
Minister of Music
First Baptist Church, Woodbridge, VA

Called To Worship is thorough in its scope of the study of worship. It is incredibly inspiring and spiritually challenging. I can readily say that this study of the progression of worship through the scriptures has changed my perspective on God's plan for my personal worship. From the innocence of worship in the garden, to the worship of David and Solomon, and the exciting culmination of "perfect worship in a perfect place," heaven, we can see God's hand in drawing us to Himself.

Vernon Whaley skillfully informs us from the scriptures and then challenges us to follow God's call to worship in a way that "transcends time and culture."

—**Don Marsh**
Composer/Arranger
Christian Recording Producer

Called to Worship may be the most thorough, complete, concise book on Biblical worship that I have ever read. In a day where worship has such a broad range of emphasis and resource it is encouraging to have a book that covers the worship perspective from creation to revelation, from private to public, from heaven to earth, and from mind to heart.

Dr. Whaley's systematic approach to the history of worship is both informational and inspirational. Every believer needs to take a good hard look at the scriptural commands to worship God. This book provides a compelling argument that worship is God's strategic plan for ALL creation. Worship is not an option, it is a command!

—**Terry W. Williams**
Team Strategist
Music & Worship Ministries
Florida Baptist Convention

There are three reasons why Vernon Whaley is a major leader in the community of worship scholars. First, he did graduate work in the disciplines of both music and theology. Second, he is somewhat of a Renaissance man having worked in the local church as a minister of worship, and as a university professor in academia, and as a publisher and producer in the music industry. Third, and most importantly, he has a passion for the Lord and for studying His Word for principles and values to guide each of us in praising the Lord. This work beautifully reflects all of this.

—**Don Wyrtzen**
Composer and Author
Professor of Church Music
Southwestern Baptist Theological Seminary

Vernon M. Whaley has written a wonderful book that gives us a glimpse into that beautiful calling that is on all of our lives . . . worship. Vernon is doing more to impact the importance of worship in our churches and in our lives than anyone else I know. And by reading this book, you will understand why Vernon is so passionate about the importance of worshipping our Lord and Savior Jesus Christ.

—Jonathan than Falwell
Senior Pastor,
"Thomas Road Baptist Church, Lynchburg, Virginia

This is a biblically-based and practical book which, if carefully read and applied by worship leaders and pastors, would very significantly impact the church of Jesus Christ worldwide! I found it informative, convincing, and accurate in presenting the essential whys of biblical worship both private and corporate. I particularly appreciate the author's attempt to establish the cannon-wide priority of worship. Well done, Vernon. You have made a significant contribution to the ongoing dialogue on this all-important issue.

—Dr. Gordon L. Borror
Professor of Church Music and Worship
Southwestern Baptist Theological Seminary

Having just turned the final pages of Dr. Whaley's engaging work, I feel as though I have just completed a worshipper's pilgrimage through the pages of time. In fact, my sandals still bear the dust of this extraordinary walk. Both educational and inspirational, thought provoking and captivating, this work is a must for any child of God who has worshiped like a son or daughter at the feet of the Father.

—Dr. Ron Upton
Minister of Family Music & Worship
Idlewood Baptist Church

CALLED TO WORSHIP

CALLED TO WORSHIP

FROM THE DAWN OF CREATION
TO THE FINAL AMEN

VERNON M. WHALEY

THOMAS NELSON
Since 1798

NASHVILLE   DALLAS   MEXICO CITY   RIO DE JANEIRO

Published in Nashville, Tennessee, by Thomas Nelson. Thomas Nelson is a registered trademark of Thomas Nelson, Inc.

Thomas Nelson, Inc., titles may be purchased in bulk for educational, business, fund-raising, or sales promotional use. For information, please e-mail SpecialMarkets@ThomasNelson.com.

Scripture versions used:

THE AMPLIFIED BIBLE: NEW TESTAMENT. © 1958 by the Lockman Foundation (used by permission).

THE HOLMAN CHRISTIAN STANDARD BIBLE (HCSB). © 1999, 2000, 2002, 2003 by Broadman and Holman Publishers. All rights reserved.

The Holy Bible, King James Version (KJV).

The Living Bible (TLB). © 1971. Used by permission of Tyndale House Publishers, Inc., Wheaton, Illinois 60189. All rights reserved.

The Message by Eugene H. Peterson. © 1993, 1994, 1995, 1996, 2000. Used by permission of NavPress Publishing Group. All rights reserved.

The NEW AMERICAN STANDARD BIBLE (NASB)® © The Lockman Foundation 1960, 1962, 1963, 1968, 1971, 1972, 1973, 1975, 1977, 1995. Used by permission.

The New Century Version (NCV) ®. © 2005 by Thomas Nelson, Inc. Used by permission. All rights reserved.

The HOLY BIBLE: NEW INTERNATIONAL VERSION (NIV)®. © 1973, 1978, 1984 by International Bible Society. Used by permission of Zondervan Publishing House. All rights reserved.

THE NEW KING JAMES VERSION (NKJV). © 1982 by Thomas Nelson, Inc. Used by permission. All rights reserved.

The Holy Bible, New Living Translation (NLT). © 1996. Used by permission of Tyndale House Publishers, Inc., Wheaton, Illinois 60189. All rights reserved.

The NEW REVISED STANDARD VERSION of the Bible (NRSV). © 1989 by the Division of Christian Education of the National Council of the Churches of Christ in the U.S.A. All rights reserved.

The REVISED STANDARD VERSION of the Bible. © 1946, 1952, 1971, 1973 by the Division of Christian Education of the National Council of the Churches of Christ in the U.S.A. Used by permission.

ISBN 978-1-4016-8008-4 (TP)

Library of Congress Cataloging-in-Publication Data
ISBN 978-1-4185-1958-2

Printed in the United States of America
13 14 15 16 17 — 5 4 3 2 1

To Beth Whaley:

My wife, companion, best friend, encourager, strength, and worship partner—Thank you for your support, your love, and your patience with all my inattention, one-sided conversation, and long nights.

CONTENTS

FOREWORD

I FIRST LEARNED OF VERNON M. WHALEY THROUGH MY COLLEGE-age son, Jordan, who was studying under Dr. Whaley's leadership at Liberty University's Center for Worship. Growing up as a pastor's son and actively involved in local church music ministry, Jordan understands much about worship and is generally unimpressed with superficial and trendy approaches. Yet, the depth of insight and personal care expressed by Vernon Whaley awakened in Jordan a fresh passion for the presence of God and a keen desire for excellence in worship.

I have been a Senior Pastor of large churches for almost 25 years. In that time, God has allowed me to lead my congregations in extraordinary experiences of worship-based prayer through prayer summits, all-night prayer meetings, weekly prayer times, seasons of fasting, and national conferences hosted at our church. Still, my heart yearns for more. *Called to Worship* has stimulated even greater thirst through a deeper understanding of how vital worship is to my soul and how pleasing it is to God.

Today, as I have the privilege of speaking and leading renewal events in dozens of churches and conferences each year I see the good, the bad and the ugly of worship. I am more convinced than ever that Dr. Whaley's thorough, biblical treatment of worship like the one offered here is desperately needed.

In Ephesians 3:18–19, Paul prayed that we "may be able to comprehend with all the saints what is the width and length and depth and height—to know the love of Christ which passes knowledge; that you may be filled with all the fullness of God." His understanding of these truths compelled him to worship with these words, "Now to Him who is able to do exceedingly abundantly above all that we ask or think, according to the power that works in us, to Him be glory in the church by Christ Jesus to all generations, forever and ever. Amen."

Called to Worship helped me experience the answer to Paul's prayer as each page called me to comprehend with biblical clarity and genuine passion the "width and length and depth and height" of all that is ours through a loving relationship of worship with God through Christ. It gave me fresh faith to long for His glory in the church, in this generation and for many generations to come.

Vernon Whaley will help you see the *width* of biblical worship as these chapters give you a clear look beyond our narrow understanding of our cultural biases. *Called to Worship* takes us past the "worship wars" that result from our myopic preoccupation with personal preferences. In this book you'll discover the grand experience of the human soul throughout human history in countless forms, locations and unique experiences of worship.

You will be amazed with the *length* of biblical worship as you see its span from eternity past to eternity future. From creation, through the Garden of Eden, within Old and New Testament history and into eternity future the line of God's loving heart is drawn here. You will see that worship invites us beyond our brief life and past the millennia of earthly time to the very presence of our holy, almighty God reigning on the throne of His eternal heavens.

The *depth* of genuine worship presented in each chapter will allow you to look into the heart of God to His profound purposes and gaze upon the deep experiences of common people in uncommon moments in God's presence. You will find yourself longing for a deeper personal experience of the privilege and power of worship.

Finally, *Called to Worship* will inspire you with the *height* of worship. As I read this book, the expectation and experience of worship seemed to crescendo to the grand finale of worship in eternity. Whaley leaves us at the height of our everlasting preoccupation with the glory of God and the worthy Lamb that was slain. It is almost as if we can hear the mighty chorus of the redeemed as we sing a new song and shout hallelujahs with the angels of heaven and the saints of the ages. As Whaley reminds us, "We're not home yet. The best is yet to come."

I often define worship as the "response of all I am to the revelation of all He is." The book will motivate you to respond in ways you never have before. The revelation of God and His plan for worship is presented with unprecedented insight and application. As you experience the width, length, depth and height of worship you will embrace the one who *is* able to do "exceedingly abundantly above all that we ask or think, according to the power that works in us" and you will cry out, "to Him be glory in the church by Christ Jesus to all generations, forever and ever. Amen." And you will long for all of this to start anew, in your own heart.

Today, I know Vernon M. Whaley as a colleague and friend. I concur with my son Jordan's assessment and I count it a privilege to commend this book to you. It thrills me to know that a new generation of worship leaders is learning from Dr. Whaley's experience, depth of insight and personal passion. It excites me even more to know that his expertise and teaching can now be reproduced in individuals and churches around the world through this extraordinary resource.

— Dr. Daniel Henderson,
President & Founder
Strategic Renewal

INTRODUCTION

IT WAS ABOUT NOON, AND HE SAT DOWN BY A WELL, TO REST.

Enter, a Samaritan woman.

Jesus asked for water. He was seeking.

The woman was seeking too.

Jesus knew her: her history, suspicions, questions, fears. He also knew her *needs*—and how to meet them. A life of failure, of disappointment—perhaps even abuse—had left her hard, bitter—and very thirsty.

Jesus could quench her thirst. And He told her so.

But the woman was incredulous. She had already tried drinking from the wells of tradition, failed relationships, religion, and sexual promiscuity. Sadly, she'd discovered that water from those sources did not satisfy. Yet *this* man—what was His name?—was presenting a different type of water, and with it, *hope*.

What was that He had said? "You'll never thirst again"? Jesus was offering something more, something eternal—that would fulfill this woman's deepest yearnings and heal the hurts in her heart. He was offering a *relationship* with God—through worship.

The Samaritan woman's perception of God—her "theology"—was a half-breed mix of Hebrew doctrine and the pantheism of the cultures around her. "You Samaritans worship something you do not understand," Jesus told her (John 4:22 NCV). But desperate to bring her to understanding, He said, "[My] Father . . . is *actively seeking* . . . people to worship *him*" (v. 24 NCV, emphasis added).

The Father was seeking *her*.

GOD IS SEEKING WORSHIPPERS!

As I sat outside of my cabin at Camp NaCoMe, Bible in hand, I breathed in the smell of frying bacon and gazed toward the eastern horizon. A picturesque sunrise flaunted stunning reds, oranges, and ambers. *Wow,* I thought. *God has really outdone Himself.*

Opening my Bible, I glanced down at John 4—and saw it for the first time: "The Father is actively seeking . . ."

Hmm . . .

I knew God loved me. He had forgiven me, saved me, healed me, and called me into ministry. But *seeking me?*

Suddenly, I "got it." This was one of those "aha" moments you hear about. *God is in pursuit,* I thought. *Of ME!*

I know what you're thinking. "Do you mean to tell me that God is actually pursuing *me* as a worshipper?"

Yes. *Actively.*

The Bible tells us that "the eyes of the Lord are always upon [us]" (Deut. 11:12 KJV), and as He watches, His spirit is ever at work, moving, convicting, suggesting, *calling.* And today, God is calling men and women, boys and girls, from every race and culture. He's calling the professional and the laborer. He's calling me—and He's calling *you*—to worship Him.

WHAT IS WORSHIP?

But, wait. What *is* worship? What do we mean when we use the word? *Merriam-Webster's Collegiate Dictionary* (11th ed.) defines worship as "reverence offered a divine being" as well as the "act of expressing such reverence." So, we are to show God *reverence.* But how? What acts demonstrate reverence for God? Does the Bible offer guidance?

In Scripture, the Hebrew word for worship is *shachah,* meaning "to kneel, stoop, prostrate oneself, or throw oneself down, in reverence." Closely related are the Hebrew words *shabach,* "to shout to the Lord"; *yadah,* "to worship with uplifted hands"; *halal,* "to celebrate God foolishly and boast about His attributes (love, mercy, goodness, etc.)"; and *tehillah,* "to sing spontaneous songs of praise."

In the Greek, the word for worship, *proskuneo*, means to express deep respect or adoration—by kissing, with words, or by bowing down. Associated words include *epaineo*, "to commend or applaud"; *aineo*, "to praise God"; and *sebomai*, "to revere."

That's a lot of words, with diverse definitions. And these aren't the only biblical terms that relate to worship. *Strong's Exhaustive Concordance*[1] offers a wealth of information regarding the various words for *worship* and its synonyms. But how can we make all of this information relevant? When we tie all of these words and their meanings together, what does it all boil down to?

Love. Deuteronomy 6:5 says, "Love the LORD your God with all your heart, with all your soul, and with all your strength" (NKJV). Jesus repeated this command three times in the New Testament (Matt. 22:37, Mark 12:30, Luke 10:27). Why? Because it's what we were made for—to love God. And if we are in *love* with Him, we will naturally want to worship Him (*shachah*). He's done so much for you and me that it only seems right to fall down before Him (*cagad*), to throw up our hands in surrender (*yadah*), to sing His praises (*zamar*)—to *worship* Him.

But, again, how?

NOT THROUGH RITUAL AND ROUTINE

Recently, I attended a popular and well-known "worship conference" packed with pastors, worship leaders, and laypersons eager to learn techniques for successful worship ministry. Famous practitioners, anxious to demonstrate their latest worship "tools," lined the exhibit hall. Some peddled how-to books on worship. Others presented sound, lighting, and stage design concepts. Worship "artists" shared personal stories as well as principles of songwriting, programming, and praise-team building, all designed to develop a *better* worship experience.

Soon, though, it became obvious that not only would there be no extended prayer for God's guidance in these sessions, but there would also be no serious study or discussion of the *biblical* principles of worship. It was all about *routine*—with no explanation of why we go through such routine.

Sadly, statements from the distinguished panel of worship "profession-als" revealed deficiencies in their knowledge of the Bible's clear teachings on how mankind is to worship God. These experts also seemed unaware of any scholarly works on biblical worship. They simply knew what they liked, and liked what they knew, and that's all they taught, with little regard for the opinions of the broader evangelical community—or God Himself.

Since that conference, I have traveled to many others and have found that the lack of biblical understanding of worship is not unique. People all over, from pew to pulpit, have heads full of misguided notions on the kind of worship that pleases God. Yet hundreds of books, articles, pamphlets, CDs, and DVDs abound on the topic, and more are produced each year by the "seasoned" worship gurus of our age.

So, why another book? Why read *Called to Worship?*

WHY ANOTHER BOOK ON WORSHIP?

In recent years, a generation of younger evangelicals has joined the ranks of ministry. They need fresh resources that present worship in concise language that represents their postmodern experiences. *Called to Worship* meets this dynamic need.

But a second generation—today's high school and entry-level college students—is also in need of resources. These passionate student musicians are the ones leading youth groups in worship *every week*. They desperately need a firm grasp on the principles of genuine worship that they can teach to their peers in the *here and now*. This book will meet their need for solid, biblical material on worship that they can apply in today's culture.

Called to Worship also meets the need of the academic community. In answer to the growing interest of young people to skillfully practice and lead worship, evangelical colleges around the world are establishing wor-ship curriculum and degrees. But in the past, professors have discovered a shortage of resources to address the diverse dynamics of their students and prepare them as worship practitioners. This book is designed to help these educators convey the truth about worship to their hungry classrooms.

Finally, this book will meet *your* needs. Whether you're a Sunday school teacher, a cell-group leader, a conference speaker, or a homeschooling parent, *Called to Worship* is an easy-to-understand teaching tool that will help you present God's story about worship to your audience—of one, or a thousand and one.

FEATURES OF *CALLED TO WORSHIP*

Called to Worship is not intended as an exhaustive exegesis or treatise on worship. It is instead informal, almost casual, in communicating truth to a twenty-first-century audience.

In *Called to Worship*, you will read the history of Yahweh worship—offered first by the hosts of heaven in eternity past, and then by mankind, from Creation to the present day. We'll study the battles that have been waged against worshippers—and worship itself—through the ages, as well as the challenges we face today as we seek to worship God in a manner that brings Him pleasure. At the end of each chapter, in a separate "Principles of Worship" section, I will offer an abstract to guide you in a *lifestyle* of worship, as well as practicable approaches that you can use in your time with God. These are meant to prepare you for *eternal worship*, which we'll study in the book's final chapter.

Above all, you will read about God's love for you, demonstrated through His repeated revelation of Himself to mankind. It is my hope that in seeing God's continued show of love to humanity, you will be inspired to a greater love for Him—and a deeper worship.

But before you and I can love God, and consequently worship Him, we must first *know* Him. So, let's start at the very beginning. Before there was a sun. Before there was a moon. Before there was you—or me. And, let's meet the One—the *only* One—worthy of our love . . . and our worship.

PART I

Old Testament Principles of Worship

Be exalted, O God, above the heavens.

Let Your glory be above all the earth.

—Psalm 57:5 NKJV

I

CREATION: A CALL TO WORSHIP

IT SEEMS AS IF JUST YESTERDAY MY BROTHER, RODNEY, AND I stood outside the doghouse of our Siberian husky, Chena, as she gave birth to a litter of six puppies. At eleven and thirteen, we had no idea that nature was simply acting out a normal, God-ordained process. But intuition told us we were witnessing a miracle. We had absolutely nothing to do with this phenomenon. We could neither cause nor prevent the births of these canine babies. But we could be witnesses: Chena allowed us to watch. And in her presence, we were eyewitnesses of the breathtaking event that is birth.

In her book *God's Story*, Anne Graham Lotz uses the word *eyewitness* while explaining how God made the world: "Who was the eyewitness of Creation?" she wrote. "The simple yet astounding answer is God Himself!"[1] God was the one writing, telling, and acting out the drama. He Himself developed the plot, prose, characters, and dramatic tension of a script placed in His heart long before the dawn of creation. And as the ultimate Storyteller, He alone is responsible for the pacing and continuity of the storyline. He's also the only one with authority to edit the manuscript.

As God began to present the plot of his eternal story in the first book of the Bible, a strategy called *revelation*[2] was unveiled: God initiated the task of *revealing* Himself to man through Creation. He gave an eyewitness account of the events of the ages and opened the windows of heaven to reveal His glory, character, love, and wisdom so that we can know Him. Why? Our instinctive response in knowing God personally is *worship*. And worship is His strategic plan for all of creation.

In the book of Genesis, God began to show us *how*.[3]

God's work of revelation was first presented in Creation; was fulfilled through God's Son, Jesus; and will be perfected when saints of all ages join in worship around the throne of heaven. And from beginning to end, God stays on task. He divided His creative work into days and time, thus providing structure. He crafted his artistic tapestry with care, color, and detail, providing wonder. He developed a framework for making Himself most clearly known by the *human* heart and mind and, in so doing, provided relationship. He gave example for worship by proclaiming approval of His own work. Then He provided time for repose, contemplation, restoration, and response, giving us a model for worship. The Creation account is, in fact, God's *call* to worship, for in it, He reveals to us His *person*, *presence*, *power*, *plan*, and *purpose*.

THE PERSON OF GOD REVEALED

At the risk of minimizing the Creation[4] account, I must point out that Genesis was not written primarily to explain how God created the universe. Rather, its purpose, first and foremost, is to reveal the *person* of God.

God is first defined as the *Creator*, or "one who made something out of nothing."[5] But who *is* this Creator, this Person? It is *Elohim*[6]: the God Most High—the all-powerful, one Creator, the God of heaven, the Holy One, the righteous sovereign.[7] Because God is creative, His very first act was to *create*[8]: He formed us in His image and placed within us the desire to know Him, fellowship with Him, love Him supremely—and worship Him.

He continued by revealing Himself as sustainer, life giver, provider, companion, and caregiver of all creation—a precursor of the relationship He seeks with His *best* product: humankind. God revealed His love in the effortless way the earth revolves around the sun, birds fly, and animals procreate. He demonstrated His divinity by creating everything there is, without soliciting help from any other being—angel or spirit. He displayed His knowledge as He crafted all things to work together seamlessly, in perfect harmony. And He daily showcases His architectural skill as nature continues to function according to His sacred, overarching plan.

God created out of an act of free will. Nothing in the universe commanded, "Go create." No hidden agenda or motive drove Him to do His work. He did not construct the cosmos to stroke His ego or meet an inner need, to become *more* God or *more* powerful. God is complete in and of Himself. He didn't have to ask permission to produce—He didn't need it. And it wasn't necessary to requisition funding to carry out His act of creation: He already owns it all. He sought no advice on the height, depth, or breadth of His construction. He already knew what He wanted to do: He wanted to create.

But *why?*

God created to establish *relationship* with those who are *like Him* (see Genesis 1:26 NLT)—and because He loves us—and loved us—even before we were born. He wants to reveal Himself as Lover of our souls.

This God, then, who created us to reveal Himself *to* us, did exactly that by using creation itself to show us His plan and purpose for life. It is as though lifted high is a flashing sign that reads, LOOK WHAT GOD HAS DONE! Why? He wanted us to know He is *there*.

THE PRESENCE OF GOD REVEALED

My wife and I lived for a number of years in Pensacola, Florida. The rich, blue waters of the Gulf of Mexico provide a backdrop for God's majesty in motion. Nothing is more breathtaking than standing on a pier on a moon-lit night, feeling the wind blow across the water, watching the waves and falling stars, and enjoying the presence of God. *No matter where you are,* He seems to whisper, *My presence is there too.*

In the beginning, the Bible tells us, "God's Spirit was moving over the water" (Gen. 1:2 NCV). Though the earth was formless and void, God was busy. The universe was static, but His Spirit was not. He wasn't waiting for administrative approval to take an active role in the grand, defining moment of history. He was in motion. Even in the darkness, God was making His presence known.

While we cannot see God's Spirit, we can sense His presence. And just as His Spirit moved across the waters, His presence today proves that He is still moving about, ever working, fully involved and carrying out His plan to be with His created. In a moment of time, God reveals His presence. Why? Because He wants to be *with* us.

How does this apply to our worship? Without His presence we will not worship. But when God is with us, when He is *present*, worship is our immediate response. And when we respond to His nearness with worship, we can begin to know Him—personally—and to feel and understand His power.

THE POWER OF GOD REVEALED

How powerful is God?

He *could* have stretched out His finger and forged a valley or carved out of nothing a river. He could have reached across the universe, tapped an angel, and gestured for a flurry of light. He could have sent a heavenly wind to propel His sparkling stars across the sky, or gathered molecules from another galaxy to shape and multiply the animals. He could have used all sorts of gaudy gimmicks and flashy fireworks—even a big bang—to create. Yet he chose not to. Instead, He simply spoke. "*And it happened*" (Gen. 1:9, 11, 15, 24, 30 NCV). *Life* happened. There is power in the very voice of God, and through God's creative voice, we can see the magnitude of His power.

The voice that spoke at Creation was the same one that said, "Snake, you are cursed." This voice later called to Moses from a burning bush, then chiseled in stone the commandments for all humans to obey. Later the same voice announced, "This is My beloved Son" (Matt. 3:17 NKJV), forever identifying Jesus as one to whom worship is due. And it is the voice of God that will one day declare, "Time is no more."

Today God's voice whispers peace to our hearts at the bedside of a dying saint. Likewise it whispers, "Come to Me" (Matt. 11:28 NKJV) and offers rest. But before all of this, with the sovereign power of His voice, God created a world.

That God spoke things into existence is no less significant than the fact that He created out of nothing. In speaking, God confirmed the words of His mouth as absolute authority.[9] As He speaks, He demonstrates His supreme self-sufficiency and self-determination. It is "through His power," Paul wrote, that "all things were made—things in heaven and on earth, things seen and unseen, all powers, authorities, lords, and rulers . . . He was there before anything was made, and all things continue because of Him" (Col. 1:16–17 NCV).

Consider the sequence of this sovereign chain of actions in Genesis 1: God *said*; God *made*; God *named*; God *saw*; and God *blessed*.

God *said*:

- "Let there be light."
- "Let there be sky."
- "Let there be lights *in* the sky."
- "Let there be plants."
- "Let there be fish in the sea and birds in the air."
- "Let there be animals." And, finally,
- "Let there be humans."

And it happened.

Then God *made*. He *made* the air and placed water both above and below it. He *made* the sun for day, the moon for night, and the stars to twinkle before children's wondering eyes. He made every bird and its distinct song, all animals large and small, and commanded each to produce more just like itself. God *made*.

Then He *named*.

Have you ever noticed how often we look to see where our clothing, cars, furniture, and other consumer goods are made? That's because we place great value on where and how these products are manufactured. Some garments proudly display, "Made in China" or "Made in America." Certain automobiles "made in Japan" or "made in Germany" evidence good craftsmanship. Furniture labels declaring "Made in Amish Country" imply quality manufacturing. We label our merchandise to reveal its superior workmanship and to indicate its value.

When our Creator stamped "Made by God" on His creation, He promised matchless workmanship and placed great value on what He created. He labeled His works with His own hand. And He guarantees His work with a warranty that will outlast the ages.

God reveals His esteem for His handiwork by supplying names. They provide identity and designate purpose and function. Names are important to God. He Himself has no fewer than twelve names that identify His roles and His character,[10] so you can bet He knows *your* name and deeply cares about you. In creating the earth, God named the light "day," the darkness "night," the air "sky," and so on.

Then God evaluated His labor. Six times in Genesis 1, He took a look at what He had made and assessed it (vv. 10, 12, 18, 21, 25, 31). And when Creation was complete and He "saw everything that He had made," He named it all "good" (v. 31 NKJV), bestowing upon His works His official seal of approval.

The fact that God grants approval is important as we learn to worship Him. In the Old Testament, Job, Abraham, David, and others were commended and rewarded by God for their faithful worship. In the New Testament, God approved of the disciples when they recognized Jesus for who He really was and worshipped Him. Mary was celebrated for her worship as she anointed Jesus' feet (John 12:1–7). And saints of all the ages will receive God's approval when He says, "Well done, good and faithful servant" (Matt. 25:23 NKJV).

We are born with the need to be seen and approved. And God wants to give us His divine approval. When we worship Him, He will do this wholeheartedly by *blessing* us. After Hannah's faithful worship, God blessed her by answering her prayer for a child with many children (see 1 Samuel). He'll answer our prayers too, when we worship Him in spirit and in truth. Why? Because He *approves*. Our worship fulfills His *plan* for our lives.

THE PLAN OF GOD REVEALED

Creation reveals that God had a plan. Moment by moment and day by day He demonstrated a commitment to prove His love for life by purposely creating an atmosphere in which things—and people—could live. He painted a broad backdrop of sky, filled with color. He moved the waters together and formed dry land, on which He placed both flora and fauna. He called seasons into existence and established weeks and years, creating a timeline for the fulfillment of His foreseen redemption. And finally, God created His most precious gift: humankind. He fashioned man, in His own likeness, from dust, and breathed into his body the breath of life. Then He furnished man a mate—a woman—and blessed the human race, giving them the ability to reproduce so they could fill and master the earth, ruling over every living thing. And He concluded his labor by saying to man, "This is all yours—and I am yours. I will look at you and see in your face the reflection of My own glory. That is your end. You are created to worship Me, to glorify Me . . . as your God forever."[11] He created humanity to *worship*, and He gave us the principles to do so through the act of Creation.

Evening Passed, and Morning Came

Six times in Genesis 1, we see the words *"evening passed, and morning came"* (NCV). What does this teach us about worship?

1. *It teaches us that practicing worship takes time.* Each time we read "evening passed, and morning came," it reflects God's dedication to time. Though He was both inventor and comptroller of time, He allows Himself to work within its limitations. He completed Creation within the constraints of *days*, six of them, and at the conclusion of each of these, *evening passed*; then *morning came*. With the lights that He set in the sky, God established times—days, nights, years, seasons—because He knew that our lives would be constrained by time. Ecclesiastes 3:1–8 says:

> To everything there is a season,
>   A time for every purpose under heaven:
>   A time to be born,
> And a time to die;
>   A time to plant,
> And a time to pluck what is planted;
>   A time to kill,
> And a time to heal . . . (NKJV)

And a lot of other "times to" as well.

For God, there was a time to *create*. And though He could have shaped all that exists in one celestial swoop, He chose to express His creative genius over a series of days, a span of *time*. He took His *time* fashioning all the aspects of the universe, visible and invisible, that He knew we would enjoy. In turn, if we are to worship Him in a manner that *He* enjoys, we need to take *our* time: we must walk away from the busyness of life and spend time with God.

2. *It teaches us that worship is a process.* Again, though He certainly could have, God did not complete the whole of Creation in an instant. He spent individual days followed by individual nights to carry out a *process*. God is dedicated to process. This is seen in the way He allows all things to *develop*. Consider the butterfly. Its transformation from creepy caterpillar to creature of beauty is a process that takes place in the cocoon. All of life, in fact—education, a lasting friendship, a solid marriage, successful parenting—involves process.

One cannot hurry a process. God did not get in a hurry when He created. He committed Himself to a process. Further, everything He crafted requires a predetermined process in order to reproduce and grow. If we, like the Lord Himself, will commit ourselves to process—becoming students of worship and applying what we learn to our worship experience— our understanding of God and relationship with Him will *grow*.

3. *It teaches us that worship requires growth.* As God created the heavens, the earth, and all that is within them, He day by day "grew" His universe. It began with light, then atmosphere; later, things with gills and things with wings, and so on. From creation to creation, God constructed the growing cosmos—again, working within the parameters of time and process. Time allows for growth, for maturation. And each time evening passed and morning came, God was allowing things to grow. Growth is essential to development and maturity. This applies not only to the mighty redwood that sprouts from a seed, but to our worship, which springs from our first recognition of who God is. Growing as a worshipper is part of God's plan to reveal Himself. The more we *learn* about Him, the more we will want to *worship* Him. The more we worship Him, the more we'll want to *know* Him. The more we know Him, the more we'll want to be *with* Him . . . then *love* Him . . . then *serve* Him. And on and on it goes. Just as God daily *grew* His universe, we must *grow* our relationship with God.

4. *It teaches us that worship requires order.* While our heart's response to God may be somewhat spontaneous at times, there should be order in our worship, just as there was a divine order to all of Creation. Those of us who are creative, right-brain types often bemoan our inability to "color within the

lines." Simply put, we don't like to go by the rules. Yet the words "evening passed, and morning came" reveal God's willingness to follow the "rules," that is, to adhere to a divine *order*. He is too disciplined to disregard the prescribed boundaries that He Himself set. We should be too. When we worship God, we need to do so within boundaries, to prevent disorder. Perhaps the apostle Paul said it best: "Let all things be done *decently* and in order" (1 Cor. 14:40 NKJV, emphasis added). (As you read on, it will become clear that every *inde-cent* act of "worship"—cutting of flesh, sex at the altars, child sacrifice, you name it—started when the boundaries were ignored and disorder set in.)

5. *It teaches us that our worship should be fresh.* Each time evening passes, a new morning follows. Darkness dissipates, and there is a sense of anticipation of something new. That's because God's mercies are "new every morning" (Lam. 3:22–23). And just as fresh *compassion* is part of God's morning routine, fresh *worship* should be part of ours, renewed each day at sunup. When we worship in the freshness of sunrise, God is hon-ored. He sees that we have placed Him first in our day. As a result, He refreshes us with His presence, restores our energy, transforms our outlook, and deepens our friendship with Him.

6. *It teaches us that worship is part of God's cycle of life.* Just as dawn is an expected part of our life cycle, worship is also to be a part. God expects it, as surely as we expect the sun to rise. All day, every day, we are to work for Him and, along the way, worship. At night, as we rest, God restores our physical, spiritual, and emotional beings so we can arise in the morning, begin our day with worship, secure His presence in our lives, and thus fulfill His purpose.

THE PURPOSE OF GOD REVEALED

The final disclosure from Creation is God's supreme purpose: *dwelling with man.* Four details illustrate His intention:

First, *God rested on the seventh day.* Now, God was not tired. He had neither written too many e-mails nor stood too long on the assembly line. As He had not overextended, He had no need to rebuild His physical or emotional energy. In fact, He had no need of *anything.* But we do. So God rested—as an example for *us.*

God created us with a need for balance in our lives, labor balanced with rest. When we rest, our bodies have time to restore. So do our minds. As we shut down the everyday hustle and bustle, we are able to rest and *focus on God*. This gives us an opportunity to meditate on Him, listen to Him, and enjoy Him.

It is most curious that God provided us a pattern for worship by resting, not by doing. *Go ahead*, He seemed to be saying, *and stay busy all week—I was—but don't forget to set aside some time to rest with Me*. God expects us to reserve time for Him so that He can refresh us as we fellowship with Him.

Second, *God created man*, enduing him with three essential life elements: breath (God's *own*);[12] will, ensuring his desire to be his own person; and freedom of choice, the power to exercise that desire. All three elements reflect the image of God. And all three are essential to our ability to dwell with—and worship—God.

Third, *God placed in the heart of man a desire for companionship*. God desires friendship. This longing was in His heart at the time of Creation. He yearns to bond and build relationship, and because we are *like Him*, we, too, have a built-in desire for connection, for rapport, for *bond* with our Creator. When we respond to that desire with worship, we are fulfilling His purpose for us. He is pleased to dwell with us.

Fourth, *God created the reproductive cycle*. In Genesis 2:18, God said, "It is not good for man to be alone." Though Adam had all the birds of the air and beasts of the field, he did not find a companion comparable to or right for[13] him. But God met man at his greatest need by providing a partner: a woman. Then, together, they began to fill the planet with more and more people for God to love—and *dwell with*.

PRINCIPLES OF WORSHIP FROM THIS CHAPTER

Our examination of Creation is essential to the study of worship. Through Creation, God established precedent for building relationships with people and showing them how to worship Him. In the Genesis account, four principles profoundly affect our obligation—and *should* affect our desire—to worship:

First, the *wonder of God* demands our worship of Him. God is supernatural; He was not created. He was the Cause; we, the effect. God is spirit, so He cannot be contained in or restricted by any manmade edifice. He is free to move as He wills and dwell where He chooses. And He chooses to dwell with *us*, His created. This should arouse the human heart to praise Him.

Second, the *work of God* demands our worship of Him. His work in Creation is beyond our comprehension, and through it, He demonstrated His redemptive plan. In Genesis, He said, "Let there be light," thus bringing the universe from darkness to illumination. His plan of redemption brings *man* from darkness to illumination; that is, from ignorance to understanding of Him. Through Creation, we can know God and be recipients of all of His benefits—including our redemption!

> *Bless the LORD, O my soul; and all that is within me, bless his holy name!*
> *Bless the LORD, O my soul, and forget not all his benefits.*
>
> —PSALM 103:1–2

The narrative of Genesis 1 provides a stunning outline of the benefits of knowing God:

God *said*—this is the first we hear of the voice of God. As He spoke the world into being, He also speaks to us—through His Word—demonstrating that we are precious to Him.

God *made*—He handcrafted every one of us, giving us each an individual identity, laced with His own attributes. As we know Him more and more, we become more like Him.

God *named*—just as He named night and day, identifying them for all time, He named and identified us—as His own (1 John 3:1; John 15:15).

God *saw*—He *sees* us (one of God's many names is *El Roi*, the God Who Sees). And as we begin to seek Him and know Him, He gives us His approval, just as He did when He "saw" each of the products of His creative week.

God *blessed*—He provides for us.

Third, the *wisdom of God* demands our worship of Him. Everything He made has its own place and purpose for existence. Every leaf on a tree, petal on a flower, feather on a wing, and song in the air only serves to make that which He created, better. That is its end. But only *humanity's* end is to dwell with God and be His children, "fearfully and wonderfully made" in His very own image (Ps. 139:14 NKJV). Those who "get" this can't help but praise Him.

And finally, the *wishes of God* demand our worship of Him. "Let Us make man," He said (Gen. 1:26 NKJV). But why make man? Why not stop at the birds, the fish, the four-legged critters? Because God wanted *relationship*. Today, He *still* wants relationship—with you and me. And He wants it to last *forever* (see John 3:16). For that, we should adore Him.

> "The whole import and substance of the Bible teaches us that the God who does not need any thing nevertheless desires the adoration and worship of His created children."
>
> —A. W. Tozer, twentieth-century pastor and theologian[14]

In summary, all of creation demands that we worship God. How can we help but worship the exclusive contractor of all nonliving matter—and the sole architect, carpenter, and building inspector for all that breathes? The only one who could create *anything* out of *nothing*? The one who, though Maker of all, is also *Father* of all (Deut. 32:6)? And the One who wants to dwell *with us*?

The moon was full and bright, casting its wonder upon the Alaskan snow. In front of me was my younger brother, with his energetic sled-dog team. I followed close behind with my own team of huskies, equally skilled at maneuvering through the ups and downs of the narrow dog trails. It was a five-mile run that the two of us had done many times before. I held on to the sled for dear life as my team sped through the night with purpose. Occasionally, I would holler out to my dogs, "Come on, boys; take us on home." Sometimes I'd hear my brother, shouting to his team. But mostly, we would travel through the night in silence. I still remember the crackle of snow beneath the runners of that old sled.

The moon reflected brilliantly off of the sparkling snow—no need for headlights, flashlights, or lanterns out there. The stars—Big Dipper and all—silently applauded God. The northern lights, red and blue and beautiful beyond words, noiselessly sang the great Creator's praise. And the breeze rustling past my furry parka offered moments of refreshing glory. Each time I breathed in the cold, I felt close to God—I experienced His presence.

I recall sensing as a teenager on nights like these, the awesome bigness of God. I marveled that the One who made the universe also lived in my heart. I will never forget experiencing, for just a moment in time, the thrill of uninterrupted, focused, holy communication with God as I prayed to Him—and worshipped.

Now, years later, I still walk out into the night from time to time. When I look to the heavens, once again, I see that moon, those stars—indeed, the *wonder of God* in full display. And it brings me to my knees.

In *worship*.

| 2 |

WORSHIP BEFORE THE FALL

OUR TWENTY-FIRST CENTURY IS A POSTMODERN, INFORMATION age. Machines talk to machines, info is measured in bits, and travelers purchase airline tickets without human intervention. Automated checkouts loudly bark prices with prerecorded, mechanical precision. With a click of a mouse, an e-mail has replaced the routine of licking a stamp, driving to the post office, and communicating with a *human being*.

Digital technology makes communication easier—but intimacy scarce. We pay our bills online, order our clothes through virtual boutiques, and shut out the unwanted distractions of a self-centered world by plugging in our MP3 players, iPods, iPod nanos, iPod shuffles, iPhones, BlackBerrys . . . My, how things have changed.

The way we establish relationships has changed too. Internet dating is today's substitute for traditional courtship, and virtual marriage counselors now provide cyberspace advice void of physical encounter. But in spite of our electronics explosion, cell-phone dependency, and IM addiction, we are a lonely generation. Parents spend less time with their children. Kids are left alone to play video games or text their friends, while Mom and Dad scramble to make money and accumulate things—that is, if Mom and Dad are even together; more than half of American marriages end in divorce. As a result, more and more children are reared in single-parent homes, spending ever more of their time flying solo. But youngsters aren't the only ones who suffer the bane of being alone. Grandparents, too, live in isolation in nursing homes, forgotten by a generation deluged with data—yet themselves just as isolated—and lonely. Loneliness is the unspoken disease of the soul. But God never intended for us to experience it. He created us to enjoy *relationships*, because He is the God of relationships.

At the end of your life, no one will remember much about what you have achieved in wealth or position. What people will recall is how you treated them. You will be remembered—or forgotten—based on the love you showed—or didn't show—to those around you. They will recollect the *relationship* you had with them. That's because all of life is about relationships. In fact, everything we do reflects *something* about the relationships we have—or don't have—with friends, families, coworkers . . . and God.

In chapter 1, we established that the way to a relationship with God is through worship. When we worship Him, we get to know Him. The more we know Him, the more we want to be with Him. And as we spend time with Him, we long to shower Him with love and worship. In turn, He rains down His love upon us, with reckless abandon—because we have worshipped.

Try to imagine perfect worship. Picture yourself closing your eyes at the end of a busy day and feeling the arms of God around you as you fall asleep, worshipping in His embrace. Imagine waking in the morning, after a night of uninterrupted rest, still secure in God's love for you and filled with love for Him too. All through the day you sense His guiding presence. And in the cool of the evening, you return to Him, walk with Him, and worship Him.

This is just a glimpse of worship before the fall—before humankind decided to strike out on their own and live in rebellion. Earth's first human inhabitants, Adam and Eve, enjoyed God, loved Him supremely, and derived great pleasure from worshipping Him. They loved to be with Him. Likewise, God loved to be with them. In fact, He dwelt with them.

The camaraderie Adam and Eve had with God was unprecedented. God made Himself directly available to them. Because Adam and Eve comprehended God, they found Him to be approachable: He was their friend and Father, and they were His sinless children, His trophies, made in His image and gifted with the privilege of worshipping Him.

God made [Adam] in His own image; in the image and likeness of God made He him; and He made him as near to being like Himself as it was possible for the creature to be like the Creator. The most godlike thing in the universe is the soul of man.

The reason God made man in His image was that he might appreciate God and admire and adore and worship; so that God might not be a picture, so to speak, hanging in a gallery with nobody looking at Him. He might not be a flower that no one could smell; He might not be a star that no one could see. God made somebody to smell that flower, the lily of the valley. He wanted someone to see that glorious image. He wanted someone to see the star, so He made us and in making us He made us to worship Him."

—A. W. TOZER[1]

THE PRIVILEGE OF WORSHIP

Man and woman are the only life forms who can enjoy the *privilege* of worshipping one in whose image they are made. Though the angels in heaven worship God, and even the stars were made for it, we alone were crafted with a *desire* for Him. He has placed an inner yearning in your heart and mine, what some have referred to as a "God-sized hole." It is this desire for God that sets us apart from all living creatures. Leonard Sweet, of SpiritVenture Ministries, defines this desire as a "Quest" for a *GodLife relationship*: "Part of the uniqueness of humanity, beings created in the image of God, is our instinct to seek and to enjoy the pleasures of seeking. It is born in us to dare, to desire, and to delight in the Quest. Questing-made-possible is who we are. Some say it's our sole advantage as a species. But the Quest is not a set of questions. The Quest is the mystery of getting lost in the GodLife relationship."[2]

Down through the centuries, men and women have been on a quest to know God, to feel His presence, to experience a relationship that transcends time and understanding. In the wilderness of Judah, David proclaimed, "O God, you are my God, I seek you, my soul thirsts for you; my flesh faints for you, as in a dry and weary land where there is no water" (Ps. 63:1 NRSV). Another psalm begins, "As a deer longs for flowing streams, so my soul longs for you, O God (Ps. 42:1 RSV). The Bible lists story after story of those who sought after God. Kings. Fishermen. Prostitutes. And God has a promise for all whose hearts are hungry for Him: "You will . . . *find* Me, when you search for Me with all your heart" (Jer. 29:13 NKJV, emphasis added).

In the beginning, Adam and Eve searched for God with "all their hearts" and worshipped Him. That's what they were created to do: worship God . . .

But worship Him *where?*

THE PLACE OF PERFECT WORSHIP

The garden of Eden was *God's* dwelling place. Yet Genesis 2:15 says that God put "man in the garden of Eden." Why? Well, for one thing, the verse continues, "to care for [the garden] and work it" (NCV). Adam was given a job to do, a responsibility. But why else, do you suppose, was he placed where God Himself was? So God could enjoy fellowship with him and all of his family—and so they could enjoy fellowship right back. God wanted His children to find peace and companionship *in Him* and to worship Him—right where He dwelled.

The garden of Eden was a place of unparalleled exquisiteness, filled with crystal clear rivers, pleasant fragrances, precious stones, and one-of-a-kind foliage:

> The LORD God caused every beautiful tree and every tree that was good for food to grow . . . In the middle of the garden, God put the tree that gives life . . . A river flowed through Eden and watered the garden. From there the river branched out to become four rivers. The first river, name Pishon, flows around the whole land of Havilah, where there is gold. The gold of that land is excellent. Bdellium and onyx are also found there. (Gen. 2:9–12 NCV)

Bdellium is an expensive, sweet-smelling resin, like myrrh. Onyx is a gem. There were at least nine precious gems in the garden, including rubies and emeralds (Ezek. 28:13). Four rivers watered the nations, and trees bore sumptuous fruit to both sustain and delight the garden's inhabitants. I don't know if they had steak and potatoes in Eden, but I do know that what they had was good, because God said so, six times in Genesis 1. All of humanity's needs were met in the garden—the need for food, water . . . and relationship. It is as if God was saying, "Adam, Eve, this garden of unsurpassed beauty is all about you and Me."

God planned for man to enjoy earth's beauty forever. He knew that the nature's splendor would inspire mankind's worship, because even in the flora and fauna, he could recognize and know God Himself, His character, His personality: "Through everything God made," says Romans 1:20, one can "clearly see [God's] invisible qualities—his eternal power and divine nature" (NCV). *The Message* puts it this way: "By taking a long and thoughtful look at what God . . . created, people have always been able to see what their eyes as such can't see: . . . for instance . . . the mystery of his divine being." Adam and Eve certainly did. They saw all that God had made and, with Him, agreed that it was "very good" (Gen. 1:31 NKJV)—and that *He* was very good. And they worshipped God in that garden.

Note that God placed Adam in a *specific* location. God had just created a whole universe, including planet earth, in all its vastness. Yet the Bible says, "God planted a garden in the east, in a place called Eden, and put the man . . . into it" (Gen. 2:8 NCV). Why did He choose a particular setting in which Adam and Eve would live, work, interact with God, and worship? Because the place of worship is important to God. The word *Eden* means "fruitful."[3] God knew that man and woman's efforts to worship Him could be fruitful in the garden.

With all the world at their disposal, and all of its goings-on, it would have been so easy for Adam and Eve to get distracted—so much to see; so much to do; so much to be involved in (sounds like life today). But in the peaceful quiet of a pristine garden, Adam and Eve could focus. They could enjoy undistracted communion with God, in a setting devoid of any element that would detract from a perfect relationship with Him.

They could worship God without the encumbrance of outside interferences. As such, their worship was natural, not contrived. It was, in fact, perfect worship:

1. It was *uninhibited*. As worshippers, Adam and Eve were free to express. They could exalt God without reservation, making their worship spontaneous, effortless, unforced. No religious establishment had ascended to God's throne, so to speak, imposing its manmade limitations on worship. And there was no pressure to conform to the worship standards of any other culture.

2. It was *unlimited* and *untimed*, never quantified. They had no prescribed time *limits* and were never compelled to rush through their adoration of God in order to "get worship done" so they could move on to the "next thing" on their agenda.

3. It was *uninterrupted*, free from obstruction or disturbance. No taxicabs speeding through the garden. No land lines ringing. No TVs blaring. No meetings to get to. No schedule to adhere to or corporate ladder to climb.

4. It was *unafraid*, bold, confident, courageous. Adam and Eve's worship style had never been compared to anyone else's, so it was unbound by a compulsion to "measure up." They were free from the fear of judgment or rejection. Thus, their worship was always genuine, never "put on."

5. It was *unblemished* by the cares of a carnal world. Sin had not yet entered the picture, so mankind's worship was without egotism or ulterior motives. And without the presence of sin, the effects of sin were absent as well. There was no war, no violence at all. Neither was there guilt, jealousy, lack, or disease. Adam and Eve felt no threat from wild animals. In fact, God placed them over the animals. There was no apprehension whatsoever, because there was safety in the garden. Worship never had to compete with worry.

6. In reality, their worship was *undefinable*, because until the fall of man, worship was *perfect*. Now we live in an *imperfect* world

filled with *imperfect* people using *imperfect* worship methods in *imperfect* settings. We are finite, bound by physical limitations and constrained by sensuality. How can we begin to offer *anything* "perfect," much less perfect worship?

But Adam and Eve, the first to be afforded the awesome privilege of worshipping God, practiced perfect worship. And what's more, they did so in a perfect place. Not until the final amen (more on this in chapter 21) will we be able to do the same. Until Christ begins His eternal reign with His Bride, we will continue to see everything, including worship, "imperfectly as in a cloudy mirror" (1 Cor. 13:12 NLT) or, as the King James Version puts it "through a glass, darkly."

But there are still lessons that we can learn from man's worship in Eden. What have we seen so far?

PRINCIPLES OF WORSHIP FROM THIS CHAPTER

1. *God is all about relationship.* He proved it by creating man — in His image. He wanted to associate with someone *just like Him.* And He wanted that "someone" to worship Him. So He strategically placed within the heart of the first man and woman an impulse to pursue, comprehend, love, and ultimately worship Him. That impulse persists in the heart of *every* man and woman today. In our sin we lack the power to know Him. But the moment we repent and begin to seek Him, we will find Him. He promised that. We will have a fresh encounter with the living God, and we'll love what we find in Him. It satisfies our inner craving — and it will bring us to our knees in worship. In turn, God will activate an intentional and individual relationship with us. It's what He wanted from the beginning. And when we

> "We need the courage of . . . a right relationship with the Creator . . . God is a mystery, not a master's thesis. We have much to learn about the truth of God that is revealed only through relationship."
>
> —Leonard Sweet[8]

respond to His call to relationship—and worship—we fulfill the purpose for which He made us.

Here's how A. W. Tozer illustrates the importance of fulfilling the purpose for which a thing is made:

A piano is made with a specific purpose: to produce music. However, I happen to know that someone once stood on a piano in order to put a fastener of some kind in the ceiling. Some artistic women have used piano tops as family picture galleries. I have seen piano tops that were cluttered filing cabinets or wide library shelves. There is an intelligent design in the creation of a piano. The manufacturer did not announce: "This is a good piano. It has at least 19 uses!" No, the designer had only one thought in mind: "This piano will have the purpose and potential of sounding forth beautiful music!"[4]

We, like the piano, were meant to sound forth "beautiful music" to God. Our worship is truly music to His ears. It glorifies Him, and according to the Westminster catechism, to glorify God and enjoy Him forever is the chief end of man.[5] But that end can only be realized by those who commit themselves to lifelong rapport with God.

2. *Where we worship, matters.* Adam and Eve's relationship with God in the garden was an experience we can only imagine. They participated in perfect worship with a perfect God in a perfect place. Only two specific sites in time and eternity have the distinction of being perfect places for worship: Eden and heaven. And until God makes us totally whole and perfect—in the new heaven and earth—we will never be able to worship God at the level that Adam and Eve enjoyed. But we can still enjoy God—in our own special *place of worship.*

Shut in with God in a secret place,
There in His presence, beholding His face,
Finding more power to run in this race.
Oh, I long to be shut in with God.

—AUTHOR UNKNOWN

Perfect worship cannot take place where noise is abundant and distractions are many. Our special place cannot be teeming with myriad faces: we will fail to see the face of God. We cannot worship fruitfully where there are countless voices, all vying for our attention. We'll miss *God's* voice. We cannot worship perfectly where the clock is king. God Himself must be our King, and we must spend time with Him, in a place unoccupied by anything that would seek to manipulate our worship, rendering it manufactured rather than a natural outflow of our love for God. We must find our own personal "Eden," an individual "secret garden." In other words, we need to get alone with God. Only then can we hope to experience worship that is "fruitful"—that brings us into the very presence of God and deepens our relationship with Him.

3. *Worship brings "multiplication."* We don't know how long God allowed man and woman to live in Eden. But we do know that it was in the garden that creation multiplied. There will be "multiplication" in your personal Eden, as well. And in mine. As we come before God in our "set apart" place, he will multiply our joy. In fact Psalm 16:11 says that in His presence there is "fullness of joy" (NKJV), and as we experience it, we will, predictably, praise God. As C. S. Lewis exclaims, "All enjoyment spontaneously overflows into praise."[6] God responds to our praise by giving us *multiplied* joy, over and over as we worship.

Now, think about this: Adam and Eve's every *need* was met in the garden where they worshipped. They were *protected* there too. God is in still in the security business today. He is also in the "need-meeting" business. He is ever engaged both in protecting us in the unsafe society in which we live, and in providing for us. In other words, God *multiplies* our benefits.

But friends, dare not expect these multiplied benefits if you refuse to walk with God as His friend and companion—and worship Him. You and I were made for His worship, and it is a privilege afforded only to members of the human race. Let's not take it for granted.

As we continue our study together, remember that God's specific design and purpose for our lives—individually and collectively—is worshipping

Him. "If we do not honor this purpose," wrote Tozer, "our lives will degenerate into shallow, selfish, humanistic pursuits."[7] We *must* worship God, as best we can. We know that we are imperfect people in an imperfect world. Our worship now is colored by the reality that we are part of a fallen race. But we'll worship God anyway, to the best of our ability, because we know that one day, when He calls us home, we will be perfect, and the place where we'll worship Him will be perfect. Our worship itself, in fact, will be perfect, as all worship once was.

Before the worship wars.

| 3 |

THE WORSHIP WARS

IN THE LAST CHAPTER, WE LEARNED THAT, ONCE UPON A TIME, there was perfect worship in a perfect place—until man became *misguided*. How did it happen? Another god arose, and Adam "turned in his keys," so to speak, so he could bow before that other god. What was its name? *Self*. And sadly, from the moment Adam and his wife bowed before the god of self, their unspoiled fellowship with the God who had made them was broken.

Let's backpedal, though, for a moment. Adam and Eve weren't the first to worship the god of self. In this chapter, we will examine the *worship wars*, beginning with the very first case of mistaken worship. But first . . .

WHAT *IS* A WORSHIP WAR?

In recent years, a variety of pastors, parishioners, church leaders, parachurch groups, and denominational executives have voiced concern about the use of various modes and methods of public worship. Personal preference over issues such as song style (traditional or contemporary?), musical instruments (all, some, or none?), and approach to worship (formal? casual? liturgical? animated?) has become the basis for deliberation, debate, and division among believers. In some cases, intense differences of opinion develop into grave conflict. Serious discord ensues, unity between friends is broken, feelings are hurt, and the body of Christ is distracted and discouraged. The fallout is often very damaging to the body and cause of Christ. Leaders refer to such clashes as "worship wars."

War is a state of open and declared hostile conflict. It is usually a struggle between opposing forces whose desired outcomes differ. At the heart of most war efforts is a wish to eradicate something or, in some cases, someone. The consequence is destruction—of property and life. And the devastation worsens with each battle.

The battle for worship is more intense, sinister, and dangerous than one could ever imagine. This "war" does not focus on musical style or instrument preference alone. The focal point of this conflict is the *object* of worship. What—or who—is worthy of man's praise?

Remember that all things were created to worship God. When He formed the heavens and the earth, "the morning stars sang in chorus," and "all the angels shouted praise" (Job 38:7 MSG). Worship began in the *spirit world*, long before man was made. And it was here that the battle for worship began.

This chapter will cover three battles for worship in Genesis. The first of these was the foundation for every worship war that followed, and its effects have impacted all of life history and the eternal destinies of every succeeding generation—including ours. It was the war between Satan and God.

WORSHIP WAR #1: SATAN VS. GOD

This battle for worship, launched ages before Creation, continues to this day. Let's take a look at what this "worship war" entails.

The Players

The author of the first worship war was a character named *Satan*. The entire battle came from the imaginations of his heart. Who is this ominous creator of conflict?

Satan is a spirit being who belongs to the order of angels called cherubim (Ezek. 28:14). He is known as:

- the *adversary*

- the *accuser*

- the *devil*

- the *tempter*

- a *liar*

- a *murderer*

- the *ruler of darkness*

He is also called a *dragon* (Rev. 12:9) and a *serpent* (20:2).

Through the ages, men have debated over the existence of Satan. Many believe there *is* no such character. But Satan is a real, live, literal figure. Eighteenth-century evangelist Charles Finney said of him, "You try opposing him for awhile and you'll see if he's literal or not."[1] Today Satan exists in the spirit world as the "prince of the power of the air" (Eph. 2:2 NKJV) and, by his own admission, is the enemy of God.

At one time in history, Satan was the most powerful and beautiful angel in heaven, the epitome of God's creation. His name then was *Lucifer,* meaning "Star of the morning,"[2] and he held a position of great authority in an unparalleled habitation. "Before his fall," wrote radio-preaching pioneer Donald Grey Barnhouse, "he . . . occupied the role of prime minister for God, ruling possibly over the universe but certainly over this world."[3] The *New American Standard Bible* calls Satan the "mighty angelic guardian" (Ezek. 28:14). This is what God had to say about him: "You were the model of perfection, full of wisdom and perfect in beauty. You were in Eden, the garden of God . . . You were anointed as a guardian cherub, for so I ordained you. You were on the holy mount of God; you walked among the fiery stones. You were blameless in your ways from the day you were created . . .

"Till wickedness was found in you" (Ezek. 28:12–15 NIV). Satan became jealous of God's eminence in the universe and declared war against Him. "I will ascend to heaven," he said. "I will raise my throne above the stars of God; I will sit enthroned on the mount of assembly, on the utmost heights of the sacred mountain. I will ascend above the tops of the clouds; I will make myself like the Most High" (Isa. 14:13–14 NIV).

As guardian of God's holiness, Satan already had access to heaven. Imagine! Always in the presence of God, and favored *by* God. But that wasn't enough for him. Satan wanted equality with God. Though God had created the angels to serve Him, Satan coveted their service—and worship—

for himself. He wanted to rule over not only the angels, but the whole universe. He wanted to compete with God. In fact, he wanted to *be* God.

The Personalities

Satan is not just some nondescript being. He has a personality and a free will, and he willingly disobeyed God. Satan is intelligent, capable of slick strategizing. He is crafty, engaging in clever war games. But above all, Satan is "puffed up with pride" (1 Tim. 3:6 NKJV). "Your heart became proud on account of your beauty," God accused, "and you corrupted your wisdom because of your splendor" (Ezek. 28:17 NIV). Satan thought he was "all that." So he drafted a battle plan to take God down—and he genuinely believed he could win.

The Process

Satan's war strategy is straightforward: he seeks to steal, kill, and destroy (John 10:10). He wanted to steal God's rank, kill our Creator, and destroy all who stood in the way. So he amassed an army. Revelation 12:4 says, "[The great dragon's] tail drew a third of the stars of heaven and threw them to the earth" (NKJV). Most theologians agree that the dragon in this verse is none other than Satan himself, and that the "stars" he cast to earth were angels he convinced to wage war with him against God. That Satan was not alone in his sin is proven by 2 Peter 2:4: "For if God did not spare the angels who sinned, but . . . delivered them into chains of darkness, to be reserved for judgment . . ." *The Message* puts it this way: "God didn't let the rebel angels off the hook, but jailed them in hell till Judgment Day." Other angelic beings rebelled too, but Satan was the root of it all.

Though mighty in strength, Satan does not possess the attributes that belong to God alone: omnipresence, omnipotence, and omniscience. He lost the revolt, and the penalty was stiff.

The Penalty

"Through your widespread trade you were filled with violence, and you sinned," God thundered. "So I drove you in disgrace from the mount of God, and I expelled you, O guardian cherub, from among the fiery stones . . . I threw you to earth; I made a spectacle of you before kings"

(Ezek. 28:16–17 NIV). Because of Satan's conceit and envy, his once intimate relationship with God was forever severed. His title and influence were removed, and he suffered the defeat of the ages. And as if that were not punishment enough, he will someday also suffer the "eternal" (Matt. 25:41 NIV) "fires of hell" (MSG), which were prepared for him and "his angels." But the cost of Satan's rebellion wasn't to him alone. All of humanity has had to pay the price.

The Price

The effects of Satan's sin were widespread. It cost everyone. It affected other angels and *all* people, from every nation of the world (Rev. 12:7; Rom. 5:12, 18; Rev. 20:3). It also positioned Satan as the ruler of this world (Eph. 2:2; John 16:11).

Still, Satan lost the war. He could not defeat God. So he decided to *hurt* God by strategically turning his attention to God's greatest handiwork.

Man.

WORSHIP WAR #2: SATAN VS. MAN

As with most wars, every battle for worship involves at least two parties, one warring against another. This second conflict was between Satan and mankind. But this time, Satan didn't look like an "anointed cherub" (Ezek. 28:14 KJV). He looked like a snake.

The Players

We know the players in this story. Their story has been told around the world. The characters' names were Adam and Eve, and they were a constant torment to Satan. *He* had once been close to God, but now, here *they* were, worshipping God in his place. Who knows what he was really thinking. But what we do know is that Satan is eye-catching, intimidating, convincing, and oh-so-wily. He knew that if he could replace mankind's worship of God with worship of self, he could remove them from God's grace — and from the garden. So he convinced them to follow his example and defy God.

The Personalities

Adam and Eve were innocent and trusting. They were intellectually, emotionally, and physically healthy—without fear and void of any suspicion. Having experienced nothing but peace and the truth of God, there had never been a reason to entertain doubt. So when the father of lies approached, Eve took his falsehood at face value.

We have already seen Satan's personality. He is self-serving, envious, and wants to be like God. And so, to establish his "godhood" over Adam and Eve, he engaged in a cunning process of pretext.

The Process

Satan is a master of disguise, famous for dressing himself as something else, even an angel of light. Then, with his deceptive beauty, he distracts, allures, and destroys. So his strategy for winning this worship war was deception, "pure" and simple. Though compared in Scripture to a roaring lion (1 Peter 5:8), he came to Eve in the form of a harmless and subordinate creature: a serpent, over which she was to have dominion.

Satan's use of a serpent, or snake, is noteworthy. The ancient Semitic goddess Asherah is represented by the serpent and worshipped as a mother goddess. The goddess Qudshu, in the Canaanite tradition, was also linked to a serpent, and revered as "the holy one." But according to God's Word, the serpent is *un*holy, bringing conflict, destruction, and death. Biblical references to snakes/serpents are always negative.[4]

Satan first approached Eve, not Adam. And his first tactic was to challenge the word of God. God had strictly commanded, "Do *not* eat the fruit of the tree of the knowledge of good and evil." If they did, he warned, they would die. But Satan told Eve that was not true. "You will *not* die," he lied. He placed doubt in Eve's heart. Suddenly she questioned God's integrity. Then she questioned His motives.

"God knows that if you eat the fruit from that tree . . ." Satan continued. He was implying that God was holding out on her. Eve listened, and Satan robbed her of her faith. ". . . you will learn about good and evil and you will be like God!" he concluded (Gen. 3:5 NCV). Now he robbed her of her contentment. She was persuaded that God's restrictions were not in her best interests. A spirit of jealousy arose within her. She wanted what belongs to God alone. So she rationalized: the fruit provided nutrition, aesthetic value, and wisdom. *It is good for me*, she reasoned. *I need it. I deserve it.*

Eve fell for Satan's propaganda—and bowed to the idol of "self." In so doing, she lost her innocence.

Several years ago I heard Dr. James Dobson, then president of Focus on the Family, share an experience he and his son had in Washington, D.C. His son was very young, perhaps only three or four, and together they stood in one of the many lines tourists often endure in the capital city.

Suddenly a man in front of them began cursing loudly, spewing language that the Dobson youngster had never heard before. The boy looked in disbelief at his father and asked him what those swear words meant. In his story, Dr. Dobson expressed great sorrow over the fact that his little boy was no longer a stranger to profanity. He had tried so hard to protect his son from such obscenities.

In much the same way, God sought to protect Adam and Eve from the same devastating results of Satan's disobedience. His motivation in forbidding them to eat the fruit was not egoism, but a desire to guard the very relationship mankind was created to enjoy. He wanted to spare them the cost of *war*.

But Satan sold Eve a bill of goods. She bought it—hook, line, and sinker.

She took.

She ate.

She gave to her husband.

And he willingly disobeyed.

The Penalty

There is always a penalty for doing wrong. Crime, once committed, can never be undone. And the price and punishment are far-reaching.

The serpent was condemned eternally to crawl on the ground and eat the dust of the earth. Hostility between his offspring and the children of man—forever—was set in motion. And someday, Satan's would be crushed (Gen. 3:15 NIV).

For her part in the crime, Eve, along with women of all ages, would experience painful childbirth. The culture in which women would live from that day forward also changed. In the new cultural hierarchy, women would be ruled by men (v. 16).

Adam was cursed to a life of hard labor. The ground would never effortlessly yield her fruit again. Man's work would now be toilsome. And worse, Adam's disobedience brought death to the entire human race, beginning with him. God told him, "Dust you are, and to dust you shall return" (v. 19 NKJV). The moment Adam and Eve took the fruit, their bodies began to shed the perfect image of God they were originally given. Their one errant act proved to be lethal to all humanity.

And Adam was driven from the garden, never to return.

The Price

We will never know the real cost of this war until God calls us home to heaven and we are shown what our lives could have been, had sin not entered our world. The collateral damage is unthinkable, as with any war.

Recall photographs of war-torn Berlin after the final invasion of the Allied troops at the close of World War II. Hundreds of homes and businesses lay in ruin. Graphic images of post–atomic bomb Hiroshima and Nagasaki show buildings, industries, infrastructures, and people in total disrepair. War always has a price—lives, resources, self-esteem, hope. All lost.

In one fell swoop, the battle for worship was lost. Mankind was condemned to death. Their relationship with God was severed. And all of life—humanity, earth, the animal kingdom, and even the spirit world—changed.

Such were the battle scars after the fall. Everything changed, including man's worship. Where once it was natural and free, it was now inhibited because of mankind's altered physical proximity with God. Communication was now from afar, and affected further by a feeling Adam and Eve had never known before: guilt! And they wouldn't be the only ones guilty. The child of their own loins would be the next to sink beneath the weight of sin and guilt.

When he lost the third worship war.

Worship War #3: Cain vs. Abel

The third worship war was between Cain, Adam and Eve's firstborn, and his brother, Abel. This conflict involved an actual act of worship. A difference in *attitude* in worship, coupled with a difference of opinion in the *presentation* of worship, was food for this notorious, one-sided battle.

The Players

The first player is Cain, a farmer. His younger brother, Abel, is a shepherd. As the story unfolds, each brother brings an offering to the Lord.

The Personalities

One gets the impression that Cain was somewhat arrogant, as an older brother can often be. He certainly had a patronizing spirit as he made his sacrifice to the Lord. He seemed to lack the sincerity required when approaching the throne of grace. The Bible says that he brought an offering of "the fruit of the ground" (Gen. 4:3). But he did not bring God the best of the fruit. He performed his obligation, but not from a heart of love. In fact, Cain's temperament "demonstrate[d] the intense paganism of his worship," wrote author Noel Due. "He hoped to build up credit with God."[5] And God rejected Cain's gesture.

Abel, on the other hand, brought God "the best of the firstborn lambs from his flock" (Gen 4:4 NLT). He could have brought a lesser gift. But the Bible says he brought his best, that which was most valuable. His was an expression of genuine, personal devotion and worship. And God accepted Abel's sacrifice.

Martin Luther once wrote, "God is not interested in any works, not even those which he himself has commanded, when they are not done in faith."[6] Interestingly God also recognized Abel's offering as an act of faith (Heb. 11:4).

We are not sure what the Lord's actual commandment was regarding sacrifices, but Leviticus 2 indicates that God accepts offerings of grain and cereal. So Cain's sin was not in the item offered, but the spirit in which the offering was made. I get the impression that it was a "thrown-together" package that did not represent Cain's potential for giving or, for that matter, a creative expression of love to God. Instead, it was prideful, as if he were saying, "Look what I've grown." Cain considered neither the quality of the gift nor the nature of his actions, important. God refused the gift, and Cain reacted with deep resentment: he "became very angry and felt rejected" (v. 5 NCV).

God gave Cain an opportunity to make things right. "You will be accepted if you do what is right" (v. 7 NLT). But Cain would have no part of it. He had done all he was going to do.

As a teacher, I've learned that there are generally two kinds of students. The first type takes advantage of any opportunity to learn. She follows through with assignments, documents all her research, and completes her work with excellence, taking time to make sure it is neat and well organized. She then hands in the work on time. Teachers *love* this kind of student. Awarding an A to such a pupil gives an instructor great satisfaction.

The second student seldom takes advantage of the learning process. He does not finish his work, does a poor job at gathering materials, and fails to sufficiently document his sources. He pays little attention to organizational structure and skips class often, resulting in his turning in work either late or incomplete. It becomes a struggle for both teacher and student at grade time. The teacher dreads the student's response to the poor grade, and the student is fretful about the grade.

Ironically, all students are given the same assignments and the same resources at the beginning of the semester. They each have the same opportunity to receive high marks. But this second type of student generally tries to blame someone else for his lack of discipline, sometimes even insisting it's the teacher's fault. "You just don't like me," he may accuse. And if the teacher actually gives him a second chance, recommending he redo the work, the student resents the teacher's audacity.

I imagine Cain was like the second student. He had the same opportunity as his brother to worship acceptably. But he chose to give God a second-best effort, and God did not accept it. So Cain became mad—and jealous.

And he murdered his brother.

The Process

"Let's go out into the field," Cain said to his brother, Abel. And there, Cain attacked his brother and killed him (Gen. 4:8 NCV).

This is a sad day in the history of man. It reveals the consequences of misdirected, self-centered gestures of worship. It also demonstrates the extreme measures man will take to prove that his own worship methods are acceptable. Says Due:

> The first murder in human history relates to the acceptability (or not) of the first recorded act of worship after the Fall. False worship arises in the flesh, breeds jealousy and anger, and ends in death. Anger at God, expressed in a brooding and fallen countenance, is expressed as anger to the brother, who is made in God's image. To kill him is to strike out at God (Genesis 9:5–6). Conversely, where one knows that one's worship is pleasing to God, there is peace and a good conscience . . . even if this is opposed with violence.[7]

All worship wars are essentially fought in the spirit world. That's because the battle for worship is *spiritual*. The conflict between Lucifer and God, declared before the days of men, continues today in a dimension that mortal eyes cannot see. But the battle for worship between Cain and Abel was unique in that the conflict was almost entirely in the heart of one man. Whereas Abel gave his best worship, Cain didn't, giving instead an offering of *convenience*. (His theme song could have been "I Did It My Way.") When his worship was rebuffed, instead of endeavoring anew to gain God's approval, he remained interested only in nursing his wounded self-esteem.

The worship battles we face today are often driven by self-interest. Unwilling to accept new, exciting venues for the expression of worship, many folks just stir up conflict. One way or another, today's worship wars are energized by the same "I want to do it my way" spirit that captivated Cain centuries ago. For example . . .

Some people prefer a particular musical style—hymns, contemporary "praise music" (P&W), classical, Christian country, Christian rock—and are *unbendable* about it.

And volume? The young folks want it loud. The older folks cover their ears. Often, both refuse to budge.

And what about worship *style?* Do we worship the Baptist way? the Catholic way? the Pentecostal way? the Methodist way?

What Scripture translation should we use? Perhaps you believe a Christian should only read from the King James Version. But others in your fellowship like the NIV. And your *pastor,* why, he uses the New American Standard Bible.

Other factors, too, such as lighting, location, pulpit placement, and manner of dress, can influence people's willingness to worship. Such personal preferences result in disagreement between brothers and sisters, pastors and parishioners, and their differences of opinion prohibit their worship of God. They have even been known to destroy the work of ministry—all because someone says, "I want it *my* way." The battle for worship then takes on a deadly posture, becoming in reality a battle for *control.* Even after reprimand, Cain was still determined to have absolute control. No one was going to tell *him* what to do. And the rest, as they say, is history.

War is never without fallout. Innocent people are caught in the crossfire. When Cain took Abel's life, he robbed Abel of his worship. Likewise, today when we wage our own little worship wars—over style or preference or what have you—someone is sure to get robbed in the process. And that's wrong.

Cain never admitted to being wrong.

The Penalty

The penalty for Cain's scuffle was stiff. "Now you will be cursed in your work with the ground," God decreed, "the same ground where your brother's blood fell and where your hands killed him. You will work the ground, but it will not grow good crops for you anymore, and you will wander around on the earth" (Gen. 4:11–12 NKJV).

The Price

War always affects innocent people. If you don't believe it, look at the statistics for World War II, "the single deadliest conflict the world has ever seen."[8] Germany, the nation most responsible for the war, lost more than 5.5

million soldiers. And that's only the beginning. Look at the military-death totals of just a few of the nations involved in the Second World War:

Bulgaria (Axis)	22,000
China (Allied)	3.8 million +
France (Allied)	212,000
Hungary (Axis)	300,000
Italy (Axis)	306,400
Japan (Axis)	2 million +
Romania (Axis)	300,000
Soviet Union	10 million +
United Kingdom (Allied)	382,600
USA (Allied)	407,300[9]

All told, "the total estimated human loss of life [in] World War II was roughly 72 million people," including approximately 47 million civilians.[10] Tens of millions of lives lost—and not *just* theirs, but also the lives of all of the children they might have brought into the world. Each casualty was a soul robbed of his or her future generations. And all because of the evil heart of one godless man—Adolf Hitler.

Because of Cain's evil heart, Abel, too, lost his life, but again, not his alone. Abel has no descendants; he lost his potential posterity. That's a terrible price to pay for Cain's misguided worship. The price to Adam and Eve, too, was terrible: one-half of their offspring—lost—and not only that, but all of the grandchildren and great-grandchildren they might have enjoyed (perhaps even great-great-great-*great* grandchildren—people lived longer in those days) had Abel lived.

The cost to Cain was the greatest of all. First, he would never be able to enjoy his brother's companionship again. Sure, brothers fight. But in the end, they're still brothers—and friends. But in an act of brutality over worship, Cain destroyed his closest friend and the one who could have tutored him in how to worship God.

Cain was driven "away from the Lord" to "the land of Nod, east of Eden" (Gen. 4:16). This move affected not only him, but his family and his sphere of influence. His future family never understood or experienced the peace of God. His existing family, Adam and Eve, were lost to him; he was separated from them. But worst of all, he was separated from God.

What about the fallout to all of humanity? Cain's murderous act set precedent for all the generations to follow. Murder, though not acknowledged by civilized society, became an acceptable alternative to peaceful negotiation. Cain's sin also established a pattern for Canaanite worship, which amounted to nothing more than ritual, coercion, and deceit to gain the gods' favor, relying on humility, not true adoration. And though condemned throughout the Bible, such worship still exists today in various forms.

PRINCIPLES OF WORSHIP FROM THIS CHAPTER

The stories in this chapter are heartbreaking; yet they provide some lifetime lessons that we can apply to our worship today.

First, misguided worship begins in the heart. The very first seeds of it sprouted in the heart of Satan. He wanted to bring down the Creator of the cosmos and end all worship of Him in heaven. But his seeds did not come to full fruition. So he planted some more in the heart of Eve, Adam, and then Cain. He wants to plant them in your heart too.

Satan is alive and well, my friend. And he wants to wipe out your worship of God. Most folks can't be hoodwinked into worshipping Satan directly, but people throughout the world worship him indirectly when they bow to the idol of "self" — by trying to worship "their way." They add insult to injury when they seek to *enforce* "their way." Like Cain, they do permanent harm to innocent people. Examples of this include the Spanish Inquisition, the Taiping Rebellion — and every church that has ever split over differences in worship styles.

But God is a God of second chances. He proved this by providing Adam and Eve another son: Seth, the head of the messianic line. Through him came "the Desire of All Nations" (Hag. 2:7 NKJV) — Jesus Christ. We are to worship Him and Him alone — *His* way.

If we do, it will bring a life filled with *promise*.

| 4 |

WORSHIP AND PROMISE: THE WORSHIP OF ABRAHAM

THREESCORE AND TEN YEARS — SUCH ARE THE DAYS OF MAN. My dad, who went to be with the Lord at the age of seventy-four, often reminded me that God only promises us seventy years. The older he got, the more he talked about "living on borrowed time." "Anything more than seventy's an extra gift," he would say. Ronald Reagan ran for office as a second-term United States president at age *seventy-six*. But I remember thinking, as a child, that *forty* was ancient.

Today in America, people are living longer. At older ages than ever before, they are enjoying richer, more fulfilling lives. Even so, most plan to be retired well before seventy. Somewhere in our sixties, the majority of us will say good-bye to the world of work and will instead live off of our traditional or Roth IRAs, Social Security (if it's still there!), and/or any pensions we may receive. Some of us will get an RV and travel the country. Others of us will just "kick back" in our rocking chairs, or spend our golden years fishing or crocheting. Where once we were active, we will become more sedentary as the days wax on toward our seventy-fifth birthdays. And to most of us, that sounds like a plan.

But not to Abram. At the age of seventy-five, he was just getting started.

ABRAM: A MAN OF WORSHIP

Prior to Abram's story, we read about the fall of man, the first murder, the great Flood, and the Tower of Babel, where God confused the languages.

These were wicked times, wherein people were driven by self-indulgence. In fact, "the LORD saw that . . . every intent of the thoughts of [their] heart[s] was only evil continually" (Gen. 6:5 NKJV). "I am sorry I ever made them," He concluded (v. 7 NLT). Mankind was given over to lust, drunkenness, and violence. But these characteristics contrast sharply with the personality we will study in this chapter: Abram.

Abram Worshipped by Obeying

We are first introduced to Abram as the son of Terah. Abram was married to his half sister, Sarai. She was a woman of great beauty, even at the age of sixty-five—but she was also barren.

Abram came from a place called Ur of the Chaldeans (or Chaldees), a city in ancient Sumer, of the lower Mesopotamian region. This whole area was known for its many massive temples, dedicated to the worship of numerous pagan gods and goddesses. Ur itself was the sacred city of Nanna, god of the moon, and Abram's father, brothers, and wife all got their names either from this "god," his associates, or the moon itself.[1] (Ironically, the moon-god Nanna was also known as *Sin*. Isn't that appropriate, since his worship often involved religious prostitution?[2]) In Ur, Joshua 24:2 tells us, Abram's father "worshiped other gods" (NIV). The Talmud indicates that he, in fact, worshipped no fewer than twelve deities.[3]

But by the time we meet Abram, he has already established himself as a follower of the only *true* God, something unheard-of in his polytheistic culture. And though fiercely loyal to his family, he broke away from their false deities and dedicated himself to worshipping the Lord[4]—Yahweh.[5]

Abram's reputation for worshipping a single god preceded him. In fact, He and Sarai were known throughout the region for their faithfulness to *one* god. This singular allegiance set Abram apart from his relatives, friends, and coworkers—and it prompted God to show up. He made His presence known to Abram and responded to his worship with both a calling and a promise: "Get out of your country, from your family and from your father's house, to a land that I will show you. I will make you a great nation; I will bless you and make your name great; and you shall be a blessing. I will bless those who bless you, and I will curse him who curses you; and in you all the families of the earth shall be blessed" (Gen. 12:1–3 NKJV).[6] What a promise! In one breath, God offered Abram (1) progeny, (2) fame, (3) protection from his enemies, and (4) blessing, not to him only, but to his family, friends, *everyone*. How did Abram respond to such a lavish covenant?

"Abram left Haran *as the LORD had told him* . . . Abram was 75 years old" (v. 4 NCV, emphasis added). Abram obeyed. In our study of worship, this detail is critical. Why? Obedience is central to worship. In fact, the first way we express love to God is through obedience to His call. How willing would *you* be at the ripe old age of seventy-five, to leave all with which you'd grown familiar, and take off to a place you had never even visited? That's exactly what Abram did. And in obeying God's orders, Abram proved his love and devotion—he, in fact, *worshipped*. That was the beginning of a relationship with God that would forever change the course of history.

Abram Worshipped with an Altar

Abram, his wife, his nephew Lot, and all his servants set out for the land of Canaan. When Abram reached the land of Shechem, the Lord appeared to him again, with another promise. This time, He told him, "See this land? I will give it to your descendants." Abram responded with awe and thanksgiving: he "built an altar . . . to the LORD" (v. 7 NCV). Then Abram traveled "to the mountain east of Bethel . . . There Abram built another altar to the LORD and worshiped him" (v. 8 NCV).

Are you beginning to notice a pattern here? Early on in Abram's story, he is identified as a builder of altars. In fact, on four different occasions in Genesis, Abram built an altar to God (12:7; 12:8; 13:18; 22:9). Obviously, Abram did not wait until his calling to start worshipping Yahweh. He had been practicing public and private worship for some time. This is clear from the fact that his reverence for God led him to build altars. He *already* knew how to honor God. He had established a *routine* for his times with God. In other words, he was already a *worshipper*.

But this "worshipper" was not perfect.

ABRAM: THE IMPERFECT WORSHIPPER (PART I)

Sometimes people feel that they must be "perfect" in order to worship God. They come to a service, and all around them, people's hearts are overwhelmed with the presence of God, yet they themselves can't seem to get involved. Maybe they feel "unworthy." They remember some failing during their day or week, and their worship is stunted. Perhaps they have just had a domestic spat, or acted inappropriately on the highway, when someone cut them off in traffic on the way to church. Whatever the case, they are riddled with guilt and have no interest in worshipping, and are certain that God has no interest in them.

But God never lost interest in Abram, in spite of his failings. What were Abraham's failings?

For one, he was a liar:

> At this time there was not much food in the land, so Abram went down to Egypt to live . . . Just before they arrived in Egypt, he said to his wife Sarai, ". . . You are a very beautiful woman. When the Egyptians see you, they will say, 'This woman is his wife.' Then they will kill me . . . Tell them you are my sister so that things will go well with me and I may be allowed to live . . ."
>
> When Abram came to Egypt, the Egyptians saw that Sarai was very beautiful. The Egyptian officers saw her and told the king of Egypt how beautiful she was. They took her to the king's palace, and the king was kind to Abram because he thought Abram was her brother. He gave Abram sheep, cattle, male and female donkeys, male and female servants, and camels.
>
> But the LORD sent terrible diseases on the king and all the people in his house because of Abram's wife Sarai. So the king sent for Abram and said, "What have you done to me? Why didn't you tell me Sarai was your wife? Why did you say, 'She is my sister' so that I made her my wife? Now, here is your wife. Take her and leave!" Then the king commanded his men to make Abram leave Egypt. (Gen. 12:10–20 NCV)

How embarrassing. Abram and Sarai were forced to tuck their tails and leave, in shame.

It was bad enough that Abram himself lied. But worse, he asked Sarai to lie too. And their "little white lie" brought dire consequences to those around them. The Egyptians were punished for Abram's sin. And the lie wasn't the worst of his trangressions. In spite of the fact that Abram *knew*

God—had heard His voice and experienced His presence—he walked in *fear*, instead of *faith*. And whatever is not of faith, is sin (Rom. 14:23). So Abram took matters into his own hands and made a willful decision to lie. Strike one.

And yet, in the very next chapter, after Abram had moved to Bethel, we see that God forgave Abram and gave him another promise: "Look all around you—to the north and south and east and west. All this land that you see I will give to you and your descendants forever. I will make your descendants as many as the dust of the earth. If anyone could count the dust on the earth, he could count your people. Get up! Walk through all this land because I am now giving it to you" (13:14–17 NCV).

Abram wasn't a perfect worshipper, but he was a worshipper. And God continued to bless him, despite his flaws. God gave him a promise, and, true to tradition, Abram worshipped God. Again, Abram "built an altar to the LORD" (v. 18 NCV).

So far we've seen two of the ways Abram worshipped God: (1) He worshipped God by *obeying* Him; and (2) he worshipped God with an *altar*, a practice Abram used routinely. In Genesis 14, Abram performed another act of worship: he honored God with the *tithe*.

Abram Worshipped with the Tithe

The storyline leading up to Abram's practice of tithing is fodder for an Academy Award–winning motion picture. It begins with a war.

The kings of Sodom, Gomorrah, Admah, Zeboiim, and Bela went out to fight in the Valley of Siddim . . . They fought against Kedorlaomer king of Elam, Tidal king of Goiim, Amraphel king of Babylonia, and Arioch king of Ellasar—four kings fighting against five. There were many tar pits in the Valley of Siddim. When the kings of Sodom and Gomorrah and their armies ran away, some of the soldiers fell into the tar pits, but the others ran away to the mountains.

Now Kedorlaomer and his armies took everything the people of

Sodom and Gomorrah owned, including . . . Lot, Abram's nephew who was living in Sodom . . . Then they left. One of the men who was not captured went to Abram, the Hebrew, and told him what had happened . . .

When Abram learned that Lot had been captured, he called out his 318 trained men . . . He led the men and chased the enemy all the way to the town of Dan. That night . . . they made a surprise attack against the enemy. They chased them all the way to Hobah, north of Damascus. Then Abram brought back everything the enemy had stolen, the women and the other people, and Lot, and everything Lot owned.

After defeating Kedorlaomer and the kings who were with him, Abram went home. As he was returning, the king of Sodom came out to meet him in the Valley of Shaveh (now called King's Valley).

Melchizedek king of Salem brought out bread and wine. He was a priest for God Most High and blessed Abram, saying, "Abram, may you be blessed by God Most High, the God who made heaven and earth. And we praise God Most High, who has helped you to defeat your enemies."

Then Abram gave Melchizedek a tenth of everything he had brought back from the battle. (Gen. 14:8–20 NCV)

The giving of 10 percent of one's substance to God is called the *tithe*. It is an act of worship. By giving a tenth of everything he had gained in battle (gold, silver, cattle), Abram was demonstrating his love for God. In other words, he was *worshipping God* with the tithe.

Some today teach that, as tithing is part of the old covenant, it is not required of today's believer. They justify this by quoting Romans 6:14, "Ye are not under the law, but under grace" (KJV). Eager to be free of the command to give a tenth of their increase back to God, they adamantly insist that "Christ has redeemed us from the curse of the law" (Gal. 3:13 NKJV). But it is important to see that this first instance of tithing came *before* the law of Moses. In fact, it predated the Mosaic law by several hundred years. So believers who use these Scriptures are in disobedience to God and are, in fact, robbing God by refusing to bring him the firstfruits of their increase. They are also robbing themselves of an opportunity to worship. The shed blood of Christ and the freedom it brings only intensify our responsibility to worship by giving to the Lord of our substance. The tithe serves as just a starting point, a bare minimum, in our worship to God and the Son He sent to die for us. Abram's gift to the high priest of Salem was an expression of appreciation—of worship. And today, we can—and must—worship Christ, our own High Priest, the same way.

ABRAM: THE IMPERFECT WORSHIPPER (PART II)

We have already seen that the great patriarch Abraham was not without his faults. In Genesis 12, he lied, and it wouldn't be the last time. But Abram also had a problem with unbelief.

> After [Abram rescued Lot], the Lord spoke . . . to Abram in a vision: "Abram, don't be afraid. I will defend you, and I will give you a great reward." But Abram said, "Lord God, what can you give me? . . . You have given me no son, so [Eliezer] a slave born in my house will inherit everything I have."
>
> Then the Lord spoke his word to Abram: "He will not be the one to inherit what you have. You will have a son of your own who will inherit what you have."
>
> Then God led Abram outside and said, "Look at the sky. There are so many stars you cannot count them. Your descendants also will be too many to count . . . I am the Lord who led you out of Ur of Babylonia so that I could give you this land to own."
>
> But Abram said, "Lord God, how can I be sure that I will own this land?" (Gen. 15:1–8 NCV).

"How can I be *sure?*"?!? God promised, and His *word* is sure. But Abram wanted more. He wanted a guarantee. And God didn't get mad about it.

Abram Worshipped God with a Blood Sacrifice

The Lord then ordered Abram to bring Him a cow, a goat, a sheep, a dove, and a pigeon (v. 9). True to form, Abram obeyed. He killed the animals and cut the larger animals in two, then laid them before the Lord. When the vultures swooped down on the carcasses, Abram chased them away. Then he waited for God's response to his act of obedience.

As the sun was setting, Abram fell asleep, and a "very terrible darkness came" (v. 12 NCV). Then the Lord spoke to Abram: "Your descendants will be strangers and travel in a land they don't own. The people there will make them slaves and be cruel to them for four hundred years. But I will punish the nation where they are slaves. Then your descendants will leave that land, taking great wealth with them. And you, Abram, will die in peace and will be buried at an old age. After your great-great-grandchildren are born, your people will come to this land again" (vv. 13–16 NCV).

Another promise! But this wasn't God's only response. Abram was a worshipper, and God answered Abram's obedient worship by showing up and "showing out." After the sun set, "a smoking firepot and a blazing torch passed between the halves of the dead animals" (v. 17 NCV). Abram saw the consuming fire of God. He was the only one in his family to see it. But God still wasn't through.

"On that day the Lord made an agreement with Abram and said, 'I will give to your descendants the land between the river of Egypt and the great river Euphrates.'" In a night, God promised Abram long life, an inheritance of land, and successors. And yet . . .

Ten years went by—*tick, tick, tick*—and still no son. Sarai couldn't take it anymore. So she went to Abram and told him to have sex with her servant, Hagar. "If she has a child, maybe I can have my own family through her," Sarai reasoned (16:2 NCV).

One can only guess what was going through Sarai's mind when she suggested that her husband of many years have sexual intercourse with a slave. Perhaps she didn't *really* mean it. Or it could be that she was so frustrated at being childless that she would do *anything* to ensure that a nation would be born through Abram. Or just *maybe* she was reacting to Abram's constant fretting over God's timing. After all, it *had* been ten years, and Sarai was already seventy-six. She may have been feeling insecure. Only God really knows. Whatever the case, Abram tamely did what Sarai said—and sinned.

You know the story. Sarai's plan worked. Hagar became pregnant and gave birth to a son, Ishmael. But that's where everything went haywire. God Himself predicted that Ishmael would be "like a wild donkey. He will be against everyone, and everyone will be against him. He will attack all his brothers" (v. 12 NCV).

Things got ugly on the home front. Hagar began to hate her mistress, perhaps because, though *she* had given birth, it was Sarai who was entitled to call Ishmael "*my* son."[7] Conversely, Sarai became jealous of Hagar and began punishing her for no reason. And these were just the immediate effects of Abram's sin. There were also lasting effects. Ishmael became the father of the Arab nations,[8] and God's prophecy about him proved true. To this day, the descendants of Ishmael live in hostility with their "brothers." Evidence of this is the never-ending Arab-Israeli conflict that we see on the news every day. And all because of one sin — and not the sin of adultery.

Abram's extramarital sex *was* a sin, of course, but the greater sin was his lack of faith in God. After all the promises God had made, Abram still didn't believe. He and Sarai decided to "help God," to speed things along, to hasten the promise. Abram committed an act of infidelity to his wife — and to God.

It's a terrible thing when we imagine that the Almighty needs *our* help. But we often do. Instead of waiting on God to answer our prayers, we take matters into our own hands. Nothing good ever comes from it. Because of Abram's impatience, he was caught in the middle of Hagar and Sarai's squabble. Then, after *herself* suggesting that Abram sleep with Hagar, Sarai actually blamed Abram for the bad blood in the household. Worse, God later made Abram send Hagar and her son away. This was *not* the heir that God promised him. In sorrow, Abram had to watch Ishmael, not the promised one but still the son of his loins, walk away.

Liar, doubter, adulterer—Abram had quite a rap sheet. But also on his list of descriptors was this word: *worshipper*. He still loved God with all his heart. So how did God respond to this wavering worshipper named Abram?

He gave him a new name.

ABRAHAM: FATHER OF NATIONS

When Abram was ninety-nine, God came to him again. "I am Almighty God," He said. "Walk before Me and be *blameless*" (17:1 NKJV, emphasis added). Notice that God didn't spend any time browbeating Abram for his past sins. He knew that Abram was well aware he had blown it. So God didn't scold him. He simply issued a new command: *be blameless.* Then he also issued Abram a new name: Father of a Multitude[9]—*Abraham.*[10]

> "I am making my agreement with you: I will make you the father of many nations. I am changing your name from Abram to Abraham because I am making you a father of many nations. I will give you many descendants. New nations will be born from you, and kings will come from you. And I will make an agreement between me and you and all your descendants from now on: I will be your God and the God of all your descendants. You live in the land of Canaan now as a stranger, but I will give you and your descendants all this land forever. And I will be the God of your descendants." (Gen. 17:2–8 NCV)

Every time God reveals Himself to man, an expression of worship follows. Worship is the normal and natural response to God's presence. As early as Genesis 11, each time God revealed Himself to Abram, he worshipped. So, what do you suppose his reaction was to this revelation of God? Facedown worship. The King James Version says that Abram "fell on his face" (v. 3).

After this, God told Abra*ham* (he is never called *Abram* again) his part of the deal: he would have to be circumcised, himself and every male in his company: servants, warriors, and offspring. We read in chapter 17 that Abraham was circumcised that very day, along with every man and boy in his household. Abraham sure knew how to worship God through obedience.

But he was still a "doubting Thomas," long before the disciple of Christ was a twinkle in his father's eye.

"I will also change the name of your wife . . . , to Sarah," God told Abraham. "I will bless her and give her a son, and you will be the father. She will be the mother of many nations. Kings of nations will come from her" (vv. 15–16 NCV).

After all of the promises Abraham had received to date, he must have fallen on his face in thanksgiving to God. Right? Well . . . no. The Bible said he "fell on his face and *laughed*" (v. 17 NASB, emphasis added). And he wasn't the only one. Later, when God appeared to him again outside of his tent and made the same promise, Sarah overheard—and she laughed too. She was, after all, ninety years old, way past childbearing age.

"Why did you laugh?" God asked her.

"I *didn't* laugh," Sarah lied (seems lying runs in the family).

"*Oh*, yes, you did," God replied.

But in spite of Abraham and Sarah's oft-repeated questioning of God's integrity, He kept His promise. Isaac[11] was born a year later, the child of Sarah.

ABRAHAM, THE SOLD-OUT SACRIFICER

Why would the God of heaven put up with a man who was so unsteady, whose faith consistently wobbled on one leg? Because in his heart of hearts, Abraham was a worshipper, and God knew it. He had great plans for Abraham and his future generations. But, first, Abraham had to pass the ultimate test of worship, and all that he had gone through to now, was God's preparation.

Abraham was now 115 years old. Forty years had passed since God's first recorded revelation to him. He had had several years, by now, to enjoy his son Isaac. What a treasure in his old age. They had no doubt laughed together—played, hunted, and fished together—father and son.

But then God gave Abraham a test—the ultimate test of his devotion to God. He asked him to sacrifice his son.

Abraham Worshipped God with Complete Surrender

"Abraham!" God called one day.

"Here I am," Abraham answered.

Then God said, "Take your only son, Isaac, the son you love, and go to the land of Moriah. Kill him there and offer him as a whole burnt offering" (Gen. 22:1–2 NCV).

So, naturally, Abraham kicked and screamed, telling God how unfair it was to ask for his only son, after it had taken *so* long to get him . . . right? No. The Bible says:

Abraham got up early in the morning and saddled his donkey. He took Isaac and two servants with him. After he cut the wood for the sacrifice, they went to the place God had told them to go. On the third day Abraham looked up and saw the place in the distance. He said to his servants, "Stay here with the donkey. My son and I will go over there and worship, and then we will come back to you."

Abraham took the wood for the sacrifice and gave it to his son to carry, but he himself took the knife and the fire. So he and his son went on together.

Isaac said to his father Abraham, "Father!"

Abraham answered, "Yes, my son."

. . . "We have the fire and the wood, but where is the lamb we will burn as a sacrifice?"

Abraham answered, "God will give us the lamb for the sacrifice, my son."

So Abraham and his son went on together and came to the place God had told him about. Abraham built an altar there. He laid the wood on it and then tied up his son Isaac and laid him on the wood on the altar. Then Abraham took his knife and was about to kill his son.

But the angel of the Lord called to him from heaven and said, "Abraham! Abraham!"

Abraham answered, "Yes." . . .

"Don't kill your son . . . Now I can see that you trust God and that you have not kept your son, your only son, from me."

Then Abraham . . . saw a male sheep caught in a bush by its horns. So Abraham . . . killed it. He offered it as a whole burnt offering to God, and his son was saved. . . .

The angel of the Lord called to Abraham from heaven a second time and said, "The Lord says, 'Because you did not keep back your son, your only son, from me, I make you this promise by my own name: I will surely bless you and give you many descendants. They will be as many as the stars in the sky and the sand on the seashore, and they will capture the cities of their enemies. Through your descendants all the nations on the earth will be blessed, because you obeyed me.'" (vv. 3–18 NCV) *rawn out of a heart of worship will always pass the test—no matter how difficult.*

And there you have it. Abraham was a man of faith. His faith produced obedience, and his obedience exemplified honest worship. Our worship, too, must be driven by obedience and faith, because faith that is drawn out of a heart of worship will always pass the test—no matter how difficult.

PRINCIPLES OF WORSHIP FROM THIS CHAPTER

Abraham: an ordinary man, made extraordinary through worship. What lessons can we glean from his life of worship?

1. Worship Begins with Obedience

These days, people often equate "worship" with the singing of songs, the raising of hands, the shouting of praises, or some other *demonstration* of adoration to God. But true worship begins with obedience. Without it, every song is meaningless and ceases to be worship. In fact, if we are not eager to obey what God asks of us, we are not even *ready* to worship.[12] That's because obedience is at the heart of worship. It is worship's very foundation.

When we look at Abraham, we see a man who was "at the ready," no matter what God told him to do. *Leave your country.* "Yes sir." *Sacrifice a heifer.* "Yes sir." *Sacrifice your son.* "Yes sir." If we are to worship God, we must be at the ready too.

2. Worship Doesn't Begin with a Perfect Vessel

Abraham was a two-time liar. He told the same lie—"She's not my wife; she's my sister"—*twice* (Gen. 12 and 20). He was an adulterer, all too eager, at the mere suggestion, to sleep with a woman who was not his wife. And he was a doubter. But God still loved him. He loves you too. And while none of us are perfect vessels, He can make us vessels of honor if we humble ourselves and worship Him. He can take all of our weaknesses and shape us, as pottery, into something beautiful. Look at what He shaped out of Abraham: the nation of Israel.

What could He shape out of *you?*

3. Worship Involves Routine

Authentic worship requires a regular worship *routine*. Abraham was a builder of altars. It was his custom, his *routine*. We need altars too. And while it's true that one can worship God anywhere, at any time, God is not impressed when the only worship He gets from us takes place

- in the car, on our way to work
- at the stove, as we cook
- in the yard, as we mow and weed-eat
- in our beds, as we struggle to not snore
- in front of the TV, as we channel surf . . .

You get the idea. God doesn't want your only worship to be *divided* worship, mingled with other pursuits. We saw this in chapter 2, where we discussed the *place* of worship. You need to meet with God at a special time in a previously appointed place—a place where He has visited before—that is free of distractions from the world around you. As you worship, God will begin to make comfortable in your own heart a process— again, a *routine*, if you will—that is best suited for your personal worship. Your activities during this time may vary, alternating between confession, repentance, prayer, praise, singing, Bible reading, intercession, maybe even a dance. But whatever your procedures, by setting a special time and identifying a "set-apart" place for private worship, you will have established a routine for spending time with God and giving him your *undivided* attention. He deserves no less.

4. There's More Than One Way to Worship

In this chapter we have seen that Abraham worshipped God several different ways. He worshipped God by obeying. He worshipped at an altar.

He worshipped with the tithe. He worshipped with sacrifices. And he worshipped with complete surrender. Thanks to the blood of Jesus, we will never again have to offer blood sacrifices, but we can always obey. We can meet with God at the altar. We can give of our substance. And we can surrender our all. Isaac was Abraham's "all," yet he was willing to give him up for the love of God. Surely *we* can offer God our lives—to His service.

5. Worship Brings God's Revelation of His Presence

Every time Abraham was faithful to God through worship, God made His presence known and reconfirmed His relationship with Abraham by revealing more of Himself. Remember, God is all about relationship. As we worship Him, He will favor us with His presence, and as our relationship with Him grows, He will reveal more and more of who He is. And finally . . .

6. Worship Brings Reward

By now I hope you can see that there are promises captured and rewards gained through worship. Abraham was blessed for his unceasing worship of the one God. God promised him a nation, a people, *descendants*. And He delivered. It will be the same for you as you practice biblical worship, from your heart. God will deliver, and you will reap the promises of God.

5

WORSHIP AND DELIVERANCE: THE STORY OF MOSES, PART I

DURING THE 1950S AND EARLY '60S, AFRICAN AMERICANS WERE discriminated against in many ways. Often, they couldn't eat in the same restaurants, attend the same schools, or drink from the same water fountains that white citizens used. They were forced to ride at the back of public buses, and unreasonable laws made it difficult—if not impossible—for them to vote in public elections. These were chaotic days, marked by bigotry and oppression. Social, moral, and political injustice prevailed across society's landscape.

Then, in August 1963, more than two hundred thousand people gathered in our nation's capital to rally for racial equality. On the steps of the Lincoln Memorial, a young, charismatic, African-American preacher named Martin Luther King Jr., told the mammoth crowd of his dream for a future in which blacks and whites—and all other races—would coexist as equals. His "I have a dream" speech became the landmark statement of civil rights in America:

> I have a dream that one day this nation will rise up and live out the true meaning of its creed: "We hold these truths to be self-evident; that all men are created equal" . . . I have a dream that one day every valley shall be exalted, every hill and mountain shall be made low, the rough places will be made plain, and the crooked places will be made straight, and the glory of the Lord shall be revealed, and all flesh shall see it together. . . .

And when this happens, and when we allow freedom to ring . . . from every village and every hamlet, from every state and every city, we will be able to speed up that day when all of God's children — black men and white men, Jews and gentiles, Protestants and Catholics — will be able to join hands and sing in the words of the old Negro spiritual, "Free at last! Free at last! Thank God Almighty, we are free at last!"[1]

Now rewind, thousands of decades, across the miles, to the days of the ancient Egyptian monarchy. Here we find another story of bigotry, oppression — and slavery. An ethnic majority is being denied equal rights — and especially its right to worship.

You know the history. A young Hebrew man, Joseph, sold by his jealous brothers into slavery, became a head of state in the land of his captivity. With wisdom from God, this man saved his part of the world from famine. And under his rule, the nation of Israel, begun by his great-grandfather Abraham, grew strong in the land of Egypt. The Hebrew people "had many children and grandchildren . . . They multiplied so quickly that they soon filled the land" (Ex. 1:7 NLT). More than four hundred years passed as the nation continued to flourish. But then . . .

"There arose a new king over Egypt, who did not know Joseph" (v. 9 NKJV). What he did know was fear — and insecurity. He became intimidated by the Hebrews' growing political and financial influence. And their sheer numbers terrified him. *They're different from us*, he reasoned. *What if we go to war? They might turn on us and join our enemies!*

So Pharaoh,[2] king of Egypt, made slaves out of Israel, forcing them to perform backbreaking labor under cruel slave drivers. But their numbers only increased, as did Pharaoh's fear. So he initiated Plan B.

"Kill the Hebrew babies," he told the Egyptian midwives. "Every boy that is born."

But the midwives feared God. So they lied. "Those Hebrew women are stout," they told Pharaoh. "Their babies are born before we even get there." So the Hebrews continued to multiply, becoming more and more powerful.

I'll fix them! plotted the insecure king, and desperate to control the Hebrews' exploding population, he hatched his most evil scheme: genocide. Pharaoh decreed that all their newborn males would be thrown into the Nile.

Yet one very important baby boy survived. We know him as Moses—the child whose mother hid him in a waterproofed, floating basket along the riverbank, so he would not be murdered.

But the child was found—by the daughter of the king himself, and she adopted him and raised him in the palace, as the son of royalty. But as Moses grew older, he knew who he was: a Hebrew, not an Egyptian. And one day, as he watched an Egyptian taskmaster beating a fellow Hebrew, something snapped. In indignation, he killed the Egyptian and buried his body.

Unfortunately, someone saw. He reported the murder to Pharaoh—and Moses became a wanted man. Frightened for his life, he fled into the wilderness.

You remember the story. Moses found work in the fields of Jethro, the priest of Midian. And God blessed Moses there with a home, a wife, a family . . . and a *calling*.

Moses spent forty years in his new land. Meanwhile, the old king of Egypt died. But the people of Israel were still enslaved, so they cried out to God—and God heard them. "He saw [their] troubles . . . , and he was concerned about them" (Ex. 2:25 NCV). He also remembered the covenant He had made with Abraham, then to Isaac and Jacob, so many years before. And God devised an escape plan . . .

GOD PREPARED MOSES FOR WORSHIP

Moses was in the wilds, tending his father-in-law's flocks and minding his own business, when suddenly, he saw a bush ablaze. But though the bush was engulfed in flames, it did not burn up. Puzzled, Moses went closer for a better look.

"Moses!" God called from the burning bush.

At once, Moses responded: "Here I am!" These three words are pivotal to our study of worship. They were the very same words uttered by both

Abraham and Jacob, centuries before (Gen. 22:1; 46:2). The prophets Samuel and Isaiah would repeat these words, centuries later. But what's so important about them?

In the last chapter, we learned that obedience is at the core of worship. In fact, all authentic worship begins and ends with a heart that is willing to obey. Moses' immediate "Here I am!" was a sign to God that he fully intended to obey. So God told Moses to take off his sandals, because the place was sacred: Moses was standing on "holy ground." Instantly, Moses took off his sandals, because he respected God. And God revealed His identity to this submissive man.

"I am the God of your ancestors," He thundered, "the God of Abraham, Isaac, and Jacob." Hearing that, Moses covered his face in fear. He desperately wanted to show his reverence for God. Then God revealed His plan to save the nation of Israel—using *Moses*.

"I am sending you to the king of Egypt," God announced. "Go! Bring my people, the Israelites, out . . . After you lead the people out of Egypt, all of you will worship me on this mountain" (Ex. 3:10–12 NCV).

The cruel king had robbed Israel of their worship. Beneath their heavy burdens, they had long been stripped of any personally compelling reason to worship their God. But our relational God craved their companionship. He wanted a *relationship* with them. He wanted to bring them out of Egypt, away from the world system they knew, to a better, more obliging place in which He could *dwell* with them and give them rest and satisfaction. All of this would be accomplished through worship, so . . . He wanted their *worship*.

And He was willing to fight for it.

But Moses was hesitant. "When I tell the Israelites that the God of their ancestors sent me, they won't believe me," he fretted. "They'll say, 'What is his name?' What do I tell them?"

"I AM WHO I AM," God answered. "Tell them, 'I AM sent me to you'" (v. 14 NCV).

But Moses was still uncertain, and a tug of war began between him and God. "I'm a nobody." "I'm not a good speaker." "I get tongue-tied." Some theologians believe that Moses actually stuttered. True or not, Moses made every excuse in the book. He just could not bring himself to believe that

God could use an *ordinary* man in an *extraordinary* way to achieve an *impossible* task.

Unbelief is a terrible thing. It cripples ambition and renders strong, valiant soldiers impotent in battle. Unbelief smothers the fire of vision, kills dreams, and halts the wheels of progress. Its loud, clanging confusion drowns out the song of victory. Remember, it was unbelief that wreaked havoc in Abraham and Sarah's household. Unbelief is the tool of Satan. It kills faith in its tracks, and God hates it.

Over the years, I've watched talented, promising young men and women turn from obeying God's will because they listened to whispers of doubt from well-meaning friends or family members. Though once convinced of God's calling on their lives, these tender, easily persuaded young people now opt for an easier road, one that ensures financial security, status, and career progression. But years later, often after a divorce or economic failure, they realize they have made a serious mistake.

God desperately wanted to prevent this from happening to Moses. So He did two things to remove all of Moses' defenses: (1) He gave him the ability to perform signs and wonders, and (2) He appointed Moses' brother, Aaron, to be the spokesman. Aaron agreed.

So there they were: Aaron, age eighty-three, and Moses, age eighty, standing before a king. And thus began . . . another worship war.

Pharaoh vs. I AM that I AM

In Chapter 3, we studied three worship wars in the book of Genesis. Now, in Exodus, we see another battle for worship, a worship war unlike any other in the history of man.

"We came to tell you," Moses and Aaron said to Pharaoh, "that the God of Israel says, 'Let my people go! They must hold a feast for me in the desert.'"

"Who is the Lord?" the king scoffed. "Why should I obey him . . . ? I do not know the Lord, and I will not let Israel go."

"[But] the God of the Hebrews has met with us . . . Let us travel three days into the desert to offer sacrifices to the Lord our God. If we don't . . . , he may kill us" (Ex. 5:1–3 NCV). But the king showed no regard for the lives of the Hebrews, and absolutely no deference to their God. Pharaoh had gods of his own—and was considered a god himself.

The ancient Egyptians were very religious. Their culture and faith were based on an odd mixture of pantheism and animal worship. Their inanimate gods were fashioned from gold, silver, brass, and stone, into the forms of various animals, because animals were considered to be incarnations of these gods. One of their many deities was Horus, the god of light. He was "depicted as a falcon, his left eye being the moon, and the right, the sun."[3] The king was thought to be a manifestation of this god, making the very word *Pharaoh* as much an institution as a political position. Pharaoh was also the central protector of *maat*,[4] the universal ethical principle that stood for justice, order, and truth. *Maat* was considered "the perfect order toward which humans should strive."[5] So, "by adhering to Pharaoh, . . . humans were aligned with nature, and thus also with maat. What Pharaoh did and said, was theoretically beyond the understanding of normal human beings, and to be understood as revelations. By giving up freedom, humans could achieve peace with the universal powers and the gods."[6]

It is easy to see why the king of Egypt was so deeply offended at Aaron and Moses. They had marched right into *his* domain and demanded that he free *his* slaves, so they could worship *their* God. Yahweh worship was a threat to Pharaoh's prestige. It was his status as a god-king that had elevated him to his position of power. He needed no competition from "I AM." To him, this god was no more important than any other deity, including himself. (After all, he *was* divine.) So what did Yahweh, the "I AM," do about this arrogant "god-king" called Pharaoh?

He took him on. Head-on—Pharaoh *and* his "gods."

Yahweh vs. the God of the Nile

The God of Israel will not share worship. His people are to "serve him only" (Deut. 6:13 NIV). So a battle for worship ensued between Yahweh and Pharaoh—and the entire Egyptian pantheon. God declared war: He sent ten plagues upon the land of Egypt. Each plague was worse than the last. And each was an assault upon the deity of Pharaoh and his gods.

Pharaoh was a god by office . . . . responsible for the welfare of Egypt, including the Nile and maat. . . . When Yahweh assailed Egypt with the ten plagues, he was casting the universal order of creation (maat) into chaos. This was a direct challenge to the power and sovereignty of Pharaoh: could he maintain maat or could he not? In the face of Yahweh, the maker of heaven and earth, Pharaoh's real status is exposed. His lack of divine power shows that he is no god, or at least no god like Yahweh.[7]

The Egyptians worshipped the Nile River and its god, Napy, so it's no surprise that the Nile was the first thing God attacked. "The LORD said to Moses, 'Tell Aaron: "Take the walking stick in your hand and stretch your hand over the rivers, canals, ponds, and pools in Egypt." The water will become blood everywhere in Egypt, both in wooden buckets and in stone jars'" (Ex. 7:19 NCV). So, in plain view of the king, Aaron raised his stick and struck the water—and it turned to blood.

All the fish died, and the river began to stink. The Egyptians couldn't drink the water, from there or anywhere, because blood was *everywhere*. For a full week the blood remained, but Pharaoh wouldn't release his slaves. So God launched another attack on Egypt's pantheon.

Yahweh vs. the Goddess Het

"Let my people go, so they can worship me," God demanded. "If you refuse, I'll punish Egypt again—with frogs." Pharaoh *flat* refused, and God sent His second plague: pesky little amphibians, throughout the land. Hippity-hoppity, all over the people. Frogs in their beds, frogs in their ovens. God was making a mockery of Het, the frog-headed goddess of fertility. She couldn't rein in the frogs that He dispatched. *He* had to call them off.

"Pray to the LORD to take the frogs away," Pharaoh begged Moses. "I will let your people go to offer sacrifices to the LORD" (8:8 NCV). Liar. He had no intention of freeing his slaves, not even for three days. And God knew it. Nonetheless, when Moses prayed, the frogs all died. But as soon as they did, Pharaoh went back on his word. So God toppled another one of Egypt's "divine beings"—by covering the Egyptians with gnats.

Yahweh vs. the Earth God

God instructed Aaron to raise his walking stick and strike the dust. When he did, all over Egypt, the dust turned to gnats.[8] They were everywhere, on man and animal alike. This was an embarrassment to all worshippers of Geb, the "god of the earth," to whom Egyptians paid homage for the fertile soil. Yet from this same soil came a pestilence that Geb himself could not destroy. Was Pharaoh dissuaded? No. The children of Israel were building huge cities for the king. He *wouldn't* do without them. So God next slapped the "bug god" soundly in the face.

Yahweh vs. Khepfi

The fourth plague God sent upon the stubborn Egyptian monarch was an influx of insects. Many Bible versions call them "flies," but this word was not in the original. Moses simply wrote that great *swarms* covered the land. Some scholars suggest that the swarmers were actually scarabs,[9] which were used to represent the god Ra.[10] Whatever these critters were, they were a humiliation both to Ra and to Khepfi, god of insects.[11] They tormented rich and poor, prince and pauper, *everyone*—except for God's chosen people, Israel.

In panic, Pharaoh decided to release the slaves to worship. But all too quickly, he changed his mind. And this time, God affronted a gaggle of gods and goddesses.

Yahweh vs. Apis, Hathor, Isis, Khnum, Ptah . . .

A horrific disease smote the animals. Remember, Egyptians worshipped their animals. But now, all were dying: horses, donkeys, camels, goats, sheep, and cattle. This scourge from God was an affront to Apis,[12] the bull-deity; Hathor,[13] the cow-deity; Isis, the heifer-loving goddess;[14] Khnum, the ram-headed god[15]; Ptah, who manifested himself as a bull[16]; and every other Egyptian god with the head of a farm animal. But Pharaoh just couldn't get enough disgrace. His own head was as hard as granite.

Yahweh vs. the Healing Deities

Next God sent boils upon the Egyptians—painful, inflamed pustules all over their bodies. This outbreak flew in the face of both Imhotep, the once-mortal "god" of medicine and healing[17]; and Thoth,[18] the god from whom physicians received their power to heal.

One by one, the deity dominoes fell. God was proving to the Egyptians — and to any Israelites tempted to join them in worship—that their gods weren't worth the stories made up about them. But God the True was not through mortifying the "god-king" and his deaf deities. He next sent a plague from the sky.

Yahweh vs. the Goddess of the Sky

"Tell the 'god-king' that the God of the Hebrews says, 'Let my people go to *worship Me*'—and tell him *that's an order!*" (Ex. 9:13, author translation). But the king said no, and from the heavens came a scourge of hail. These hailstones, and the lightning that accompanied them, inflicted the worst storm-related devastation since Egypt became a nation. They destroyed crops and trees, homes and lives, both human and animal. And where was the sky goddess, Nut, all this time? God proved her impotent in the face of His judgment.

Yahweh vs. Neper, Osiris, and Renenutet

Right before Pharaoh's eyes, God had made quick work of a slew of Egyptian deities. At any time, had he chosen to, the conceited king of Egypt could have repented of his stubbornness, denounced his counterfeit gods, and declared for all of Egypt to hear that they were to worship Yahweh, the God of the Hebrews.

But Pharaoh's heart was proud, rock hard, ice-cold. So God sent locusts to destroy what the hail had left behind. The creatures covered the land so the ground could not be seen. Meanwhile, the god of grain was silent. The god of vegetation was powerless. And there wasn't a thing the goddess of the harvest could do.

Then God sent darkness.

Yahweh vs. the Sun God

With His ninth plague, Yahweh confronted Re, the god of the sun. Originally named Amon-Ra, the sun god was, at different times, also associated with creation, fertility, victory in war, and justice for the oppressed.

So when darkness covered the land of Egypt, it was an insult to the whole of the Egyptian belief system. And the darkness was so thick it could be felt. Pitch-black—for three full days.

Pharaoh decided he'd better let the *people* go for that feast—but he wouldn't surrender the animals. "No way," said Moses. He would need the animals for sacrificing. So the king of Egypt stiffened his neck one more time.

"Get out of here!" he bellowed at Moses. "Don't ever let me see you again!"

"Very well, I will never see you again" (10:27–28 NLT), Moses told him, adding one last warning:

Yahweh vs. the Progeny of Egypt

"At midnight tonight," God told the hardheaded king, through Moses, "I will go through Egypt—and *every firstborn son* will die: your slave's son—and *your* son. *Even* the sons of your beloved cattle. Egypt will be filled with cries, but not from *My* people. Then your officers will beg—facedown—for My people to leave" (Ex. 11:4–8, author translation).

The Egyptians had until the stroke of twelve. But in the meantime, God wasn't sitting idly by, waiting to unleash his horrors. He was preparing His people to be a community of worship.

GOD PRESERVES HIS PEOPLE THROUGH WORSHIP

Moses called the elders of Israel together and told them to get animals ready for sacrifice and to instruct each Hebrew family on how to worship God at midnight. The rules were very specific. As each lamb was killed, the household was to take a branch of the hyssop plant, dip it into a bowl of blood from the slain lamb, and paint the blood on their doorframes. No one was permitted to leave the house until morning. Every home obedient to these instructions would be spared as the death angel passed through the streets of Egypt, fulfilling God's vow to kill all firstborn sons. After Moses related God's instructions, the people "bowed down and worshiped the LORD" (Ex. 12:27 NCV).

At midnight, for the first time, Israel would worship God *together*. Though every family would be in their individual home, worshipping privately, all families would be worshipping collectively as well, as a nation, all following God's directives at the same time. And the directives He gave were for an observance that would come to be called *Passover*.

Israel's obedience/worship on this first Passover would accomplish two things: (1) it would protect them from the deaths of their own firstborn; and (2) it would institute an annual celebration to commemorate their divine protection and their deliverance from bondage.

At midnight—just as God had warned—all the firstborn Egyptian males began to die. From palace to prison, cries were heard as the death angel executed God's slaughter. Even the livestock fell victim to the curse.

Horror-stricken, the king called for Moses. "Leave us!" he cried. "Go away! Go and worship the LORD!" (v. 31 NLT). The Egyptian people chimed in. "Hurry up," they urged, "or we'll *all* die."

Moses immediately moved the children of God into action. They got up and left Egypt.

GOD PROTECTS HIS CHILDREN FOR WORSHIP

You know the rest of the story. Realizing that his workforce was gone, and furious that his reputation as a god had been compromised, Pharaoh angrily sent his army to pursue the children of Israel and bring them back. He caught up with them at the edge of the Red Sea.

Yahweh vs. Yamm, God of the Sea

When they realized they had reached a dead end at the seashore, the Israelites were terrified. But we know the outcome. God split the sea, humbling one more Egyptian god: Yamm, god of the sea. The Israelites crossed on dry land.

When the Egyptians tried the same thing, Yamm didn't protect them. The sea crashed in on them. Chariots, riders, horses, all were crushed beneath a wall of water. The king's army was utterly destroyed. It was a *total victory* for God.

"So that day the Lord saved the Israelites from the Egyptians," wrote Moses, "and the Israelites saw the Egyptians lying dead on the seashore. When the Israelites saw the great power the Lord had used against the

Egyptians, they feared the Lord, and they trusted him and his servant Moses" (Ex. 14:30–31 NCV).

THE FIRST SONG OF WORSHIP

The defeat of the eminent god-king, Pharaoh, was a defining moment in the life and history of Israel. The people forever learned the value God placed on them as a people created to worship and fellowship with Him. So now, with their enemies floating dead in the sea, the children of Israel took time to worship. In concert, Moses and the people—the *delivered* people—sang the first national song of worship to the Lord:

> I will sing to the LORD,
> For He has triumphed gloriously!
> The horse and its rider
> He has thrown into the sea!
>
> The LORD is my strength and song,
> And He has become my salvation;
> He is my God, and I will praise Him;
> My father's God, and I will exalt Him.
>
> The LORD is a man of war;
> The LORD is His name.
>
> Pharaoh's chariots and his army He has cast into the sea;
> His chosen captains also are drowned in the Red Sea.
>
> The depths have covered them;
> They sank to the bottom like a stone . . .
>
> Who is like You, O LORD, among the gods?
> Who is like You, glorious in holiness,
> Fearful in praises, doing wonders? . . .
>
> The LORD shall reign forever and ever . . . (Ex. 15:1–18 NKJV)

What a song! Look at those lyrics. And what you see here is only a part of the victory song Israel sang that day.

In many musical and literary forms, composers write an extension to their pieces, known as a *coda*, or *recapitulation*. This device serves as a conclusion, a means to summarize the work as a whole. The Song of Moses used this device. In verse 19, the recapitulation reads, "For the horses of Pharaoh went with his chariots and his horsemen into the sea, and the LORD brought back the waters of the sea upon them. But the children of Israel went on dry land in the midst of the sea" (NKJV). The song began with praise for God's deeds, and ended the same way.

Then Miriam, Moses' sister and Israel's new "worship leader," exhorted the people to sing some more. "[God] is highly exalted," she crooned, grabbing the nearest tambourine (v. 21 NASB). The Israelite women followed suit, also taking up tambourines and dancing in worship. What a service this must have been! Don't you wish *you* could have been there?

The good news is, we can worship God the same way every day. We, too, can praise Him for His mighty acts. We can applaud His strength and acknowledge His power to defeat Satan, this world's "god-king." Along with Israel, we can proclaim that God is holy. And we can—and must—recognize God as our Deliverer, because just as He freed the Israelites to worship, He will free *you* from all that hinders your worship. Ego, depression, anger, fear—like the soldiers of Egypt, these will all drown. God wants to free you—*today*.

PRINCIPLES OF WORSHIP FROM THIS CHAPTER

Pre-deliverance, Israel was caught in a web of heathenism, surrounded by strange religious rites in worship of a host of spurious gods, including Pharaoh himself. This vicious god-king tried with all his might to eradicate worship of the one true God, the only One who could bring him down. He oppressed God's people, striving to take away their every reason to worship any god but himself. And he set himself up as a "king of kings" and an equal with God.

But there is only one King of kings, and He has no equal. So God's response to Pharaoh's arrogance? *THIS MEANS WAR!* God denounced the king and his mythological gods. Yahweh Himself emerged victorious.

Today, Horus is no longer worshipped. Neither is Re. No temples of Isis remain. And no one bows to Geb. The gods of Egypt have been long forgotten, the ancient religious infrastructure overthrown. But across the globe, the God of the Hebrews—*our* God—is worshipped today.

So what does this story teach us? First, it demonstrates that God will fight for His worship. He will also defend His worshippers. Our enemy, the devil, seeks to destroy our worship. He, like Pharaoh, will afflict us and try to rob us of our joy and reason to praise God. But God will only put up with it for so long. He wants to be our song. So He will go to battle for us. What a comfort that should bring to you and me as we worship.

But how do we approach God, as we seek to worship Him? In this chapter, Moses taught us how.

When God identified Himself to Moses from the burning bush, Moses instantly covered his face. Why? Because of his fear and respect for God. We, too, need to approach God with fear—not in the sense of terror or dread. Perfect love for God casts out that kind of fear (1 John 4:18). Instead, we are to fear God in the sense of reverential *awe*. "Our God is an awesome God," sang the late Rich Mullins, and we need to be in awe of Him. In His presence, we will be.

So come before Him. Worship Him. Be *awestruck* by His presence. Each time you do, you will be changed, because wherever you worship—in your special, set-apart place—it is "holy ground."

We have not seen the last of Moses. In chapter 6, we will read of his journey to Mount Sinai. There Moses will learn what God has planned for Israel: He wants to make them His very own. He wants to *dwell* with them, as He wants to dwell with *you*. Let's see how the Israelites respond to His deepest desire . . .

| 6 |

WORSHIP FROM THE TENT:
THE STORY OF MOSES, PART II

THE ISRAELITES WERE FINALLY BEGINNING TO *FEEL* FREE. THE nightmares had stopped. The stripes from Egyptian whips had healed. People were no longer looking over their shoulders. No army would be coming after them. And they'd never have to labor making Egyptian bricks again. They didn't even have to labor in the kitchen, for that matter. God Himself was feeding them, bread and meat, every day. And now they had reached the Desert of Sinai. Here they would learn God's plan and purpose for them.

GOD'S DESIRE FOR ISRAEL

Moses decided to climb the mountain to "appear before God" (Ex. 19:3 NLT). When he reached the top, God called out to him: "Tell the people . . ." He began, "'If you will obey me . . . , you will be my own special treasure . . . my kingdom of priests, my holy nation." (19:4–6 NLT).

My own special treasure . . . Hmm . . . What does one *do* with a treasure? He *hides* it, *treasures* it. Keeps it *safe*. And keeps it *close*. After the Egyptians had shown Israel they were of no more value than a beast of burden, God demonstrated to them that they were of *infinite* value to Him. He wanted to keep them safe—and close. He wanted the Israelites to abide in Him, and He in them. But that's not all . . .

A kingdom of priests . . . Hmm . . . What do priests *do*, exactly?

Let's skip ahead, for a moment, to the book of Ezekiel. Here the Lord commended a group of priests with whom he was pleased. Though, in this same chapter, He had rejected the service of some, of these priests He said, "[They] shall stand before Me . . . They shall enter My sanctuary; they shall come near to My table to *minister to Me*" (44:15–16 NASB, emphasis added). That's what the Lord wants from His priests. He wants them to "minister" to Him. But how does one do that — "minister" to the Lord?

He *worships* Him.

In Exodus 19, when God promised to make His newly liberated people "a kingdom of priests," He was expressing once more His deep desire to bind Himself to a people who would worship Him (and, as priests, would lead other nations to do the same). Moses went down the mountain and told the people God's desire.

"Oh, yes!" they responded enthusiastically. "We'll do *whatever* God says!"

The Lord then told Moses, "Have [the people] spend today and tomorrow preparing themselves. They must wash their clothes and be ready by the day after tomorrow. On that day I, the LORD, will come down on Mount Sinai, and all the people will see me" (vv. 10–11 NCV).

God wanted to be with them! What an honor! The God whose power was sufficient to conquer both Pharaoh and his whole horde of "holies" was requesting audience with *them*. Excitedly, Moses returned to the people and helped them prepare for God's visit. They washed their clothes.

But they didn't wash their hearts.

THE LAW OF GOD REVEALED

On the third day, thick clouds filled with smoke and lightning covered the mountain. God was there! And there, in the people's hearing, He began instructing them in how to live to please Him. First off, He told them, they were to have only *one* God. They were not to make idols of gold or silver. "Do not worship these gods in addition to me," He told them (Ex. 20:23 NCV). After years in a polytheistic culture, in which they no doubt participated, God was drawing a line in the sand. He wanted them for His own, and He wanted them to want *Him* and worship *Him* alone.

But the people didn't know Him; they knew terror. The Bible says that when they saw the smoke and the lightning, "they shook with fear and stood far away from the mountain" (v. 18 NCV). "Speak to us yourself," they begged Moses, "and we will listen. But don't let God speak to us, or we will die."

"Don't be afraid," Moses told them. "God has come in this way to show you his awesome power . . . Let your fear of him keep you from sinning" (v. 20 NLT). But they stayed back, "in the distance" (v. 21 NLT). Not one of them craved God's presence enough to venture forward and meet the One who had saved them. Yes, they were understandably afraid, but also, in their own way, they were rejecting God. They wanted no real part of Him—because they weren't *prepared to worship.*

So God told Moses to go into the cloud and climb higher on the mountain. And he was there—in the presence of God—for forty days and nights. During this time, God showed Moses His plans to dwell with those he loves. He commanded Moses to construct a movable house of worship—a tabernacle, God's dwelling place for Himself—among His people.

Historians, theologians, and teachers of worship will agree that any in-depth treatment of Old Testament worship needs to include a serious study of the Tabernacle. After all, it is a type of Christ. Every piece of equipment, measurement, item of furniture, cloth, metal, board, pillar, and provision for worship typifies Christ and His redeeming work for mankind. But for now, we will concentrate on the actions of Moses and the people, and what they teach us about worship.

On the mountain, God told Moses everything that His children would need to know to effectively worship Him. He gave guidelines for bringing offerings, as well as specific directions for the feasts Israel was to celebrate with Him. He even taught Moses how they were to treat *one another.* Then God gave Moses two stone tablets inscribed with His commandments— written with His own finger. This was serious. His instructions to Israel were important, the difference between life and death, because the penalty for worshipping any other god was *death.*

But old habits die hard.

THE GOLDEN CALF

"When Moses failed to come back right away," says Exodus 32 (v. 1 NLT), the people became impatient. Here God was, composing for Israel the laws that would keep them free, yet the very ones He had rescued were now weary in their waiting for Moses. *Moses has forsaken us*, they presumed. They needed *another* god to take them into the promised land. So they went to Aaron, Moses' brother. "Make us gods!" they demanded.

"OK," he agreed. Dupe. You'd think he'd know better. Yet all too quickly, Aaron—the *priest*—said, "Give me your gold." He then took that gold (which the Hebrews had gotten *only* because of God's own genius), melted it, and formed a statue—of a calf.

You may remember that with His fifth plague upon Egypt, a cattle disease, God discredited both of Egypt's bovine-headed deities. Yet Aaron had created just one more cow, and *then* had the audacity to say, "This is your god, O Israel, who brought you up from the land of Egypt" (v. 4 NASB). Worse, he added, "Now, let's *party*!!!"

And party they did. The next morning they got up at the crack of dawn and offered both burnt *and* fellowship offerings to their idol, effectively mixing image worship with Yahweh worship. They ate and drank. They danced. And had illicit sex. "It turned into a wild party!" (v. 6 MSG). And God saw the whole thing.

SAVED BY THE SKIN OF THEIR TEETH

"Quick! Go down the mountain!" God told Moses. "Your people . . . have corrupted themselves. How quickly they have turned away from the way I commanded them to live!" (32:7 NLT).

The blatant disobedience and disregard of God's law by the Israelites—and Aaron—made God furious. "Don't try to stop me," He said. "Give my anger free reign to burst into flames and incinerate them" (v. 10 MSG). In other words, *Let Me at 'em!* No longer did God want to *treasure* them; now He wanted to *destroy* them.

Moses reacted quickly. He knew how dangerous God was about to get. So, reminding God of the covenant He had made with Abraham, Isaac, and Jacob, he begged the Lord to withhold His judgment. And God was merciful. He permitted the people to live.

But Moses would want to kill them himself before it was over.

A HARSH LESSON

When Moses got off that mountain and heard the sounds of revelry—and then saw that golden calf—he lost it. Angrily, he threw down the stone tablets on which God had written, and they broke. Then He whirled around to his badly behaved brother.

"What did these people do to you," he spat, "to make you bring such terrible sin upon them?" (32:21 NLT).

"Don't be *angry*, master," Aaron answered good-naturedly. "These poor folks just couldn't help themselves. They were so worried about *you* that they said, 'What happened to our *dear* Moses? Oh well, guess someone else will have to lead us . . . *make us some gods.*' So . . . I did. They gave me their gold, and I put it in the fire . . . and out came this calf!" (vv. 22–24, author translation).

Can you believe that? That old calf just *magically* appeared, right out of the flames. I don't think Moses was fooled. He was *hot*. The Bible says that he melted that calf down, cooled the liquid, ground it to powder, threw it in the Israelites' water—and made them drink it! Then, standing at the edge of the camp, he said, "Anyone who wants to follow the *Lord*, come to me." The tribe of Levi instantly stepped up. "Get your swords," he told them. "Then go from one end of this camp to the other and kill *every-one*, friend, family, and foe."

And they did. Like a skilled surgeon cutting a deadly cancer from his patient's body, the Levites eradicated three thousand calf worshippers.

But God was still angry. "Moses," He said, "I can still get the children of Israel into the promised land, but an angel will have to lead them. *I won't go.* I'd only end up killing this rebellious bunch" (33:1–3, paraphrased).

The presence of the Lord would no longer be with them! When the people heard this, they were horrified. The Bible says they mourned (v. 4).

Since the days of their escape from slavery, God's people were blessed because of His presence. It was His presence—in the form of a cloud by day and fire by night—that set them apart from the heathen nations. God's presence between them and Pharaoh's pursuing army had prevented the slaughter of thousands of ex-slaves. His presence hovered over the Israelites, protecting them and giving them a sense of security. And now, they grieved at the very thought that God was withdrawing His presence from them. Even though they had substituted a lifeless image for the living Yahweh— and had *just* reveled in all kinds of uncontrolled depravity and sexual immorality—they knew what it would mean to lose the presence of God. They were beginning to understand the consequences of their sin. And if that weren't bad enough, God sent a plague upon them too.

EXPOSED! THE ESSENTIALS OF WORSHIP

In contrast to all of Israel's madness and the penalty that their folly received, Moses did something wise—and reaped great rewards. He went outside of the camp and set up a "Meeting Tent." Whenever Moses entered the tent, the pillar of cloud that was God's presence would descend from the sky and enter the tent door. Moses and God would then spend time together. (Sometimes Joshua, his assistant, would go with him.) Moses liked to go into the tent every day, because he *craved* God's presence. He could not be without it, even if the people were destined to be.

1. *Worshippers Need to Crave God's Presence*

When I was a little boy, whenever my cousins Brenda and Linda came over, we would play "tent." Our tent was constructed of a queen-size sheet, a mop handle, four big rocks, and two clothespins. Linda was especially good at building the "tent." She had a five-step process: First, she'd assign each of us a rock. Then she would spread the sheet across the back lawn. Next, she'd crawl under the sheet and plunge the mop into the ground, thus erecting the "tent." The rest of us would then place our rocks on the sheet's four corners. Finally, Linda would scoot out from under the tent, lift up one side, clip on the clothespins to create a door, and, voilá! We were ready to play "tent."

Playing "tent" was so much fun. We'd drink Kool-Aid in there, and sometimes eat brownies our mothers brought to us. We'd sing silly songs and tell funny stories—and we didn't even mind having guests—in fact, the more the better. To this four-year-old boy, nothing was more gratifying than being in that makeshift dwelling.

But now that I look back, I realize that it really wasn't the *tent* that was so special—it was the *people* gathered within. I wish I could be with them today, right now, in that tent. I crave their presence. That's because the real joy of our tent was the presence of my family.

The real joy of Moses' "Meeting Tent" was the presence of God.

I can only imagine how fulfilling and enriching it was for Moses to encounter God in the Tent of Meeting. That's where He found companionship with God, mentoring, divine equipping, and counsel. It's also where He went to worship God—in the Meeting Tent.

Do you have a "Meeting Tent," a special place to meet with God? Have you found somewhere to go and hide so you and God can be alone? Are you finding solace, encouragement, strength, and purpose as you meet alone with Him? If not, God wants to give you all of that, just as he did Moses. God built a relationship with a faithful, loyal, loving servant in that Meeting Tent. He will do the same for you. See, Moses wasn't the only one who could use the Meeting Tent. Exodus 33:7 says that "anyone" (NCV) and "everyone" (NLT) could go to seek the Lord there and make requests of Him.

But on this day, it was Moses in the Tent. And as he met with God, the principle of a unified worship leader and congregation was demonstrated for all future generations:

"Whenever Moses went out to the Tent, all the people would . . . stand at the entrances of their tents, watching . . . When Moses went into the Tent, the pillar of cloud would . . . come down and stay at the entrance of the Tent while the LORD spoke with Moses. Whenever the people saw the pillar of cloud . . . they stood and worshiped" (vv. 8–10 NCV). They praised God as families, each man taking the role of spiritual leader of his home as he worshipped under the leadership of Moses. And Moses was setting a good example. He was there to seek God's face. More than anything else, he wanted to cultivate a *friendship* with God.

2. *Worshippers Must Cultivate Friendship with God*

How can you worship someone you don't know? The answer is, you can't. If you haven't taken the time to get to know someone, really know him, then how is it even possible to say much either *to* or *about* him?

Moses knew God. In fact, every time he went into the Meeting Tent, the Bible tells us, "the LORD spoke to Moses face to face *as a man speaks with his friend*" (Ex. 33:11 NCV, emphasis added). The dependent clause that describes this relationship is no small deal. The word *friend* as it is used there, implies a deepening relationship in an already close bond, as with a *brother, companion, fellow, lover,* or *neighbor.* For example:

"A friend loveth at all times." (Prov. 17:17 KJV)

"There is a friend that sticketh closer than a brother." (Prov. 18:24 KJV)

"Iron sharpeneth iron; so a man sharpeneth the countenance of his friend." (Prov. 27:17 KJV)

"Abraham believed God . . . and he was called the Friend of God." (James 2:23 KJV)

"Greater love has no one than this, than to lay down one's life for his friends." (John 15:13 NKJV)

What does God ask of His friends? "You are My friends if you do whatever I command you" (John 15:14 NKJV).

What kind of friendship did God and Moses share? And what kind of friend was Moses? There are, after all, several different types of friends. There is an *acquaintance,* for example, someone you simply know and with whom you have a casual relationship. In your lifetime, you will have hundreds—maybe even a thousand—of these.

A smaller group, consisting of scores of people, is made up of your *associates.* An associate is someone with whom you build a professional or social relationship. You may attend church together or be part of the same civic organization. You share common goals and interests. You may even enjoy each other's "friendship" at a cookout, class party, or company gathering. But your overall relationship is still rather distant—and kept at a distance. *God does not want to be your associate.*

Another type of friend is a *colleague.* Your inventory of colleagues is smaller still. A colleague is simply a coworker, collaborator, or partner. One or two outside forces bring these types of friends together—a Little League team, for example, that you coach together, or a Sunday school class, business relationship, or mutual friend. You might invite colleagues to your home, and allow your children to develop closer relationships with them. But they're not like your . . .

Best friend. This kind of relationship is special and rare. You will only have five to ten of these close friendships throughout your life. These are people with whom you can share your burdens and tell your accomplishments. You feel accepted by your best friends and wouldn't hesitate to invite them over for picnics, after-church activities, or to play cards, because you thoroughly enjoy their presence. Willie Morris gives an example of this level of friendship in his story of Jackie Robinson, famous African-American baseball player, and Pee Wee Reese:

> One example of friendship remains with me as vividly as the moment I first heard of it as a boy. In his first seasons with the Brooklyn Dodgers, Jackie Robinson, the first black man to play Major League baseball, faced venom nearly everywhere he traveled—fastballs at his head, spikings on the bases, brutal epithets from the opposing dugouts and from the crowds. During one game in Boston, the taunts and racial slurs seemed to reach a peak. In the midst of this, another Dodger, a Southern white named Pee Wee Reese, called timeout. He walked from his position at shortstop toward Robinson at second base, put his arm around Robinson's shoulder, and stood there with him for what seemed like a long time. The gesture spoke more eloquently than the words: This man is my friend.[1]

But there is a closer friend than this, with whom your relationship is higher and deeper: your *comrade.* You will only have one or two of these in your entire life. Your comrade accepts you at face value—through thick and thin, good and bad, no matter what happens. He wants to be identified as your friend, because he likes being around you. This friend is a forever friend—he would die for you. And your relationship grows richer and stronger as the days go by. *This* is the friendship God had with Moses. And it's the same kind of friendship God wants to share with you. It was for this level of relationship that Jesus went to the cross. And it is this type of friendship that will bring you into a worshipping relationship with Him.

Hymn writer Will L. Thompson aptly described this kind of close, intimate friendship:

> Jesus is all the world to me, my life, my joy, my all;
> He is my strength from day to day, without Him I would fall.
> When I am sad, to Him I go, no other one can cheer me so;
> When I am sad, He makes me glad, He's my Friend.
>
> Jesus is all the world to me, I want no better Friend;
> I trust Him now, I'll trust Him when life's fleeting days shall end.
> Beautiful life with such a Friend, beautiful life that has no end;
> Eternal life, eternal joy, He's my Friend.[2]

Friendship with a comrade is built on mutual trust, fellowship, communion, time together, and genuine, unreserved love. The Lord is this kind of friend. As Joseph C. Ludgate contends, Jesus is . . .

> A Friend when other friendships cease,
> A Friend when others fail,
> A Friend Who gives me joy and peace,
> A Friend when foes assail!
> A Friend when sickness lays me low,
> A Friend when death draws near,
> A Friend as through the vale I go,
> A Friend to help and cheer![3]

It was exactly this brand of friendship that Moses enjoyed in the Meeting Tent. Good thing. His success as Israel's patriarch depended on his friendship with the Ancient of Days. But more important to him than success was his relationship with God. "Don't leave us," he begged the Lord, "or we will be just like every other nation."

In chapter 2, we learned the importance of relationships. *Nothing* in life is more significant than our relationships with our families, friends, coworkers, neighbors—and God. Our relationship with family establishes our character and lifetime habits. Relationships with friends reveal our inner character. Our relationships with coworkers are reflections of the connections we have with family, friends, and God, and often determine our career opportunities.

But our relationship with God has eternal consequence. And Moses knew that. Nothing was more important to him than his friendship with God. God was, in fact, *all* Moses wanted. He loved God and faithfully maintained healthy communication—and relationship—with God. And because of *this* relationship, the children of Israel were given another chance. It was certainly not because of their own faithful worship. God felt compelled to withdraw His threat to abandon them *only* because of His friendship with Moses, nothing else. He would lead them to the land of promise—Himself. "I will personally go with you, Moses," He said (Ex. 33:14 NLT). "You are my friend." Then, to top it off, God gave Moses the gift of gifts. He said, "I am pleased with you" (v. 17 NCV).

Friend, you and I should long to hear those words from God. We each, like Abraham and Moses, must become a *friend* of God. If God identifies you as His friend, then He will also affirm you, just as He did Moses.

What will that mean for you? Author John Trent gives us an idea in his story of Mary, a young girl born with a cleft palate.

The setting: 1950s, in an elementary school. Mary's classmates were teasing her relentlessly. She was not only deformed, but she also had hearing loss in her left ear. She had grown up knowing she was different from every other kid in her school.

But Mary had a teacher who showed genuine love to children like her. Her name was Mrs. Leonard, and Mary dearly loved her too.

In the '50s it was common for teachers to give their students an annual hearing exam, called the "whisper test." The test was usually administered in front of the class. Each student would stand by the classroom door, turn sideways, and cover one ear. The teacher would then say something to the student, in a soft whisper. In return, the student would repeat the teacher's words or answer a question the teacher had asked. Mary, determined to hide her handicap from the other students, pretended to cover her good ear, so she could still hear the teacher.

Usually teachers would say such things as, "The sky is blue," "I like your dress," or, "What color are your shoes?" But Mrs. Leonard changed her words to Mary.

What did she say?

"I wish you were *my* little girl." And these seven words of affirmation changed Mary's life forever.[4]

The power of spoken affirmation cannot be measured. Words like:

> *"I'm proud of you"*;
> *"Good job"*;
> *"You're the best!"*;
> *"I knew you could do it!"*;
> *"You are really special to me"*;
> *"I trust you"*; and
> *"Well done"*

can change a young person's entire perspective on life, including his vision for the future.

And the God of the universe gave Moses just such an affirmation: "I'm *pleased* with you." And if that weren't gift enough, He also *enlarged* their relationship: He let Moses see Him.

A RELATIONSHIP ENLARGED

In chapter 1 we saw that the more we *learn* about God, the more we want to *worship* Him. And the more we worship Him, the more we want to *know* Him. Moses had learned about God in the Tent of Meeting. He knew that God was capable of being pleased, and He was pleased with Moses. This made Moses want to worship God all the more, and to *know* Him more. "Show me your glory," He pleaded (Ex. 33:18 NIV).

But Moses didn't know what He was asking. The Hebrew word for glory, *kabowd*, denotes that which surrounds the throne of God the King, plus everything that makes up the Almighty—His majesty, His integrity—

indeed, the very power of God. It's more than any human can take.

"No, it will kill you," God replied. "But I *will* do this . . ."

Remember, Moses was a worshipper—and a *friend*, tried and true. He loved God, and God knew it. And from the beginning we have seen that God's desire is to reveal Himself to those who love and worship Him, to *enlarge* the relationship. So . . .

"I will cause all my goodness to pass in front of you," God said, "and I will announce my name, the LORD, so you can hear it . . . But you cannot see my face, because no one can see me and live.

"There is a place near me," He continued, "where you may stand on a rock. When my glory passes that place, I will put you in a large crack in the rock and cover you with my hand until I have passed by. Then I will take away my hand, and you will see my back" (vv. 19–23 NCV).

And that's exactly what God did. He came down in a pillar of cloud and called out His own name. "It's Me," He said, "the Lord." And *the Lord* did as He promised: He let Moses experience all of His "goodness." And even that was more than the man could take: "Moses immediately threw himself to the ground and worshiped" (34:8 NLT)—man's built-in response to the presence of God.

PRINCIPLES OF WORSHIP FROM THIS CHAPTER

What have we learned about worship that we haven't seen before?

In this chapter, we read that God stated that His desire for His people was for them to be "a kingdom of priests," an enclave of people set apart to *minister* to—that is, to *worship*—Him. It is why they were made. It is why *we* were made. But in order to worship God in a way that pleases Him, one's heart must be prepared. Moses' was. Israel's weren't. They had washed their clothes, but they hadn't cleansed their hearts. They wanted to have God, yet still cling to their idols. Today, worshippers often try to do the same. They want to serve God while still cleaving tenaciously to their pet sins. Their priorities are out of order. Their jobs come first. Their mates come first. Their "stuff" comes first. You get the picture.

But God will not tolerate dual allegiance. He made this clear to both

Old Testament and New Testament believers. "Love not the world," says 1 John 2:15, "neither the things that are in the world. If any man love the world, the love of the Father is not in him" (KJV). God wants to be your one and only, the sole object of your worship. "I will follow You alone, Lord," He longs to hear. "Please take me as Your own." If that is our prayer, the unfeigned cry of our hearts, how will God respond? He'll say yes—and make us His own "special treasure" (19:5 NLT).

I want to be treasured by God, don't you? Then, together, let's find out how by reviewing the essential principles of worship that this chapter has exposed.

First, we must crave God's presence. When Moses wanted to escape and spend time with God, he would steal away to the Tent of Meeting. There he could shut out all that was going on around him and concentrate on God. Where is your Tent of Meeting? Do you have a special somewhere to commune with the Lover of your soul? If not, I can't emphasize it enough: you must find a place to get alone with God, a place where you can hide away and find Him when your soul longs for His company.

And second, we must cultivate our friendship with God. He doesn't want to be a casual acquaintance, someone we say hi to, in passing. And He doesn't care to fellowship with us only in the pew, once a week, twice if He's lucky. He wants to be our *comrade*—*your* comrade, your day-by-day, devoted, lifelong friend. He was willing to die for you. What are you willing to do for Him?

Crave Him. And if you're not quite there yet, ask Him to place a hunger in your heart for Him. He will. Then, through your heartfelt worship, cultivate your friendship with Him. He will enlarge it. He'll show you all His goodness. He'll reveal Himself to you, more and more. He'll affirm you and call *you* "friend." He'll give you victory over the enemy. And you will love Him for it.

GET THE GLOW!

After his encounter with God in the cleft of the rock, the Bible says, Moses came down from Mount Sinai. He had spent an awesome time in the presence of the Lord, worshipping Him, talking to Him, *loving* Him. I dare you to do the same. You'll be just like Moses, fresh off that mountain. What kind of shape was he in, anyway, after being in the "glorious presence" of God (Ex. 33:18 NLT)?

He glowed![5]

7

PREPARATION AND CHOICE: THE WORSHIP OF JOSHUA

MY FRIEND BOB MACKENZIE, LONGTIME NASHVILLE RECORD producer and publisher, had a saying that regularly brought things into focus for us aspiring musicians, arrangers, and publishers. After a rather lengthy dose of wisdom on how to survive the comings and goings of the Music City Christian music industry, he'd say, "Now, remember, the longer the line of preparation, the greater the opportunity." In short, Bob was telling us to stick to the task, stay focused, and use every moment as an occasion for preparation, because God was *getting us ready* for bigger and more important opportunities.

Thorough preparation is critical to so many professions. An aspiring physician will often spend more than a decade preparing to practice medicine. Schoolteachers devote years to learning to instruct students. Pilots invest hundreds of hours in preparation for flying with a commercial airline—longer for the military. Plumbers and electricians complete an apprenticeship to fulfill their preparation process. And it takes hours of preparation for a sound engineer to qualify for work in a world-class studio.

Does it surprise you that one must also prepare to worship?

The longer the line of preparation, the greater the opportunity. This bit of wisdom articulates well the lives of Abraham, Jacob, Joseph, and Moses. God used their relationships, circumstances, experiences, and life lessons as a means for preparing them for greater things—which they achieved through worship. Though these men struggled constantly with distractions from the cultures and situations around them, God used their trials to reveal His faithfulness through it all. As He witnessed their authentic commitment to Him and their personal dedication to worship, in spite of their obstacles, He rewarded them. And each became a model of authentic worship to all future generations.

Worship has its limitations if it is not exemplified, taught, and passed on. To worship God is glorious, yes. We have already seen what personal worship can effect for the worshipper. But to practice worship *and* epitomize it for others—now, that's really praiseworthy. And that's what Moses did.

In chapter 6 we learned of Moses' effective witness to the nation of Israel as he *properly* worshipped God. Moses' worship was acceptable worship. God confirmed this by saying, "I am pleased with you." But now it was time for Moses to leave this earth and to pass the leadership baton to another—a man he had effectively trained in the art and science of Yahweh worship: Joshua.

A HANDPICKED VESSEL

No one was more qualified to succeed Moses as commander in chief than Joshua. More than once, he had been with Moses in the Tent of Meeting as he came to worship God. And even after Moses had left the tent, Joshua would often remain, in the presence of the Lord.

Joshua had learned much about worship, both from his mentor, Moses, and from God Himself. Above all, he'd learned that obedience was the groundwork for authentic worship. So when God commanded Joshua to lead the Israelites across the Jordan River into the promised land—to become a kingdom of priests who would *minister* to the Lord through worship—Joshua obeyed without hesitation. And he would do well. Why? Because Joshua was uniquely prepared to lead a nation of worshippers.

THE PREPARATION PROCESS

Joshua's preparation process actually began on the west side of the Red Sea, some eighty years before the crossing of the Jordan. He was born a slave in Egypt and spent about forty years there. An active participant in the Exodus, Joshua also served as Moses' military commander when Israel defeated the Amalekites a couple of months later. Joshua then spent forty years in the wilderness, being mentored by Moses and serving as his aide. He was also one of the twelve spies Moses sent to scope out Canaan—one of only *two* who had actually believed God was capable of delivering the land to Israel. Joshua had proved faithful, so God selected him to succeed Moses. At God's bidding, Moses presented Joshua to Eleazar the priest, in the eyes of all the people, to bless him and confirm his appointment (Num. 27:18–22). Then, just before his death, Moses himself inaugurated Joshua (Deut. 31:14–23 NCV), formally transferring the mantle of leadership. Joshua would devote the last twenty-five years of his life to escorting God's special treasure, national Israel, into Canaan, Yahweh's gift to His holy nation.

But first, Joshua would have to carry out a critical order given by God. He was to *remove* all other nations from the promised land, killing the inhabitants, eliminating entire communities, even slaughtering the livestock. Israel was to rid itself of all other influences in their midst, a hard task, but if they would obey, the Lord would reward them with victory, long life, and rest. He had promised.

But why such a tall order? *Why* kill all the other nations—and their cows? Because God knew the hearts of His people. He was well aware that, left to their own devices, they would naturally do wrong—*just like before*. Aaron had said it best: "These people are always ready to do wrong" (Ex. 32:22 NCV). God wanted to remove their temptation to marry into heathen cultures and adopt their way of life—and their religion: *idolatry*.

The completion of Joshua's mission would completely alter Israel's history—and in the process, reveal the glory of God. But to bring this plan to fruition, Joshua would first have to accomplish three strategic tasks.

1. Crossing the Jordan

First, Joshua was to lead Israel across the Jordan River. To the human eye, that would be no small task. It was the harvest season, and the Jordan was always at flood stage during harvest. The river was overflowing its banks. Sure seemed like the wrong time of year to cross it. It was, in fact, an *impossible* time, and an equally impossible time to go to battle. But

God *is* the God of the impossible, and He had issued a mandate: *Cross the river.*

The first thing Joshua did was dispatch a pair of spies into the land—Jericho, in particular—to evaluate the conditions for battle. Joshua's secret agents furtively slipped into the city. There they met a prostitute named Rahab. This woman, sin stained though she was, recognized a disparity between her people and the Hebrews. The children of Israel had something her people did not: *the very presence of God.* She determined to help the Israelites—if they would help her. She promised to hide the spies from the king's soldiers and get them safely back to the Israelite camp. They, in turn, promised to spare her family when the Israeli army invaded her land. The spies then returned to Joshua with the news: *Jericho can be defeated.* "The people in the land are terrified of us," they told him (Josh. 2:24 NLT).

Time for a pep talk. As a football coach rallies his team, strategizing and inspiring his players, Joshua now began to motivate his people. No doubt, he relived their triumphant escape from Egypt and reminded them of their victory over the Amalekites. Then . . . he gave them a critical directive: "Make yourselves holy, because tomorrow the LORD will do amazing things among you" (3:5 NCV). Holiness. This was vital to their success. They were to *purify* themselves, to *sanctify* themselves. Simply put, they were to separate themselves from all that was common and unclean. *Then* God would do great things in their midst.

Whenever God is to reveal Himself in a special way, special preparation is demanded. This includes repenting of sin, petitioning God for help, and *worshipping.* So the people obeyed, acting out their worship through physical and spiritual cleansing, and Joshua was pleased. He knew that Israel's obedience would guarantee God's involvement in their war endeavor. "Today you will know that the living God is among you," he told them. "Think of it! The Ark of the Covenant, which belongs to the Lord of the whole earth, will lead you across the Jordan River!" (Josh. 3:10a, 11 NLT).

The ark of the covenant was a sacred chest built by Moses at God's command. Made of wood and covered with the purest gold, it contained various sacred articles, including the second set of stone tablets on which God engraved His commandments after Moses broke the originals. But most important, the ark was God's throne, and the presence of God resided within it. By taking the ark into battle, God intended to show both His own nation and the surrounding kingdoms, that He was alive, active, and *present* with Israel.

So they set out for the river, dressed in war garments and ready for war, with the "Ark of the LORD" (v. 13 NLT) in tow. The priests, who carried the ark, led the procession.

The instant their feet touched the water, God caused the river to stop flowing. The floodwaters were cut off at Adam, about eighteen miles north of Jericho, and the riverbed dried.

God instructed His people to follow six-tenths of a mile behind the ark. Remember, the ark itself signified that God was present among them. But this six-tenths-mile separation also had a meaning to Israel. It was God's reminder that He is *separate* from his people; that is, different—in character, holiness, righteousness, and glory. By separating the people from the priests who bore His presence, God was stressing that He was to be respected, feared, and *worshipped*. Israel was not to treat Him casually.

Soon the people were on the other side. Now Joshua would complete his second task: he would erect a memorial—for worship.

2. Establishing a Sacred Place

Here is the picture. All of God's people led by forty thousand warriors, had crossed to the western side of the Jordan. But the priests had stopped, in the center of the river, to allow the people to pass. Now, as they stood in the middle of the riverbed, with the ark of God hoisted upon their shoulders, Joshua instructed twelve men, one from each tribe, to each get a boulder and carry it ashore. The men did as they were told.

Meanwhile, Joshua built a memorial, right in the middle of the Jordan, with twelve stones of his own. Then he and the priests came ashore.

As soon as their feet came out of the Jordan, the waters returned to the river, and it again began to overflow!

Joshua now told the men his plan for the stones they had carried from the river. They were to pile them up at their campsite, as a memorial. The stones would forever mark the location where God had worked marvels for His people. "In the future your children will ask you, 'What do these rocks mean?'" Joshua said. "Tell them, 'Israel crossed the Jordan River on dry land. The LORD your God caused the water to stop flowing until you finished crossing it, just as the LORD did to the Red Sea . . . so all people would know he has great power and so you would always respect the LORD" (Josh. 4:21–24 NCV).

So the Israelites built their memorial, thus creating *a permanent site for the worship of God.*

But there was one more task to fulfill before they could enter their covenant land.

3. Circumcising the Flesh

You may remember that all of the men who had come out of Egypt had been circumcised in the wilderness. It was a symbol of their covenant relationship with Yahweh. But forty years had passed, and all of those who had served as soldiers after the Exodus had died. Now there was a new generation of Hebrews, those who had been born in the desert. And none of these bore the mark of their covenant with God. So God said to Joshua, "Circumcise them." And it had to be done *before* they entered the land of promise.

Why was this so important? Because Israel was different from all other nations. And they were to *remain* different, separate from the ways of the cultures around them. By now, the Israelites were close enough to the enemy to be observed. To be circumcised before their eyes was a sign to them that Israel was set apart. They were, by an act of will, putting off the sinful flesh and identifying themselves as a nation eternally bonded with the *only* God who chose to covenant with His people.

But what timing! The ritual God was requiring was an act that would temporarily weaken the Israelites—every soldier—right before battle. And remember, Jericho's watchmen could see them.

God wasn't a bit concerned. The battle wasn't Israel's anyway. It was the Lord's.

Joshua, dutifully submitting to the Lord's command, circumcised Israel's males. Then the Lord told him, "Today I have rolled away the shame of your slavery in Egypt" (Josh. 5:9 NLT). And they named the place *Gilgal*, "to roll away." Then "they rested in the camp until they were healed" (v. 8 NLT) and celebrated Passover. In fact, just before Israel's collective status changed from *wanderer* to *conqueror*, the women baked their Passover bread made with grain *from Canaan*.

They never ate manna again.

JOSHUA MEETS . . . CHRIST?

The people now began their ascent to the hill city of Jericho. But as Joshua was approaching the city walls, he looked up suddenly and saw a strange man standing in front of him, sword in hand. "Are you an enemy, or a friend?" Joshua asked him.

"Neither," the man replied. "I am [the] commander of the Lord's army" (5:14 NLT).

Of the Lord's *army!* This was no ordinary man, then. He was supernatural! Who could he be? And why was he here?

Many Bible scholars believe this "commander," or "captain" (NASB) was Jesus Christ Himself, because when he identified himself, Joshua instantly fell with his face to the ground and worshipped. Now, remember, God had hand selected Joshua to lead His people. He had the Spirit of God all over him. As such, Joshua would never have bowed down to any *ordinary* man. Yet he bowed to this commander, absolutely prostrate, giving him "Divine honours."[1] What's more, the commander received Joshua's show of deference, and "by his acceptance of adoration . . . , which a created angel durst not admit of,"[2] proved he was no created being. An angel would have put a stop to such worship, as did the angel in Revelation, at whose feet John fell and assayed to worship. "Don't worship *me!*" he told John. "I'm just God's servant—like you!" (19:10, paraphrased). But the commander of the Lord's army made no move to correct Joshua. He was the Son of God.

"Does my master have a command for me?" Joshua asked (Josh. 5:14 NCV).

"Take off your sandals," the captain answered, "because the place where you are standing is holy." These were the very same words God had spoken to Moses, decades before (Ex. 3:5). Now Joshua was hearing them. The place was holy because of the captain's presence—again, no mere angel—and Joshua was ordered to remove his shoes. This was God's prerogative alone.[3]

Joshua immediately obeyed. Then the Lord said to him, "March around the city with your army once a day for six days. Have seven priests carry trumpets . . . and have them march in front of the Ark. On the seventh day march around the city seven times and have the priests blow the trumpets as they march. They will make one long blast on the trumpets. When you hear that sound, have all the people give a loud shout. Then the walls of the city will fall so the people can go straight into the city" (vv. 3–5 NCV). God's instructions were to be followed to the letter, because *this* battle would actually become a time of worship to the Most High God.

Notice that the presence of God Himself, represented by the ark of the covenant, was in the center of the entourage. This was *the* crucial detail. By requiring the Ark's presence, God was showing Israel—and its enemies—that He was in attendance and that He was, in fact, marching with them. God had more at stake than the people of Israel. His very reputation was at risk. If Israel failed, He failed. And that would never happen. He was—and is—God.

But imagine how strange this convoy must have appeared to the inhabitants of Jericho. Israel's whole war strategy must have looked crazy—disjunct, unorganized, and juvenile—but it all made perfect sense to God, so for almost a week, seven horn-blowing priests marched in front of the ark of the covenant.

On the seventh day, a war cry was heard. The walls crumbled. Soldiers charged into the city and, without delay, killed all the citizens—cattle, sheep, and donkeys too. The only lives spared were a Jerichoian hooker (Rahab) and her family. Finally, Israel claimed the land God had sworn to their forefathers.

GONE TO GLORY

Israel saw many more victories with Joshua as their leader. They defeated Ai. They destroyed kings—north, south, east, and west of them. But time passes swiftly, and soon, "many years passed, and Joshua grew very old" (Josh. 23:1 NCV). It was time for him to die.

Joshua gathered all the tribes of Israel to Shechem, and they presented themselves before the Lord and worshipped. In general, the people of God were living in greater faithfulness to the Lord. They obeyed His Law. They worshipped in His sanctuary. They sought His presence. And yet . . . there was still a tendency on their part to abandon Yahweh and worship foreign gods instead. Joshua was keenly aware of their mind-set. He knew he had just one more chance to impart a word that might keep them true to God.

So, in his farewell speech, he reminded Israel of God's mighty exploits on their behalf. He challenged them to remember the Lord and keep His law, and to love Him alone. Then he gave them a choice: they could worship false gods, he said, or they could worship the true God. Whichever they chose, though, the choice was theirs *alone*—and they would pay the price for it. Listen to Joshua's parting words:

> "I am now very old . . . It's almost time for me to die. You know . . . that the LORD has done great things for you . . . Every good promise that the LORD your God made has come true . . .
>
> "Now respect the LORD and serve him fully and sincerely. Throw away the gods that your ancestors worshiped . . . Serve the LORD. But if you don't want to serve the LORD, you must choose for yourselves today whom you will serve. You may serve the gods that your ancestors worshiped . . . or you may serve the gods of the Amorites who lived in this land. As for me and my family, we will serve the LORD." (Josh. 23:2, 14–15; 24:14–15 NCV)

After that, Joshua sent the people home. Then, at the ripe old age of 110, Joshua himself went home—to glory. But his final words would ring in the Israelites' ears for years to come. *Choose for yourselves today whom you will serve.* The choice was *theirs*.

And today, the choice is yours. Tell me, friends, whom will *you* worship?

PRINCIPLES OF WORSHIP FROM THIS CHAPTER

At last, Israel was in the land God had promised them. *At last*, they could become the "kingdom of priests" God wanted them to be—a holy nation, a special treasure, a collection of saints who would *minister to* God. Keep in mind, God led the Israelites out of Egypt for the sole purpose of giving them freedom to worship. And all along the way, during their long, diffi-cult journey to Canaan, God was teaching them lessons that they could apply to the practice of worship for all time. What did they learn?

1. *There Will Always Be Obstacles to Worship*

The city of Jericho was bordered by a huge retaining wall, about fifteen feet high. On top of that was another wall, even higher and six feet thick. Behind this was a hill that led up to the city, which was surrounded by yet another seemingly impregnable wall.[4] The Israelites on their own could have never penetrated the city.

But God knew that on the other side of those walls was the territory *He* had promised them, the land where they would become the kingdom of priests He wanted them to be. There, on covenant ground, Israel would minister to the God of the universe and *worship* Him. He wanted their worship. He wants yours too.

But there will always be obstacles to worship. Before God's people could enter the land and worship their Deliverer there, they would have to overcome all that stood in the way. You will too. Like the overflowing waters of the Jordan River, circumstances in your life may hinder your worship. Perhaps you long to worship God, but you can't seem to cross that "river" because of what you see before you. Crippling uncertainty. Never-ending troubles. Unconquerable sin. *Swollen waters.*

But how did the Israelites cross their river? By faith. They didn't wait until the obstacle was removed to approach the river. They marched right up to the bank—and took a step of faith.

You may not feel like worshipping. Difficulty may be all you can see ahead. Your life, like a river, may be overflowed with questions, problems, pain. But don't wait for these obstacles to move before you worship. Take a step of faith. Plunge your feet into the river—and worship. Then watch those waters recede.

"But I'm not *good* at worshipping," you say. Well, your worship may seem awkward at first, your every effort halting and clumsy. But don't let this stop you. Your discomfort is just one more obstruction—one more swollen river—that God will move out of your way. In the meantime, by faith, press in and continue to *practice worship*. Great baseball players become better by practicing. Incredible musicians sharpen their skill *only* through practice. Nothing can take its place.

You want to grow in the Lord, don't you? Then practice the worship of God. But before you do, make *sure* your heart is prepared.

2. Authentic Worship Requires Holiness

Before God would ever accept Israel's worship and consequently demonstrate His power to them, His people first had to prepare their hearts. How were they to do this? "Make yourselves holy" (Josh. 3:5), He told them. They were to put off all that was unclean—and *repent*. The rules haven't changed.

Before we can ever expect to satisfy God with our worship, we must first repent of our sins. To come to God with unrepentant hearts—full of sin that we refuse to part with—will guarantee God's *nonattendance* in our worship experience. But we need Him *there*, in attendance. The Israelites learned early on that God's presence was essential to their every step. Without His presence, they were destined to fail. So are we. We need—*you* need—the presence of God. His presence can rid you of guilt, oppression, and fear. It can provide protection that is stronger than any fortress, more reliable than any gun, sharper than any sword, and more sophisticated than any wartime technology. God's presence will protect you from disease, from deceit, from *yourself.* In short, the presence of almighty God can bring victory in your every situation, just as it did for Joshua. God's presence rendered his enemies helpless. It will do the same to *your* enemy, the devil. But first you must "make yourself holy." How? Come before God in humility, recognizing Him as the Forgiver, and confess your sins to Him. And then . . . turn away from them. This is the true meaning of repentance. Only then can you worship Him authentically. But when you're ready to do that, remember this:

3. Authentic Worship Needs a Home

Think back for a moment. Once the Israelites had made it safely across the Jordan River, what's the first thing they did? They stopped and took the time to build a memorial, a *permanent site* for worship. This twelve-stone monument was erected to provide a special place for moms and dads to

bring their children to remember God's goodness. At this special
spot, the story of God's miracles would be freely shared with gen..
after generation. That would lead to worship; the site itself had been *designated* as a place of worship.

In chapter after chapter, we have seen that we, too, must designate a *place of worship*, a special setting in which we meet with God. Can we worship outside of such a place? Absolutely! But designating a *particular* meeting place is important because it sets a precedent for you to convene with God. God sees that you have made Him your priority, and your "special place" becomes a "secret place," the sanctuary for Him to communicate with you *alone*. It becomes your "holy ground." So choose a place, a *special* place. Then choose to worship. After all . . .

4. Worship Is a Choice

Practicing worship involves a choice. There will always be a thousand and one things to distract you from *doing* worship. To worship, we must put action to our faith, because genuine worship is active, energetic love for God, demonstrated in our *choice* to obey. "Choose today whom you will serve," Joshua dared the Israelites (24:15 NLT). He knew not only that the practice of worship engaged the heart, soul, and mind, but that it was, in fact, an act of the will.

"I cannot give up my will," wrote Oswald Chambers. "I must exercise it. I must will to obey . . . 'Choose you this day whom ye will serve.' It is a deliberate calculation . . . It is not an impulse, but a deliberate commitment."[5] By an act of his *will*, Joshua made a "deliberate commitment"— and declared his home a household of *worship*.

Will you?

8

WORSHIP IN THE BOOKS OF HISTORY, PART I: FROM JUDGES TO KINGS

IN THIS CHAPTER, WE WILL BEGIN AN EXAMINATION OF WORSHIP in the Historical Books, the eleven Old Testament books that tell the story of early national Israel. These books (specifically, Joshua, Judges, Ruth, 1 and 2 Samuel, 1 and 2 Kings, 1 and 2 Chronicles, Ezra, and Nehemiah) contain many stories of worshippers. Though we will not explore every book in the histories, we will examine the best of what they have to offer. Their tales, both good and bad, can teach us timeless truths about how to worship God today.

We have already looked into one of the books of history, Joshua. Under his leadership, the children of Israel became conquerors. In fact, Joshua 12 lists thirty-one kings and their cities that Israel destroyed (vv. 8–24). What had made them so successful? "The people [had] served the LORD during the lifetime of Joshua" (Judg. 2:6 NCV). In return, the Lord gave them victory—and rest, in the promised land.

But now Joshua was dead. What would Israel do? Would they be faithful to the One who had gift-wrapped one military conquest after another for them? Would they *exclusively* worship Yahweh, who had delivered Canaan to them on a silver platter?

No. Sadly, the people failed to pass their faith on to their children. Though they had seen mighty feats of God, with their own eyes, performed on their behalf, Israel's old-timers did a poor job of retelling the stories to their offspring. So when the old generation died, the "children grew up and did not know the LORD or what he had done for Israel" (Judg. 2:10 NCV). Inevitably, they "quit following the LORD" (v. 12 NCV) and started worshipping idols instead. It wasn't hard to do, because Israel had begun intermarrying with the heathens who lived among them. They were *supposed* to drive these nations out. Instead, they merged with them. Israelite men married pagan women and gave their daughters to pagan men — then worshipped their pagan gods (3:6).

The Lord became angry and "handed them over to robbers" (v. 14 NCV), who stole their possessions. When Israel fought back, "they always lost, because the LORD was not with them" (v. 15 NCV). In desperation, then, the people cried out to God, and He felt sorry for them and assigned new leaders — judges — to save them from their foes. The first was Othniel, then Ehud, Shamgar, and so on. Each judge, as best he or she could, would restore religious order, and the people would live in peace — for a time. Under Deborah, the peace lasted for forty years.

But Israel just couldn't — or wouldn't — remain faithful to the I AM. They went back, like a dog to its vomit (see Proverbs 26:11), to their God-provoking ways. So the Lord allowed the Midianites to swarm like locusts upon their land, destroying their crops and stealing their livestock.

It wasn't long before Israel was running back to the Lord, tails tucked firmly between their legs. God answered them through a prophet: "I forced the Canaanites out of their land," He told them, "and gave it to *you*. Then I said . . . , 'I am the LORD your God. Live in the land of the Amorites, but do not worship their gods.' But you did not obey me" (6:8–10 NCV, emphasis added). His verdict? *I won't help you anymore.*

But the people begged for forgiveness, and God, rich in mercy, once again showed pity: He appointed a very special judge to deliver them from their enemies and reestablish their compromised worship:

DOUBTING . . . GIDEON?

We all know the story of "Doubting Thomas." But there was another doubter long before him: Gideon. His familiar story has been food for many a sermon on faith.

One day, an angel appeared to Gideon. "The LORD is with you, mighty warrior!" he announced (v. 12 NCV).

"Really?" Gideon responded, incredulous. "Then how come the Midianites are *eating our lunch*?" (He didn't realize he was talking to an angel.)

The Lord Himself answered Gideon. "*You* will save Israel."

"How?" Gideon wanted to know. "I'm a *nobody*—the least important member in my family, from the least important family in Israel."

"I'll be with you," God answered.

But Gideon wanted proof. "If it's *really* You, Lord," he said, "and You're *really* on my side, then wait here. I want to bring You an offering."

The Lord agreed, and Gideon scurried into his tent and prepared a roast goat and some unleavened bread. Then he brought out the bread, meat, and a pot of broth and set it before the angel. But the angel told him to place the platter on a nearby rock and pour the broth all over the offering. Gideon did as he was told.

As soon as Gideon set the platter down, the angel touched it with a stick. Fire instantly leaped from the rock and burned up the bread and meat. And the angel disappeared!

That's when Gideon finally got it. "Lord GOD!" he cried out. "I have seen the angel of the LORD face to face!" (v. 22 NCV), and he swiftly built an altar to "worship the LORD" (v. 24 NCV).

Then God gave Gideon an assignment.

The people of Israel had forsaken God and were now worshipping Baal, the Canaanite god of rain, clouds, wind, and therefore fertility.[1] Not only did they make images of this deity, but they also kissed them, just as the Canaanites did. Worse, Israel had also embraced Asherah (also called Ashtoreth), goddess of the sea, and erected tall idols in her honor. They were called "Asherah poles," and God hated them. They represented Israel's effort to mingle false religions with the worship of Him—they even believed that Asherah was His *wife*. "Don't you *dare* set up an Asherah idol next to the altar you build for Me," He had told Israel, long before (Deut. 16:21). Yet the land was full of them.

"Tear down your father's altar to Baal," God now told Gideon. "And cut down that Asherah idol next to it. Then I want you to build an altar for *Me*. Sacrifice a bull on it. And use the wood from *Asherah* for kindling!" (Judg. 6:25–26 paraphrased).

Why do all of that? Why not just command Israel—again—to stop worshipping counterfeit gods? Wouldn't that have sufficed?

No. As long as the idols remained, Israel would be tempted to worship them. They had to be removed. So that's exactly what Gideon did. He tore *down* the idols. Then, with God at his side, he tore *up* the Midianites. With just three hundred Israeli men, Gideon defeated the entire army of Midian.

There They Go Again . . .

"You saved us!" cried the Israelites, as Gideon returned from the war. "Now we want you to rule us."

"No!" Gideon replied, in horror. "*The Lord* is your ruler! But . . . Gideon did want one tiny favor. "Bring me a gold earring, each of you, from your plunder." So the Israelites did. Now, that was a lot of earrings. In all, Gideon collected nearly forty-three pounds of gold. From it, he made a holy vest—with the noblest of intentions.

But the people worshipped it. It was just one more idol. It even became a snare to Gideon—*and* his whole family (Judg. 8:27). And after Gideon died, Israel made a full-scale swing back to idolatry. In spite of all God had done for them, crushing their nemesis and giving Israel the spoils, they "did not remember the LORD." Instead, they "followed the Baals" and "made Baal-Berith[2] their god" (vv. 34, 33 NCV).

I know what you're thinking. *Those hardheaded Israelites! They never learned! I would never worship another god! And I'd certainly never bow to some idol!* Oh, really? But Paul the apostle wrote that when we even *think* the wrong thing on a consistent basis, we're doing exactly that: bowing to an idol. "Put *all evil things* out of your life," he warned, "sexual sinning, doing evil, letting evil thoughts control you, wanting things that are evil, and greed. This is *really* serving a false god" (Col. 3:5–6 NCV, emphasis added).

Today, God's people are repeatedly lulled, just as Israel was, into worshipping "false gods." Which ones, you ask? The "idols" of fantasy, pornography, illicit sex, alcohol, drugs—in other words, gods of *self*-indulgence, *self*-centeredness, *self*-abandonment . . . You understand. Satan, the god of this world (2 Cor. 4:4 NASB), wants *self* to be your epicenter, because if you serve your*self*, then you're essentially serving *him*, and he has your worship. You are bowing at Satan's feet.

But God wants to be the object of your worship, and for this to happen, you must tear all of your idols down—and keep them down. Israel had a hard time with this. Under judge after judge—and, later, king after king—they bowed to the image of every false god they encountered. And today's Christians do the same. Of course, our "idols" are not actual statues of wood or gold. Ours are those sins we can't let go of. But our fate as we worship them is the same as Israel's. Whenever the Hebrews erected (or re-erected) their nauseating idols, the Lord caused them to be defeated in battle—"every time" (Judg. 2:15 NCV). We will be defeated too—*every time*—as long as we worship at the feet of sin, that is, of idols.

Gideon tore his idols down (Judg. 6:25–28). And so must we. As Paul the apostle wrote, we must "lay aside every weight, and the sin which so easily ensnares us" (Heb. 12:1 NKJV), being careful not to hang on to even a trace of our besetting sins. Why? Because sin has "legs," and if we cling to bits and pieces of our favorite transgressions, these idols will rise from the ashes again. And we will bow the knee to them—again.

Get rid of your idols, and don't allow even a vestige of them to remain to trap you. They may seem harmless, but remember: by something as seemingly innocuous as a "holy vest," Gideon was trapped, and all of Israel with him. It was just one more idol, added to their collection. But they couldn't worship both idols *and* God. And neither can you. God said so Himself.

> "You can't worship two gods at once. Loving one god, you'll end up hating the other. Adoration of one feeds contempt for the other." (Matt. 6:24 MSG)
> ". . . You cannot serve both." (NCV)

But Israel sure tried. After the holy-vest fiasco, their abominations only got worse. In time, the people added the gods of Ammon, Aram, Moab, Sidon, and the Philistines to their list of divinities. God wouldn't have it. It was Him, or them. And the people chose *them*. They "abandoned the LORD and no longer served him *at all*" (10:6 NLT, emphasis added).

Enter Samuel—A Special Calling to Worship

Samuel was the last of the fifteen great judges of Israel. He faithfully served the Lord as prophet, priest, and judge. He loved God and worshipped Him all his life.

The setting of his story is the pre-king era in Israel, in the town of Shiloh. The Lord still dwelt in the Ark of the Covenant. The ark rested in the Holy of Holies within the House of the Lord.

Eli was priest at Shiloh and had two sons, also serving in the House of the Lord, who did not honor God. The brothers were guilty of indulging in sexual promiscuity and gluttony. Often, they had sexual relations with the women serving at the entrance of the Meeting tent (1 Samuel 2:11–17; 22–25). Eli the Priest did nothing to curb the carnal appetites of his sons.

God brought Samuel in to the story of redemption through the heart of a mother, Hannah. She was a godly wife of Elkanah, son of Jeroham, but she was unable to have children. Each year, she joined her husband in worship at Shiloh. Hannah and Elkanah journeyed to the house of God every year to worship. Elkanah participated in the regular worship ritual and sacrifices. Hannah's heart was heavy. She sought God and prayed for a child, saying, "Lord All-powerful, see how sad I am. Remember me and don't forget me. If you will give me a son, I will give him back to you all his life, and no one will ever cut his hair with a razor" (1 Sam. 1:10–11, NCV).

God honored Hannah's plea with a son, and she kept her promise. Hannah named him Samuel because she asked the Lord for him. At the time Samuel was weaned (approximately 3 years of age), Hannah took him to the House of the Lord to live with Eli. Samuel grew in stature and in favor with the Lord and with people and ministers before the Lord. As a little boy, he obeyed the Lord.

Samuel lived with Eli and his family. He observed Eli's two sons, Hophni and Phinehas, do evil. Samuel learned about the prophecy against Eli. Even though Eli was disobedient, Samuel continued to faithfully serve the Lord under Eli in the House of the Lord.

Practice of Worship. One evening, while Samuel was still a little boy, God spoke. Eli was lying in bed. Samuel was also in bed in the Lord's house. The Lord called Samuel, and Samuel answered, "I am here!" Samuel ran to Eli's bed and said, "I am here." You called me." But Eli said, "I didn't call you. Go back to bed." Samuel did as he was told. A second time God called. Samuel again went to Eli and his response was the same. A third time, the Lord called to Samuel. Samuel got up again and went to Eli and said, "I am here. You called me." Then Eli realized that the Lord was calling the boy. So he told Samuel, "Go to bed. If he calls you again say, 'Speak, Lord. I am your servant and I am listening.'" So, Samuel went to bed.

This time, the Lord stood by Samuel's bed and said, "Samuel, Samuel." Samuel answered, "Speak, Lord. I am your servant and I am listening." God told Samuel that Eli and his sons were going to be punished. He stressed the fact that his sons acted without honor and that Eli did nothing to stop them from doing wrong.

The next morning, Eli approached Samuel and asked about the Lord's message. Samuel told Eli all that God has spoken to him. Eli responded, "He is the Lord, Let him do what he thinks is best" (1 Sam. 3:11–18 NCV).

It is doubtful that on the day Hannah left her little boy in the care of Eli the priest, she understood all Samuel was to become in the service of God. God honored her faith by making Samuel one of the most important prophetic voices in the history of Israel.

Place of worship. Now, God took a little boy and used him to deliver judgment to a disobedient priest. Samuel worshipped God while on his bed and in the House of the Lord. God chose to speak to this little, innocent boy, in the quiet of the night. God took him and made his life great for purposes larger than any human could have ever imagined.

Though but a child, Samuel was nonetheless called by God. That God did not call Eli or his sons, the more obviously qualified adult candidates, is startling, because it calls into question the deeply cherished assumption that the experienced, the educated, and the privileged are the vessels through which God works. In Israel's case, all of those types had wandered from the ways of Yahweh, and thus God chose a child, through whom the word of the Lord was to be delivered. It is a characteristic of God, who chooses the second-born Jacob rather than the firstborn Esau and the politically and economically weak Israel rather than the rich and powerful Egypt, to align Himself with such figures—a fact that should compel us to reach out to the marginalized as well.[3]

Samuel's response to God's inquiry? "Here I am." This was the same response uttered by Abraham centuries before when faced with the presence of God. Jacob spoke "Here I am" when at Bethel. Standing before the burning bush, Moses came into the presence of God. His response? "Here I am." God's test for true worship is *always* obedience.

God was so patient. After Gideon, other judges came to the fore, each giving Israel one more shot at redemption. But some of these judges, like Samson, for instance, were spiritually unstable, and so, the entire aspiration of national Israel began to change. They no longer wanted either God or His system of leaders.

They had a new agenda now . . .

A NEW ORDER

"We want a king! We want a king!"

Imagine, if you will, the vast throng of Israel, jaws collectively set as they made their demands. "Give us a king . . . like all the other nations" (1 Sam. 8:5 NCV).

Years had passed, and Israel had lived through fifteen judges—and they did not want another one.

Yet the judge system had originated with God Himself. After Joshua's death and the ensuing spiritual chaos, God chose judges to administer justice among the people and to restore religious order. But the people wouldn't listen to them. Some of them weren't so hot, anyway, they reasoned. Samuel, for instance? Sure, he was a righteous man. But his sons! They were too corrupt to fill his shoes. (See 1 Samuel 8:3–5.)

But Israel didn't want another judge, anyway. Neither did they want another priest, nor another prophet. They wanted a king, *like everyone else.*

But God didn't want them to have a king. Kings, in those days, were often worshipped as gods. They demanded veneration. Only God is worthy of veneration, and He wanted to be their only King. Still . . .

"Give us a king! Give us a king!" Israel clamored. They wanted to worship a *human*.

As a teenager, I worked as a bagger at a grocery store, and I'll never forget the many children I'd see at the cash register, wheedling and whining at their mothers. Here they'd come—candy or toy in hand. "Mommy, can I have this? Can I have this?"

"Not today," their mothers would answer. "You don't need that."

Some children meekly accepted the decision. Others would transform into monstrous creatures, kicking and screaming with rage, to the embarrassment of their moms. Still others would simply persist, hammering their frazzled mothers with "Please, Mommy? Please, please, *please?*"

Sometimes, a mom could muster up the courage to resist her child. But others, in total despair, caved in to the persistent nagging. "Well, it's not good for you," I'd hear them sigh, "but . . . OK. You can have it."

Remember Samuel? What God did that night in Eli's tent was prepare Samuel to be the one single character to make the transition from a government run by judges to a monarchy. Samuel grew up with God's favor upon his life. All Israel knew, recognized, and respected Samuel as a true prophet of the Lord. Samuel's prophecies never failed to come true.

This is much the same way the Lord agreed to give Israel its monarch. It wasn't good for them. It wasn't in their best interests. It was not God's plan. But the Israelites wanted a king—and not the King of kings, either. So, like kids in a candy store, they bleated relentlessly at their weary old prophet. "*We want a* KING!" And it broke Samuel's heart.

While Samuel himself did not approve of the shift to kingdom rule, he faithfully obeyed God and anointed Saul as the first of Israel's kings. "Don't be sad," God told the heartbroken prophet. "They haven't rejected *you*. They've rejected *Me*. They don't want Me as their King."

Still, Samuel tried to persuade them. "You don't know what you're asking," he warned. "If you get a king, he'll take your sons away from you and make them fight. He'll take your daughters and make them cook in the palace. Your slaves will become his slaves. Your flocks will be his flocks; your vineyards, his vineyards . . ."

But the people wouldn't listen. "We want a king to rule over us. Then we will be the same as all the other nations." How dangerous it is when God's people want to be like everyone else. But God gave them just what they asked for, and the theocracy ended.

A new order had begun.

THE FIRST KING OF ISRAEL

At age thirty, a man named Saul became Israel's first king. He definitely looked the part: he was tall (a head taller than any other Israeli man), dark, and handsome.

His story began in the mountains of his homeland. His father's donkeys were lost, and Saul was charged with finding them.

Saul looked and looked, but to no avail. Finally, his servant said, "There's a seer in this town, a real man of God. He could probably help us. Everything he says comes true." The seer was Samuel, Israel's last judge, and he *knew* Saul was coming. God Himself had told him, a day ahead of time. As Saul approached, the Lord spoke again to Samuel. "This is the man I told you about," He whispered. "He will be Israel's king."

"Excuse me, sir," Saul said. "Can you tell me where I can find the seer?"

"I am the seer," Samuel answered, "and you're just in time. Go with me to worship; then let's eat. Oh, and don't worry about those donkeys. They have been found. Besides, soon *all* the wealth of Israel will belong to you."

That night, the servant and Saul stayed at Samuel's house, and Samuel fed the future king.

In the morning, Samuel called for Saul. "I have a message for you—from God . . . He has chosen *you* to lead His people. Oh, you want proof?

"After you leave, you'll meet two men at Zelzah. They'll tell you your father has found his donkeys. When you reach the big tree at Tabor, you'll run into three more men, on their way to worship. Go on to Gibeah of God. There you'll meet some prophets, coming back from worship. They'll be prophesying. When you meet them, the Spirit of the Lord will come upon *you*, and you'll prophesy too. And you will be a different man!"

That's exactly what happened. As soon as Saul met the prophets, a surge of divine power rushed through him. His heart was changed, and he began to prophesy (sing and speak under heavenly influence).

THE WORSHIP (??) OF SAUL

Oh, Saul got off to a good start. But as author David Broder once said, "A man who does not listen cannot lead."[4] That was Saul all over. Though chosen by God, anointed by Israel's premier prophet, and divinely equipped for the task of leading Israel, he never learned to listen to God. All through his reign, he was characterized as an impetuous king who habitually disobeyed the Lord. For instance . . .

Strike One

Not long after Saul was crowned, Israel decided to go to war against the Philistines. But before the Israelites could engage in battle, Samuel the priest was to offer a sacrifice to the Lord, so that He would bless Israel's war efforts. *Only* an ordained priest was allowed to make such a sacrifice.

But Samuel wasn't there.

Saul waited. And waited. For seven days he waited. Meanwhile, the Philistine forces were pressing in on every front, and Saul's soldiers began deserting.

Finally, in his impatience, Saul performed the sacrifice himself, totally disregarding God's sacrificial laws. Though Saul's motive may have been ever so noble (he *just* wanted the Lord's approval), and seemingly justifiable, by human accounts (how could he fight with no army?), God considered Saul's deed a hasty, gross, and deliberate act of disobedience, not to mention a violation of His worship.

Strike Two

Now fast-forward a bit. Another day, another war, but this time, it was against the Amalekites. "Destroy *everything*," Samuel told Saul. "Let *nothing* live. Kill men, women, children, and every animal you see. This is the offering God requires of you" (1 Sam. 15:3, paraphrased).

But that's not the offering God got. Saul spared not only the enemy king, but the choicest sheep and cattle—then rationalized his disobedience. "I saved them," he told an angry Samuel, "so I could *sacrifice* them to the Lord." And maybe Saul really did intend to use the animals in the worship of God, but, remember, that's not what God had ordered. The animals' deaths *in battle* were to be Saul's sacrifice, so his "worship" was to no avail. Worship without obedience isn't worship at all. God doesn't respect—or accept—it.

Worship without obedience isn't worship at all.

Samuel didn't either. "Why didn't you just *obey* the Lord?" he railed. "Obedience means more to God than *any* sacrifice." Then, in rage, Samuel himself killed the Amalekite king. The Bible says he cut him to pieces.

"God has rejected you, Saul," Samuel told the king. "The kingdom will no longer belong to your family." And Samuel left. He never saw Saul again, and, worse, Saul never heard from the Lord again.

Strike Three—Saul's Out!

Saul's reign was not entirely without success. First Samuel 14 says that "everywhere Saul went he defeated Israel's enemies" (v. 47 NCV). He even remembered to honor the Lord after defeating the Philistines; he built an altar to God (v. 35). But he just didn't have it in him to *obey* God, so his worship was a sham. Saul was his own god—he even erected a monument "in his own honor" (1 Sam. 15:12 NCV). And that's not the worst of Saul's story.

But what, if anything, does Saul's story—or Gideon's, for that matter— have to do with us? More specifically, how do these antiquated accounts relate to our worship? Can we learn anything from them that will ensure that worship in our century is authentic? Let's take a look . . .

PRINCIPLES OF WORSHIP FROM THIS CHAPTER

In this chapter we looked at a judge who started out strong and destroyed the idolatry in his community—only to become the catalyst for its reemergence. We then beheld a king who also started out strong, defeating enemies left and right—only to bow to the greatest enemy there is. What can we capture from these character sketches?

From Gideon

We've already discussed the danger of allowing any hint of idolatry, once eliminated, to resurface. Gideon tore down multiple idols, but then made a new one—and obviously worshipped it himself. (Remember, the Scripture said it snared him.) We do this too—every New Year's! Oh, come on. How many "New Year's resolutions" have *you* made? "I'm not going to do *that* anymore!" you'll say, in reference to some longtime sin or habit that has garnered your devotion. It's happened to all of us. So we tear that idol down. But . . . by the third day of the new year—the fourth or fifth, if we're *really* good—either we've bowed to that loathsome idol all over again, or we've erected a new one in its place. New Year's is just an example. Truth is, we fight the issue of idolatry constantly. It's a *day-to-day* battle—with sin. Once again, let me quote the apostle Paul: "I do not understand the things I do . . . I do the things I hate . . . It is sin living in me" (Rom. 7:15, 17 NCV). Sounds like Paul, too, struggled with idols, sins that insisted on being served. But as frustrated as Paul got at times, he always knew the answer, and he shared it with us: "Remove . . . the sin" (Heb. 12:1 NCV); that is, tear down your idols. And keep them torn down. Anything that would prompt you to bow again, get it out of your sight. That may require you to rethink the company you keep. Do your friends entice you to worship "idols"? Then *remove* yourself from fellowship, and *remove* their influence from your life. Finally, *remove* your idols, whatever they may be. And, unlike our unsuspecting friend Gideon, never allow another one to compete with your worship of God.

From Samuel

Samuel was the faithful worshiper. He learned how to worship as a child and continued his entire life. How did he do it? First, Samuel *made himself available to God*. He was obedient all the days of his life. Even in giving his farewell address, near the time of his death, Samuel honored God (1 Samuel 12:1–24). He reminded all of Israel to serve the Lord, cast away their idols, sin no more, worship only Yahweh, and remember the wonderful things He did for them (1 Samuel 12:20–22, 24).

Second, Samuel *served the Lord*. He first learned this lesson under Eli's authority. Even though Eli and his family did not obey God, Samuel still served. His service was to the Lord and not to Eli. God knew this and rewarded Samuel with favor. All of Israel respected and admired Samuel. His reputation was above reproach.

Third, Samuel *heard the Lord and immediately answered*. His response was simply, "Here I am." And, when he was told that the voice might be that of the Lord, he responded quickly. Obedience demanded the straightforward response, "Here I Am."

Fourth, Samuel *listened for the Lord*. God honored Samuel's worship by giving him a heart that listened for the Lord's voice. When God visited the fourth time, *the Lord came and stood* by Samuel's bed and called, "Samuel, Samuel" (1 Samuel 3:10–13). Samuel said, "Speak, Lord. I am your servant and I am listening."

Fifth, Samuel *obeyed God's word*. God rewarded Samuel's faithfulness to worship Him through obedience. Because of Samuel's faithful obedience, the Lord continued to show himself at Shiloh. And, God confirmed Himself to Samuel through His word.

This lesson of obedience is one we will see over and over again as we study the relationship between God's revelation and worship. When God reveals Himself—no matter how seemingly insignificant that revelation may be—our response, if indeed we have worshipping hearts, is always obedience. Worshippers must say, "Here I am."

From Saul

What *about* Saul? Are there lessons to be gotten from his life? He didn't bow to idols, did he?

Well, actually, he did. He bowed to an idol named *Narcissism*. See, he was in love, not with God, but with himself. He proved it time and again by disobeying the Lord—*and* setting up a monument to honor none other than himself. It is from King Saul that we learn the difference between pseudoworship and the "real McCoy." Oh, Saul made a show of worship. Remember? When he offered sacrifices in the priest's place? But it was against God's law, and you cannot worship God "above the law."

Yet people try constantly. "Oh, I'm a Christian," they say. Every weekend, they're in God's house, singing enthusiastically along with the worship leader, perhaps even raising their hands, or shouting hallelujah. Like Saul, they're making a show of worship. But then these same "worshippers" go home and worship at the feet of Internet pornography or sex-filled romance novels. Their TV viewing is uncensored; the movies they watch, abhorrent.

Their speech is laced with profanity—and gossip. Alcohol hides in their cupboards; lust and envy lurk in their hearts. They are worshippers, all right, but of whom? Themselves. They're certainly not worshipping God, because they are endeavoring to worship above the law, and that's idolatry.

"Oh, but I give 20 percent of my salary to the church," they'll tell you, with puffed chests. "*And* I donate to charity!" They're *sacrificing* for the Lord. But what did Samuel tell King Saul? "It is better to obey than to sacrifice" (1 Sam. 15:22 NCV). God has no interest in our "sacrifice" if we don't obey Him. That's just one more attempt to worship above the law. If we continue, then—like Saul—we'll be brought down.

We know how Saul's tragic story ends. He died—at his own hand—a broken and hated man. But first, he would meet his successor—a boy who smelled of sheep. What was his name? "King" David.

Now, *there's* a man who can teach us how to worship!

9

WORSHIP IN THE BOOKS
OF HISTORY, PART II:
THE WORSHIP OF THE KINGS

DAVID WAS JUST A YOUNG MAN — AND AN INSIGNIFICANT ONE, at that — when God chose him to be the leader of Israel. The youngest of eight boys, David tended his father's sheep on the rugged hills of Judah, and he tended them very well — he saved the flock from both a lion and a bear.

Any other shepherd would have cut and run at first sight of a bear, and *faint* before the "king of the beasts." But not David. He was brave — so brave, in fact, that he killed not only these bloodthirsty animals, but also a giant — that not a single soldier in King Saul's army was willing to fight. Yes, David certainly had courage. You've read about it, in 1 Samuel.

But David had more than just courage; he also had talent. David was a skilled composer of music, with a golden voice. King Saul even hired him to play the harp and sing in the palace, to calm his royal nerves. "No one found anywhere in God's Word is so versatile," says author Henrietta Mears. "He is David, the shepherd boy, the court musician, the soldier, the true friend, the outcast captain, the king, the great general, the loving father, the poet, the sinner, the brokenhearted old man, but always the lover of God."[1]

May I add that he was a worshipper?

The Sheepherding King

David was only eighteen when God told Samuel to anoint him as Israel's next king. Yet David waited until age thirty to actually wear the crown. Why? He respected his predecessor; God Himself had chosen Saul. So, instead of usurping the king's authority, David waited until Saul's rule was over before assuming the position of sovereign. In the meantime, David served Saul dutifully.

But Saul was insanely jealous of his court musician. *This whippersnapper is getting too big for his britches!* he thought. David was very popular, and Saul wanted him dead.

David became an outlaw, hunted like an animal by an insecure king. Meanwhile, Saul was losing the esteem of both the priests and his own people. At the same time David was increasing in favor, with both God and man. There were many who would gladly have made him king right then. Yet David refused to seek the throne until Saul was dead.

THE WORSHIP OF DAVID

Eventually, Saul did die, and David became king. And with each passing year, "David became more and more powerful, because the LORD Almighty was with him" (1 Chron. 11:9 NIV). Why was the Lord with David? Because David was committed to the proper worship of God, not only personally, but nationally. During his reign, David unified his people religiously, reinstituting Yahweh worship as the center of Hebrew life. For forty years, there was no idol worship in Israel. Neither was there intermarriage with heathen nations. Instead, he conquered those nations, and each time he did, he burned all of their idols. He didn't want his subjects to become rooted in idolatry again. Instead, Israel, along with their king, became firmly rooted in God.

> David's rootedness in God continued through all the seasons of his life. When he became king and won victories in war, when he established Jerusalem as the political and spiritual hub of the nation, and as he planned for the construction of the Temple, David held God central. Through all his successes and popularity, David kept the focus on God, not himself, and continued in his inner worship of God.[2]

David's "inner worship" brought God near, and God's presence was David's lifelong compass as he ruled his nation. How—and where—did he develop such a strong inner experience? David's worship of God was shaped, at least in part, in the solitude of the hillsides and plains where he had once kept his father's sheep. He obviously had a lot of time on his hands as his lambs grazed. So, while loyally guarding the flock, David spent the long, lonely hours composing love songs for Yahweh and worshipping Him with his harp. Day and night, in the quiet company of his sheep, David connected with the "Great Shepherd of the sheep" (Heb. 13:20 NCV).

David also connected with God during his dark years as a fugitive. Some of his sweetest psalms were penned during his political exile. As David witnessed, again and again, Saul's failed attempts to catch him, he captured a glimpse of God's provision, protection, and power—and sang about it. Some of David's compositions praised God as the "rock" of salvation. Others told stories of His mighty exploits through the ages. Still more exploded with admiration of God's creative handiwork. But all were filled with praise; David *lived a life* of praise. We'll take a detailed look at some of his "praise choruses" in chapter 12. But for now, let's just take a sneak peek . . .

> Praise the Lord!
> Praise God in his Temple;
> > praise him in his mighty heaven.
> Praise him for his strength;
> > praise him for his greatness.
> Praise him with trumpet blasts;
> > praise him with harps and lyres.
> Praise him with tambourines and dancing;
> > praise him with stringed instruments and flutes.
> Praise him with loud cymbals;
> > praise him with crashing cymbals.
> Let everything that breathes praise the Lord.
> > Praise the Lord! (Ps. 150 NCV)

David *loved* the Lord, not only His person, but His Word as well. The book of Psalms is filled with references to its value. For example:

The law of the LORD is perfect, converting the soul;
    The testimony of the LORD is sure, making wise the simple;
The statutes of the LORD are right, rejoicing the heart;
    The commandment of the LORD is pure, enlightening the eyes;
The fear of the LORD is clean, enduring forever;
    The judgments of the LORD are true and righteous altogether.
More to be desired are they than gold,
    Yea, than much fine gold;
    Sweeter also than honey and the honeycomb.
Moreover by them Your servant is warned,
    And in keeping them there is great reward. (Ps. 19:7–11 NKJV)

Over and over David testified of his dependence on and commitment to the precepts and statutes of the Lord. In God's Word, the Lord *Himself* is revealed. David knew that, so he soaked up the Word of God. And what, do you think, was his response to it? (You'd *better* know the answer by now!) Yes, worship. Anyone who truly adores the Lord will also treasure His Word, and it will lead that individual to a deeper worship experience. David spent a lifetime loving both God and the Word that came forth from Him—and thus became a model of worship.

Sure, David made mistakes—heinous ones. We know the stories about adultery, murder, and general disobedience. How could the man after God's own heart have taken such monstrous missteps? Satan targets and tempts the authentic worshipper. He certainly targeted King David. And David fell, more than once. But God forgave the worshipping king and made both his name and his kingdom great. Again and again, the once-adulterous king conquered his foes because of his *un*adulterated worship. He praised God constantly, and God inhabited his praise (see Psalm 22:3). The presence of the Lord was with David, not only personally, but also in the Ark of God.

But something still troubled David . . .

The Dream of a King

Many years had passed, and King David was living a life of luxury. All of his enemies had been conquered, and Israel was at peace. So, why was he suddenly perturbed?

"Look at me," he said one day, to Nathan the prophet. "Here I am, living in a palace of cedar, while the Ark of *God* is out there—in a *tent*!

"I've got it!" he said. "I'll build a temple for God, a special place He can call *home*."

But the Lord said no. If God was to have a temple, He wanted a man of peace to build it. David had shed too much blood over the years. Still, David couldn't let go of his passion for the idea. He longed to see a beautiful structure built to testify to God's greatness—a structure that all eyes would see.

God honored the king's desire and gave him the temple blueprint. David's son, Solomon, would complete the project. Excited, David assumed the role of "public relations coordinator" and began to execute the capital-giving campaign. His efforts exceeded everyone's expectations: he secured *total* funding for the project. And through his dedication to the cause of God, we catch our deepest glimpse of David's heart of worship:

> "I have done my best to prepare for building the Temple of God. I have given gold . . . and silver . . . I have given bronze . . . and iron . . . I have given wood for the things made of wood and onyx for the settings. I have given turquoise gems of many different colors, valuable stones, and white marble. I have given much of all these things . . . but *now I am also giving my own treasures* of gold and silver, because I really want the Temple of my God to be built . . . Now, who is ready to give himself to the service of the Lord today?" . . .
>
> [Then] the leaders gave willingly and completely to the Lord. The people rejoiced . . . , and King David was also very happy.
>
> Then David said to all the people . . . , "Praise the Lord your God." So they all praised the Lord, the God of their ancestors, and they bowed to the ground to give honor to the Lord and the king. (1 Chron. 29:2–5, 9, 20 NCV).

Wow! Do you see what happened here? David praised the Lord, in front of his whole kingdom, and they followed his example. They worshipped God the same way. It wasn't difficult; they had watched their king do it for years. See, David wasn't afraid to worship, in private *or* in the presence of others. You remember his wife's embarrassment when he "danced before the LORD" after defeating the Philistines (2 Sam. 6:14 NKJV). It didn't matter who was watching; David would worship.

The Death of the Worshipping King

At the end of David's life, in his last public prayer, the king once more praised the Lord, in front of all the people. In this final orison, David gave Israel one last lesson in worship:

> "We praise you, LORD, God of our father Israel. We praise you forever and ever. LORD, you are great and powerful. You have glory, victory, and honor. Everything in heaven and on earth belongs to you. The kingdom belongs to you, LORD; you are the ruler over everything. Riches and honor come from you. You rule everything . . . Now, our God, we thank you and praise your glorious name." (1 Chron. 29:10–13 NCV)

And David died "at a ripe old age" (v. 28 NLT).

THE WORSHIP OF SOLOMON

In his book *The 21 Irrefutable Laws of Leadership*, John Maxwell shares the story of a Cuban-born businessman named Roberto Goizueta. Educated at Yale, Goizueta answered a newspaper ad in 1966 for a bilingual chemist at Coca-Cola, and was hired. But under the mentorship of Coke patriarch Robert W. Woodruff, Goizueta would become much more than a chemist. Within fourteen years, Robert Goizueta would become Coke's chief operating officer. It happened in 1980.

One year later, the company was valued at $4 billion. But under Goizueta's leadership, Coke's value rose to $150 billion by the mid-1990s—a 3,500-percent increase—making Coca-Cola the second most valuable corporation in American history.

At Goizueta's death, the company was stronger than ever. Why? Because during his tenure, (1) he had made the company as sound as possible, and (2) he had meticulously prepared his successor. Goizueta's integrity as a leader left a permanent mark on the organization.[3]

At David's death, the worship culture of Israel, like Coca-Cola, was stronger than ever. David, too, had made a permanent mark—on national Israel. He had wisely prepared his son, Solomon, to take over, praying, "Help him always obey your commands" (1 Chron. 29:18 NCV). Solomon was ready.

Solomon was anointed king of Israel at the young age of twenty, and at his father's death, he immediately "took firm control of the kingdom, for the LORD his God was with him and made him very powerful" (2 Chron. 1:1 NLT). The entire nation of Israel "stood in awe of him" (1 Chron. 29:25 NLT), and all of the people obeyed him.

On the day Solomon became king, the people sacrificed burnt offerings to the Lord—a thousand bulls, a thousand sheep, and a thousand lambs. They also brought drink offerings and celebrated with great joy in the presence of the Lord, feasting and anointing their new king "before the LORD" (v. 22 NLT). Solomon was loved from the get-go.

After the feast, Solomon addressed the people. Then together, sovereign and subjects went to the place of worship in Gibeon, where God's Meeting Tent, in which the Ark of God still dwelled, was erected. A bronze altar stood in front of the tent, and there, Solomon and the people worshipped God. Then, with the eyes of all Israel on him, Solomon himself approached the altar and offered a thousand burnt offerings. Clearly, Solomon had learned from his father: worship is meant to be taught.

Almost immediately, Solomon began the work envisioned by his father: a great temple for the Lord. David had received the "blueprint" from God Himself and had handed it to Solomon. The new king would follow that blueprint to the letter, honoring every detail of God's instructions.

But first, he enlisted some foreign aid. He wrote a letter to Hiram, king of Tyre, saying:

> "I [am going to] build a temple for worshiping the LORD my God, and I will give this temple to him. There we will burn sweet-smelling spices in his presence. We will continually set out the holy bread in God's presence. And we will burn sacrifices every morning and evening, on Sabbath days and New Moons, and on the other feast days commanded by the LORD our God. This is a rule for Israel to obey forever.
>
> The temple I build will be great, because our God is greater than all

gods. But no one can really build a house for our God. Not even the highest of heavens can hold him. How then can I build a temple for him except as a place to burn sacrifices to him?

Now send me a man skilled in working with gold, silver, bronze, and iron, and with purple, red, and blue thread. He must also know how to make engravings. He will work with my skilled craftsmen in Judah and Jerusalem, whom my father David chose.

Also send me cedar, pine, and juniper logs from Lebanon. I know your servants are experienced at cutting down the trees in Lebanon, and my servants will help them. Send me a lot of wood, because the temple I am going to build will be large and wonderful. (2 Chron. 2:4–10 NCV)

King Hiram answered promptly. "Praise the LORD, the God of Israel, who made heaven and earth!" he wrote. "He has given King David a wise son . . . who will build a temple for the LORD" (v. 12 NCV). And Hiram promised his help.

Chapters 3 and 4 of 2 Chronicles describe the building of the temple, in all its opulence. What a magnificent structure it must have been. And God appreciated it, without a doubt. It represented the best of man's efforts, using the best of God's resources. But for the Lord, the joy wasn't in the edifice itself; it was in the heart of worship behind it. And when construction was complete, God met Israel there.

A Worship Service Extraordinaire

God now had His temple (even though it was something He didn't ask for). It was time to worship Him in it. Second Chronicles 5 tells us that King Solomon called for the elders, asking them to bring "the Ark of the Agreement with the LORD" (v. 2 NCV) to Jerusalem. So the priests brought the Ark to Solomon, and there, gathered before the Ark, the people and their king "sacrificed so many sheep and bulls no one could count them" (v. 6 NCV). Then the priests carried the Ark into the Most Holy Place, inside the temple. The sacred box, made as a place for God's presence to dwell, now had a home. And the people held a worship service the likes of which may only be seen again when we—the unified body of Christ— stand before our Messiah:

All the Levite musicians . . . and all their sons and relatives—stood on the east side of the altar. They . . . played cymbals, harps, and lyres. With them were one hundred twenty priests who blew trumpets. Those who blew the trumpets and those who sang together sounded like one person as they praised and thanked the LORD. They sang as others played their trumpets, cymbals, and other instruments. They praised the LORD with this song: "He is good; his love continues forever." (vv. 12–13 NCV)

Did you catch that? The singers and the musicians "sounded like one person." And, in unison, they praised the Lord together, spontaneously, with *one* unified song. That's because their hearts were of one accord before they ever got there. The people had arrived with one agenda: to worship God—as one. They checked their egos at the door and joined together, in unity, to give God praise. How the Lord loves our praise. So what do you imagine was His response to Israel's passionate, united praise and worship?

God Shows Up—in Solomon's Temple

My father was a pastor. Often, he would invite guest evangelists to come and preach a "revival." I remember, as a boy, witnessing those special times when God would suddenly visit our congregation. The spirit of God would begin to move in the hearts of people, sometimes during prayer, other times as we sang. Occasionally it would happen right during the sermon. People would start to weep, then spontaneously run to the altar, confess their sins, pray for unsaved loved ones, and freely worship the Lord. It was not uncommon during these times for people to receive Christ, for marriages to be reconciled, or for wayward children to be reunited with their estranged families. The glory of God filled the house, and His presence was so powerful that the preacher had to quit preaching.

That was the scene in Jerusalem that day. "The Temple of the LORD was filled with a cloud" (v. 13b NCV). We've seen a cloud before, haven't we? God led the Israelites out of Egypt with a *pillar of cloud*. And here He was again, with His people, in a cloud of grandeur. The priests had to stop what they were doing. Man's work was no longer important. The glory of the Lord Himself had filled the house.

Breathless, young Solomon cried, "Praise the LORD, the God of Israel" (6:4 NCV), and he raised both hands to heaven in worship. Then, in the sight of all Israel, he knelt at the altar, hands spread toward the sky, and prayed. "LORD, God of Israel, there is no god like you in heaven or on earth . . . Forgive your people who have sinned against you . . . Look at us. Listen to the prayers we pray in this place. [And] now, rise, LORD God, and come to your resting place" (vv. 14, 39–41 NCV).

And God did—quickly, decisively, and deliberately. Fire fell from the sky and consumed the sacrifices. Then the Lord's glory filled the temple. When the people saw this, they "bowed down on the pavement with their faces to the ground" and "worshiped and thanked the LORD" (2 Chron. 7:3 NCV).

The importance of fire from heaven cannot be understated. It symbolized God's sanctioning of Solomon's worship. God was pleased with the worship of the king, and with His holy fire, He was *proving it*!

Solomon wouldn't always get it right. We know from history that, one day, he would unite with foreign wives, and even worship foreign gods. But we also know that he would repent, and the wisdom from his life would be recorded in the book of Ecclesiastes. At the end of his road, King Solomon would write, "I give my final advice: Honor God and obey his commands, because this is all people must do" (Eccl. 12:13 NCV). Solomon never forgot about that time when God showed His pleasure with Solomon's worship—and proved it by fire!

Now, about that fire . . . Can you imagine—can you even imagine?— what it would be like for fire to fall in response to God's pleasure with *your* worship? *my* worship? the *church's* worship?

I don't know about you, but it sure makes me want to "get it right."

PRINCIPLES OF WORSHIP FROM THIS CHAPTER

In this chapter, you have read about the worship of two of Israel's most unforgettable kings. Each of these critical characters has shown us something about worship that we can apply in our own experience. What wisdom can we extract from the stories of Kings David and Solomon?

From David

Unabashed and authentic worship brings God near. Just ask David. He poured all that he had into the worship of God—not only his own, but his kingdom's. King David established the worship of the true God as the heart of society. No idol worship existed during his reign. What were the results? Peace and order. And all because of David's uninhibited worship. Recall how he danced before the Lord, to his own wife's chagrin. He didn't care what *anyone* thought of his zealous displays of adoration. We shouldn't either. Yet, in so many churches today, many miss out on the nearness of God because they are afraid to worship without inhibition.

I'm the only one raising my hands! And the phalanges slip self-consciously down to our sides.

[Gasp!]My mascara is running. So the tears are stifled.

I'm a man—I can't cry. And the joy—or repentance—is stymied.

I don't see anyone else kneeling, so why should I?

Hmm . . . no one else *is doing that.* And the Spirit is quenched, all because of what people *might* think about us.

But David only cared about what God thought. So he sang his heart out. Cried a river. Danced shamelessly in the worship of God. And God came and brought peace, forty years of it.

Do you want the peace of God in your life? Then, no matter the circumstances, no matter the company, worship Him. Brazenly. Barefacedly. Without reserve. And Yahweh-Shalom, "the Lord [Our] Peace" (Judg. 6:24) will "move in" (see Psalm 22:3) and bring sweet peace to you. Not only that, but you'll be a channel through which God broadcasts authentic worship to those around you. And what will result? More worship. Remember, the people followed David's *example.* They'll follow yours too.

From Solomon

Perhaps one of the most challenging times for a choral conductor is when a melodic line must be sung in perfect unison. *Perfect* unison requires *perfect* balance—in volume, intonation, timbre, rhythm, diction . . . Everyone must work together, with a single goal. It's no time for individual showcasing. A hundred voices must sound like *one.* Only then does the melody, sung in unison, have corporate power. Otherwise, it's just noise. The same is true of collective worship.

There's power in corporate worship. If you don't believe it, revisit Solomon's story. When the Ark of God was brought into the newly built temple, the kingdom worshipped God together, in unison. And they "sounded like one person" as they praised and sang to Yahweh (2 Chron. 5:13 NCV). Their hearts were in accord. And what happened? Fire fell, because God was in the house.

Do you want God "in the house"? Then remember: when we come together to worship, it's not about us. It's about Him. No human voice should stand out among others (except, of course, the worship leader's). And no one is a "star." All hearts should instead be directed toward the *morning star* (see Revelation 22:16). When we worship God like that, He'll make His presence known, just as He did for Solomon. Our profound, God-exalting worship, no matter how many of us there are, will reach heaven as one earnest, *unified* voice of praise.

And that, my friend, is when the fire will fall.

WORSHIP IN THE BOOKS OF HISTORY, PART III: DEVOTION IN A DIVIDED KINGDOM

IN CHAPTER 9 WE STUDIED THE WORSHIP OF TWO GODLY KINGS. First, we looked at King David, Israel's second monarch, and a man after God's own heart, whose reckless abandon to the worship of God has been celebrated throughout history. Next, we looked briefly at Solomon, son of David, whose worship brought fire down from heaven.

It wouldn't be the last time fire fell from on high.

By now, the first three kings of national Israel—Saul, David, and Solomon—were dead. A new order had arisen; Solomon's son Rehoboam, was crowned. But Rehoboam's reign would not be one of peace. He was weak, easily influenced by his friends. He was unwise, preferring the imprudent counsel of the young and impulsive to the wisdom of his elders. He was unjust to his people, and he made a lot of enemies. Of him the Chronicler wrote, "He was an evil king, for he did not seek the LORD with all his heart" (2 Chron. 12:14 NLT). Indeed, at the pinnacle of his power, Rehoboam forsook God. And the kingdom was divided.

Those in the south, two of Israel's tribes, remained loyal to Rehoboam. But the people of the north, ten tribes in all, chose a king of their own: Jeroboam. The once-strong and unified kingdom of Israel was now split in two: the Northern Kingdom, Israel, and the Southern Kingdom, Judah. And the two were continually at war.

Thus began a shameful history of kingships on both sides, north and south, which eventually led to the destruction of both realms. Of the nineteen kings that reigned over the Northern Kingdom before its fall in 722 BC, *not one* was good. Beginning with Jeroboam, who molded golden calves for his kingdom to worship, every succeeding northern king worshipped "the calf."[1] Some also worshipped Baal.

To give you an idea of the state of Israel:

Nadab (Jeroboam's son) . . .	"did what the Lord said was wrong" (1 Kings 15:26 NCV).
Baasha . . .	"[did] many things the Lord said were wrong" (16:7 NCV).
Elah . . .	"sinned and led the people of Israel to sin" (v. 13 NCV).
Zimri . . .	"sinned in the same way as Jeroboam" (v. 19 NCV).

And that (including Jeroboam) was just the first five.

The Southern Kingdom fared a little better. A *few* kings worshipped Yahweh, but only a few. Asa, Judah's third king, "did what the LORD said was right" (1 Kings 15:11–12 NCV). He got rid of the idols that his predecessors had erected and put an end to prostitution in the house of worship, even forcing the prostitutes into exile. He also removed his Asherah-worshipping grandmother, Maacah, from being queen mother. He was a good king, the first one the Southern Kingdom had known. In fact, the Bible says that "Asa was faithful to the LORD all his life" (v. 14 NCV). And his faithfulness to God was obviously both taught *and* "caught" . . . by his son, Jehoshaphat, whom we'll talk about momentarily.

Too bad the Northern Kingdom didn't learn a thing from Asa—*not one good king* in Israel. All were wicked. But one did more "to make the LORD . . . angry" (1 Kings 16:33 NCV), or as the New King James puts it, "to provoke the LORD" than any of the kings that preceded him. His name was Ahab. And speak of the devil . . .

AHAB, THE MALEVOLENT MONARCH

Ahab, son of Omri and the seventh king of Israel, was a rotter! Yet, interestingly, Ahab considered himself a worshipper of the God of Israel. Several times, the Bible records, he received counsel from God's prophets (20:13, 14, 22, 28; 22:8). A student of these stories will easily see that, at one time, anyway, God was even in Ahab's "corner." Perhaps the man had once genuinely loved God. If not, he at least *thought* about Him: in later years, three of his children's names would even incorporate God's divine name (Ahaziah, "held by Jehovah"[2]; Athaliah, "whom Yahweh has afflicted";[3] and Jehoram, "Jehovah-exalted"[4]).

But Ahab made a fatal error, early in his reign: in disobedience to God, he married an infamously impious foreign princess: Jezebel.

Jezebel was the daughter of the priest-king of Sidon, mother city of Tyre. Remember, the Lord had strictly forbidden intermarriage with the people of Canaan (Deut. 7:3), of which Tyre was a part. In fact, Israel was supposed to have destroyed them when they entered the promised land. But now Ahab had married a Tyrian who both practiced witchcraft and worshipped idols (2 Kings 9:22), in particular, Baal, Tyre's chief deity. And because Jezebel "wore the pants" in her household, she personally authorized—with her husband's blessing—the funding of 450 Baal prophets (plus 400 prophets of Asherah) from Israel's treasury. It wasn't long before Ahab not only worshipped his wife's statues, but began to patronize the Canaanite cult within his own kingdom.

First, he built a temple to Baal and placed an idol there that he had cast himself. Then he made an image of Asherah too. Finally, at Jezebel's prodding, he began to aid her in persecuting those who refused to worship these deities. These were dark and desperate hours for Israel as Ahab persistently ignored God's warning, given through Moses centuries before: "Be careful, or you . . . will turn away to . . . worship other gods. If you do, the Lord will become angry with you and will shut the heavens so it will not rain. Then the land will not grow crops" (Deut. 11:16–17 NCV).

Enter Elijah.

ELIJAH, THE PLUCKY PROPHET

Elijah was a rugged and forceful prophet of the Lord, from Gilead, a rough region in the Transjordan. One day, he showed up, seemingly from nowhere, to jog King Ahab's memory of the consequences of breaking God's covenant. "The God of Israel is about to send a drought," Elijah announced. "Not one drop of rain will fall until I say so" (1 Kings 17:1, paraphrased).

Canaanite mythology divided the universe into four parts: The heavens belonged to the high god; the underworld was ruled by the god of death; and the sea and earth between were controlled, in part, by Baal. Elijah's announcement of an impending drought was a direct challenge to the pre-fabricated power of Baal. After all, he *was* the presumed god of rain, wind, storm, and water, and was pictured brandishing a lightning bolt. But Elijah had issued an *"en garde"* to Ahab's pseudogod. Then . . .

Elijah disappeared, as quickly as he'd come. And Jezebel was beside herself. "Find him!" she screeched. "And *kill* him!"

For three years, Elijah was missing in action. Meanwhile, the entire region groaned under the curse of the drought. There was no food. No water. Finally, Ahab and his palace overseer went in opposite directions to search every spring in the land for even a drop of moisture. And Ahab's armies were still on the prowl, searching doggedly for God's prophet. But then . . .

"Go back to Ahab," the Lord told Elijah, who had been in hiding. "It's time for a showdown!" So Elijah headed for the palace.

Face-Off with a False God

"Troublemaker!" Ahab spat as, once again, he faced the spirited seer from Gilead.

"Ahab," Elijah roared boldly, "YOU have brought trouble to Israel, by following the Baals!

"Tell all of Israel to meet me at Mount Carmel," he ordered. "And bring your '*prophets*' with you." So Ahab sent for the citizens and their prophets, and together they met with Elijah at the mount.

"How long will you waffle, back and forth, between two gods?" Elijah challenged the assembled horde. "If God is the true God, then *worship* Him—alone. If Baal is, worship *him*. You can't have them both!" You know he was speaking to Ahab more than anyone else. Ahab *still* professed to be a follower of Yahweh, even while cleaving to the gods of his shrew, Jezebel. But God was through with it. The time had come for Ahab, and all of Israel, to choose one way or the other.

Then Elijah added fuel to the fire: he defied the prophets. "There are 450 of *them*," he taunted, "and only one of me. Have your 'prophets' bring a couple of bulls." So the Baal prophets brought two bulls to the altar on Mount Carmel. "Now, kill one," Elijah told them, "and cut it in pieces; then lay it all on this altar." So they did. Elijah did the same. Then he turned to the prophets. "Now, you pray to Baal, and I'll pray to the Lord. Whoever answers by fire—*that's* the true God."

Sounded like a plan, the people thought, so the prophets of Baal began to pray. And pray! . . . And *pray* . . . They prayed all morning. "'O Baal, answer us!'" But there was not a sound, "not so much as a whisper of breeze" (1 Kings 18:26 NCV). So the false prophets began to dance dizzily about, with more and more fervor as the day dragged on.

And Elijah was loving it.

About noon, Elijah started making fun of Baal's misguided mystics. "'You'll have to shout louder than that,' he scoffed, 'to catch the attention of your god! Perhaps he is . . . sitting on the toilet, or maybe he is away on a trip, or is asleep and needs to be wakened'" (v. 27 TLB).

That only piqued their passion. "They prayed louder and louder," the writer tells us, "cutting themselves with swords and knives—a ritual common to them—until they were covered with blood." This went on until evening, as they "used every religious trick and strategy they knew to make something happen on the altar, but nothing happened . . . not a flicker of response" (vv. 28–29 MSG).

"Enough!" Elijah said, as he shooed the prophets away. "Now . . . watch this!"

The people gathered around Elijah as he rebuilt the altar, in honor of the Lord, and dug a trench around it. Next he placed the wood, and then portions of beef, on the altar. Finally, he did what must have seemed most peculiar: he soaked the firewood and the sacrifice with four buckets of water—three times—to rule out any suggestion of chicanery on his part. "No cheating, now," he teased.

In contrast to the baalists' dizzy display, Elijah now prayed a simple, succinct prayer: "O GOD, . . . make it known right now that you are God in Israel . . . Answer me, GOD . . . and reveal to this people that you are . . . the true God" (36b–37 MSG).

Immediately, fire fell from the sky, drying up the wood, burning meat and altar—rocks and all—and even licking up the water! The people then fell on their faces and cried, "Jehovah *is* God! He *is*!"

"Oh yeah?" Elijah answered. "Then grab those bogus prophets! *Get 'em!*" And they captured the false prophets. Then Elijah slaughtered them. *Every last one.*

You know what happened next. Elijah prayed for rain, and rain came. A *heavy* rain, the Bible says (v. 45 NCV). And it slaked the thirst of Israel's parched land.

Now, you may be saying, "That's a nice story, and I've heard it a gazillion times before . . . but what's the *point?*" Indeed, what *does* this tale have to do with you and me—and our worship?

PRINCIPLES OF WORSHIP FROM ELIJAH

There are so many ways to worship God. Some like it "hot," as they say. Boisterous, exuberant, with lots of demonstration. And their hearts are really in it, so God "shows up." Hey, He's all for it, *whenever* worship—and the worshipper—is authentic.

But what about those folks who prefer a deep, meditative, internal worship experience? Their worship is just as heartfelt, but there is little outward demonstration. In a society on a quest for "more bang for the buck," these quiet worshippers are often misunderstood. Is their worship any less valid than that of the "movers and shakers"? Obviously, Elijah didn't think so.

The prophets of Baal worked themselves into a froth at Mount Carmel, slashing themselves, pleading and squalling, and dancing themselves to dizziness. They were sure making a lot of noise, but to no avail. Baal didn't show.

Then comes Elijah, a man of few words. He prayed briefly, worshipped without pageantry, and—again—fire fell from heaven.

Thunderous, demonstrative worship can be a wonderful thing—unless it's offered from immoral hearts. God won't accept such praise; it's contrived, whipped to an artificial but fruitless froth. Says A. W. Tozer:

> The adolescent taste which loves the loud horn and the thundering exhaust has gotten into the activities of modern Christians. The old question, "What is the chief end of man?" is now answered, "To dash about the world and add to the din thereof" . . . We must begin the needed reform by challenging the spiritual validity of externalism. What a man is must be shown to be more important than what he does. While the moral quality of any act is imparted by the condition of the heart, there may be a world of religious activity which arises not from within but from without and which would seem to have little or no moral content. Such religious conduct is imitative or reflex. It stems from the current cult of commotion and possesses no sound inner life.[5]

What a man is? More important than what he does? Well, what *was* Elijah? A moral man. A steadfast servant. A faithful follower. A one-track worshipper. His heart was in right moral condition. As such, he didn't have to make a big noise to get God's attention. We don't either. Now, if that's your style, then more power to ya. King David liked it like that. I do too. But "performance" alone won't make God happy. Just ask Ahab. He was humiliated that day, on Mount Carmel, when all that he believed in was put to shame.

But as Ahab licked his wounds over the murders of his prophets, a new king was ruling the Southern Kingdom. This was Jehoshaphat, son of Asa, whose story we told at the beginning of this chapter. Jehoshaphat was a good king, like his father, and was a worshipper of the only true God, Yahweh. In fact, I guess you could say that King Jehoshaphat took worship to a whole new level.

The Worship of Jehoshaphat

In the heart of Pennsylvania's Dutch Country Roads Region lies a U.S. Army facility known as Carlisle Barracks. This site is home to the United States Army War College, the Army's most senior military educational institution.[6] Valuable during both George Washington's presidency and the Civil War, today the Barracks has the distinction of being *the* place for officers to be trained in the art of war. At the elite Army War College, students are schooled in military strategy and prepared for the highest-level leadership positions. These upwardly mobile trainees will shape America's future war policies and procedures.

Imagine if, today, this group of prestigious war planners was ordered to march into battle—against our most formidable enemy—with the U.S. Army Chorus leading the charge. No tanks. No stealth bombers. No grenades. Just singers . . . singing—and *without* night vision, bazookas, or "shock and awe." Simply the sounds of voices trolling "The Caissons Go Rollin' Along." The average war strategist would look at his superior and say, "Have you lost your mind? We are *not* going into battle led by a covey of crooners!"

But that was the exact scenario in 2 Chronicles 20.

Jehoshaphat ruled in Judah for twenty-five years, and because "He wanted very much to obey the Lord," God was with this king. Second Chronicles tells us (17:6 NCV) that he removed all of the images of Asherah from the land. Then, in the third year of his reign, he sent priests all over the kingdom to instruct the people in the law (v. 7). From town to town, sixteen leaders took their "traveling school" and taught from the "Book of the Teachings of the Lord" (v. 9 NCV) so the people would turn from their pagan religious practices. Later, the king himself went out among them and "turned them back to the Lord" (19:4 NCV). Then he appointed judges to pastor the people. "Always serve the Lord completely," he told this group of priests before dispatching them to their respective sectors. "You must fear him" (v. 9 NCV). Jehoshaphat's deepest desire was to rule a kingdom that feared, that is, worshipped, Yahweh.

God rewarded Jehoshaphat's devotion. All of the surrounding nations were afraid of this king—and his God. No one would go to war with

Jehoshaphat. Even the Philistines, Judah's longtime enemy, paid tribute to him (v. 11). Better still, because of Jehoshaphat's single-hearted worship, the Lord blessed all of his efforts. His wealth was great, his army vast, and cities strong and walled. No one could invade his domain.

But one day, someone tried . . .

Whispers of War

"A huge army is on their way to attack you!" messengers told Jehoshaphat one day. "We saw them coming from Edom. Ammonites, Meunites, and Moabites." (Oh my!) These rival nations were ready for war, and the king was afraid.

What will I do? he wondered. But Jehoshaphat already had a built-in response to crisis: *I'll ask the Lord.* So the first thing he did was call a fast. All of the people of Judah were to abstain from food and instead go to the temple for a national "Day of Prayer." From every town they came and met in the temple's courtyard. Then Jehoshaphat stood up and prayed:

> "LORD, God of our ancestors," he cried out, "you are the God in heaven. You rule over all the kingdoms of the nations. You have power and strength, so no one can stand against you. Our God, you . . . gave this land forever to the descendants of your friend Abraham. They lived in this land and built a Temple for you. They said, 'If trouble comes upon us, or war, . . . we will stand before you and before this Temple where you have chosen to be worshiped. We will cry out to you when we are in trouble. Then you will hear and save us.'
>
> "But now here are men from Ammon, Moab, and Edom . . . The Israelites . . . did not destroy them. But see how they repay us for not destroying them! They have come to force us out of your land, which you gave us as our own . . . We have no power against this large army that is attacking us. We don't know what to do, so we look to you for help (20:6–12 NCV).

Notice the elements of Jehoshaphat's prayer. First he lauded God's *power.* No one, the king said, was God's equal. Then he reminded the Lord of the *past,* and how good the Israelites had been to the enemy nations, sparing their lives. Finally, he mentioned the *promise* of God. The land given to Abraham was to be Israel's forever, but now it was threatened. In humility, the king concluded, "We do not know what to do, but our eyes are upon you" (v. 12 NIV).

You know the saying: "There's power in numbers." You will remember that, in the Upper Room, it was when all of the worshippers were "with one accord" (Acts 2:1 NKJV) that God came on the scene.

That's exactly what happened in the temple courtyard on this day. *All* of Judah's men, women, and children stood reverently before the Lord and worshipped him. This was no private worship service. The whole kingdom was in attendance, all seeking God together.

Suddenly, the Spirit of the Lord entered a musician named Jahaziel, and he stood. "Listen, King," he said, "the Lord told me to tell you, '*Don't be afraid!* The battle is not yours. It's Mine. Go out to that battlefield. You won't even have to fight. Just get out there, hold your places, and watch *Me* save you!'" (2 Chron. 20:14–17, paraphrased).

Can you imagine? Think of the many conflicts our nation has seen over the last hundred years. World Wars I and II. The Korean and Vietnam conflicts. The Persian Gulf confrontations. The "war" on terrorism. Try to picture the president's reaction at hearing God say, in any of those cases, "Your soldiers won't *have* to fight; I'll win for you"?

How do you suppose Jehoshaphat reacted? He hit the ground, face-down—him and the whole Southern Kingdom. Verse 18 says that "all Judah and the inhabitants of Jerusalem fell down before the LORD, worshiping [Him] (NASB). They hadn't seen the outcome of the battle yet. They were taking it by faith. But, many times, that's how we have to worship God—*before* we see the answer with our physical eyes. Judah knew that if there was to be any divine intervention, their priorities must be in the right order. So they worshipped God, faces to the floor . . . till someone started praising.

Then, Judah had a "glory service," and what a time it must have been. The people rose from the ground and began to "praise the LORD God of Israel with voices loud and high" (v. 19 NKJV). They had no doubt that God would save them. The Lord had spoken, and when He gives a word, it's a *sure* one. Judah accepted the victory by faith.

Jehoshaphat's Wartime Chorus

Early in the morning, Jehoshaphat's army went out into the desert of Tekoa, and there the king concocted the most ridiculous war plan in the history of mankind. It would baffle strategists for centuries to come.

Jehoshaphat chose a band of singers—*singers*, not *warriors*. Their job? Sing. To the Lord. Why? Because it was good war strategy? No, because, quite simply, God "is holy and wonderful" (v. 21 NCV), and now, this burly, all-male choir was instructed to march in front of the army and sing about Him: "Give thanks to the LORD, for his love endures forever" (v. 21b NIV).

The King James Version says the lyrics were actually "Praise the LORD; for his mercy endureth for ever." Another version renders it, "Give thanks to GOD, His love never quits" (MSG). Still another, "Give thanks to the LORD, for His lovingkindness is everlasting" (NASB). And a fourth, ". . . for His faithful love endures forever" (HCSB). The important thing is that, in the face of what looked like certain doom, this husky gospel choir was to testify to the enemy nations—in song—of God's all-sufficient love for Judah. No weapons would be on the front line, no chariots, no swords, no bullets—only a chorale of brawny men, whose hardest-working "muscles" would be their vocal ones. The warriors—with all their arms and ammo—would follow *behind* them.

A God-size Victory

"As they began to sing and praise God," the Scriptures say, "the LORD set ambushes for the people . . . who had come to attack Judah. *And they were defeated*" (v. 22 NCV). But, how?

They say that the great Roman Empire was destroyed from within. That was exactly the case with these enemy armies. God Himself arranged a surprise "assault" on the three hostile nations—in the form of mass confusion. The Ammonites and the Moabites began to attack their allies, the Edomites. When they had killed them, they turned on each other. Next thing you know, all three armies were destroyed.

When Jehoshaphat's army reached the battlefield and gazed across the desert, they saw no approaching militants. Instead they saw corpses. Dead bodies everywhere. Not one enemy soldier was alive, and there was pillage for the taking—booty, loot, spoils, swag, whatever you want to call it—it was more than they could carry away. It took three days to gather the plunder that would be Judah's war prize.

Isn't that just like God? He gave more than Jehoshaphat expected. And He'll do the same for you—if you will worship Him. Whatever your "Ammonites" (et al) may be, God Himself will go to battle for you and turn terror into triumph, violence into victory, dismay into delight—and give you more, *abundantly* more, than you could ever ask or think (see Ephesians 3:20).

An All-out "Praise-athon"

How do you react when God blesses you? What is your response when God exchanges your sadness for His gladness? Do you stop and thank Him? Do you celebrate Him with joy and music? That's what Jehoshaphat did, after his battle. He held an all-out "praise-athon"! To any outsider, the odds were against the king's success, yet God had invisibly stacked the odds in Judah's favor, and Jehoshaphat's army had *won*. So the people went straight for the temple—harps, lyres, and trumpets in hand—to praise the Lord.

Jehoshaphat was an indisputable worshipper. And God's overall impression of him? "[He] was good" (2 Chron. 20:32 NCV). Not only that, but he exhibited true faith in the face of peril—he worshipped *before* he saw the answer. Now, that's faith! Televangelist Joyce Meyer wrote, "God has a plan for our deliverance before the problem ever appears. God is not surprised when the enemy attacks. He is not in heaven wringing His hands trying to figure out what to do. Our part is to focus on Him . . . , worshiping Him and praising Him for the manifestation of His solution."[3] That's what Jehoshaphat did, and God blessed him for it.

Obviously, you're not being confronted with an enemy army today. But perhaps the problem you're facing is, from your point of view, just as life-sized. Again, quoting Joyce Meyer, "God has a plan for [your] deliverance," and He had it before the problem ever raised its ugly head. Are you doing your part? Are you worshipping and praising God, as Jehoshaphat did? Are you thanking Him for the answer *before* it manifests? If not, let me encourage you today. Do it. Praise God in the heat of your trial. Worship Him in the face of perplexity. God honored Jehoshaphat for it. He'll honor you too.

PRINCIPLES OF WORSHIP FROM JEHOSHAPHAT

Now, what purpose does *this* story serve in a book on worship? Is there really anything in this narrative that relates to worship here and now?

Sure there is. The same worship principles that applied to Jehoshaphat still apply today. What are they?

When Jehoshaphat's too-numerous enemies marched on Judah, intent upon wiping them out, did the king scramble about, frantically mustering an inadequate army to wage inadequate warfare? No. *He took it to the Lord.* Then he sent his singers—his *worshippers*—into battle first. And Judah didn't have to lift a finger. God Himself was the Conqueror. The victory was won through *worship*.

When our enemy, the devil, comes to wipe *us* out, sure, we can take matters into our own hands. But our warfare will be inadequate. Still, we try. With hands a-wringing, we try with all our might to figure it out, when what we ought to do is recall Jehoshaphat's "melodious" military maneuver. We should, like his "army" of singers, send up a song of praise to our Conqueror, worship God in the face of fear, and let *Him* fight the battle. It worked for Jehoshaphat. Then, centuries later, it also worked for Paul and Silas, in a cold, dark prison. And it'll work for *you*.

Put down your earthly sword, Christian, and worship your way to victory. And when it comes, don't forget to praise the Lord. Remember, when Jehoshaphat's enemies were beaten, dead at his feet, he held a whole-hearted "praise-athon." You do it too.

Too Much, Too Little, Too Late

Though Jehoshaphat learned from his desert experience, poor old Ahab never did get it right. After all he had seen and heard, he persisted in his folly. Though Ahab had witnessed firsthand the triumph of the God of Israel, Ahab still opted for pseudogods. As a result, he came to a bitter end: he died with an arrow in his heart. Equally bitter was the end of his priestess-queen. She got thrown out a window — and was eaten by dogs.

But worse than that, though fire had fallen from the heavens, and the people had seen it with their *own eyes* — had even hailed Yahweh as God — their puckered lips were soon pressed again to the face of an idol. So were their kings' and queens'. One monarch after another kissed the image of a lifeless god. Consequently, the people "lived as their evil kings had shown them" (2 Kings 17:8 NCV). "They built places to worship gods in all their cities . . . They put up stone pillars to gods and Asherah idols on every high hill and under every green tree. [They also] burned incense everywhere they worshiped, just as the nations who lived there before them" (vv. 9–11 NCV).

God was very patient with them. He "used every prophet and seer to warn [them] . . . But the people would not listen . . . [They] rejected all the commands of the LORD their God. They molded statues of two calves . . . They worshiped all the stars of the sky and served Baal. They made their sons and daughters pass through fire and tried to find out the future by magic and witchcraft . . . [and God] removed them from his presence" (vv. 13–18 NCV). Such was the fate of the Northern Kingdom. "Only the tribe of Judah was left" (v. 18b NCV).

But they didn't do much better. Jehoshaphat's reign was followed by three evil monarchs in a row. Oh, there were a couple of good rulers sprinkled throughout Judah's history — Josiah, for example. When the long-forgotten Book of the Teachings was found in the temple, its words broke this king's heart. Recognizing that the people were not living up to God's holy standards, Josiah immediately burned everything made for "Baal, Asherah, and all the stars of the sky" (23:4 NCV). He also burned "Asherah" and ground her to dust. He then demolished the place where people sacrificed their children to Molech, the Ammonites' god, and even burned items used for sun worship. So convicted was Josiah by the Word of God that he broke down all of the altars of foreign gods, "smashed them to pieces and threw their dust" into the valley (v. 12 NCV). Then he trashed the places where the people had worshipped Ashtoreth, goddess of the Sidonians; and Chemosh, god of Moab. He went on to remove *all* the temples for worship of gods other than Yahweh. Finally, he killed their priests — right on the altars where they sacrificed.

This good king tried with all his might to get his people to turn their hearts back to the Lord. He even commanded them to celebrate Passover again, in the eighteenth year of his reign. And the celebration was unlike any since the days of the judges. There was never another Passover like it during the rule of the kings. And even that was not enough for his worshipping heart. He continued his work of purging by destroying every fortune-teller and house god he could get his hands on. Josiah left no stone unturned.

But it was too little, too late. Though Josiah himself "obeyed the LORD with all his heart, soul, and strength" and followed "all the Teachings of Moses" (v. 25 NCV), his subjects did not. Like pigs wallowing in the mud, the people continued to flounder in their sins, kissing their inert idols, burning their babies as sacrifices, even worshipping the planets that God's own hands had made.

After Josiah's death, God gave Judah four more chances to get it right. Four different kings reigned before the end of the Southern Kingdom— but all four did wrong, as did their subjects. Israel was a failure, and now Judah was too.

And God was sick of it . . .

Worship in the Books of History, Part IV: A Nation Captive— Then Set Free

Yahweh, God of Israel, is not a plaything. But His people had been radically unfaithful for centuries now. And God knew just how to get their attention.

In 722 BC, Samaria, capital of the Northern Kingdom, fell to the Assyrians. Less than a century and a half later, in 586 BC, the Southern Kingdom fell too, when Nebuchadnezzar, king of Babylon, attacked Jerusalem, Judah's beloved capital city. First he barricaded the city walls, to stop trade, and the people began to starve. Then he broke into the city, capturing Judah's last king, Zedekiah, and slaughtering his sons, right before his eyes. Then Nebuchadnezzar gouged out the king's eyes, put him in chains, and took him prisoner to Babylon. Solomon's magnificent temple was burned to the ground by the beastly Babylonians, and thousands of Jewish people were slaughtered at the hands of these merciless infidels. Those who remained "were led away from their country as captives" (2 Kings 25:21 NCV) and were forced to be slaves under Nebuchadnezzar.

But God never took His eyes off of His people. They cried out to Him, and their cry was heard from heaven. Forty-seven years later, Babylon also fell—into the hands of the Medes and Persians. And it was under Cyrus, king of Persia, that God's people would be given another chance.

Cyrus: A King with a Calling

This is what Cyrus king of Persia says:

> The LORD, the God of heaven, has given me all the kingdoms of the earth, and he has appointed me to build a Temple for him at Jerusalem in Judah. Now may the LORD your God be with all of you who are his people. You are free to go to Jerusalem.

Did you hear that? The king himself had decreed that the Jews could go *home*! In 536 BC, a man named Zerubbabel led 42,360 souls back to Jerusalem (a second group followed in 455 BC), and he himself laid the foundation for a second temple. It was completed in 516 BC.

But the temple's construction was inferior compared to Solomon's glorious masterpiece. This new, substandard edifice only reminded the people how far they had fallen. Jerusalem itself was fallen still, its walls charred and in disrepair.

Now, in those days, a city's walls were of great importance. All strong Middle Eastern cities had them. They were massive, typically made of stone, and from the tops of them, soldiers could survey the landscape and determine, from great distances, who was approaching the city.

To enter the city, travelers would pass through great, guarded gates that served as gathering places for the city fathers. Here, relationships were built, business was transacted, and civic and religious matters were decided. In short, a city's walls and gates served as testimony of community health and well-being. Their condition could be either a matter of pride or of reproach. Jerusalem's walls were a pile of ash and rubble, and its inhabitants were vulnerable to attack. The city was not safe.

Then . . . along came two men, who, together, would bring safety—both physical and spiritual—back to God's people.

NEHEMIAH: REPAIRER OF THE (PHYSICAL) BREACH

Nehemiah was the royal cupbearer for King Artaxerxes I and lived at the palace of Shushan, in Persia. The year: 446 BC. And Nehemiah was not happy. He had just learned of Jerusalem's sorry state, both physical and spiritual, and he was devastated.

So the cupbearer began to pray, earnestly, from December till the next April. He prayed; he fasted; he sought the face of God. And then . . .

Four months later, God wrought a miracle in the heart of the Persian king. With his blessing, Nehemiah was allowed to lead a group back to his hometown to rebuild Jerusalem's once-mighty walls. The king even provided Nehemiah a large escort; letters to the *pashas* (leaders) of all the provinces he would pass through; and an order to Asaph, keeper of the royal forest, to afford any assistance that Nehemiah would require.

Upon his arrival in Jerusalem, Nehemiah began reconstruction on the city walls. The job wasn't easy. The cupbearer and his crew faced many obstacles: mockery, the anger of their enemies (Neh. 4:1–3, 6–9), discouragement (v. 10), threat of bodily harm (vv. 11–23), fear, and intimidation (6:1–8, 10–14). Nevertheless, in just fifty-two days, the walls were complete (6:15), and the enemies of God's people were stifled.

With his construction work complete, Nehemiah promptly chose priests and singers to begin to bring religious order back to Judah's fair city. Jerusalem's walls stood tall and proud. Judah's dignity was restored. Now it was time to restore their worship.

In recent years, I have been privileged to participate in several ministry endeavors in Romania. This beautiful country is filled with lush forests, quaint mountain homes, and gorgeous countryside farms. But it was once the home of a merciless Communist killing machine.

One evening, as I visited with numerous church leaders and worshippers in this small European nation, I was amazed at their stories of suffering during the decades-long rule of Communism. Christians were persecuted by the hundreds of thousands. There were tortures, imprisonments, house arrests, confiscation of property, deportations, and executions.

But in December 1989, as the news media reported protests, rioting, and killing, Christians joined together in prayer all across the country. Evangelicals from every denomination sought God's face, pleading for deliverance. First they prayed in houses, storefronts, and chapels. Then they moved to school buildings and large fellowship halls. Finally, they prayed in the streets, actually kneeling on the pavement—by the thousands—and asking God to redeem their country. As a result of those nationwide prayer meetings, the murderous, oppressive, ungodly regime of Nicolae Ceaușescu fell.

Liberation! People falsely imprisoned for their faith were set free. Public worship—Bible reading, hymn singing, and gospel preaching—was finally permitted. Revival spread throughout the land. Thousands received Jesus Christ as Savior. People once denied the right to hear the reading of Scripture, now clamored to hear the Word.

The story of the Romanian police state is much like the tale of God's people. The Jews were taken from their homes, just like many Romanians, and moved to unfamiliar lands. On top of that, this entire people group was forced to learn another language under pagan rule. But, unlike the people of Romania, Israel's exile resulted from its own wrongdoings. The entire Hebrew nation was at fault. Though they knew better, they gave themselves over to the worship of gods of carnal desire. And, true to God's warning, they were dispersed into enemy hands. *Seventy years*, separated from God and forbidden to worship. It would have never happened if Israel had stayed true to God.

But now, freedom. *At last.* More than forty-two thousand people were settled in their own towns, enjoying the liberty that God had given them. And with that liberty, God also restored to each callused Hebrew heart a hunger for Him. What, do you imagine, was their first request? "We want to hear the Word of God."

"All the people of Israel gathered together in the square by the Water Gate. They asked Ezra the teacher to bring out the Book of the Teachings of Moses, which the Lord had given to Israel" (Neh. 8:1 NCV).

Just think about it. Families were finally, *really* able to meet together and worship Yahweh, for the first time in seventy years. For the young, it was the first time *ever*. Now they were gathered, in one mind and for one purpose, to seek and to find God—and to worship Him. But who would repair the breach in their fellowship with God?

EZRA: REPAIRER OF THE (SPIRITUAL) BREACH

Public reading of the Law was required by God as an "every seventh year" practice. But during the Hebrews' long period of captivity, this tradition had been abandoned. Now the people begged for its return.

But Ezra the priest had retired into private life, devoting his time and energy to constructing a complete edition of the Scriptures. Yet when God's people demonstrated their intense desire to hear the Word of God again, Ezra obliged: "On the first day of the seventh month, Ezra the priest brought out the Teachings for the crowd" (Neh. 8:2 NCV). And the people's response provided us a lasting model for worship. Look at what happened:

1. *The People Listened Attentively*

"Ezra the priest brought out the Teachings . . . All who could listen and understand had gathered" (v. 2 NCV). And listen they did. As Ezra stood on a high wooden platform, facing the square in front of the Water Gate, he read aloud from daybreak until noon. According to my wristwatch, that's six hours of uninterrupted reading of God's Word. Yet the people listened with rapt attention.

Now, remember, this was no small gathering of ten or fifteen people. There were thousands in attendance. Men; women; wiggly little children, no doubt; and perhaps even a few howling babies, whose mothers would not be denied the chance to hear the Word. Imagine the din such a multitude would make, even at their quietest. The subtle movement of thousands of robes. The sounds of shuffling feet. And, too, the occasional bleating of a distant lamb. The barking of neighborhood dogs. The braying of donkeys. How could the people possibly hear God's Word?

Perhaps they practiced what has come to be known as the *cocktail party effect*. At a party, many people are talking at once. A band is playing. Glasses are clinking and chairs scraping. But in the midst of it all, somehow you can concentrate on the whispers of your friend. It was the same with the Hebrews. Amid all of the background noise, they were able to focus their listening attention on one speaker, Ezra. Why? They were ready to worship God again, but first, they needed to know Him. He would reveal Himself through His Word, they knew, so they wanted it read, and they wanted to *listen*. Listening is an integral part of worship. This is often forgotten by today's worshipping community.

We live in a busy, hurried world. "Noises" from all of life—work, family, relationships, ambitions—all compete for our concentration, and all at once. Satan wants to distract us by turning our attention to other things.

Even in the middle of our worship, we look around and see things we need to attend to. We remember calls we need to make, errands we should run, bills we'd better pay—and our worship is hasty. We go through the motions, often peppering our "worship" with requests from our "wants list." Meanwhile, we neglect any time for learning at the Lord's feet. We need to remember the cocktail party phenomenon, and block out all other influences so we can focus on hearing from God through His Word. It has the power to convict, instruct, comfort, and reinforce us, but only to the extent that we make it a part of our worship.

2. They Stood in Respect

"Ezra opened the book in full view of everyone, because he was above them. As he opened it, all the people stood up" (Neh. 8:5 NCV). Why'd they do that? Because they respected God's Word, and by showing their respect for His Word, they were also showing their respect for *Him*. God had performed a miracle for them: He had moved upon the king's heart and, once again, set them free. He performed another miracle by causing the city walls to be reared in fewer than eight weeks. The Hebrew people admired their miracle-working God. So when they stood—families, leaders, and servants, both old and young—they demonstrated their admiration for both God and the Word that would bring them into harmony with Him. This was worship from the heart—unrehearsed, *spontaneous*.

Sometimes our standing is planned, nothing more than one part of the order of events during worship. But at other times, we spontaneously rise as admiration for God swells within us. This is what the Hebrews did on this poignant day. Artlessly, they stood in worship. Then . . .

3. They Lifted Their Hands

"Ezra praised the LORD, the great God, and all the people held up their hands" (v. 6 NCV). When the priest saw that the people had risen to their feet in impulsive worship, he began to praise God. Then the people began to express their own praise—with uplifted hands. Ezra didn't tell them to. He didn't say, "OK, your turn." He simply proclaimed the greatness of God. The people, then, also aware of God's greatness, impulsively responded to Him by lifting their hands in surrender. They were ready at last to forfeit control of their lives to this "great God" (v. 6 NCV), so they raised their hands, pledging their lifelong fidelity and submission to Him.

Are your hands raised right now?

4. They Shouted, "AMEN!"

"[Then] all the people . . . said, 'Amen! Amen!'" (v. 6b NCV). As old Ezra shouted his enthusiastic praises to God, the people agreed with all that they were hearing. So they joined in the worship, participating with their preacher: "Amen!"

The practice of saying amen is seen in several places in the Bible. In Deuteronomy 27, the Israelites were commanded to say amen repeatedly during the catechism of the curses of the Law. The word *amen* was also used (1) to close several of the psalms; (2) by Jesus, in concluding the Lord's Prayer in Matthew 6:13; (3) in many of the doxologies found in the book of Romans; (4) at the conclusion of each epistle penned by the apostle Paul; and (5) at the very end of the Bible, in Revelation 22:21. What is the significance of this one-word interjection?

"So be it," or today, "*We agree.*" In the Hebrew tradition, it meant "God is our trustworthy King." During the 1970s, it may have been rendered "Right-on!" But any way you look at it, as Ezra passionately broadcast the preeminence of almighty Yahweh, God's people were making a concerted pronouncement, for all the nations to see and hear: "We *agree.*" And notice that it was a double *Amen.* That was like saying, "We really, *really* agree." The Hebrews would serve the Lord, and all of their enemies knew it. The people had publicly pledged allegiance to the one true God. No longer would they be loyal to evil spirits that would haunt and oppress them. Neither would they bend the knee to statues their *own hands* had made. On this day, during the Feast of Trumpets, as Ezra extolled Yahweh alone, the people agreed.

Right-on!

5. They Bowed Down in Worship

"Then they bowed down and worshiped the LORD with their faces to the ground" (v. 6b NCV). Not only did God's people stand together and shout amen together, but they also bowed low and worshipped—together.

Maybe it's time for us to reinstitute this practice: standing; lifting our hands; bowing; and shouting, "Amen"—together. This historic worship, led by Ezra, was rich, expressive, and maybe even more complete as the people praised God *together*.

6. The Priests Read the Scripture . . .

"[The] Levites . . . read from the Book of the Teachings of God and explained what it meant so the people understood what was being read" (vv. 7–8 NCV).

Perhaps this is the most difficult part of worship—reading and assimilating the Word of God. Why? It requires the most discipline. But the people were ready for discipline, so the priests brought them the Word. Most scholars believe that Ezra himself read the Word in Hebrew, and the Levites (priests) translated it sentence by sentence into Chaldean, expounding the religious and cultural significance so the people could comprehend it.

Imagine the difficulty in this exercise. The Israelites had been in Babylon for a long time, forced to learn its national language. Many could not speak their native tongue, Hebrew. So this read-and-translate process was a time-consuming pursuit. But the people were hungry for God. They were willing to pay the price to hear from Him.

Are you?

7. . . . And the People Wept

The Hebrew word for "wept" or "weep," *bakah*, occurs seventy-one times in the King James Version. Here it means literally the shedding of tears in humiliation—or joy. Either way, the emotion is always deep. As the people heard God's Word, they were deeply sorry for their shameful, disobedient, idolatrous history. Tears of sorrow often accompany honest confession of sin and repentance. Such was the case on this day in Israel's history. As the Word came forth, the people's hearts were enlightened, and they realized how much they had missed—how much their children had missed—by being separated from God. They wept—bitter tears of grief, but at the same time, tears of joy also. Why? After more than half a century of separation from God, they were back together as a nation with the freedom to seek—

and find—their God. And find Him they did as they confessed their sins, repented, and enjoyed the forgiveness of the God who had *never* stopped loving them. And in that moment, these postexilic Hebrews experienced the warmth and wonder of true, sincere biblical worship.

Some years ago, I took a group of college students on an extended ministry, leading worship, singing, and proclaiming the Word of God at churches, schools, and recital halls. One young lady had dedicated herself to memorizing entire books of the Bible and could quote them verbatim, so, during this spring tour, we designed the entire choir program around the reading of 1 Peter. The program was divided into five sections to correlate with the five chapters in the epistle.

On the first night of our tour, as one song concluded, my student began passionately quoting the fourth chapter of 1 Peter. That's when it happened: people all across that large congregation spontaneously began to weep. Without any provocation, people stood to their feet, raised their hands to heaven, and *wept*. In a moment's time, we witnessed the power of God's Word—spoken aloud. It moved people to tears. It moved the choir to tears; it moved *me* to tears.

For the next eleven nights, the same thing happened. As the choir finished a choral number, and the Word of God was uttered, its simple presentation brought weeping to the sanctuary. Every evening, people stood on impulse, in tears, and moved to the altar, where they knelt, confessed their sin, and, worshipped.

I can only imagine, after that personal experience, the depth of the Hebrews' encounter with God at the foot of Ezra's pulpit. They wept. And then . . . they were comforted.

"This is a holy day to the LORD your God," Ezra told them. "Don't . . . cry . . . Go and enjoy good food and sweet drinks [and] send some to people who have none, because today is a holy day to the Lord. Don't be sad" (Neh. 8:9–10 NCV). And Ezra calmed the people. "Shhh . . ." he whispered. "Be quiet. This day is holy" (v. 11, paraphrased).

I really love this next verse: "Then all the people went away to eat and drink, to send some of their food to others, and to celebrate with great joy. They finally understood what they had been taught" (v. 12 NCV). So *now* what did they do?

8. They Celebrated

When was the last time you "celebrated" God? This is often the most overlooked part of worship, but it wasn't overlooked on this day in history. These liberated folks celebrated with great *joy*. They were *glad* they had heard the Word. God had revealed Himself through it. They were *glad* to repent. It brought freedom; the chains of their long-enduring sin were broken. And they were *glad* to be forgiven. It brought restoration. Their fellowship with God was renewed. Now, *that's* cause for celebration!

Have you read God's Word today? Can you see His love for you in its pages?

Then celebrate!

Have you, like me, ever been bound by sin? Has the truth of God set you *free*?

Then celebrate!

Was your fellowship with God once broken? Has it now been restored? Do you feel shiny, new, and at peace with God?

Then celebrate! Celebrate love, liberty, renewal. Celebrate *God*!

And worship.

PRINCIPLES OF WORSHIP IN THIS CHAPTER

This concludes our study of worship in the Historical Books. Have you learned anything? Look back at chapters 8, 9, and 10. A lot of worship principles emerged as we examined some of the characters from the books of history. I hope they've taught you something about worship that pleases the heart of God.

But what about this chapter? What can you take from it that will help you as you seek to validly worship God? I hope you've learned that a knowledge of His Word is essential to your worship experience. Indeed, how can any of us worship Him whom we do not know? But when we do know Him, through His written revelation, it arouses our worship. Then, in turn, our warm worship arouses God's love for us. We feel it, so we love Him more, and He loves us back. To quote an old gospel song, His love just gets "richer, deeper, fuller, sweeter . . . as the days go by."[1]

It's so powerful when the Word of God is part of our worship time.

When postexilic Israel began their worship with the Word, it changed their lives. And as they worshipped at the feet of Ezra the priest, they unwittingly provided all future generations with a model for corporate worship that pleases God. They stood reverently before the Lord; they wept tears of joy *and* repentance; they knelt in deference; they raised their hands; they shouted; they celebrated—all because of the Word of the Lord. It convicted them. It cleansed them. It comforted them. And it will do all of this for *you*.

When you and I remember to bring our Bibles into our "Tent of Meeting," and we seek God's face through His written Word, what will He do? He'll reward our interest in Him. He'll rain down His presence, quenching our spiritual thirst. He'll shower us with love. He'll reveal *Himself*. Think about that. You'll feel Him, know Him, and *understand* Him. Then, like the people of Nehemiah's day, you'll celebrate Him. You may want to stand in His presence—or touch your face to the ground in awe. You may wish to whisper sweet "somethings" to Him—or shout boisterously, with uplifted hands. You may want to perform a dance for Him and Him alone. Or . . . you may just want to reach out and touch His face. But whatever your style, when He reveals Himself to you, you'll want to *worship* Him. And when you do, it'll be just like the stories in the books of history. Fire will come down from heaven. Oh, not literal fire, perhaps. Not the type that burns up both bull and altar. But there will be fire, and when it falls, it'll set *your* soul on fire. And . . .

It'll make you want to sing.

| 12 |

WORSHIP IN THE PSALMS

NOW, OPEN YOUR HYMNALS TO PAGE . . .

What? You think I'm kidding? But that's exactly what the book of Psalms is: a hymnal, filled to the brim with *songs*.

God's people have always been lovers of song. Throughout the Bible's pages, saints of God used music to express both their joy and their sorrow. We read anthems of gladness—and sadness; airs of adoration—and detestation; and arias of gratitude—and grievance. Ballads were sung to inspire prophets, enthrone kings, drink to the harvest, exorcise evil spirits, celebrate marriages, and lament deaths. And music accompanied incantations, feasts, labor, merrymaking, war, and worship.

The first mention of music in sacred history is in Genesis 4, where we meet a man named Jubal, "the father of all who play the harp and flute" (v. 21 NIV). Man has been playing these instruments ever since. Playing and *singing*.

Singing has long been a part of the worship of God. Even the stars, says Job 38:1, once sang. The word *sing* itself is used more than 120 times in God's Word, some 60 mentions of singing in the Old Testament alone. In Exodus 15, the Israelites sang what is known today as the Song of Moses, a carol of praise to God for delivering them from Egyptian slavery. Another well-known Old Testament song is in Judges 5, the Song of Deborah. And remember King Jehoshaphat? His armies went to war, led by a male vocal ensemble. Singing was, and is, an integral part of worship. But *when* did it become such an essential element of our praise and veneration of God? And who so deeply embedded the use of music into man's worship?

Before we delve into the subject of this chapter, the book of Psalms, let's look into its history . . .

DAVID THE SONGWRITER

King David is credited with structuring music for use in temple worship. You remember David. He was the rosy-cheeked son of Jesse who spent his boyhood on the hillsides, tending his father's sheep. A skilled harpist and songster, David soon found himself in the royal palace, commissioned to play his harp to soothe the spirits of a neurotic king—whom he would one day replace. We read about him in an earlier chapter.

Singing with the Ark

David did finally become king of Israel. But before the crown had even settled on his brow, David had a sudden awful recollection: the Ark of God—that is, God's very throne on earth—was not in Jerusalem! It was in a town called Kiriath Jearim. Now, remember, the Ark represented God's presence among His people. Without it . . . ooh! David didn't even want to think about it. What he did want was to bring the Ark back—posthaste. So the new king gathered his subjects to retrieve their sacred treasure.

As the Israelites carried the Ark toward the seat of the kingdom, they were filled with joy, and they celebrated—with music. "With all their strength," the Bible says, "they were singing and playing lyres, harps, tambourines, cymbals, and trumpets" (1 Chron. 13:8 NCV).

We know from history that the Ark didn't make it back to Jerusalem this time. One of David's men made a critical error: he touched the Ark—and died. David was afraid to continue the Ark's transfer to Jerusalem, so he left it in the home of a man named Obed-Edom.

But with the passage of time, King David's desire for the presence of the Ark of God returned. By this time he had his palace, wives, and houses all over Jerusalem. He had also prepared a special place for the Ark. Now if he could just arrange transportation . . .

This time, to avoid any needless deaths, David set some ground rules for the Ark's transport. It would be carried on special poles—no risk of touching it with human hands. Furthermore, the only men allowed to bear the Ark would be *Levites*.

Singing at the Tent of God

The Levites were priests chosen by God Himself to serve Him for eternity. All Levites were skilled musicians charged with the unique responsibility of conducting and overseeing Israel's worship. These musician-priests were also prophets and often used harps and percussion as they proclaimed God's Word. But on this historic day, their assignment would be to convey the ark of the covenant to the tent David had set up for it.

First, though, King David instructed the Levite leaders to "appoint their brothers as singers to play their lyres, harps, and cymbals and to sing happy songs" as the Ark entered the capital city (1 Chron. 15:16 NCV). A man named Kenaniah (or, Chenaniah) was chosen to be "in charge of the singing, because he was very good at it" (v. 22 NCV). Then the Levites selected three more men to serenade the Ark's arrival: Heman, Asaph, and Ethan. (These names are important; you'll see them again.) Not only would this trio sing, but they would also keep the rhythm on cymbals of bronze (v. 19), accompanied by a string section (vv. 20–21). Another cluster of priests would lead the procession, with trumpets (v. 25).

So joyful were they, at the Ark's homecoming, that the Levites offered sacrifices of bulls and sheep, while the people worshipped God: shouting, blowing horns, and playing cymbals and stringed instruments. Soon the Ark of God was nestled safely in its pavilion. Then David began to organize the *permanent* worship of God through music.

His first step was appointing a team of priests to serve as professional musicians before the Ark of God. Their job? To lead worship, give thanks, and praise the Lord (1 Chron. 16:4). Asaph was installed as Israel's official choir director; his relatives, as the Levitical choir. These choral members "were chosen by name to sing praises to the LORD" (v. 41 NCV).

From that moment on, the prophet/priest/musicians would serve daily before the Ark. Each morning and evening, as offerings burned at the altar, the choir would descant to the sounds of trumps, chimes, and gongs. And music would be forever tied to the worship of the Almighty.

Singing in the Temple

Decades later, as we have already read, King David passed his crown to Solomon. But first, David appointed four thousand Levites who would praise the Lord with song in the soon-to-be-built temple. As other priests cared for the holy place and offered sacrifices at the various feasts and New Moon festivals (1 Chron. 23:28), the choiring priests would belt out lyrics of praise, accompanied by musical instruments that the aged king had crafted himself (v. 5).

Once again, Asaph was at the center of Israel's worship. While he preached the Word, under order of King David, Heman (David's seer), Jeduthun (he preached too), and all of their sons complemented the discourse with instrumentation. That's a lot of instruments. Heman alone had fourteen boys, and all of them made "music for the Temple of the LORD with cymbals, lyres, and harps" (1 Chron. 25:6 NCV). Now, *that's* a praise band!

Can you imagine the beauty of the temple worship? Every service a symphony. Not one musical component was missing. There was percussion (timbrels and cymbals); wind instruments (flutes, trumpets, and ram's horns); and strings (the harp, the lute, and the lyre). And not a single sour note, because all of David's musicians and their kin—288 in all!—"were trained and skilled in making music for the LORD" (v. 7 NCV). Better yet, they had voices of gold. How the Lord must have loved to hear them sing!

But what exactly, *did* they sing? Why, psalms, of course. And now, we will discuss the melodious book of Psalms, the official hymnal of the Hebrew nation.

THE WORSHIPFUL, TUNEFUL BOOK OF PSALMS

Psalms, or the Psalter, is an entire book of the Bible devoted to expressing truth through melody. Its title in the Jewish Bible is *Tehilim* ("praises" or "hymns"), though the word itself only occurs in the heading of one psalm (145). The *New Century Version* calls Psalms *The Songbook of Israel*. But just what kind of "songbook" is it?

The book of Psalms is a collection of poems—prayers, really—that were set to music. They were written in different time periods, by different people, to express different emotions and truths. Some of the psalms express faith in God; others mirror distress. The first psalm compares two different lifestyles:

one good and one bad. The last psalm is a canticle of exuberant praise. But every psalm is a stand-alone musical composition, accompanied by instruments often named in the heading: strings for Psalm 4; flutes for Psalm 5; a *gittith* (zither) for Psalm 8, and so on. As a whole, the book of Psalms affords the sincere worshipper a comprehensive model for the expression of his love and praise to God.

The Psalms are divided into five sections, also referred to as "books." Combined, these books contain 150 separate musical pieces:

Organization of the Psalms
Book 1 — Psalms 1–41
Book 2 — Psalms 42–72
Book 3 — Psalms 73–89
Book 4 — Psalms 90–106
Book 5 — Psalms 107–150

In these five books are verses of:

- praise

- history

- lament

- wisdom

- penitence

- imprecation (cursing of enemies)

- ascent (as the people went up to worship)

- prophecy (including Messianic)

- thanksgiving

- prayer

and so much more. But who penned all of these verses? And whose voices trilled the melodies in the five books collectively titled Psalms?

COMPOSERS OF THE PSALMS

God uses people to do His work. He breathes upon strategic individuals His own breath, heart, and personality, and they respond by fulfilling His desires. When God wanted to teach the world how to worship Him, simultaneously expressing His own love of music and song, He chose poets, choralists, lyricists—*artistes*. And they created masterpieces. Their hymns are the bases of many worship tunes sung today, in our century, on both sides of the globe. Let's examine these talented virtuosos, the works of art they produced, and what those musical creations teach us about worship.

David, the "Sweet Psalmist of Israel" (2 Sam. 23:1 NKJV)

The book of Psalms is often called "The Psalms of David," because David is by far the most prolific of the artists contributing to its collected works. Of the 150 psalms, David authored almost half of them. He is also the only psalmist named in the New Testament.

Some of David's psalms were written in the Judean hills, in the company of Jesse's flocks. David's long hours of solitude and repose allowed for a depth of worship that shaped his character, molding him into a man after God's own heart, a fact confirmed by his many explosive songs of love for the Lord.

But other passionate strains were penned as David fled for his life from a jealous and homicidal king, or a band of enemies, or his own bloodthirsty son. These sorrowful strains exude terror, anguish, and the pain of betrayal. Still more of David's poems were composed during moments of celebration, ease, or security. But whatever the contents, all were filled with emotion. In fact, David seemed to write about every human response. He left no stone unturned, articulating both angst and appreciation; grief and gratefulness; anger toward men and adoration for God; fear and faith. He unabashedly displayed his feelings about his foes (Ps. 5), his sinfulness (Ps. 51), his love of nature (Ps. 8), his zeal for God's house (Ps. 27), his respect for God's judgments (Ps. 9), and *especially*, his love for the Lord. And David's systematic practice of singing love songs to God gave us an example to follow. He palpably testified of God's sovereignty (Ps. 99), blessing and forgiveness (Ps. 65), healing (Ps. 3), and love (Ps. 23). He schools us in the fear of God (Ps. 34). Above all, David teaches us how to worship.

Oh, taste and see that the LORD is good. (Ps. 34:8 NKJV)

Well, what are you waiting for? Let's take a little taste. It'll make you want to worship, just as David did!

Praise the LORD, you angels;
    praise the LORD's glory and power.
Praise the LORD for the glory of his name;
    worship the LORD because he is holy.

The LORD's voice is heard over the sea.
    The glorious God thunders;
    the LORD thunders over the ocean.
The LORD's voice is powerful;
    the LORD's voice is majestic.
The LORD's voice breaks the trees. . . .
    The LORD's voice makes the lightning flash.
The LORD's voice shakes the desert . . .
The LORD's voice shakes the oaks
    and strips the leaves off the trees.
In his Temple everyone says, "Glory to God!"

The LORD controls the flood.
    The LORD will be King forever.
The LORD gives strength to his people;
    the LORD blesses his people with peace.
(Ps. 29 NCV)

What a spectacular, soulful number this is! Could anyone equal David's poetic passion? Maybe. Let's look at . . .

The Sons of Korah

Most of us have seen how sin and its consequences are often passed from one generation to another. Sometimes an alcoholic father will have an alcoholic son, and an alcoholic grandson after that. Or a grandmother will watch both daughter and daughter's daughter struggle with the same lifelong habit that she herself has fought. This could have been the fate of the Sons of Korah.

But God had other plans.

The Sons of Korah were descendants of the Old Testament priest whose name they bore. Korah himself is remembered most, not for his excellence in priesthood, but for his rebellion against Moses' authority. He died because of it (see Numbers 16).

But the descendants of Korah, and in particular the musicians known as the Sons of Korah, were ashamed of their forefather's misconduct. In reaction, they became meek and obedient to God. Rather than evidencing an arrogant leadership style, they gave themselves to humility, serving without fanfare as temple musicians and priests. The Sons of Korah wrote 12 of the 150 psalms but sought no *individual* credit. Not one attached his own name to any of these psalms. These musical expressions speak of intimacy with God, ardent longing to experience Him, and hunger for relationship with Him:

> *To the Chief Musician.*
> A *Contemplation of the sons of Korah.*
>
> As the deer pants for the water brooks,
> So pants my soul for You, O God.
> My soul thirsts for God, for the living God.
> When shall I come and appear before God? . . .
> Why are you cast down, O my soul? . . .
> Hope in God, for I shall yet praise Him
> For the help of His countenance.
> (Ps. 42:1–2, 5 NKJV)

And then there are the songs of Asaph.

Asaph

There's that name again. Vocalist, percussionist, and seer, Asaph, as you recall, was one of the three men commanded to "sing happy songs" for King David as the Ark of God was being conducted into Jerusalem (1 Chron. 15:16). Did you ever wonder where Asaph came up with those happy songs? He wrote them himself! (Or at least some of them.) Asaph was the author of eleven psalms. One of his best, Psalm 50, teaches all who would heed it the right way to worship God, from the Lord's *own* perspective. Psalms 73 through 83 celebrate God's goodness, forgiveness, mighty deeds, and righteous judgment.

Here's a sample:

> A *psalm of Asaph.*
>
> Surely God is good to Israel,
> to those who are pure in heart.
> But as for me, my feet had almost slipped;
> I had nearly lost my foothold . . .
> Yet I am always with you;
> you hold me by my right hand.
> You guide me with your counsel,
> and afterward you will take me into glory.
> Whom have I in heaven but you?
> And earth has nothing I desire besides you.
> My flesh and my heart may fail,
> but God is the strength of my heart
> and my portion forever.
> Those who are far from you will perish;
> You destroy all who are unfaithful to you.
> But as for me, it is good to be near God.
> I have made the Sovereign LORD my refuge;
> I will tell of all your deeds.
> (Ps. 73:1–2; 23–28 NIV)

Other Writers

Psalm 90 is a prayer attributed to Moses. Two psalms are credited to Solomon, son of David (72 and 127). And Heman and Ethan, the court musicians we saw earlier in this chapter, were the creators of Psalms 88 and 89, respectively. This last psalm has been the foundation for many a modern hymn and worship tune. See if you recognize verse 1:

> "I will sing of the LORD's great love forever; with my mouth I will make your faithfulness known through all generations." (NIV)

> "I will sing of the mercies of the LORD for ever: with my mouth will I make known thy faithfulness to all generations." (KJV)

But that was then—this is now. What do all of these ancient psalms mean for us today? What good, really, are the lyrical writings of David, Asaph, and others to *modern* society? Let me tell you a story . . .

On September 15, 2004, Hurricane Ivan swept through Pensacola, Florida, turning a calm Wednesday evening into one of the worst nights of terror in the city's history. For the next several days, families regrouped, while trying to make sense of the devastation. Thousands of people were without food, water, supplies, and power. In the pitch-black evenings, mothers and fathers, huddled around lanterns and makeshift power generators, comforted their frightened children.

Then came Sunday. The sun sparkled with hope as the clouds cleared and people began making their way to church. The little house of worship had seen bad weather before. Its congregation had assembled after many a storm. But this time, it was different. As two crude generators churned out just enough power to run the sound and light the front of the sanctuary, nearly two thousand people gathered. And they sang. And prayed.

Then one of the pastors spoke:

"'God is our refuge and strength, an ever-present help in trouble. Therefore we will not fear, though the earth give way and the mountains fall into the heart of the sea, though its waters roar and foam and the mountains quake with their surging.

"'There is a river whose streams make glad the city of God, the holy place where the Most High dwells. God is within her, she will not fall; God will help her at break of day. . . .

"'"Be still, and know that I am God; I will be exalted among the nations, I will be exalted in the earth.'"

"'The LORD Almighty is with us; the God of Jacob is our fortress. Selah.'" [from Psalm 46:1–5, 10–11 NIV]

When the preacher finished, a deafening silence filled the building, and in that moment, the Lord revealed His presence, breathing into our anxious hearts, *Peace . . . Be still.* Some wept. Others shouted hallelujah. But all were comforted by these precious words from the Psalms.

For centuries, men and women have uttered the psalms for comfort—at the bedside of a dying saint, or the graveside of a lifeless loved one. The psalms have also been read as devotions, both public and private; during celebrations and baby dedications; and even at the coronations and weddings of kings.

And . . . people have used them for *worship.*

But how can we use them today, you and I, in our own private times with God?

We can *pray* them. Often we don't quite know how to pray about a situation that arises. But if we turn to the blessed book of Psalms, it will show us how to dialogue with God. Don't know what to say to God in the midst of your suffering? Then choose a psalm that speaks to your anxiety or heartache, and ask the Lord to accept it as your own cry of help. Are you so blissful, so *effervescent* today, that words fail you? Do you feel foolish trying to express your great thankfulness? Then, again, use the psalms as a model, praying through a fitting passage as though its words of thanksgiving were composed by you. God loves those words. He inspired them in the first place. In reading the psalms aloud, you'll see His faithfulness in living color. Often, even the seemingly cheerless ones, those that open with sobs of complaint, end with praise and elation.

Do you have a complaint about life as you're living it? Do you wonder *where* God is, and *when* (or *if*) He's going to help you? David felt that way too. "Lord, why are you so far away?" he sobbed. "Why do you hide when there is trouble?" (Ps. 10:1 NCV). And look at this plaintive elegy:

> How long will you forget me, LORD? Forever?
>> How long will you hide from me?
> How long must I worry
>> and feel sad in my heart all day?
>> How long will my enemy win over me? . . .

> Answer me, my God . . . or I will die.
> (Ps. 13:1–3 NCV)

But, beloved, look how this same song ends:

> My heart is happy because you saved me.
> I sing to the LORD
> because he has taken care of me. (vv. 5b–6 NCV)

You see? When David faithfully worshipped God—in song—God turned his "mourning into dancing" (Ps. 30 NKJV). He'll do the same for you!

PRINCIPLES OF WORSHIP FROM THIS CHAPTER

This one's a no-brainer. I'm not even going to list principles from this chapter. You are going to discover them *for yourself*! How? By *practicing worship*.

On the next few pages you will see a full week of devotions from the book of Psalms, one for each day, to use in your personal worship time. Each exercise contains:

- an opening prayer
- a daily reading from the book of Psalms
- a short devotional
- a prayer of praise
- a prayer of intercession
- a personal application
- a "Thought for the Day"

Read the psalms and pray the prayers *out loud*. As you do, you will become more comfortable worshipping God.

Ready? Go!

Day 1—How to Live for God and Be Happy[1]

Opening Prayer: Dear Lord, thank You for this incredible day, a *new* day to live. And thank You for loving me. I love You too. I honor You. I exalt You. You alone are worthy of praise. I ask You to forgive me of any evil. Then open the eyes of my heart as I read Your Word today. In Jesus' name, amen.

Daily Reading: Psalm 1:1–3 (NKJV)

> Blessed is the man
> Who walks not in the counsel of the ungodly,
> Nor stands in the path of the sinners,
> Nor sits in the seat of the scornful;
> But His delight is in the law of the Lord,
> And in His law he meditates day and night.
> He shall be like a tree
> Planted by the rivers of water,
> That brings forth its fruit in its season
> Whose leaf also shall not wither
> And whatever he does shall prosper.

Devotional: One of the two Hebrew words for our word *blessed* is *ashrey*. It means "happiness." God is concerned with blessing His children, and He wants to bless you and me with happiness, with *ashrey*. But how can we receive *ashrey* from the Lord?

First, to be happy requires that we be *separated from the world* (v. 1). Happy folks are not influenced by the ungodly culture around them. They don't take the advice of the wicked or imitate their deeds. Why? Because they know that happiness comes by staying away from wrong and, instead, following after righteousness.

Second, happiness requires us to be *saturated with the* Word (v. 2). Today's psalm says the happy person's "delight" is in the law of the Lord. A happy soul enjoys spending time in God's presence, reading the Scriptures and seeking to know and understand God. Loving, reading, and thinking about His Word—day and night—becomes a pattern for living and a constant desire.

Third, happiness from God comes when we are *situated by the water* (v. 3), that is, always positioned in the presence of God. Every moment we live, we should be mindful of His gaze and desirous of His approval. Then, like fruitful trees, planted by the river's edge, our *lives* will bear fruit. Our work for God will prosper. He'll make us successful in our walk with Him, and we'll accomplish great things for His glory.

Prayer of Praise: Dear God, thank You for giving me the strength to shun ungodly counsel, the way of sinners, and the seat of the scornful. Thank You for giving me a thirst for You and Your Word. And thank You, most of all, for situating me by the water of life, where You will quench my thirst and shower me with *happiness*.

Prayer of Intercession: Today I pray for those who don't yet enjoy the happiness that only You can give. May they understand that You are seeking them. May they seek You too, find You, and follow after You forevermore.

Personal Application: I need to constantly, willfully sever myself from those who do wrong, separating myself from both their company and their influence. I must also meditate upon God's Word—day and night—until it becomes part of my life. Then God will become my strength and happiness.

Thought for the Day: God wants me to enjoy full, rich happiness.

Day 2—How to Worship God

Opening Prayer: Dear God, I come to You today with an open heart, hungry for Your presence and eager to know and worship You. Please teach me how. You are my One, my only, my awesome Lord of lords. Reveal Yourself to me today. In Jesus' name, amen.

Daily Reading: Psalm 51:10, 12, 15–17 (NCV)

> Create in me a pure heart, God,
>   and make my spirit right again . . .
> Give me back the joy of your salvation. . . .
> Lord, let me speak so I may praise you.
> You are not pleased by sacrifices, or I would give them.
>   You don't want burnt offerings.
> The sacrifice God wants is a broken spirit.
>   God, you will not reject a heart that is broken and sorry for sin.

Devotional: This psalm is a prayer for forgiveness. It was written by David after he had committed adultery and murder—and Nathan had called him on the carpet about it. David was humbled and ashamed. He was a broken man. But God uses broken people; He came to heal them (Luke 4:18).

Brokenness. Surrender. Obedience. These are the words we use when we talk about worship, and rightfully so. According to Psalm 51, a genuine worshipper must be broken. Brokenness is part of the process that each of us must go through if we want to be worshippers. How does this happen?

We must be broken of *self.* This means we must dispense with our *self-*centeredness. All of us deal with this issue. We want to do things "our way." *Please me! Just please me!* our selfish hearts insist. And we go on our merry ways, trusting in our own self-sufficiency—arrogance, really. But if we want to please God, we must abandon such arrogance and any sin we intractably cling to, and our hearts must be broken over our sin. Too, we must allow the Holy Spirit to break us, just as a trainer breaks an untamed horse and makes it fit for use. God wants to use us—me, *you.*

But that can only happen if we are willing to surrender. We *must* be surrendered. *Not my will, but Yours* must be our hearts' cry. If we will surrender our lives, our futures, our *wills* to God, then—and only then—we will be fit for the Master's use.

Prayer of Praise: O God, thank You! Thank you for Your wisdom, power, grace, and love. Thank You for breaking me, and for using broken people—like me—for kingdom service. I love You, and I worship You for loving me. Amen.

Prayer of Intercession: Dear Lord, please continue your work of breaking the untamed hearts of those who have not surrendered to You. Draw them into Your presence, Lord, and help them become totally surrendered to Your will—and broken. Then mend their broken hearts, O Lord, as only You can. Amen.

Personal Application: Brokenness allows us to see God for who He is in our lives: all we have and all we need. Once we are broken, we'll realize that He is also all we *want*.

Thought for the Day: *The sacrifice God wants is a broken spirit.*

DAY 3—HOW TO KNOW GOD

Opening Prayer: Dear heavenly Father, I worship You today. Thank You for your guidance, care, and love for me. Thank you for choosing to live in my heart and for allowing me the privilege of feeling your presence. I love to be in your presence, Lord. And I love *loving* You. Thank You for all that You are doing in my heart today. Amen.

Daily Reading: Psalm 119:9–16 (NIV)

How can a young man keep his way pure?
By living according to your word.

I seek you with all my heart;
do not let me stray from your commands.

I have hidden your word in my heart
that I might not sin against you.

Praise be to you, O LORD;
teach me your decrees.

With my lips I recount
all the laws that come from your mouth.

I rejoice in following your statutes
as one rejoices in great riches.

I meditate on your precepts
and consider your ways.

I delight in your decrees;
I will not neglect your word.

Devotional: There are seven steps that every true worshipper of God should follow.

First, *keep His Word.* Follow His road map—every day—and you won't get lost on the twisty turnpikes of life.

Second, *seek Him.* Seek God's face—and His heart. The Bible promises that if we seek Him, we will find Him. He *wants* you to find Him and to know Him in an intimate way. So seek Him diligently so you can know His heart, because as Charles Spurgeon said, "You can always trust His heart."

Third, *hide the Word* in your heart. Memorize it. Learn by heart all of God's promises, and stand on them. They are sure. Also commit to memory God's rules for living. They'll keep you from sinning.

Fourth, *proclaim His truth.* The truth of God will endure forever. Bless God by speaking His Word, professing His name, and proclaiming His wonders to a world that does not know His peace or forgiveness.

Fifth, *rejoice in His statutes.* Statutes, or decrees, are rulings, verdicts, judgments. God is righteous and just, always fair, always our defender. He loves to rule in your favor. Rejoice in that knowledge today.

Sixth, *meditate on His precepts and consider His ways.* Precepts are principles, guidelines, instructions. Ponder God's wisdom. Think about Him and His ways. He is good. He is holy. He is faithful. Now, that'll make you worship! And finally . . .

Seventh, *delight in His Word.* Find joy and satisfaction in reading, pondering, quoting, and *obeying* God's Word. It'll change the way you think.

Prayer of Praise: Thank You, dear, precious Father, for revealing Yourself to humanity—for giving us ears to hear, hearts to feel, and minds that can understand. And thank You for revealing Yourself—Your promises, Your commands, Your statutes, and Your precepts—to *me*! I worship You for that miracle.

Prayer of Intercession: Dear Lord, please continue to show Yourself and Your plan to the human race. And keep responding to those who seek after You. I specifically pray for my friends who doubt You. I ask you to open their eyes and show them how they can know You in a personal, dynamic way.

Personal Application: God is in the process of revealing Himself to me. He wants me to know Him in all His wisdom, power, and wonder. I do this by reading His Word. As I seek Him, He will make Himself known—to *me*!

Thought for the Day: Spending time in God's Word is *worship*.

Day 4—How to EXALT God

Opening Prayer: Dear, precious Lord, I celebrate Your majesty and wonder. I exalt You high above the heavens. And I place You first in my life today. You are so good. You are too wonderful to me. You are my reason for living. You are my song in the night, worthy of exaltation. Be blessed today. In Jesus' name, amen.

Daily Reading: Psalm 100 (NKJV)

> Make a joyful shout to the LORD, all you lands!
> Serve the LORD with gladness;
> Come before His presence with singing.
> Know that the LORD, He is God;
> It is He who has made us,
> And not we ourselves;
> We are His people, and the sheep of His pasture.
>
> Enter into His gates with thanksgiving,
> And into His courts with praise.
> Be thankful to Him,
> And bless His name.
> For the LORD is good;
> His mercy is everlasting,
> And His truth endures to all generations.

Devotional: Psalm 100 is a song of thanksgiving. It teaches us how to exalt God—in seven ways.

1. *By shouting triumphantly* to the Lord. God is our victorious King. When we cheer for Him for His mighty, triumphant acts, we exalt His name and personally bless Him for being God.
2. *By serving the Lord with gladness.* This involves both our actions—serving—and our attitude—gladness. Remember, "Whatever you do, work at it with all your heart, as working for

the Lord, not for men . . . It is the Lord Christ you are serving"
(Col. 3:23–24 NIV).

3. *By coming before Him with joyful songs.* God loves it when we
   sing to Him. He is honored and blessed with our love songs—that
   is, when they spring from pure hearts. These blissful, heartfelt
   songs make His praise *glorious*!

4. *By acknowledging that He is Lord.* Say it: "You are Lord of
   heaven and earth— always have been; always will be."

5. *By recognizing the things He has done.* He made us. He saved us.
   He redeemed us. He bought us. He loved us—and *loves* us, today.

6. *By entering His gates with thanksgiving.* "Whatever you do,
   whether in word or deed, do it all in the name of the Lord Jesus,
   giving thanks to God the Father" (Col. 3:17 NIV). Remember this
   every time you step foot in God's sanctuary—or in your own
   "secret place."

7. *By praising His name.* God has many names revealed in Scripture.
   Learn a few of them. Then praise your covenant God—by *name:*˙

Prayer of Praise: Beloved *Elohay Mishpat,* I praise You for being so just.
Precious *Elohay Selichot,* I thank You for forgiving all of my sins. *Elohay
Mikarov,* my heart sings because You are near. Loving *Elohay Mauzi,* I
brag on you to my friends, family, neighbors, and coworkers; You are my
Strength. I acknowledge today, and forevermore, that You are *Elohay Yishi,*
the God of my Salvation. You are alive, *Elohim Chaiyim,* and You alone
are *Elohay Elohim,* God of gods—and God of me. My heart and my lips
commend Your name today. Amen.[2]

˙ Elohay—God
  Elohay Mishpat—God of Justice (Isa. 30:18)
  Elohay Selichot—God of Forgiveness (Neh. 9:17)
  Elohay Mikarov—God Who Is Near (Jer. 23:23)
  Elohay Mauzi—God of My Strength (Ps. 43:2)
  Elohay Yishi—God of My Salvation (Ps. 18:47; 25:5)
  Elohay Chaiyim—Living God (Jer. 10:10)
  Elohay Elohim—God of Gods (Deut. 10:17)

Prayer of Intercession: Dear God, please persist in using the things of this earth—the sky, moon, sun, stars, hills, lakes, and valleys—to reveal Your wonder to man, especially those who do not yet know Your name. Then teach us all to praise You with our lips, our lives, our labor, and our love.

Personal Application: My whole life needs to be a model of praise to God. When I praise Him, He is exalted in my life, and when He is *exalted*, I am happy and whole.

Thought for the Day: *God wants us to exalt His name. He promises to protect all who trust in it (Ps. 91:14 NLT).*

Day 5—Trusting in God

Opening Prayer: Dear Lord, I come to You today with a heart full of love and appreciation for all You do for me. You are great, so mighty, so good to *me*. I sense Your presence in my life. I feel your sweet peace. *You love me!* And You are too wonderful for words. You supply my every need, because You are my Provider. Thank You so much. Amen and AMEN.

Daily Reading: Psalm 131:1-3 (NASB)

> O LORD, my heart is not proud, nor my eyes haughty;
> > Nor do I involve myself in great matters,
> > Or in things too difficult for me.
> Surely I have composed and quieted my soul;
> > Like a weaned child rests against his mother,
> > My soul is like a weaned child within me.
> O Israel, hope in the LORD
> > From this time forth and forever.

Devotional: This psalm teaches us how to deal with life when things are out of control. How *do* we deal with circumstances beyond our control? We learn to have childlike trust in the Lord. This is an issue of the heart. To trust God, we must come to him with an *honest* and *humble heart* (v. 1). God can't do much with the overconfident child, who thinks he already knows it all. We must come to God acknowledging that we *don't* have all the answers. Only then is He willing to come to our aid.

But we must also have a *hopeful heart* (v. 3). Our God is the God of hope (Rom. 15:13 HCSB, KJV, NASB, NIV, NKJV), and those who hope in Him *"will not be disappointed"* (Isa. 49:23 NIV).

Prayer of Praise: Thank You, Lord, for giving me joy and peace. And thank You for helping me trust in You. Every time I do, my hope overflows, just as You promised in Romans 15:13. I have no fear of the future, because I trust in You to meet all of my emotional, intellectual, physical, and spiritual needs. You have *never* let me down!

Prayer of Intercession: Heavenly Father, thousands of hurting people are living without hope today. They're sad, lonely, dejected—because they don't know *You*. They see life only through the lens of pessimism. But, God, You know each one by name. They are important to You. Please reach out to them and meet their needs. In Jesus' name, Amen.

Personal Application: I can trust God with all my heart—and with every part of my life: my relationships, my future, my finances, *all* my needs. I can count on Him to always do what's best for me. But meanwhile, I need to keep my heart *humble, honest,* and *hopeful.* If I do that, then my hope will OVERFLOW!!

Thought for the Day: *I demonstrate my greatest worship when I trust God with all my heart.*

Day 6—Remembering God's Goodness

Opening Prayer: Heavenly Father. We come to You at the beginning of another day. We want to thank You for allowing us to sense your presence and giving us a deep, inner peace. Thank You for renewing your mercies each morning. Lord, may Your voice speak to us as we remember Your goodness and seek to follow Your ways. Amen.

Daily Reading: Psalm 136:1–9, 25–26 (NKJV)

> Oh, give thanks to the LORD, for He is good!
>> For His mercy endures forever.
> Oh, give thanks to the God of gods!
>> For His mercy endures forever.
> Oh, give thanks to the Lord of lords!
>> For His mercy endures forever:
> To Him who alone does great wonders,
> To Him who by wisdom made the heavens,
> To Him who laid out the earth above the waters,
> To Him who made great lights,
> The sun to rule by day,
> The moon and stars to rule by night,
>> For His mercy endures forever . . .
> Who gives food to all flesh,
>> For His mercy endures forever.
> Oh, give thanks to the God of heaven!
>> For His mercy endures forever.

Devotional: *For His mercy endures . . .* The word *mercy* can be defined as "kindness," "forgiveness," "compassion" . . . or "love." This psalm is about the enduring *love* of God. Now, that's something to worship about!

. . . *forever.* Forever is a long time. Simply put, forever means "at all times" or "on every occasion," for all future time. God's mercy, or love, will be regular and constant—forever. That alone is more than I can fathom! But that's only the beginning . . .

He is good (v. 1). Compare our God with the petty, cruel, licentious gods of mythology, the ones who demanded child sacrifices, self-mutilation, and sexual sin *right* at their altars. Only *our* God is good—*always* good, for all eternity. Oh, and *His love endures forever.*

He is God of gods and Lord of lords (vv. 2–3), the only God known for passionately *loving* His people. *And His love endures forever . . .*

He does great wonders (v. 4). Parting seas. Stopping the sun. Healing lepers. Raising the dead. Feeding multitudes from one boy's lunch bucket. *And His love endures forever.*

He is the Creator of all (vv. 5–9): sun, moon, stars, sky . . . The big bang theory? Oh, sure. God spoke, and—*bang!*—Creation happened. And it is sustained because . . . *His love endures forever.*

He provides for us (v. 25). Not only does man eat from the hand of God, but all of creation feeds at His table. God supplies food for people, and for platypuses. He nourishes the lion—and the lemur. And He fills the belly of the anteater—and the *Actinophrys sol* (don't ask!). The God of heaven gives food—and life—to all, caring especially for those made in His image. Why? Because He *loves* us.

Oh yeah, and *His love endures forever!!*

Prayer of Praise: O God, our God, thank You for your constant, eternal, enduring, everlasting, never-ending, never-changing . . . (there are not enough adjectives!) love. You love me in so many ways. How can I thank You enough? I can't! But for the record, let me say it now. *I love You too.* And I worship You today—and forever. *For Your love endures forever.*

Prayer of Intercession: Eternally loving Father, teach Your people to love You well. And to those who don't, reveal Yourself—all that You are and do—so they will learn to love You too. Draw them to You. Help the unlovely know that You love them; those who've lost at love to know that Your love never ceases. And use Your people—use *me!*—to spread Your love from pole to pole. Amen.

Personal Application: *His love endures forever.* God proves it every day as He supplies all of my needs. And yours.

Make a list of twenty things for which you are thankful. Salvation. An affectionate spouse. A strong marriage. Healthy children. Job security. A lovely home. You get the idea. Do it now . . .

Do you have your list? Take a look at it. God created it all. "Without Him nothing was made that was made" (John 1:3 NKJV). He provided those things, for *you*. He'll *always* provide for you—because His love endures forever.

So, now, thank Him for each thing on your list, one by one. And conclude each "thanksgiving" with—you guessed it—*Your love endures forever.*

Thought for the Day: Seasons change; flowers die; colors fade; life ends. But the love of my God—for *me*—is FOREVER!

Day 7—How to Praise God

Opening Prayer: Dear God, I've come to worship You: as King; as Lord; as the Rock of ages and the Shepherd of my soul. I worship You as the Lion of the Tribe of Judah, and as the Lamb that was slain. You are my Sanctifier, my Peace, my Healer, my Provider, and my Righteousness. You alone deserve glory and honor, and I offer them to You today. Receive my praise, O God. It comes from a heart of worship. Amen.

Daily Reading: Psalm 150 (MSG)

> *Hallelujah!*
> Praise God in his holy house of worship,
>   praise him under the open skies;
> Praise him for his acts of power,
>   praise him for his magnificent greatness;
> Praise with a blast on the trumpet,
>   praise by strumming soft strings;
> Praise him with castanets and dance,
>   praise him with banjo and flute;
> Praise him with cymbals and a big bass drum,
>   praise him with fiddles and mandolin.
> Let every living, breathing creature praise God!
> *Hallelujah!*

Devotional: This is one of the "Hallelujah" psalms. The *hallel* in this word means "praise." The *jah* comes from the Hebrew *Yah*, the short form of Yahweh, the divine name of the God we worship. When we shout, "*Hallelujah!*" a word that is pronounced the same in every language, we are actually crying out, "Praise God!" This is an act we should never hesitate to do. And this psalm tells us . . .

Where: in His holy house. The NIV calls it the "sanctuary." The *New Century Version* says "in his Temple." Whichever rendering you prefer, this verse forever settles the question "Do I have to go to church to please

God?" Let me help you: *yes!* We are to attend church, and praise God there. We are also, though, to praise Him "under the open skies"—that is, anywhere and everywhere.

For what? for His "acts of power." Who but God can "[fill] the sky with clouds and [send] rain to the earth," "[make] grass grow on the hills" and "[give] food to cattle and to the little birds that call" (Ps. 147 NCV)?

But *how* shall we praise the Lord? With music! We *love* music, don't we? And why? Because *He* loves music. So we praise Him with brass, and with strings. We praise Him with woodwinds, and we praise Him with percussion. We dance; we sing. And He loves it all, from all who have breath. I'm breathing—how about you?

So stop and praise Him—right now. Here's a song to get you started:

> Praise the Lord, praise the Lord.
> Let the earth hear His voice
> Praise the Lord, praise the Lord.
> Let the people rejoice.
> O come to the Father through Jesus, the Son
> and give Him the glory,
> Great things He hath done!
> —Fanny Crosby

Prayer of Praise: Lord, I want to take time to praise you—right now—by name. You are:

> Jehovah-Jireh, my Provider;
> Jehovah-Rapha, my Healer;
> Jehovah-Nissi, the Lord my Banner (of victory);
> Jehovah-mekoddishkem, the Lord who sanctifies me;
> Jehovah-Shalom, my perfect peace;
> Jehovah-Sabaoth, the Lord of Hosts, who protects me night and day;
> Jehovah-Tsid-kenu*, the Lord my righteousness;

---

* pronounced *sid-qay-nu*

Jehovah-Shammah, the One who is *always* there; and
Adonai—my *Master*. Lord, I am Your willing bondservant, and I will
   serve You forever! *Hallelujah*.

Prayer of Intercession: Dear Lord, may Your name and fame be spread throughout the world so others may come to know You. And please use my feeble efforts to accomplish that. Help all who love you to publish your name and deeds, and so advance Your kingdom. Amen.

Personal Application: God wants my praise! He went to great lengths in Psalms to show me how. So I need to practice praise in all that I do. My deeds of kindness, my gestures of love, my gifts and offerings, and my labor are all praise—if I remember to do *all* to the glory to God.

Thought for the Day: Everything you do, have, say, and think can be a *hallel* to *Yah*.

Now that you've enjoyed a week in the psalms, I hope you will make them a part of your everyday worship. You don't have to use the psalms I have. Choose your own, a different set each week. Whichever psalms you use, they will teach you how to love, worship, and fear the Lord. And, friend, that's so important.

After all, the fear of the Lord *is* the beginning of wisdom . . .

Worship in the Books of Wisdom, Part I

The fear of the LORD is the beginning of knowledge.

—King Solomon (Prov. 1:7 NKJV)

In this chapter, we will begin looking at worship in the collection of books known as *Wisdom Literature*. This anthology of classics includes the books of Job, Psalms, Proverbs, Ecclesiastes, and Song of Solomon. We have already viewed worship in the Psalms. Now we will concentrate on two of the remaining works: Job and Proverbs. (We'll look at Ecclesiastes in the next chapter.) Both contain pearls of wisdom that we can apply to our worship of God. If you haven't read either of these books for a while, gently pull apart those stuck-together pages, and we'll begin . . .

In 1964, in Minneapolis, Minnesota, builders began construction of a 1,907-foot, eight-lane arch truss bridge that would carry Interstate 35W over the Mississippi River. Three years later, Bridge 9340 was completed and quickly became Minnesota's fifth-busiest bridge. More than 140,000 drivers per day trusted this overpass with their vehicles, cargo—and lives. They had no doubts about the quality, the soundness, the *integrity* of the steel structure that was faithfully maintained by their state Department of Transportation.

Ironically, in 2001, the civil engineering department of the University of Minnesota discovered and reported a deficiency with the cross girders at the end of the approach spans. In 2005, the bridge was studied again, and, again, it was rated as "structurally deficient." And in June 2006, the U.S. Department of Transportation noted cracking and fatigue in the structure. Simply put, the bridge's integrity was in serious question. In fact, it was compromised.

On Wednesday, August 1, 2007, at 6:05 p.m., the Mill City learned a harsh lesson about integrity. With rush-hour traffic moving slowly across the bridge, the central span of the structure suddenly gave way. The deck collapsed into the river, some parts falling more than eighty-one feet, killing thirteen people and injuring about a hundred more.[1] And all because the bridge had been lacking in integrity.

What is integrity? In the Hebrew, integrity (*tom*) refers to wholeness of mind, innocence, the absence of an evil purpose. Its use implies that its possessor is upright, perfect, and without ulterior motive. In the *New Century Version*, it is translated "honesty" (Ps. 25:21).

In English, integrity is the state of being sound or, when related to product development, undamaged. A *person* of integrity is one who consistently adheres to high moral principles or professional standards. One synonym for *integrity* is *incorruptibility*.

Everything I've just written perfectly describes one saint of God that we'll discuss in this chapter. His name is Job, and through him, we discover that integrity is a critical link between ourselves and our worship of God.

JOB'S STORY

The historical character we know as Job came from the town of Uz. He had seven sons and three daughters, and was a man of great wealth and influence. He was also a man whom God trusted. The Lord knew that Job would never betray his faith, because Job was a man of worship—and of integrity. God Himself said so . . .

One day when the angels came to report to God, Satan, who was the Designated Accuser, came along with them. God singled out Satan and said, "What have you been up to?"

Satan answered God, "Going here and there, checking things out on earth."

God said to Satan, "Have you noticed my friend Job? There's no one quite like him—honest and true to his word, totally devoted to God and hating evil."

(Job 1:6–8 MSG)

Sounds like a man of integrity to me. But Satan wasn't impressed.

"You pamper him like a pet," Old Slewfoot purred (v. 9 MSG), implying that the only reason Job honored God was because of His blessings. If all of Job's good fortune was taken away, Satan contended, he would curse the Lord.

En garde!

God accepted the challenge. "We'll see," He said. "Go ahead—do what you want with all that is his. Just don't hurt him" (v. 12 MSG).

Round 1

Job's story is known well. His children were killed when hurricane-force winds blew the roof in on them. Marauders rustled his cattle and murdered his servants; more came to make off with his camels. A lightning storm fried his sheep and his farmhands—and Job was left with nothing.

So he stomped and snorted and cussed and . . . No, that's not right. What *did* Job do?

"*He bowed down to the ground to worship God*" (v. 20 NCV). "'I was naked when I was born,'" he cried, "'and I will be naked when I die. The Lord gave these things to me, and he has taken them away. *Praise the name of the Lord.*' In all this Job did not sin or blame God" (1:21–22 NCV, emphasis added).

What an incredible testimony! He passed the test: not only did he *not* curse God, but he praised Him. Now, remember, this was long before God's written word was available to man. Job had never read the promises of God that are so comforting to us today. Yet he trusted in God, enough to praise Him in the face of immeasurable loss. That's because Job was a man of incorruptibility—of *integrity*.

Round 2

Satan is never satisfied. It wasn't enough to rob Job of all he possessed. He wanted more—namely, Job's life. Job hadn't bowed to the pressure and pain—and, thus, to Satan himself—by cursing God. Instead, he had bowed down and worshipped God. And that made the devil *mad*.

So, again, Satan came slinking into the presence of God.

"What are *you* doing here?" the Lord asked. "Oh, and, by the way, have you noticed that Job did *not fail*?" God then cheerfully reminded the Accuser that, in spite of his assault, Job still had "a firm grip on his integrity" (Job 2:3 MSG).

"A human would do anything to save his life," Satan wheezed. "But what do you think would happen if you reached down and took away his health? He'd curse you to your face, that's what" (vv. 4–5 MSG).

Satan wanted so badly to embarrass God by causing Job to stumble, fall—and then blame the Lord for the tumble. Worse, he was itching for the chance to destroy Job. Why? Because Job was a threat to Satan's kingdom.

So are you.

Job was a very influential man. In fact, the Bible makes it clear that he taught others (Job 4:3–4), so his testimony meant a great deal. Job's commitment to God was clear to all who knew him. And as he faithfully worshipped the Lord and received the benefits therefrom, it testified to onlookers of God's goodness to His worshippers. It also inspired those around Job to embrace and worship his God.

But if the devil could destroy him . . .

"OK, Mr. Know-It-All," God answered Satan. "Have at him. But you're wasting your time. Job will *not fold*, no matter how great the pressure. Do what you want. Just don't kill him."

Do you think for a moment that God was about to be blindsided? That He didn't know what Satan had up his sleeve? Of course not. God knew exactly what Satan would do. But He also knew Job. Job would not disappoint the Lord. He'd never exchange his worship for cursing of God's holy name. His personal integrity would not allow it.

There's that word again: *integrity*. What does integrity have to do with worship? Everything. Look at its definition in *Merriam-Webster's 11ᵗʰ Collegiate Dictionary*:

> Integrity: "firm adherence to a code of especially moral . . . values."

Firm adherence, when? Just when the road is smooth? No. A person of integrity is determined to do what's right, *no matter what*. Integrity, then, is a character quality. It can't be bought on the open market. It can't be earned; and it can't be taken from someone else. It is developed along with everything else that makes up one's character.

But how can you recognize a person of integrity? It has been said that character is revealed in hard times, during suffering—under *pressure*. Take Job: when he had lost all, the world saw what he was made of. Strength. Validity. Integrity. A man of integrity isn't wishy-washy; he's honest. His integrity reveals that he intends to love—and worship—the Lord, even when the going gets tough. Without integrity, he'll only worship when life is a cakewalk. Any lack of integrity on his part will eventually expose him as one whose preferred god is a "candy dispenser," not a Master; a divine Santa Claus, not the God of heaven. His worship will always be dependent upon his *circumstances*.

But Job's was not. And speaking of circumstances . . .

Job's Cataclysm

Sometimes, God uses circumstances as a platform for the growth, the maturity, the development of our worship. Remember Jehoshaphat? His worship was developed as the sound of enemy feet was heard marching toward his kingdom. Abraham's worship matured as the years slowly ticked by . . . and he remained childless. And Joshua's worship grew as he marched, day by day, toward seemingly impenetrable city walls—with an order from God to break through them. All of these *circumstances*, on the face of it, were insurmountable. An enemy army that eclipsed the "home team." A man way past his reproductive prime. And an impregnable, inde-structible barrier between the commander—with thousands of Israelites in his custody—and victory. These Bible characters were under pressure. And what about Job's pressures? Satan now had permission to unleash his worst. What sorrowful circumstances would Job face next?

Sickness. "Satan . . . put painful sores on Job's body, from the top of his head to the soles of his feet" (Job 2:7 NCV). Job was struck with raw, nasty, oozing boils. Also known as *carbuncles*, these germy eruptions began as tender, red bumps under Job's skin. They soon filled with pus, growing larger and spreading in clusters across his body, head to toe. Crawling with infection, Job then developed a fever, until, finally, the boils ruptured, leaving his flesh raw. Bacteria-filled fluid drained from every sore, making the disease ever ghastlier. His acquaintances feared that they'd get it next. Job was immediately exiled from the city.

Peer pressure. "Then his wife said to him, "Do you still hold fast to your integrity? Curse God and die!" (Job 2:9 NKJV). We don't know how long Job suffered with his skin disease, but we do know that "Mrs. Job" was tired of seeing her husband in such searing pain. She wanted him to be relieved of the torment that ravaged his body day and night. She was even willing to give him up to death, just to rid him of his pain.

Physical suffering has a way of affecting us all. Gentle, easygoing people, when tortured with bodily pain, often react in uncharacteristically harsh ways. Pain does that. It overpowers the emotions and brings despair, especially if the illness or injury is life-threatening. The caregivers, too, suffer despair, often equal to that of the afflicted. Job's wife was at her wit's end.

Condemnation. Who hasn't heard of "Job's comforters"? Eliphaz, Bildad, and Zophar: three "friends" who seek to give Job counsel.

Oh, they probably were real friends. They did, after all, devote seven full days and nights to staying by Job's side, "to show their concern and to comfort him." They even "[cried] loudly and tore their robes and put dirt on their heads to show how sad they were" when they first laid eyes on him (2:11–12 NCV). They were, undoubtedly, faithful friends.

But they were also misguided friends.

The disease ravaging Job's body was known as "black leprosy." Most people, including Eliphaz, believed it was the result of some hidden sin.

"I have had a vision!" Eliphaz pompously declared. Of course, his "vision" was relayed to Job along with an insinuation: *Your disease is the judgment of God.* "I have noticed that people who plow evil and plant trouble, harvest it," he hinted (Job 4:8 NCV). So certain was he of Job's guiltiness! And it got worse. Snide intimation morphed into direct attack. "Does God punish you for respecting him? . . . No! It is because your evil is without limits and your sins have no end. You took your brothers' things for a debt they didn't owe; you took clothes from people and left them naked. You did not give water to tired people, and you kept food from the hungry. You were a powerful man who owned land . . . But you sent widows away empty-handed, and you mistreated orphans. That is why traps are all around you and sudden danger frightens you. That is why it is so dark you cannot see and a flood of water covers you (22:4–11 NCV). *Jumpin' Jehoshaphat!*

People like Eliphaz abound today—especially in the church. Are you sick? Then you *must* have done something wrong. Suffering financially? Then surely you are *terrrrribly* wicked, and God's a-gettin' you! Beware of people like this. They can shipwreck your faith—even cause you to doubt your salvation. "You're *sinning!*" they'll opine, with wagging head and pointed finger. A man so accused, especially by Christian "brothers and sisters," will often run and hide. You won't see him in church. Why would he come, knowing everyone has already declared him guilty? He won't pray, because he feels undeserving. Then he gets mad—at God. *Why won't the Lord forgive me?* Eventually, he even blames God, and his worship is derailed. How can he dare worship God when he's so *unworthy?* He feels guiltier still for his God-directed anger—and becomes angrier still. And on it goes: guilt and condemnation, a vicious cycle . . .

But the condemnation didn't even come from God. It came from a friend, and not just one.

Two more of Job's overly critical companions—plus a whippersnapper named Elihu—put in their two cents' worth, all of it from the pits of hell. "Your children sinned against God," Bildad sniffed haughtily, "and he punished them for their sins" (8:4 NCV). "You are being punished like the wicked," Elihu added. "You are getting justice" (36:17 NCV). How self-righteous.

And not only were Job's friends self-righteous; they were also deceived. Eliphaz, for example, believed that righteousness assured one an easy road. "If I were you, I would call on God," he offered, "and bring my problem before him" (5:8 NCV). No better advice has ever been given. If only he'd stopped there. Instead, he went on to promise:

"In battle [God] will save you from the sword" (v. 20 NCV). Really? How many *godly* soldiers have died fighting in wars?

"You will be protected from the tongue that strikes like a whip" (v. 21 NCV). But how many of God's people have suffered the effects of slander? (Jesus Himself was the victim of other folks' forked tongues.)

"The wild animals will be at peace with you" (v. 23 NCV). (Even Christians get mosquito bites . . .)

"You will check the things you own and find nothing missing" (v. 24 NCV). But haven't Christian people been robbed? Haven't churches, even—houses of God—been broken into?

Can you see Eliphaz's error here? Worship the Lord *right* and all will be well. We in America are particularly prone to this type of thinking. We have more than the rest of the world—more money, more food, better health. We don't suffer the same diseases as people in poor nations. Our water is clean, and our plates are full. Our army is large, and our nation is blessed. *We're worshippers of God in this nation, you see, and are therefore exempt from evil*, the thinking goes.

And yet.

Christian people—honest-to-goodness worshippers of God—in Third World countries are being persecuted daily. Forced to be slaves to non-Christian "masters"—today. Forbidden to use community wells because of their love for Christ. Raped by religious extremists. Beaten bloody by former friends, family members, and police. These Christians' homes are burned, their churches destroyed, their property confiscated. They are denied good jobs and basic rights. One only needs to read one issue of

Voice of the Martyrs magazine to see that this is true, all over the world—and, yes, in the twenty-first century. And when such bad things happen to these good people—that is, these *saved* people—does that mean they aren't *really* saved? Eliphaz seemed to think so. Worse than that, he promised Job that if he'd get it right, "You will come to the grave with all your strength" (5:28 NCV). *Hmm* . . . When I think of all the people throughout history who were tortured and even martyred for their faith, not to mention those who are being tortured and martyred *today*, it puts a whole new light on the Eliphaz delusion. And speaking of delusions . . .

"Pray to [God]," Eliphaz went on, "and he will hear you . . . Anything you decide will be done" (22:21, 23, 27–28 NCV). There are entire movements in the church today that teach that one who is in right standing with God can have anything—absolutely *anything*—he says, no limits. Want a jet of your very own, so you won't have to suffer the inconvenience of airport delays? Well, just worship God, and then speak that jet into existence! Need a million-dollar wardrobe (despite the fact that millions of people in impoverished nations have *no* clothing)? You deserve it! Your worship is *just right* (not to mention awfully self-righteous). You've seen these people. They believe that if they just "do worship" or "do church" *right*, they'll have whatever they want. If they're sick, they can just "decide" to be well (v. 28 NCV), and it will be. If they're poor, they can elect to be rich. They have that *right*, they believe, because they are Christ-worshippers. Elihu even went so far as to say that if people will just obey and serve God, "the rest of their lives will be successful" (36:11 NCV).

But right relationship with God does not assure *anyone* a bed of roses; neither does it guarantee personal success. Read the tales of the early church. Study Paul and Silas. They were whipped and imprisoned. Examine 2 Corinthians 11:22–30. Paul was shipwrecked. (*Gasp!* Was he nursing a hidden sin?) He suffered cold, nakedness, and hunger. (Was he *saying* the wrong things?) He was stoned and left for dead. Had he done something wrong? No. So what was the problem?

The apostle Paul had an enemy. *You* have an enemy too,—Satan—and he wants to not only rob you of your friendship with God, but to rob God of your worship. He wanted the same in Job's case. Satan sought to render Job shamefaced about sins he had *not even committed*, and to so overwhelm him with shame that he couldn't even call on God. Have you ever heard a Christian say this: "Oh, I'm so troubled, I can't even pray" or "I'm so ashamed, I can't even face God!"? That's where the devil wanted Job to be: inundated, self-conscious, insecure, doubtful of God's love, and riddled with guilt. And he even tried to use Job's own friends as tools in his endeavor. Everything that was happening to Job was *his* fault, his buddies decided. His hard luck was from the hand of God—no mention of an enemy. They were seemingly ignorant of the devil's existence. God, they determined, was pouring out His judgment on their decadent friend.

But Job didn't fall for it. "Worthless doctors, all of you!" he spat. "I wish you would just stop talking" (13:4 NCV).

"I have never left the commands [God] has spoken," he went on, countering their numerous allegations (23:12 NCV). Later he added, "I've only worshipped God—never the sun or the moon. I have never desired a woman, other than my own wife. I have never denied clothing to the cold or naked. I have never hurt or withheld bread from *anyone*. And I don't flaunt my wealth" (from Job 31, paraphrased). Job had lived a life of integrity, avoiding the sins that fell so many. "The fear of God," he said, "has kept me from these things" (v. 23 MSG). Job had *respected* the Lord, all of his life. He was innocent of his friends' indictments.

Remember, the devil is the accuser of the brethren (Rev. 12:10). If he can get you to doubt yourself, wondering if your every dire circumstance is *your fault*, you'll lose the war for worship. You'll think God is mad at you—when He's not. You'll believe He's abandoned you—when He hasn't. You'll forget that, through Christ's blood, you have been declared "not guilty." *You're not fit to be called a Christian*, the accuser whispers. Believe it and your worship is arrested, all because of insinuations—and bald-faced lies. Be careful who you listen to.

Though Job could have heeded the whispers of his enemy, disguised as his friends—and even his own loving spouse—he didn't. Curse God? No way. He was a man of integrity! And he won the battle for his worship. How?

1. *Job worshipped God with his lips*. All through his anguish, he constantly affirmed the greatness of God. That's worship! Listen to some of Job's affirmations, right in the midst of his deepest distress:

God's wisdom is deep, and his power is great; no one can fight him without getting hurt. God moves mountains . . . and turns them over when he is angry. He shakes the earth out of its place and makes its foundations tremble. He commands the sun not to shine and shuts off the light of the stars. He alone stretches out the skies and walks on the waves of the sea. It is God who made the Bear, Orion, and the Pleiades and the groups of stars in the southern sky. He does wonders that cannot be understood; he does so many miracles they cannot be counted. (9:3–10 NCV)

Only God has wisdom and power, good advice and understanding. What he tears down cannot be rebuilt; anyone he puts in prison cannot be let out. If God holds back the waters, there is no rain; if he lets the waters go, they flood the land. He is strong and victorious. (12:13–16 NCV)

> God stretches the northern sky out over empty space
>   and hangs the earth on nothing.
> He wraps up the waters in his thick clouds,
>   but the clouds do not break under their weight.
> He covers the face of the moon,
>   spreading his clouds over it.
> He draws the horizon like a circle on the water . . .
> Heaven's foundations shake
>   when he thunders at them . . .
> He breathes, and the sky clears . . .
> And these are only a small part of God's works.
>   We only hear a small whisper of him.
>   Who could understand God's thundering power? (26:7–14 NCV)

This is worship, if I've ever seen it! And the more Job's faith was tested, the more he worshipped, articulating God's immensity. In so doing, he learned—from his own mouth—more of who God was, and is, and will be. And the more he learned, the more he offered praises, and the greater was his determination to do right. "As surely as God lives," he vowed, ". . . as long as I am alive . . . my lips will not speak evil, and my tongue will not tell a lie" (27:2–4 NCV).

Now, be it understood that Job didn't come out completely smelling like a rose. He was, after all, human. He wallowed in self-pity, and he cried the blues. (Wouldn't *you*?) "Why did You make me?" he sobbed to the heavens. "Oh, *why* did I have to be born?" And he cursed the day of his birth . . . but he didn't curse God. He worshipped Him.

2. *He never lost his faith.* Ill and indicted, banished and blistered, Job still refused to insult God through unbelief. "Though he slay me," Job said through gritted teeth, "yet will I trust Him" (Job 13:15 NKJV). Even if he died, Job was committed to hoping in God: "I know that my redeemer lives," he affirmed, "and in the resurrection I shall stand on the earth. After my body decays in the grave, in my flesh I'll see God. I'll stand before God and see Him with my eyes. This is my only hope" (19:25–27 NKJV).

We know what happened. After endless pages of discourse — charge and defense, complaint and counsel — God Himself interrupted, and every tongue ceased its chatter. No more advice from Job's friends. And no more pity party for Job. God was speaking — through a whirlwind. Everyone else just listened.

The Lord began to question Job. In fact, He posed *forty-nine* stiff questions, as in "a courtroom cross-examination where the defendant . . . withers under divine interrogation."[2] And all the while, He was teaching Job the difference between God and man. Sure, Job was innocent of his friends' judgments, but he was still a fallen and fallible *man*, lacking the sovereign dignity, mystery, and potency of the Creator.

How did Job respond? "I am not worthy," he stammered. "I cannot answer you anything, so I will put my hand over my mouth . . . I will not answer again . . . I will say nothing more" (Job 40:4–5 NCV). In a phrase, Job *surrendered.*

"Finally, Job went flat down on his face," wrote Henrietta Mears, "repenting in 'dust and ashes' (Job 42:6). This is the only place to learn God's lessons — on your face, with your mouth shut!"[3] And when God revealed Himself to Job, Job immediately practiced that for which he was made: worship. Was the Lord pleased? Let's see:

The LORD gave him success again. [He] gave Job twice as much as he had owned before . . . [and] blessed the last part of Job's life even more than the first part. Job had fourteen thousand sheep, six thousand camels, a thousand teams of oxen, and a thousand female donkeys. Job also had seven sons and three daughters . . . There were no other women in all the land as beautiful as Job's daughters . . .

After this, Job lived one hundred forty years. He lived to see his children, grandchildren, great-grandchildren, and great-great-grandchildren. (Job 42:10–18 NCV)

What a beautiful ending to a hard-to-read story. Job's faithful worship—in spite of everything the devil threw his way—recompensed him on a grand scale. There is a reward, friends, a compensation, for our unfailing worship.

But it may not be the reward we expect. God owes us nothing. We are the debtors. We *owe* Him our best worship, whether or not we ever receive the answers we expect from Him in this life. It is our duty to worship God, even in the absence of hoped-for benefits. But if we truly love Him, worship will never seem a duty. It will be a joy.

WORSHIP IN THE BOOK OF PROVERBS

Though the actual terms *worship* and *praise* never appear in the book of Proverbs, there is another word that closely relates to our worship. That word is "fear," *yir'ah*. References to the *fear of the Lord* abound in both Psalms and Proverbs. In fact, in the King James Version, the phrase occurs four hundred times! But what does it mean?

To *fear* God is to "to have a reverential awe of" Him.[4] This "awe," or fear, is not a slavish sort of dread, but the simple and appropriate *respect* a child feels for and demonstrates toward his or her parents. When we genuinely respect our parents, we esteem them highly, valuing them above any other earthly authority figure. When we truly respect God, that is, when we demonstrate the *fear of the Lord*, we hold Him "in the highest esteem, and [honor] and [value] Him as the God of the universe (the only God) and crowning [Him] as the Lord and reigning boss of [our] life, day by day."[5] We show Him *reverence*,[6] another synonym for *worship*.[7]

In Proverbs, the application of worship is to our *lifestyle*. How do we treat others? Are we honest with them? Generous? Fair? If not, then we can't possibly worship God pleasingly. Remember, worship is *respect*. How can we show due respect for God if we constantly disrespect those made in His image? In essence, the apostle John asked the same question: "He that loveth not his brother whom he hath seen, how can he love God whom he hath not seen?" (1 John 4:20 KJV). The book of Proverbs teaches us how to love—and respect—our "brother." Evangelist Billy Graham reads a chapter from it every day, to learn how, he said, to "get along with [his] fellow man."[8] Graham obviously understands the relation between our worship of God and our treatment of others.

So what does the book of Proverbs say about how we should treat others? It teaches us:

- to do good to them (3:27; 11:25);
- to be trustworthy neighbors (3:29);
- to lend without hesitation (3:27);
- to be faithful to our spouses (5:15, 18–20);
- to leave *other* folks' spouses alone (6:29, 32–35; 7);
- to not steal or embezzle from others (6:30–31; 10:2);
- to refuse to gossip (6:19; 10:14; 11:9, 13; 12:23);
- to tell the truth (10:32; 12:17, 19);
- to be honest in business (11:1, 3);[9]
- to avoid backbiting (11:12) and harsh words (12:18);
- to give generously (11:24–25); and *even*
- to be kind to our pets and livestock (12:10).

The book of Proverbs is filled with wisdom relating to our behavior toward others, and if we heed its wise counsel, we are not only respecting God's uttermost achievement—*humankind,* but honoring Him as well. That is, we are demonstrating the "fear of the Lord." Christ Himself said it best: "Anything you [do] for even the least-significant person . . . , you also [do] for me" (Matt. 25:40, paraphrased).

Do you want to worship God in a way that brings Him pleasure? Would you like for Him to know that you respect Him? honor him? *fear* Him? Then deal justly and considerately with those created in His image. Love your neighbor. Be kind to your mate. Be patient with your spouse. Give to the homeless. Feed the hungry. Clothe the poor. In so doing, you are obeying God's Word and thus revealing your fear, or respect, of the Lord. In a nutshell, you are *worshipping* God, in the most innocent of ways. And He won't neglect to reward you. The fear of the Lord, wrote the author of Proverbs, will bring health, long life, riches, honor, safety, peace, knowledge, and victory over sin:

- "Fear the LORD and depart from evil. It will be health to your flesh, and strength to your bones." (3:7–8 NKJV)
- "The fear of the LORD prolongs days." (10:27 NKJV)
- "The fear of the LORD is a fountain of life, to turn one away from the snares of death." (14:27 NKJV)
- "By . . . the fear of the LORD are riches and honor and life." (22:4 NKJV)
- "In the fear of the LORD there is strong confidence, and His children will have a place of refuge." (14:26 NKJV)
- "Those who respect [fear] the Lord will have security, and their children will be protected." (14:26 NCV)
- "The fear of the LORD is the beginning of knowledge." (1:7 NKJV)
- "By the fear of the LORD one departs from evil." (16:6 NKJV)

Are you beginning to get the picture?

PRINCIPLES OF WORSHIP FROM THIS CHAPTER

If you don't get anything else out of this book, get this: *Fear the Lord.* It is the beginning of knowledge. Do you want to *know* God, personally and intimately? Then begin with a respect for who He is. That's where worship begins. There can be no worship without respect, or reverence. Every biblical personality who walked closely with God, first feared Him.

But how? What actions convey our fear of the Lord?

Integrity. At all times and in all situations. We know what the Lord expects from us. Where He is concerned, God expects our unswerving loyalty, in good times and bad. We obey Him, even when it's tough. We serve Him, even when we'd rather serve our own interests. We trust Him, even when we can't see the light at the end of the tunnel. And we worship Him, even when our boat is turned upside down. We are not double minded and unstable (see James 1:5 NKJV); we are unbending and unflinching, like Job. Though he was suffering his own personal hell, and could have blasphemed and bellyached all the way through it, Job refused to. Why? Because he loved and *feared* God—and his integrity proved it. It's what God expects.

But what does He expect from us in relation to others? Again, integrity—toward our fellow man. What does that mean? It means we hold persistently to high morals and professional standards, the kind we see in the book of Proverbs. Our ethics are above reproach. We don't lie to our neighbors or "borrow" what is theirs. We don't cheat on our income taxes or take extra time on our lunch breaks. We don't beat the dog, kick the cat, and yell at our kids for looking at us wrong. I could go on, but we all know what integrity is. And if we cleave to it, we are showing the fear of God. Personal integrity is an act of worship, and we cannot *practically* worship God without it. Attempting to do so, without day-to-day integrity, is fraudulent. How do I figure? Well, if you would lie to me, you would lie to God. If I'd cheat you, someone made in God's image, then I'd just as easily cheat the Lord Himself. If we don't respect *each other*, then . . .

I've made my point. Integrity—at home, at work, at church, and on your knees—is essential for those who want to *worship* God. So . . . let's be people of integrity. It's just one small way to demonstrate our fear of the Lord. We'll never regret doing the right thing, because . . .

"Those who fear him will have everything they need." (Ps. 34:9 NCV)

| 14 |

WORSHIP IN THE BOOKS
OF WISDOM, PART II:
WORSHIP IN ECCLESIASTES

SIXTEENTH-CENTURY FRENCH REFORMER JOHN CALVIN ONCE described the human mind as a "factory" of idols,[1] wherein all of those things we so highly esteem become fashioned into objects of worship. And it's true. Our natural inclination is to worship anything and everything but God. We may start out well, but our *minds* become distracted. Other things gain our attention, and they scream for our devotion. If we're not careful, we begin to seek our fulfillment from them instead of from the Lord. Soon, we are bowing hungrily before these distractions, if only in spirit, and they steal our worship of God. They have become *idols*.

This is precisely what happened to Solomon.*

Oh, Solomon began well. When God offered the young king any gift he chose, Solomon had asked for just one thing: wisdom to rule his people well. Though he could have chosen riches, long life, or revenge against his enemies, Solomon asked *only* for wisdom (2 Chron. 1:7–10). That's because He wanted not only God's approval but His presence. Nothing was more important to the king. And God honored Solomon's request: He gave him wisdom—so much, in fact, that "he was wiser than anyone on

---

* Though Solomon's authorship of the book of Ecclesiastes has been challenged, both the early church and the church fathers accepted the view that the book was written by Solomon.[2]

earth" (1 Kings 4:31 NCV). "People from all nations came to listen to King Solomon's wisdom" (v. 34 NCV). And to this day, the wisdom of Solomon is celebrated and rehearsed the world over. We explored some of his wisdom in chapter 13, where we studied his famed book of Proverbs. In Proverbs, wise King Solomon taught us to control our tongues, to keep our hands in our own cookie jars, and, most important, to *fear the Lord*. Why? "LORD, God of Israel," Solomon once cried, "there is no god like you in heaven above or on earth below . . . The LORD is the only true God" (1 Kings 8:22, 60 NCV). Indeed He is. Yahweh is the *only* God, and the only one capable of satisfying the human heart.

Too bad Solomon forgot that . . .

SOLOMON'S IDOLS

Alas, like many of us, Solomon got sidetracked by other things, devices that vied for his affection and competed for his worship of God. *Idols.* No longer satisfied with God alone, Solomon began chasing after other alternatives. Ecclesiastes records this "chase." One diversion after another beckoned the once-wise king of Israel. And to each new amusement, Solomon bowed, if not in body, at least in his heart. Eventually, he even bowed his knee to other gods.

But these pursuits didn't fulfill him for long, none of them. Like rock musician Mick Jagger, Israel's king just couldn't "get no satisfaction."[3] Still, it didn't keep him from trying.

So, what *did* Solomon try? What did he really think could complete him apart from God? What could have possibly turned the eyes and heart of someone who had started so strong, away from the Lord?

The very same things that turn *our* eyes and hearts today, robbing God of our worship, and robbing us of our relationship with Him. Let's take a look:

Education (1:12–18; 3:1-15)

The first thing Solomon substituted for worship was "wisdom." Why did I place that in quotes, you ask? Well, remember, Solomon had asked for wisdom from God, and God had granted it. But Solomon allowed his wisdom to become a snare to him. He "decided to use [his] wisdom to learn about everything that happens on earth" (1:13 NCV). In other words, Solomon wanted to answer the age-old question, why am I here? So he began to study philosophy, and then medicine and science, law and religion—the "wisdom" of man. Eager to learn the truth about existence and causality, he sought *information*. And he got it, some true—but also some false. And it led him to wrong conclusions.

"I learned that God has given us terrible things to face," he lamented (v. 14 NCV). No wonder he went after other gods! Solomon had concluded that the world's evil is *God's fault*. Who wouldn't want another God! To make matters worse, Solomon was proud of his newfound "revelation": "I have become very wise and am now wiser than anyone who ruled Jerusalem before me. I know what wisdom and knowledge *really* are" (v. 16 NCV, emphasis added).

Sure, he did.

To no one's surprise, Solomon wasn't satisfied. So, in addition to studying human "wisdom," he also decided to "find out about . . . foolish thinking" (v. 17 NCV) (as if he hadn't already). Soon his head was full of all sorts of ideas—all wrong—and he became a depressed, disillusioned, dissatisfied individual.

How frequently this happens today. Young men and women, at countless universities both secular and Christian, dive into the philosophy of man and come out faithless. Science, they are taught, conflicts with Scripture. Atheism defies a supernatural God. Logic defies faith. These bright-eyed learners, ears now full of worldly "wisdom," become blinded to true wisdom—that which would lead them to their knees in worship of God. Finally, robbed of their worship, they are also deprived of God's presence in their lives, and they wind up like Solomon: hopelessly discontented. They need *something* to cheer them up. Just like Solomon.

Pleasure

I will try having fun, Solomon said to himself. *I will enjoy myself* (2:1 NCV). Solomon began to seek satisfaction in pleasure. He laughed; he drank; he partied—he *worshipped* . . . just not at the feet of God. But the laughter, the wine, even the music sung by choruses of singers—and accompanied by large bands and orchestras—failed to cheer him. He was worshipping at the wrong feet. So he worshipped something else for a while: himself.

Achievement

Solomon controlled the entire region west of the Euphrates, establishing Israelite colonies all around his province. As such he had a large share in the trade between countries north and south of him, and his own empire was so sizable that it was divided into twelve districts.[4] He was also famous for his architectural prowess. Everyone has heard of Solomon's magnificent temple, unequaled since its time. But he was also known for other building projects—most constructed using slave labor. For example, he built a city wall, a palace for the daughter of Pharaoh (one of his wives), cities just for storage, and a palace of his own. He planted acres and acres of orchards and vineyards, gardens filled with rare flowers and tropical plants, aqueducts, pools . . . and somehow found the time to write more than 3,000 proverbs and compose 1,005 songs (1 Kings 4:32). Solomon poured himself into work, into *human achievement*—why?—so that in the end he could say, "Look at all *I've* accomplished."

We do the same thing. We throw ourselves into careers, even ministries, with reckless abandon. And we work hard at them, doing great deeds and accomplishing great tasks—mostly to hear the accolades of men. But it fails to satisfy. Just ask Solomon.

"I was pleased with everything I did . . ." he began, "but then I looked at what I had done, and I thought about all the hard work." His deduction? "It was useless, like chasing the wind" (Eccl. 2:10–11 NCV).

You've heard the cliché: "Only one life; t'will soon be past. Only what's done for Christ will last." Solomon discovered that for himself, millennia before this phrase was ever coined. So he decided to bow at the feet of . . .

Wealth

Long before there was a "Material Girl," Solomon was the original "material guy." Still hungry for completion, he began to accumulate enormous wealth, as if he didn't have enough already! In 1 Kings we read that he owned twelve thousand horses that he kept in four thousand stalls, along with fourteen hundred chariots (4:26; 10:26). He also had myriads of slaves, as well as a palace that took thirteen years to complete (7:1).

Still not enough. So he built ships and sailed them to other lands. The vessels he sent to Ophir brought back thirty-two thousand pounds of gold (9:26, 28). Another fifty thousand was added to his coffers *every year* (10:14). Even his ivory throne was covered in gold. "Anything I saw and wanted, I got for myself," he said (Eccl. 2:10 NCV).

But in the end, after Solomon "had it all," listen to his assessment: "I hate everything I've . . . accumulated on this earth. I can't take it with me—no, I have to leave it to whoever comes after me. Whether they're worthy or worthless—and who's to tell?—they'll take over the earthly results of my . . . hard work (Eccl. 2:18–19 MSG).

Sexual Gratification

Solomon is famous for his love of women. In fact, *The Message* tells us he was "obsessed with" them (1 Kings 11:1: he had seven hundred wives and three hundred concubines. And these were not just any kind of women. "[I chose] the most voluptuous maidens for my bed," he bragged (Eccl. 2:8 MSG), "all the women a man could ever want" (v. 8 NCV).

Of course, many of Solomon's wives were chosen to strengthen political alliances and to build his personal wealth. Inter-kingdom marriage was common in those days. But the truth is, "Solomon [also] fell in love with these women" (1 Kings 11:2 NCV).

What's so bad about that? The love of many of these women was forbidden—by God. His instructions had been clear to Solomon: "You must not marry people of other nations. If you do, they will cause you to follow their gods" (1 Kings 11:2 NCV). But Solomon didn't listen. So filled with lust was he, for "the daughter of the king of Egypt, as well as women of the Moabites, Ammonites, Edomites, Sidonians, and Hittites" (v. 1 NCV), that he "gave in to every impulse" (Eccl. 2:9–10). These foreign women wound up in Solomon's bed. There they captured his heart—and stole his worship.

False Gods

Solomon's wives were his undoing. It was bad enough that he had married them in the first place, in disobedience to God—worse that he allowed them to continue worshipping their false gods. But most heinous of all, "Solomon [himself] openly defied GOD" (1 Kings 11:6 MSG) by allowing his "voluptuous maidens" to "seduce him away from God. As Solomon grew older," we read in *The Message*, "his wives beguiled him with their alien gods" (vv. 4–5). He worshipped Molech, whose child sacrifices were slowly burned to death in the open arms of his image[6]; Ashtoreth; Chemosh—a whole mishmash of deities that God hated. In time, Solomon's worship of idols led to the division of his kingdom.

His "Final Answer"

Fortunately, the story doesn't end here. After a lifetime of disappointment at the feet of idols both literal and figurative, Solomon came full circle. That's when he wrote Ecclesiastes, "the idol buster,"[7] a book that once and for all confirms the true worthlessness of *all* those things he held—and we hold—in such high esteem. After he had tried everything, and nothing filled his God-shaped hole, Solomon repented. "[My] last and final word," he wrote, "is this: Fear God. Do what he tells you. And that's it" (12:13–14 MSG). The New King James Version says, "This is man's all" (v. 13).

My translation? "It's the only thing that matters."

Principles of Worship in This Chapter

We've talked an awful lot about idolatry in the last several chapters. And it may seem irrelevant in today's world, to Christians in particular. But it's not. God's own people bow to idols every day. If you don't believe it, consider these scenarios:

I know I shouldn't drink, but I just can't stop . . . And the worshipper "bows" to Chemosh, in the form of a shot glass.

I know sex with him is wrong. We're not married. But I just can't say no. I LOVE *him.* Yep, she loves him—more than God.

It's Sunday, and I should really be in church. But it's such a nice day for fishing . . . Yes, grab your tackle. Baal is calling . . .

I need to break this engagement. She doesn't believe in God. And the

Bible says I shouldn't be unequally yoked, but . . . Ashtoreth is demanding veneration. She's just changed her name.

I shouldn't be on this Web site. It's filthy, vile . . . but just one *look won't hurt . . .*

Rationalizations. Just like the one that led Eve to take the first bite of forbidden fruit. *God said not to, but . . .* And she kneeled at the feet of Satan. Solomon rationalized too, no doubt. "But they're so *beautiful,*" he probably said of those with whom he shared forbidden love. "What harm can it possibly do? Besides, I've been serving God for *years.* Those gals won't sway *me.*" Famous last words . . .

Friends, Solomon was in a battle for his worship, and he lost. We're in the same battle today. And it's a battle we *don't* want to lose. This battle is spiritual. Satan, the ultimate deceiving spirit wants our worship, and he'll do anything to get it. "Oh, I'd *never* worship Satan!" we say. Yet, again, anytime we worship something other than God, we are committing the sin of idolatry and, in fact, *worshipping Satan,* the very spirit behind our idol worship. So it's important that we not get too self-righteous and think that idolatry was just a problem "back then." The spirit of idolatry still exists, in the pop-culture era, and I suspect you—yes, even *you*—are bombarded with temptations to bow, more often than you imagine.

Satan is subtle. He doesn't hang a big banner between two buildings that says, "Worship me." No, his "banner" looks more like a young, seductively dressed girl, or a guy with six-pack abs and a playful look. Sometimes the banner-in-disguise innocently stares at you from the top of a magazine rack, or silently beckons from your computer screen, a convenience-store cooler, or a department-store display. And it beckons one and all, from the vilest sinner to the most pious saint to the man in the pulpit or the singer at the microphone—the one leading worship. No one is above enticement, and anyone can fall. If you don't buy that, then chew on this:

- Conservative Protestant teens have their first sex at about the same time as their peers.[8]
- Around 40 percent of clergy have admitted to visiting sexually explicit Web sites.[9] As many as 30 percent of male Protestant

ministers, reported a 1997 *Newsweek* article, confessed to having had sex with women other than their wives.[10]

- Between 1950 and 2002, 4,392 Catholic priests/deacons were accused of sexually abusing a minor.[11]

Every one of these situations involves an idol. Can you guess its name? And in each case, it starts with a thought, a seed. The person begins to *think* about it, and that thought swirls about in that "factory of idols" that Calvin wrote about. Soon, an idol looms, larger than life, clamoring to be worshipped, recklessly, devotedly. Behind its beckoning voice is the whisper of none other than Satan himself, the great deceiver, weaving his illusory spell. The soul once captivated now finds it difficult to discern between right and wrong. Suddenly, the basest, most hideous sin *seems* tolerable, and that's where it begins. Solomon's wives introduced idol worship to him, and, though he didn't practice it immediately himself, he *tolerated* it in the lives of his women. It *seemed*, in his mind, to be safe enough. He'd just keep their idols at a distance. *He* wouldn't worship, but he'd allow them to continue worshipping.

Folly. Soon he was an image worshipper too. I wonder if he considered the penalty . . .

The Penalty for Idolatry

Idolatry has a penalty, and a *stiff* one, at that. What *is* God's fine against those who bend the knee to other gods? What can one expect who chooses idol worship over the worship of God?

1. *Separation from God.* Once a person chooses to worship anything other than God, he no longer enjoys the Lord's presence. Too many other things are on his mind—namely, his idols. He stops praying—he's no longer speaking to God. His Bible begins to collect dust—God's no longer speaking to him either. The relationship begins to break down, until, finally, God leaves that individual alone—with his idol. That's what happened to Solomon. As he worshipped in the groves of academia, at the altars of his wives' statues, and between satin sheets, the God of Ages was conspicuously absent from Solomon's life.

2. *A Curse from God.* Jilted by His onetime worshipper, God is not only hurt, but angry. Long ago, He warned His people what the fallout of His anger would be: "You will be cursed . . . Do not disobey the commands I am giving you today, and do not worship other gods" (Deut. 11:28 NCV). God doesn't *just* remove His blessings; he also sends a *curse*:

> You will be cursed when you go in and when you go out. The LORD will send you curses, confusion, and punishment in everything you do . . . The LORD will punish you with disease, fever, swelling, heat, lack of rain, plant diseases, and mildew until you die . . . The LORD will turn the rain into dust and sand . . . The LORD will help your enemies defeat you . . . The LORD will punish you with boils . . . You will have bad growths, sores, and itches that can't be cured. The LORD will give you madness, blindness, and a confused mind . . . You will fail in everything you do. People will hurt you and steal from you every day, and no one will save you . . .
>
> You will be mistreated and abused . . . The things you see will cause you to go mad. The LORD will give you sore boils on your knees and legs that cannot be cured, and they will go from the soles of your feet to the tops of your heads . . .
>
> You will plant much seed in your field, but your harvest will be small . . . All these curses will come upon you and stay.
> (Deut. 28:19–29, 33–35, 38, 15 NCV)

Sickness, drought, war, insanity—what a lineup. And that's only part of the list. God vows to curse those who worship at the feet of His enemy.

"That's so *mean!*" some might say. "What kind of a God does things like *that?*" The kind of God who's true to His word. His warning was clear, so His judgment is fair. God put His laws in black and white, for all to read. If they disobey, God is obligated to keep His word and administer the punishment—the curse—that He vowed to. And this curse is in force today. Age-old illnesses, unseen for more than a hundred years, have suddenly reappeared. Cholera, TB, diphtheria, and others, once nearly wiped out, are spreading globally, and in forms unaffected by antibiotics. In the U.S. alone, infectious diseases have risen by nearly 60 percent over the last two and a half decades.[12] In the last twenty years, HIV/AIDS has destroyed the immune systems of tens of thousands of people, claiming 22 million lives. And the plague continues, spread by the sexually promiscuous and drug addicted of the world. Idol worshippers. Now, don't misconstrue what I'm saying. Not all disease is the judgment of God. Good people get sick; and godly people die. But isn't it possible that the return of so many *epidemic* diseases today is the direct result of mankind's disobedience? It's not only possible; it's certain. God Himself said it: tumors and lesions that "can't be cured" (Deut. 28:27 NCV). Idolatry pays a price, and if America continues to kneel before their idols of promiscuity, alcoholism, drug abuse, pornography, and "keeping up with the Joneses"—among other things, the price will only get higher. Solomon's curse, in part, was the knowledge that his own son would fail at kinghood.

3. *The absence of God.* Many times, as the idolater sinks deeper and deeper beneath the weight of divine punishment, he or she will naturally cry out to God . . . but God will not be found; He won't hear; He won't answer (See Proverbs 1:28). Of course, when God sees that the idolater means business, He will hear that individual's plaintive cry, but until then . . .

4. *A sentence on the children.* "You shall not bow down to [idols] nor serve them. For I, the LORD your God, am a jealous God, visiting the iniquity of the fathers upon the children to the third and fourth generations of those who hate Me (Ex. 20:4–5 NKJV). *Hate?* That's a strong word. Just because one bows to an idol, does that mean he or she *hates* the Lord? God thinks so. Now, again, today we don't bow to statues, as King Solomon, and the Israelites before him, were prone to do. But we still bow to idols, from time to time. And when we do, the moment we catch ourselves in the act, then we, like Gideon, had better *cut them down*. If we don't, God says we "hate" Him. And he'll severely chastise, not only us, but "[our] children, and even [our] grandchildren and great-grandchildren" (v. 5 NCV). He punished Rehoboam, Solomon's son.

5. *Total destruction.* The very first time one embraces an idol, he or she begins a process of spiritual decline. Left unchecked, that individual will spiral ever downward until, finally, the hapless idol worshipper is destroyed. Deuteronomy 28:48 warns, "You will be hungry, thirsty, naked, and poor, and the LORD will put a load on you until he has destroyed you" (NCV). If

you need examples of this in our own day, look at the many rock stars who have died from drug overdoses. The ministers who slapped God in the face with their marital infidelity—and their ministries now lie in ruins. The once-wealthy celebrities who sit today in America's prisons because of idols they chose. And you and I can choose the same ones. But hear God's warning if we do: "You will be destroyed and suddenly ruined" (v. 20 NCV).

6. A *ruined name*. Even after the idolater is destroyed, to whatever extent—divorced, bankrupt, bedridden, or dead—the condemnation goes on. "The curses will be signs . . . to . . . your descendants forever" (v. 46 NCV). The one who engaged in long-term idolatry has totally blown it—and no one will forget it. Proof? The book of Proverbs stands forever as part of God's holy Word and a testament to Solomon's part-time wisdom. But the book of Ecclesiastes stands just as eternally as evidence of Solomon's spiritual plummet.

Oh, I can hear it now: "Whaley, you're making a big deal out of nothing. So I drink a little." Or, "So what if I'm in love with an unbeliever? I can get him saved *after* we get married." Or, "OK, so I have a little problem with lying. But God doesn't mind little *white* lies . . . does He?" I don't have to say any more. You can mentally fill in the blank with any derailing sin. And that's just it, the one word at the very heart of idolatry: *sin*.

Now, let's bring it home. I'm talking to you. (Yes, you!) Is what you're doing a *sin*? Would you do it in the physical presence of Christ Jesus? (He sees it anyway.) Would you hide your "idol" quickly behind your back if your pastor suddenly walked in the room? Does the thing you're entertaining keep you from doing what's right? Is the act itself *wrong*? But, then, do you continue it anyway?

Then it's an idol, and it makes God *mad*. First, it tells Him—and everyone who knows about it—that He is not enough. Solomon may as well have broadcasted it on the World Wide Web: *God's not "cutting it." I need more to satisfy me.* Are you sending the same signal to those around you? You're ruining your witness, friend. You're also ruining your life. And if you continue in idolatry, you'll pay a price.

The whole Jewish world paid for Solomon's idolatry. We read about it, in part, in chapter 10. Solomon's kingdom was split in two. God had said it would be:

GOD was furious with Solomon for abandoning the GOD of Israel, the God who had twice appeared to him and had so clearly commanded him not to fool around with other gods . . . GOD said to Solomon, "Since . . . you have no intention of keeping faith with me . . . , I'm going to rip the kingdom from you and hand it over to someone else. But . . . I won't do it in your lifetime. It's your son who will pay—I'll rip it right out of his grasp." (1 Kings 11:9–13 MSG)

That came to pass in 931 BC, and you'd think Rehoboam would learn from his father's gaffes. But he didn't. And neither did the kings who followed him. They worshipped those idols, as they say, "like there was no tomorrow."

But God never gave up. He offered his people chance after chance. If they wouldn't listen to Him, He'd let them hear His words of warning from someone else, a human voice. And God sent *prophets* to warn the Hebrew tribes that they'd better—once and for all—renounce their idols.

Or else.

| 15 |

WORSHIP
IN THE PROPHETIC BOOKS

THE PROPHETS, ALSO KNOWN AS "SEERS" IN THEIR DAY, WERE each considered to be the mouth of God on earth. They spoke *for* God, delivering messages directly *from* God to His people. Sixteen of the Old Testament's thirty-nine books were named for these prophets. Of these, four are considered to be the works of *major prophets*, those whose writings were greater in length. The remaining twelve books have been identified as the *minor prophets*, much shorter, but no less significant than the major prophets. Collectively, the prophets' writings make up more than one-third of God's written Word.

The ministry of the Old Testament prophets covered a span of about four hundred years, from 760 to approximately 400 BC. Their books can be divided chronologically into three groups:

1. *Pre-exilic*—those written before the Babylonian captivity; this includes the books of Jonah, Amos, Hosea, Isaiah, Micah, Nahum, Habakkuk, Zephaniah, and Jeremiah (c. 760–587 BC)

2. *Exilic*—the books of Daniel and Ezekiel (c. 605–560 BC), which were penned during the Babylonian captivity

3. *Post-exilic*–Haggai, Zechariah, Obadiah, Joel, and Malachi (c. 560–415 BC), written after God's people were allowed to return to their homeland

The prophets were God's men for their time—preachers, evangelists, worshippers, and revivalists, from all walks of life: Amos was a farmer. Zechariah was a priest's son. Hosea was the husband of a prostitute. But every prophet, whatever his background or vocation, was chosen by God to sound a trumpet, calling His people to repentance, and to warn them—at great personal cost—of things to come.

Though the prophets lived in different times and preached to different audiences—some to the Northern Kingdom of Israel; some to the Southern Kingdom of Judah—the problems they encountered among the people they were sent to lead were common—to both kingdoms and to all eras, including ours. And these problems affected the people's worship of God—and God's response to that worship.

So, what were these issues? What exactly did the prophets face? More important, what does it have to do with *contemporary* worship? Do the prophets' own responses to God teach us about worship in our postmodern world? What lessons can we learn from these men—collectively and individually? In this chapter, we will examine the prophetic books as a collection and their collective message regarding the worship of God.

SICK IN THE HEAD . . .

Well over half of the prophetic books deal with people's battle with idolatry. The problem was widespread. The book of Isaiah is filled with text condemning the worship of false gods. Jeremiah reviled it. Ezekiel did too. Daniel also rebuked it, as did Zephaniah. And in the book of Jeremiah, God told the ten tribes of Judah, "You have as many idols as there are towns . . . You have built as many altars . . . as there are streets in Jerusalem" (11:3 NCV). God's people were addicted to idol worship, and we have examined their addiction in this book, in depth. In chapter after chapter we have witnessed the people of God bowing to idols both literal—Baal, Chemosh, Asherah— and figurative—lusts, habits, aspirations . . . *Sigh*. We need say no more about idolatry here. It wasn't national Israel's only problem, anyway.

They were also plagued with *blindness*. Though God Himself had accused them of turning against Him (Isa. 1:2), the people were deluded. And their spiritual leaders weren't shedding any light. "The prophets and priests . . . tell lies," God told them. "They [say], 'It's all right, it's all right.' But really, it is not all right" (Jer. 6:13, 14b NCV). And if that weren't indictment enough, God said to Israel, "Your whole head is hurt, and your whole heart is sick" (Isa. 1:5 NCV).

Yet God's people didn't believe that they were very far from God. They actually thought they were OK. They bought into a myth—and it was the prophets' job to expose that myth and restore the people's worship of God.

Are we, perhaps, falling for the same lies today that caused the heart of God such anguish in the days of the prophets? Can the misguided worship of an ancient civilization have anything to say to worship in the post-industrial era?

Let's take a look:

"I hate, I despise your religious feasts; I cannot stand your assemblies. Even though you bring me burnt offerings and grain offerings, I will not accept them. Though you bring choice fellowship offerings, I will have no regard for them. Away with the noise of your songs! I will not listen to the music of your harps." (Amos 5:21–23 NIV)

"I do not want all these sacrifices. I have had enough . . . I am not pleased by the blood of bulls, lambs, and goats. You come to meet with me, but who asked you to do all this running in and out of my Temple's rooms? . . . I hate the incense you burn. I can't stand your New Moons, Sabbaths, and other feast days; I can't stand the evil you do in your holy meetings. I hate your . . . other yearly feasts. They have become a heavy weight on me, and I am tired of carrying it. When you raise your arms to me in prayer, I will refuse to look at you. Even if you say many prayers, I will not listen to you." (Isa. 1:11–15 NCV)

"I will put an end to all [of my people's] celebrations: her . . . festivals, and her Sabbaths. I will stop all of her special feasts." (Hos. 2:11 NCV)

"These people worship me with their mouths, and honor me with their lips, but their hearts are far from me. Their worship is based on nothing but human rules." (Isa. 29:13 NCV)

These were harsh words from the Almighty, directed at a people who were "going through the motions." Oh, their worship *looked* all right—the feasts, the offerings. And they were going mad with animal sacrifices and other ostentatious forms of worship—the key word here being *forms*. The people's form was well practiced. But God wasn't accepting any of it. He was, in fact, rejecting their worship. Why? Because it was *false* worship, and He had just one thing to say about it: DON'T BOTHER . . . *unless you repent!*

The three prophets I just quoted, Amos, Hosea, and Isaiah—among others—all preached against false, or as author Allen Ross calls it, *hypocritical worship.*[1] They were talking about worship filled with pageantry—yet empty of meaning. Even in the midst of all their pomp and circumstance, they were mistreating the poor, charging huge and unfair interest on money loaned, and practicing ethnic/racial prejudice. Judah and Israel were both guilty of it—guilty of living *immorally, blindly,* and *without fear.*

Living Immorally

The people were living decadently in the prophets' times. They were "loaded down with guilt" and "full of evil" (Isa. 1:4 NCV), God contended. "Cursing, lying, killing, stealing and adultery [were] everywhere," we are told in Hosea (4:2 NCV). A once-glorious nation now consisted of liars (Isa. 9:17), thieves (3:14), and drunks (28:7). What's worse, they weren't even ashamed of it. "They don't even know how to blush about their sins," the Lord lamented to Jeremiah (Jer. 6:15 NCV).

Maybe we need to step back at this point and evaluate our own lives a bit. We of the third millennium needn't think we are inoculated against these kinds of indulgences. And before we get all sanctimonious about "those stupid, idol-worshipping Israelites," remember that we are only aware of their depravity thanks to the *prophetic voices.* In their day, the people thought that they were A-OK. So do we, and had we lived back then, we would have been as blind as Israel was. They were reprobates, their lives overrun with sin. And, frighteningly, many of our own churches, synagogues, parishes, and Christian schools are in danger—today—of indictment for the same sins committed by the Hebrew nation and scorned by the prophets.

For months we listened as news reporters droned on about the sexual improprieties of Catholic priests with young, unsuspecting boys—right on church premises. It has been going on for years and years—and not just in Catholic churches, either. Within the last decade, Southern Baptist, United Methodist, Assembly of God, and Church of God ministers have been accused of child molestation and rape. (If you don't believe me, Google for yourself.)

We have also heard about well-known ministries misappropriating funds, operating under a cloud of questionable business and moral practices, and resisting disclosure when inquiry is made by the authorities and the media. This is in the news even now.

And what about the church youth group whose teenagers would rather play games on their cell phones during youth service than worship God and learn how to grow closer to Him? Or the worship leader who consistently pushes the envelope in his or her personal life or sexual conduct during the week—while presenting praise and worship songs on Sunday? Or the pew warmer who can unleash a string of profanities, without batting an eyelash?

Most alarming, unbelievers, like the nations around ancient Israel, look with disgust and distrust at those of us who call ourselves God's people, yet feed the flesh with an ungodly lifestyle. Our testimonies are consistently and daily eroded. David Kinnaman, in his book *Unchristian*, reveals the embarrassing truth about the newest generation of Christians:

> In virtually every study we conduct, representing thousands of interviews every year, born-again Christians fail to display much attitudinal or behavioral evidence of transformed lives. For instance, based on a study released in 2007 . . . most of the lifestyle activities of born-again Christians were statistically equivalent to those of non-born-agains. When asked to identify their activities over the last thirty days, born-again believers were just as likely to bet or gamble, to visit a pornographic website, to take something that did not belong to them, to consult with a medium or psychic, to physically fight or abuse someone, to have consumed enough alcohol to be considered legally drunk, to have used an illegal, nonprescription drug, to have said something to someone that was not true, to have gotten back at someone for something he or she did, and to have said mean things behind another person's back. No difference.[2]

But, there is more. Watch but a few moments of the many Hollywood news shows and you will quickly see how misguided some of our celebrities are about life and religion. Yet we, Christians included, celebrate them. The values espoused by the Old Testament prophets are quickly dismissed as passé, inconvenient, and inconsistent with our postmodern ideals. We have reared a generation that admires couples who "cohabitate," have illegitimate babies, flaunt their addictions, and "respect all religions equally." Some of our most esteemed heroes and entertainers seek fulfillment in all the wrong places. And, just like Israel of old, we blindly follow. It's *always* been this way. Why? Because we need intervention from a holy God. Left to our *own* devices, even we, God's people, *will* dumbly pursue decadence. That's what Israel did every time. From prophet to prophet they were, short and sweet, living immorally.

Living Blindly

God's people were also living blindly—that is, turning a sightless eye to the poverty and injustice around them. While hooked on their own careless ease and luxury (Amos 2), they were totally ignoring their social responsibilities. They refused to care for the poor. Their leaders weren't "seek[ing] justice for the orphans" or "listen[ing] to the widows' needs" (Isa. 1:23 NCV). But they *were* sacrificing, feasting, singing—and God was supposed to be impressed with it! See, for them, worship was something they did in the *house of worship*. But it wasn't trickling down into their everyday lives, to their *ethics*, to the way they treated people, conducted business, and responded to the less fortunate. Worship was just one big, pretentious charade filled with hollow rituals.

But authentic worship involves more than ritual. It also embraces protection of the needy and marginalized. Anything less is cold, arid "religion," empty of God's presence. In the words of author A. W. Tozer, "What good is all our busy religion if God isn't in it?"[3]

The prophet Amos told his generation that the Lord was grieved over His people's hypocritical veneration. "As they worship at their altars, they lie down on clothes taken from the poor," the Lord accused (2:8 NCV). Of course, the people didn't want to hear Amos's message. In fact, the prophet was ordered to stop preaching—and he wasn't the only one. "Don't see any more visions!" Israel shouted at Isaiah, probably with hands clapped over their ears. "Don't tell us the truth! Say things that will make us feel good" (30:10 NCV). They wanted a different "word."

Just like people today.

Living Without Fear

And finally, God's people were living without fear. Those who weren't worshipping fallaciously weren't worshipping at all. "People of Israel, you have become tired of me," God sadly told them (NCV). "You have not . . . honored me . . . I did not weigh you down with sacrifices to offer or make you tired with incense to burn. So you did not [even] buy incense for me; you did not freely bring me fat from your sacrifices. Instead you have weighed me down with your many sins" (Isa. 43:22–24 NCV).

"Should you not fear me," God asked them, ". . . [and] tremble in my presence?" (Jer. 5:22 NIV). They should have—but they didn't. Their hearts did not cry, "Let us fear the LORD our God" (v. 24 NIV). They had lost their "awareness of the divine"[+] and, therefore, their *respect* for Him. Little by little, they grew casual in their relationship with God.

We've done the same thing today, haven't we? In an effort to emphasize God's role as "Abba Father," there are many who refer to God as "Daddy," "Papa God," "the man upstairs," or "the big guy in the sky." He is our Father, true, and an affectionate one, at that. And, sure, we can develop a warm, loving, personal relationship with Him. But this relationship in no way gives us a license to treat the God of the universe with familiarity. To do so, says worship pastor Miller Cunningham, is to make "small the infinitely large God that is beyond our own thinking."[5] Approaching Him on a "hey, buddy" basis demonstrates both disrespect and outright arrogance. God is not our "buddy." We wouldn't worship Him if He were. What He is, is "a consuming fire" (Deut. 4:24; Heb. 12:29 NKJV), and as worshippers, we are to come before Him with deference. "Worship the LORD," wrote David. "*Tremble* before him" (Ps. 96:9 NIV, emphasis added).

My friend, the prophets were far from casual when entering the presence of God. One glimpse at God, "sitting on a throne, high and lifted up," and Isaiah cried, "Woe is me" (6:1, 5 NKJV). Ezekiel, on the other hand, was speechless—for days. He also fell flat on his face. Jeremiah did too.

Today, God is still "sitting on a throne, high and lifted up," and in our hearts, we need to keep Him there, for "when we put God back where He belongs, . . . the whole spiral of our religious direction will be upward."[6] Isn't that what we need today, brothers and sisters, an upward spiral in the direction of the church? A spiral that the whole world can see? How can we achieve that? *It is even possible?*

Yes, but it all begins with the worship—the *right* worship—of Yahweh, and that starts with recognizing the *glory* of God—and giving Him *glory*.

"Give God the Glory" . . . *How?*

"Holy, holy, holy is the Lord *of hosts; the whole earth is full of His glory!"*

(Isa. 6:3 nkjv)

What is the "glory" of God? In Chapter 6 we learned that the word *glory* comes from the Hebrew *kabowd* and means, quite simply, the total essence of all that God is. To expand on that definition, the "glory" of God is the manifestation of the fullness of His character—His solemn presence; His importance past, present, and eternal; His perfection and infinite wisdom—His every attribute. In Exodus 33:18–22; 40:34–35, and 2 Chronicles 7:1–3, this Hebrew word is used to describe the presence and power of God *coming down.*

It is *His glory* that God wants the world to see, for it is this that reveals Him to the human heart and mind, invokes man's worship, and changes his life. It changed Isaiah's. When God's glory was revealed to him from a throne, where God sat surrounded by smoke and seraphim, Isaiah cried out in despair, painfully aware of his sinfulness. After that, he was never the same. God used Isaiah to witness to a kingdom. When Ezekiel beheld God's glory in the form of a "surrounding radiance" with the "appearance of [a] rainbow" (1:28 nasb), he fell on his face—and became the most radical prophet of all time.

I haven't seen any smoke-filled temples, seraphim, or swirling rainbows lately. Neither have you, I'm sure. Yet God *still* wants to reveal His glory and change people's lives. But how is the world to see it? How will they ever witness God's glory?

Through us—you and me—as we *glorify* God.

> *"Glorify the* LORD *in the dawning light, the name of the* LORD *God of Israel in the coastlands of the sea."*
>
> (ISA. 24:15 NKJV)

What does it mean for us to "glorify God"? Obviously, we cannot add to His glory. Only He is omniscient, omnipotent, and omnipresent. God alone is perfectly and infinitely complete—i.e., glorious. So how can *we* glorify Him?

Worship in Word

"Ascribe to the LORD the glory due his name" (Ps. 96:8 NIV). When we ascribe glory to God, it means we give honor to His *person* . . . in worship. We admire who He is, and we tell Him—and others. We are amazed at His love, humbled by His goodness, awestruck by His deeds, and honored that the King of kings even gives us the time of day. This drives us to worship, and we direct our worship of God both to *Him* and to *anyone else* who will listen. In fact, we can't say enough about Him—that is, if we really know Him—and each time we effervesce about the things He's done in our lives, the prayers He has answered, the comfort He has given, we are worshipping and *glorifying* God. We worship the Lord in word *every time* we rehearse His past faithfulness to us, in the hearing of others.

I had cancer—but God healed me.

I was on drugs—but God delivered me.

My marriage was falling apart—but God turned it around.

I didn't have a bite to eat—but God supplied my need, just in time!

I was hopelessly lost—but God saved me!

And even, *Well, God didn't heal my aunt, but when she died, He comforted me in my grief. And I'll see her again, in heaven anyway!*

We glorify God every time we remind the hopeless that God is Himself *Hope.* That's what the prophets did. They declared *hope*—through God alone—and in so doing, *worshipped* and *glorified* God. We, too, glorify God when we take every opportunity to brag on God and invite our friends and families to experience Him for themselves. This, friends, is worship, and God is thrilled when we glorify Him with our words.

But what about our deeds?

Worship in Deed

We also glorify God when we allow His glory to make a difference in the way we live our lives. Do we live in *obedience* to God? If so, then we are *glorifying* God. We've talked about this at length already, but at the risk of being redundant, one absolutely *cannot* worship God without obedience to Him. When God called Isaiah, he responded instantly: *"Here am I!"* (Isa. 6:8)

Jacob said in the lonely desert, "Here am I!" (Gen. 46:2)

Moses answered at the burning bush, "Here am I!" (Ex. 3:4)

Samuel responded in the dark of night, "Here am I!"

(1 Sam. 3:4–10)

Each of these worshippers was eager to *obey* the Lord, because each knew it was critical to worship. It's no less critical today. If we desire to glorify God in deed, then we have to be ready to do what God *wants us to do.*

> *"The LORD . . . said to me, 'Get up and go out to the plain, and there I will speak to you. So I got up and went out to the plain. And the glory of the LORD was standing there . . . and I fell facedown."*
>
> (EZEK. 3:22–23 NIV)

So what *does* He want us to do to show His glory to a lost world? They can't see God's glory with their physical eyes . . . but they can see it manifested—through *you.*

Worshipper, every time you take the high road, you glorify God. Every time you offer your own food to someone hungry, stand up for someone who is defenseless, and do an honest day's work, you glorify God before all who are watching. (And they *are* watching.) Anytime you:

- gather up clothes—not the stained and tattered ones, either—for someone whose house has burned down
- take a meal to someone who is too sick to cook
- visit an elderly person whose family has abandoned him
- help that wheelchair-bound neighbor get groceries into her house
- give that single mother a break by watching her three kids while she relaxes for a night

you are bringing glory to God, because those around you can *see* the glory, the character, the *person* of God in *you*.

All through the Bible, God used *outside* influences as conduits to deliver His message. He chose a whirlwind, pottery, a big fish, an almond branch, dry bones, and more, to get across to people what He wanted them to see. He does the same today. He uses *people*—you and me—to manifest His personality, His attributes, His *glory* to those who need most to see it. Today's cynical generation can't see God's benevolence, but they can witness yours, and your acts of compassion bring glory to God. They are, in fact, acts of worship.

The Hebrew nation didn't want to worship God that way, though. They were interested in offering "moments" of worship. What they needed, before they could ever offer pleasing worship to God, was a good dose of repentance.

REPENTANCE, AN UNPOPULAR CONCEPT

Repentance. Now, that's a concept sure to *not* get applause from today's society. Yet most of God's prophets wrote about it,* many of them making impassioned pleas for people to *come back* to the Lord. Nearly fifty times in the King James Version, the word "repent" or "repentance" appears. But what does it mean, really? In Hebrew, *nacham*,[7] the word for repentance denotes sorrow (regret, grief, remorse, rue) over something that has happened in the past. It is a genuine disappointment over personal actions or attitudes, evidenced by feelings of heartache, and usually resulting in some type of apology—"Please forgive me."

> "Come back to me" (Isa. 44:22 NCV).
> "Come back to me, unfaithful people.... All you have to do
>   is admit your sin" (Jer. 3:12–13 NCV).
> "Remember what you have done and feel ashamed" (Ezek.
>   16:61 NCV).

---

* The books of Micah, Nahum, and Haggai contain no clear calls to repentance.

"We have sinned and done wrong. . . . We are all ashamed . . .
    forgive us" (Dan. 9:5, 7, 9 NCV).
"Return to the LORD your God . . . Come back to the LORD"
    (Hos. 14:1–2 NCV).
"Come back to me with all your heart" (Joel 2:12 NCV).
"Come to me and live" (Amos 5:4 NCV).
"Come to the LORD . . . Do what is right" (Zeph. 2:3 NCV).
"Return to me" (Zech. 1:3; Mal. 3:7 NCV).

The Greek word *metanoia*, repentance, indicates a change of mind for better. It is followed by abhorrence of one's past sins.[8] F. F. Bruce explains that "repentance (metanoia, 'change of mind') involves a turning with contrition from sin to God." It is precisely this type of turning from wrong that God was requiring when He told Solomon, "If my people . . . will . . . turn from their wicked ways, then will I . . . forgive their sin" (2 Chron. 7:14 NIV). This is repentance, and only after such turning from sin is a person "in the proper condition to accept . . . divine forgiveness."[9] And only when we are divinely forgiven can we offer, from pure hearts, worship that God will accept.

In chapter 7, we learned that repentance is vital to authentic worship. The prophets knew this way before we did. They preached it relentlessly and without apology. But before these men could preach *about* repentance, they had to *experience* it for themselves. Isaiah repented in the temple. Jonah repented in the belly of a fish. Ezekiel fell on his face in repentance when he saw the glory of God in a vision. But what did their "repentance" involve? And what does it involve today?

Examine Yourself . . .

In worship, repentance requires *examination*. Socrates said, "An unexamined life is not worth living." The prophet Jeremiah certainly agreed, for it was he who wrote, two centuries earlier, "Let us *examine* and see what we have done and then return to the Lord" (Lam. 3:40 NCV, emphasis added). This is exactly what the prophet Isaiah did when he saw the Lord on His throne, with His train filling the temple. He took a hard look at himself and said, "God, I am not worthy to be in your presence! I'm a sinner!" (Isa. 6:5, my paraphrase). He examined himself, saw that he was sinful, and then *confessed* his sin, another critical component of repentance. When Isaiah did this, God's forgiveness was granted, and the prophet was made clean: "One of the heavenly creatures [took] a hot coal from the altar. Then he . . . touched my mouth with the hot coal and said, 'Look, your guilt is taken away . . . Your sin is taken away'" (vv. 6–7 NCV).

Is it examination time? Is it time to confess sin, to repent, and to seek God's forgiveness? As Isaiah did, let's take a good, hard look at ourselves, examining ourselves for any flaw. And, like David of old, we should ask the Lord to examine us too: "Examine me, O LORD . . . See if there be any wicked way in me" (Ps. 26:2; 139:24 KJV). When sin is found, confess it. Ask for forgiveness. Then, friend, you can worship God, free of fear, from a heart full of love and devotion.

PRINCIPLES OF WORSHIP FROM THIS CHAPTER

The prophets have taught us much about authentic worship. What have we learned?

1. *True Worship Includes Right Actions Toward Others*

There's more to worship than what goes on at church. True worship also involves our actions toward those on the *outside*. It embraces the way we treat the impoverished, the homeless, the widowed, and the orphaned. Our coworkers, family members, and the big-eyed kid that tramps through our flower gardens. Our friends—*and* our enemies. In short, God wants our worship to actively demonstrate genuine love for, not only Him, but for all who are made in His image. If you turn up your nose at that woman at church who desperately needs deodorant, don't think you can raise your hands in the sanctuary and worship God. He won't accept it. If you piously look down on that single mother, whose child was born out of wedlock, don't even try to sing songs of praise, especially if that woman has a need, and you are in a place to meet it—but don't. If you make fun of that mentally retarded classmate or that kid with the limp, don't even attempt to worship God. In fact, be *afraid* to. God will not endure religious "activities" or accept offerings of worship from those who neglect the fatherless, ignore the penniless, ridicule the disabled, or reject the elderly. What God wants, say the prophets, is for our worship to encompass doing good, seeking justice, helping orphans, and punishing those who hurt others (Isa. 1:16–17). If it doesn't, then *don't bother*. "Execute judgment and righteousness, and deliver the plundered out of the hand of the oppressor," God commanded His people for all time. "Do no violence to the stranger, the fatherless, or the widow" (Jer. 22:2–3 NKJV). The *New Century Version* puts it this way: "Do what is fair and right. Save the one who has been robbed . . . Don't mistreat or hurt the foreigners, orphans, or widows." Put briefly, we are to actively engage in showing our love for God by loving those less fortunate. It *brings glory to God* and is an *act of worship*.

2. God Wants Worship from Repentant Hearts!

We've also learned that true worship must be offered from untainted hearts. Otherwise, we are like whitewashed sepulchers filled with dead men's bones, sweet frosting covering a stale cake, or costly perfume poured on rotting flesh. This was the condition of the people in the prophets' times. They needed *repentance*. This was the driving message of both the major and minor prophets. It is still God's message today, and it is a matter of utmost importance. God so desperately wants relationship with us. He wants to dwell with us. And He wants our worship. But He will never, ever, *ever* accept our worship unless and until we *examine ourselves*, see our sin in Technicolor, and confess it to God. He is so anxious to forgive you and cleanse you. Just listen to His plea:

> "Come now, and let us reason together . . .
> Though your sins are like scarlet,
> They shall be as white as snow;
> Though they are red like crimson,
> They shall be as wool." (Isa. 1:18 NKJV)

What sins are in your life? What have you been neglecting? Then hear the Word of the Lord: *Come home.* Can't you hear Him calling?

Come home, lost teenager.

  Come home, cynical son.

    Come home, broken addict.

      Come home, embarrassed daughter.

        Come home, helpless cripple.

          Come home . . .

Friends, this is by far the most significant principle we've learned thus far. Our ethics will take care of themselves if we will simply examine ourselves, repent of our sins, and come home to the Father. You'll see. After all, isn't it written that "deeds of justice and charity are the first fruits of repentance"?[10]

So repent, my friend, and come home. How will God respond? *"He will take great delight in you . . . [and] rejoice over you with singing"* (Zeph. 3:17 NIV).

I'm sorry to say, during the prophets' era, God's people never did give Him much to sing about. Their worship was either nonexistent or made up of ceremony without substance. Their sacrifices were boring and meaningless to them, and equally meaningless to (and unfulfilling for) the Lord. And from the very beginning, God knew it would be that way. Old Testament worship would never satisfy us *or* Him. Why? It was based on obeying the law, and the law was imperfect.

Yet God created in our innermost being a *desire* for worship. So, what to do? Give up on worship altogether? As Paul the apostle would say, "God forbid!" That would be the proverbial "throwing out the baby with the bathwater." We *need* to worship. It's just that our yearning cannot be satisfied by adherence to rules and regulations. Only *relationship* can produce worship that is vibrant and authentic. But therein lies the rub.

As humans, we are innately sinful, degenerate, depraved, and every other negative adjective that can be ascribed to our race. This puts us at odds with

God, who is totally holy and pure. Beginning with the Fall, our relationship with God was impaired, our fellowship broken. Therefore, our pitiful attempts at worship throughout history were a disappointment to God. He was displeased with our sacrifices before we ever offered them, because they were given from impure hearts. We needed *someone else* to make our sacrifices, someone who could bridge the immense relational gap between us and God, someone qualified by virtue of Virtue Himself. Then along came Virtue, in human form. And His name was JESUS.

PART II

New Testament Principles of Worship

But when the time had fully come,
God sent his Son,
born of a woman, born under law,
to redeem those under law,
that we might receive
the full rights of sons.

—GALATIANS 4:4-5

THUS FAR, WE HAVE STUDIED WORSHIP THROUGHOUT THE books of the Old Testament. We saw that, from the beginning, God wanted relationship. Fellowship. Friendship. So He created humanity and then communed with them, revealing Himself to them.

How did God's people respond to His revealed presence? They worshipped Him. It's what they—and we—were made for. With varying expressions of veneration, the Old Testament saints made known their love for God. They worshipped with sacrifices. They worshipped through simple obedience and by living lives of integrity. Some built altars. Others danced. Or shouted. Or banged on drums. Or sang songs. Some of these songs were slow, soft, and heartfelt; others were loud, fast, and spicy. But all were written to the glory of God, because that's what worship is—giving glory to the God who wants to *dwell* with us.

What did we learn about worship *posture* in Part I? Some Old Testament characters worshipped on their feet, often with upraised hands. Others worshipped on their knees. But some, overcome with awe and adoration, simply fell—facedown.

We discovered in Part I that our *place* of worship is important. Mankind's first worship took place in a garden. Later, men and women worshipped at altars, in a tent, on a mountaintop, on a battlefield, and in a temple, among other places. But wherever they worshipped, the dynamic personalities we studied in the first half of this book taught us valuable principles about worship:

First, *we are born with a desire to worship*. It's innate. Our hearts long to worship *something*. Evidence of this can be seen through all the foibles and fumbles of mankind through the ages. We've bowed to the sun and moon, to animals and trees, to idols of wood and gold. But only the worship of Yahweh has that "personal touch." We worship Him in spirit, and

He responds to our spirits. He is the *only* One who does, so *only* our God can fulfill the unquenchable thirst of the human race to worship God.

Second, *we are born to worship* ONE. While the Egyptians, Canaanites, and so many others through time worshipped a myriad of deities (none of whom *ever* responded), we worship one God, Yahweh, because there *is* only one God. He is the Giver of all life, Father of all joy, and Creator of all peace. He didn't require a cocreator to construct the heavens, leaving Him just the earth to shape. He didn't need someone else to fling the stars into space, as He created the oceans. No, He did it all, and as such, He deserves *all* worship. He alone is worthy to receive it. Therefore, throughout history, God has rejected any and all worship that was not . . .

> *to* Him alone,
>> *of* Him alone, and
>>> *for* Him alone!

He demanded that worship be focused on Him *only* — free from agenda, personal ambition, and distraction.

But God's children throughout time have had their own agendas (to sin), their own ambitions (to sin some more), and plenty of distractions (do I need to say it?). Israel was addicted to sin and consequently, always in trouble. Raiders stole their goods. Strangers took them captive. But somehow, with the exception of a few, mostly prophets, Israel could never make the connection between their crises and their vacillating worship. Overcome with the problems they reaped from the infidelity they sowed, the Israelites couldn't pinpoint their *real* problem.

At the conclusion of the Old Testament, the nation of Israel is worshipping God in a second temple — one built to replace the glorious temple of Solomon, which was destroyed because of their rebellion. For years, they had been captives to a foreign nation, Babylon. But then, by the grace of God alone, they were set free by a decree from Cyrus, king of the Medo-Persian Empire, allowing all Jewish captives to return to Judah. (Sadly, only a small remnant of the multimillion-member nation known as Israel actually returned.) They were also given some other freedoms: though Palestine continued to be under Persian control, the Israelites were allowed to form a quasi-province in Jerusalem under the governor of Syria.

Alas, though God's people could manage their government, they still couldn't manage their worship. We've studied together the frustration of the prophets, who tried with all their might to get the Hebrew people back on track. But they just couldn't—or wouldn't, more precisely—stay on the straight and narrow.

Finally, Yahweh was fed up with His rebellious, disloyal people, and His weariness set in motion a sad epoch in history. We know it as the *intertestamental period*. But what it really was, was silence—four hundred years of it. God did not speak at all. And during this time, Israel continued its struggle to exist as once again, a stronger nation overtook them.

Alexander the Great won victory over Greece, Persia, and Syria in 331 BC. Once more, the Hebrew nation was not its own. Still, Alexander did allow the Jews to retain self-government, and even to worship "their" God. But they didn't worship Him. They worshipped everything else. They were swept away by the Hellenistic culture that engulfed them after Alexander's death. So God remained silent, and soon Israel's "optional" worship was no longer an option.

In 170 BC, Antiochus Epiphanes took Jerusalem by force and instituted compulsory idol worship, erecting a statue of Zeus on the altar—in the Hebrews' own temple![1] He burned the Scriptures, prohibited worship of the Hebrew God, and even forced the Jews to eat pork, something the law had strictly forbidden. During this time, hundreds of Hebrew people were martyred. But that was only the beginning of sorrows for the chosen-but-traitorous nation.

By 63 BC, Rome was the law of Palestine. Twenty-six years later, Herod the Great, aided by Roman troops, became the supreme ruler of the Jews. Now, not only were they subject to his command, but they were also obliged to pay taxes to Rome.

Still, this could have been a glorious time for God's people. True, Herod was evil, but he did rebuild the temple, and on a grand and glorious scale, at that.[2] He also restored dignity to the Jewish way of worship. During this era, two great sects emerged as Israel's spiritual leaders: the Pharisees and the Sadducees. Unfortunately, these influential scribes and lawyers were mostly just corrupt pawns in Herod's government. Further, they led the Hebrew people in a self-righteous "worship" for which God had no respect, so He maintained His silence . . . for a time.

Here, we must heave a heavy sigh. The once-celebrated nation of Israel was still someone's puppet. They were politically and religiously "free," but still under Rome's jurisdiction. They needed someone to save them, both politically and spiritually. But they hadn't heard a word from God in centuries.

Still, they had hope. God had promised them a *Messiah*, a savior. The books of Psalms, Isaiah, and Jeremiah—among others—all talked about Him. Haggai called Him the *desire of all nations* (2:7 KJV). Jeremiah portrayed Him as the *righteous Branch* (23:5 KJV). Then, in the Old Testament's final book, Malachi described the Messiah as the *Sun of righteousness* (4:2 KJV), who would enable Israel to "tread down the wicked," their enemies, and make them "ashes under the soles of [their] feet" (v. 3 KJV). Next the Messiah would establish a new kingdom—a glorious kingdom—that would eclipse the empires of Assyria, Babylon, Persia, Greece, and Rome, Then He, the long-awaited Messiah, would be worshipped forever, and would *change* worship forever. Israel believed this. It was their one enduring hope.

But God was still stone silent.

Interestingly, though He had nothing to say to Israel during this time, God was still busily working. He was, in fact, preparing the way for a permanent change in worship.

First, He initiated change in the *place* of worship. In times past, all of Israel worshipped in one central temple. Before that, they worshipped in a *single* tent. But just prior to the years of God's silence, Ezra and Nehemiah set up synagogues all over, in many different towns. This permitted people to receive spiritual education, celebrate the Jewish festivals, and participate in worship, close to home. This change in locale was the foundation for worship in the early church, which we'll study in Chapter 17.

Next, God initiated change in the availability of Scripture. The Pentateuch was translated into Greek (the *Septuagint*) around 285 BC. By this time, Jerusalem was a very cosmopolitan, Greek-speaking society. This new, Greek translation made God's law more accessible to the people. It was also a precursor of the living word to come. (Remember, Jesus is the *incarnate Word*, and He was, and is, accessible to all.) God was setting the stage for the Messiah. Remember, the last Israel heard from God, Malachi was crying, "The Messiah is coming."

In the first book of the New Testament, Matthew proclaimed, "Messiah is here."

WORSHIP IN THE NEW TESTAMENT

So, what will we see in the New Testament?

We will see Jesus, the hope of all nations, the only begotten Son of God. The *Messiah*. And we know He is the Messiah, because only Jesus Christ so completely satisfied the fulfillment of messianic prophecy. While I'm only scratching the surface in offering proofs of Jesus' messiahship, here are just a few of the prophecies that were fulfilled in Christ: The Messiah was to be born in Bethlehem (Mic. 5:1). Jesus was. He was to come from the tribe of Judah (Gen. 49:10). He did. He would reveal His kingship from atop a donkey's back (Zech. 9:9), then be arrested, tried, tortured, killed, and buried in a rich man's tomb (Isa. 52–53; Ps. 22)—only to rise from the dead, the best evidence of all! And all of these prophecies were fulfilled *to the letter* in Jesus the Christ.

But who was this Jesus? He was an agent of change. From the time of His birth from a virgin's womb, He was worshipped as equal with God. Why? He *was* God, in the flesh. And while He walked on our very planet, He forever changed the way worship was done. Our worship today is no longer under the rigorous, unflinching law of Moses. Jesus ushered in a new dispensation: grace. Neither is worship confined to the tabernacle. Christ Himself became the tabernacle.

Do you remember the tabernacle? It was the "dwelling place" that God instructed Moses to build, in the Old Testament. It was very important to God—so important, in fact, that its construction and purpose required fifty chapters to explain.[3] This movable structure was full of symbols, all revealing the glory of God—in Christ. As a matter of fact, *every part* of the tabernacle pictured Him. The furniture, pillars, ropes, curtains, priestly garments—*all* speak of the Messiah. For example:

- The Ark spoke of Christ's person.
- The tablets represented Christ as *living word*.
- The golden pot of manna typified Christ as Bread of life.
- Aaron's rod connoted the Resurrection.
- The mercy seat denoted Christ's purpose.
- The table illustrated Christ's humanity.
- The golden lampstand and its branches indicated Christ's deity.
- The oil for the lamps symbolized the Holy Spirit's working.
- The veil epitomized God's righteousness.
- The colors in the curtains suggested Christ's attributes.[4]

But the tabernacle is gone, and we can no longer—*need* no longer—go there to worship. But what does that knowledge mean to the body of Christ? What does it do for *us*?

It takes us full circle. From the beginning, God has desired to dwell among His people. That's what the tabernacle was for. And today, God's yearning is still the same: to dwell with us and have relationship with us. He made that longing known anew through Christ, the New Testament tabernacle, who lived and walked among His people: "The Word became flesh," wrote John, "and made his dwelling among us. We have seen his glory, the glory of the One and Only, who came from the Father (John 1:14 NIV) . . . and his name is the Word of God (Rev. 19:13 NIV).

Jesus dwelled among us, on this earth, taking on human form and suffering the same temptations that are common to all humankind. He lived the life of a man—working, weeping, thinking, reacting, and responding to the culture around Him. He saw our sin firsthand. He got up close and personal with our addictions. And He saw the futility of the law to make us any better. No amount of animal sacrifices could cleanse mankind. Worse, up to now, anyone who disobeyed the law was condemned to death. The world would need a once-for-all sacrifice to pay for their sins *and* to free them—once and for all—from sin's tyranny.

Christ would be that sacrifice, the one *perfect* Lamb that would atone for our sins forever. He would, in fact, *save* us. With His atoning death, out went the law of Moses, which brought only "sin and death," and in came the "law of the Spirit that brings life . . . God did what the law could not do. He sent his own Son to earth with the same human life that others use for sin. By sending his Son to be an offering for sin, God used a human life to destroy sin" (Rom. 8:2–3 NCV).

It should have been us. The sins were ours, not Christ's. The whole world should have been condemned to death.

But Jesus took that death upon Himself. He changed places with us and put Himself under our curse. In so doing, He took away the penalty of our sins and gave us a clear, unobstructed path to worship Yahweh. This, my friends, changed worship *forever*. What's not to worship? Not only has God made it abundantly evident that He *loves* us, wants to *dwell* with us, and desires above all things a *relationship* with us, but now He's even provided a once-for-all-time payment of our sin debt—His Son, Jesus. "Those who are in Christ Jesus are not judged guilty," says Romans 8:1 (NCV). Better still, through Jesus, God has made our road to heaven—where we will spend eternity in relationship with Him—accessible, not by fulfilling the letter of the law, but by believing on the Son of God and worshipping Him.

There's so much to cover in the last half of this book—Jesus as the High Priest, the new and better covenant, and so forth—but I don't want to give too much away. For the moment, just understand that the focus of worship now centers on one person—*Jesus Christ*. Through Him we have been given a whole new reason to worship: eternal life through the salvation that He purchased for us *with His own blood*. Because of His substitutionary work on the cross, we are privileged to enjoy worship, free from the bondage of the law. Old methods and models for worship are passed away. Now we will worship to a new "tune."

In his book, *God's Big Picture*, Vaughn Roberts depicts God as a composer of music. After creating the world and all its inhabitants, He gave clear instructions—the "score," so to speak, so that we—the musicians— would know how to live.

But we ignore the notes. We try to play "by ear." We seek to create our own melodies and apply our own dynamics to our own rhythm, instead of following the melodic line of our Great Composer, God. We also ignore the conductor. We can "conduct" ourselves, you see. The results? In the words of Vaughn, "a terrible cacophony."[5] Without a conductor, there is no hope for unified presentation, but rather, dissonance and rhythmic chaos—in short, a musical *mess*.

But in our worship, we must see Jesus as our Conductor, who came to this world to direct a magnificent symphony that puts us in harmony with God and each other. And if we will let Him, Jesus will restore order out of chaos and transform our ugly discord into beautiful music for the glory, honor, and praise of the Most High God.

And that's what Part II is about. We will learn how to follow our Conductor, Jesus, as He leads us—with His tempo, His tune, and His dynamics—through the musical masterpiece of life that was composed for us by God. We will love this music. It was made for us, and as we follow our Composer and Conductor, we will fall in love all over again with Yahweh, the God of the Ages.

And we will *worship*.

WORSHIP IN THE GOSPELS, PART I

"When you do a charitable deed, do not let your left hand know what your right hand is doing, that your charitable deed may be in secret; and your Father who sees in secret will Himself reward you openly."

—JESUS CHRIST

IN THE DAYS LEADING UP TO THE END OF WORLD WAR II, Western Allies pushed into Germany, liberating prisoners from the death camps at Auschwitz, Buchenwald, Bergen-Belsen, and Dachau. By this time, not only had countless blind, deaf, mentally ill, and crippled Europeans been murdered, but Poles, Slavs, Gypsies, and *six million* innocent Jews had also been deliberately exterminated—all because of Adolf Hitler's dream of creating a master race.

This was an ugly time in world history, and in the aftermath of the Holocaust, Allied troops discovered these chilling words written on a cellar wall in Cologne, Germany:

> *I believe in the Sun even when it is not shining,*
> *I believe in Love even when I cannot feel it,*
> *And I believe in God even when he is silent.*[1]

Silent. No doubt, all Jews felt that God was silent during Hitler's implementation of the "Final Solution." And this was not the first time they had sensed His silence. Between the Old Testament and the New, the children of Israel had lived through *four hundred years* of it. From the closing of the book of Malachi to the first page of Matthew, God had said nothing. *Not a word.*

No prophecy.

No words of comfort.

No revelation.

The heavens were, for lack of a better term, "as silent as the grave."

But even in the silence, some believed. They looked for a savior. They yearned for a King. They prayed for the Messiah to come. And they hungered for their silent God.

Then, one Sabbath day, at the time when incense was offered, God spoke. Through an angel, God told Zechariah, an elderly temple priest, that he and his aged wife, Elizabeth, were going to have a baby: "I am Gabriel," the angel began. "I stand in the presence of God, and I have been sent to . . . tell you this good news . . . Your wife Elizabeth will bear you a son, . . . John . . . He will be filled with the Holy Spirit . . . Many of the people of Israel will he bring back to *the Lord* . . . And he will go on before *the Lord* . . . to . . . make ready a people prepared for *the Lord*" (Luke 1:19, 13, 15–17 NIV, emphasis added).

Not long after, God spoke again through Gabriel to a young virgin named Mary—who would become the *mother* of "the Lord": "Greetings!" the angel said to her. "Listen! You will become pregnant and give birth to a son, and you will name him Jesus . . . The Holy Spirit will come upon you, and the power of the Most High will cover you. [And] the baby will be . . . called the Son of God" (Luke 1:28, 31, 35 NCV).[2]

But God wasn't through speaking yet.

Shaken by the news that Mary was pregnant, Joseph, her husband-to-be, decided to divorce her. But again, God sent an angel: "Joseph," he told him, "the baby in [Mary] is from the Holy Spirit . . . he will save his people from their sins" (Matt. 1:19–21 NCV).

And in the fullness of time, God spoke once more. To a group of shepherds in a field, an angel announced, "'I [bring] you good news that will be a great joy to all the people. Today your Savior was born in the town of David. He is Christ, the Lord' . . . Then a very large group of angels from heaven joined the first angel, praising God and saying: 'Give glory to God in heaven'" (Luke 2:10–11, 13–14 NCV).

Wow! After forty painfully silent decades, not only did God begin speaking again, but His words promised to fulfill the great hope of mankind: He was sending a Messiah—*the* Messiah—to save His people from the guilt of sin. His name would be Jesus, or in the Hebrew, Yeshua.

How did He come? You know the story. It is told in every language, in every nation, on every continent: *"The Word became flesh and made his dwelling among us"* (John 1:14 NIV). Yes, God the Son took on human form and was born, not in a four-star hotel or a well-appointed palace, but in a stable, without fanfare, where His first bed would be an animal's feeding trough.

But this Jewish baby boy would change worship *for all eternity.*

WORSHIP IN THE GOSPELS

In this chapter and the next, we will take a look at worship in the Gospels, that is, the first four books of the New Testament: Matthew, Mark, Luke, and John. Out of the sixty New Testament uses of the word "worship," *proskyne*, more than half appear in the Gospels, and it is in these of writings that we discover Jesus Himself is the *fulfillment of worship.* He is both the superlative worshipper of God the Father *and* the One to whom worship was, is, and forever will be offered. And He taught every man, woman, boy, and girl how to worship God, both by His teachings and by personal example.

So how did Jesus worship?

FAST FACT:

Q: What did *worship* mean to New Testament worshippers?

A: Among Oriental peoples, especially Persians, worship meant "to fall upon the knees and touch the ground with the forehead as an expression of profound reverence" or (NT) "by kneeling or prostration to do homage (to one) or make obeisance."[3]

Worship by Jesus: Teaching Worship by Example

Jesus Worshipped in the Sanctuary

In chapter 12, "Worship in the Psalms," we learned that Psalm 150:1 forever settles the question, "Do I have to go to church to be pleasing to God?" The verse reads, "Praise God *in the sanctuary*" (KJV, emphasis added), or as *The Message* renders it, "Praise God in his holy house of worship." From the earliest times, we learn that Jesus Himself did just that. He was engaged in the worship of Yahweh *in the temple*. In fact, in the well-known story of twelve-year-old Jesus getting "lost" during a trip to Jerusalem to celebrate the Passover, his parents' found the adolescent in the temple, the Jews' house of worship—where He *chose* to be (Luke 2:41–49). If this isn't enough to convince the excuse seeker that God's people are to make His house a place of regular attendance, perhaps this verse will: "And [Jesus] came to Nazareth . . . and, *as his custom was*, he went into the synagogue on the sabbath day" (Luke 4:15 KJV, emphasis added). The *New Century Version* says Jesus went there *"as he always did."* By this time, Jesus was a man, capable of choosing—or not choosing—to engage in worship in God's house. Where do we find Him? In the house of worship—by choice. Worship in the house of God was a deliberate and customary part of Jesus' routine. And if it was good enough for the King of kings, it is certainly good enough for me—and you. He set the example for all of humanity to worship God in His house.

What other examples did He set for us as He worshipped His Father?

Jesus Worshipped by Submission

Immediately after the story of Jesus as a boy in Jerusalem's temple, we read of John the Baptist. This John is the second cousin of Jesus, and the son of Zechariah and Elizabeth, to whom God spoke first after His centuries-long silence. John is also the one of whom God said, in the last book of the Old Testament: "I will send my messenger, and he shall prepare the way before me: and the LORD, whom ye seek, shall suddenly come to his temple" (Mal. 3:1 KJV). John would be, the Lord told Malachi, the forerunner of the Messiah.

In Luke 3, we find John in the wilderness, preaching "a baptism of changed hearts and lives for the forgiveness of sins" (v. 3 NCV): "Prepare the way for the Lord," he cried to all who would hear him. "Make the road straight for him" (v. 4 NCV). And he baptized in water any who were willing.

One day, Jesus Himself came to the river. He wanted to be baptized too. But as soon as John saw Him, He cried out, "Look, the Lamb of God, who takes away the sin of the world!" (John 1:29 NCV). And when he realized that Jesus intended to be baptized—by *him*—he said, "Why do you come to *me* to be baptized? I need to be baptized by *you*!" (Matt. 3:13 NCV, emphasis added). But Jesus replied, "We should do all things that are God's will" (v. 15 NCV).

John baptized the Son of God.

A bit of review is in order. In chapter 4, as we studied Abraham, we discovered that *obedience* is central to worship and is, in fact, the first way we express our love to God. True worship begins with obedience. Jesus knew that His baptism in water was the Father's will and that it was necessary to "fulfill all righteousness" (v. 15 NKJV). And so, the perfect, sinless Son of God submitted Himself to what He knew to be God's bidding and stood alongside sinners to be baptized by a fallen man—whom He would one day die to save. And Christ's obedient act of worship so pleased the Father that heaven opened, and God's Spirit came down on him like a dove. Then, "a voice from heaven said, 'This is my Son, whom I love, and I am very pleased with him'" (v. 17 NCV).[4] God publicly endorsed Jesus! Why? Because Jesus demonstrated to all generations that authentic worship begins with a heart that is willing to obey. Without it, all worship "demonstrations" are mere exhibits—wasted, insignificant, futile. Jesus refused to engage in that type of worship. Instead, He would worship by submitting.

A NEW TESTAMENT WORSHIP WAR

Jesus was 100 percent God. Students of God's Word know this. They also know, though, that, fully God, Christ was also fully human. And Satan is out to kill, steal from, and eternally destroy all humans—because we are made in the image of God.

The enemy wants above all things to steal our worship; destroy our relationship with God; and make sure we are consigned to eternal hell. We read about this in chapter 3, "The Worship Wars." Doesn't it stand to reason, then, that Satan wanted precisely the same for Jesus? to replace Christ's worship of God with worship of *him*? to take His life? to send not only all of humanity but Christ Himself to hell forever? You can bet he did, so once again, Satan declared war—against God in the flesh.

Immediately, after His baptism, Jesus was led by the Spirit into the wilderness, "to be tempted by the devil" (Matt. 4:1 NCV). Satan knew he could never defeat Jesus as divinity. He had tried that in heaven before being unceremoniously cast out (Ezek. 28:13–19; Luke 10:18). But now, here Jesus was—in the flesh—and He was fasting! *What an opportunity!* the devil must have thought. *I'll attack His humanity.*

Match 1: The temptation began with an effort to get Jesus to doubt God's word. We've seen this before, with Eve in the Garden. "If you are the Son of God," Satan teased, "tell these rocks to become bread" (Matt. 4:3 NCV). Jesus knew He was the Son of God. His Father had broadcast it from heaven just weeks before: "This is My beloved Son" (Matt. 3:17 NKJV).

"But are you *really*? Satan mocked. "And aren't you *hungry*?"

"Jesus answered by quoting Deuteronomy: 'It takes more than bread to stay alive. It takes a steady stream of words from God's mouth'" (4:4 MSG). And besides, *He* was the bread of life (John 6:33, 35, 48), and He knew it.

Christ–1, Satan–0. But the game wasn't over.

In the second match, Jesus was on top of the temple (Matt. 4:5). "*If* you are the Son of God . . ." Satan coaxed again, "jump off." Then, stooping as low as he could go, the unholiest of creatures dared to quote God's Holy Word: "[After all, the Scriptures say,] 'He has placed you in the care of angels. They will catch you" (v. 6 MSG, from Psalm 91:11-12).

Jesus must have looked at Satan as if he were crazy. Shaking His head, He answered, "[Yeah, but the Scriptures also say,] 'YOU SHALL NOT PUT THE LORD YOUR GOD TO THE TEST' (v. 7 NASB, from Deuteronomy 6:16).

Christ—2, Satan—0.

Third match: Jesus and the tempter stood at the top of a high mountain, where, deliberately and unapologetically, Satan tried to entice Jesus to worship him. Pointing to the kingdoms below, he said, "Go down on your knees and worship me, and they're yours" (vv. 8-9 MSG).

They were *already* His. Jesus is already Lord of all creation. Why would He ever entertain Satan's offer? This was nothing more than "a ploy to bring the Son captive to himself," wrote Noel Due. "Satan want[ed] to force Jesus to choose a method of inheritance: by worshiping Satan or by worshiping God."[5]

But Jesus refused to yield to Satan's will; He refused to *worship* him.

"Beat it, Satan!" Jesus shouted. "[The Scriptures say,] 'Worship the Lord your God, and only him'" (v. 10 MSG, from Deuteronomy 6:13).

Christ—3, Satan—0. Jesus passed the test and *won* the worship war.

Notice that Satan attacked Jesus during the very time that He was seeking to obey the Spirit, who had *led* Him into the wilderness. Satan does the same thing to you and me. Often, it is when we are trying to obey the Spirit's voice as He is leading us to pray or worship, that Satan tries to lure us away. We become distracted, sleepy, or restless. This, friends, is when we must press in all the more. We are in a battle--a spiritual one. Adam and Eve lost the battle for worship in the garden (Gen. 3:1--7). Mankind has been paying ever since. But when Jesus faced a personal, one-on-one worship war with Satan, Jesus prevailed. Every time Satan cast his bait, Jesus recommitted Himself to the Word and will of God--and won! And because He won--*in His flesh*, we can win too.

Jesus Worshipped in Prayer

Prayer. We haven't talked a whole lot about it thus far, because *prayer* and *worship* are two different things. And yet . . .

1. Prayer should never be offered without worship.
2. Prayer is one of the elements of worship.
3. Prayer *is* worship.

Let's talk about these assertions.

Prayer should not be offered without worship. In Matthew 6 and Luke 11, we see Jesus teaching His followers how to pray. In both Gospels, the prayer begins the same: "Our Father in heaven, hallowed be Your name" (Matt. 6:9; Luke 11:2 NKJV). Notice that the first thing out of Jesus' mouth was not His list of wants and needs. No, He began by giving God praise. Now, were Christ's words meant to teach us that if we praise God first, He'll be more inclined to answer us? Are we to try to manipulate God with praise? Of course not. He'd see through that anyway. But we are to recognize that He and His name are "hallowed." The word *hallowed* means "holy," and before the King of kings ever began running down His "prayer list," He first took the time to revere—to worship—the *holy* name of God.

Centuries before, another king had also worshipped the *name* of the Lord. Hear the praises of King David*:

* All of these verses are from the New King James Version.

"I . . . will sing praise to the name of the Lord Most High." (Ps. 7:17)

"O Lord, our Lord, how excellent is Your name in all the earth." (Ps. 8:1, 9)

"I will sing praise to Your name, O Most High." (Ps. 9:2)

"Therefore I will give thanks to You, O Lord, . . . and sing praises to Your name." (Ps. 18:49; 2 Sam. 22:50)

"Oh, magnify the Lord with me, and let us exalt His name together." (Ps. 34:3)

"In God we boast all day long, and praise Your name forever." (Ps. 44:8)

"I will praise Your name, O Lord, for it is good." (Ps. 54:6)

"Not unto us, O Lord, . . . but to Your name give glory." (Ps. 115:1)

And that's just a few.

Fellow worshippers, "the name of the Lord is a strong tower; the righteous run to it and are safe" (Prov. 18:10 NKJV). David wrote that "our help is in the name of the Lord" (Ps. 124:8 NKJV). God wants us, when we go to prayer, to praise His *name*, and yet so many times, we approach the Lord as if he were a pop machine, where we plunk in our quarter-sized prayers, all laced with "gimme, gimme, gimme," and expect Him to deliver, with nary a word of thanks or praise.

Jesus knew better. He knew that His heavenly Father was, is, and ever will be "worthy to be praised" (Ps. 18:3), so He made it a point to teach both the world that then was *and* the world to come that prayer should include praise.

And it stands to reason. Which would you, as a parent, rather have your child do: come straight in the door after school and say, "Hi, Dad! Can I have fifty bucks?" or rush into your arms, "love on" you, and then ask for whatever it is he wants? I think the answer is clear. Jesus did too. When teaching His people to pray, He showed them, in two different Gospels, that the way to win the heart of God is through praise.

Now, let's keep things in perspective here. Prayer itself *is* about asking, not worship. Jesus said, "Whatsoever ye shall *ask* in prayer . . ." (Matt. 21:22 KJV, emphasis added). But whenever we appeal to God, we should always worship Him for who He is: Father, Provider, Healer, Savior—not to butter Him up so we'll get what we ask for, but because our love and awe for Him are real.

Prayer is one of the elements of worship. So many Scriptures record the prayers of Jesus. He prayed:

> at His baptism (Luke 3:21)
> before choosing the Twelve (Luke 6:12)
> on the mountain (Luke 9:28–29)
> before His death (Matt. 26:36)
> for Himself (17:1)
> for little children (Matt. 19:13)
> for His disciples (John 17:6)
> for *all* who would one day follow Him (John 17:20)

And today, He "ever liveth to make intercession"—for you and me (Heb. 7:25 KJV)!

Why did Jesus pray, do you suppose? Why did He bother? First, I believe, He just wanted to talk to His Father—alone. Getting alone with God was a regular part of Jesus' daily life. In Matthew 14:23, we read that Jesus "went up on the mountain by Himself to pray" (NKJV). Jesus must have loved the solitude of the mountains, because we also see Him praying there in the books of Mark (6:46) and Luke (6:12; 9:28). Luke 6:12 tells us that once He got to the mountain, He "continued all night in prayer to God" (NKJV). Obviously, this private time with God was a source of guidance, strength, comfort, and joy. It was an opportunity to get away from the "busy" so he could worship God *privately*, pray about what mattered to Him, and seek direction as He worked to fulfill His mission.

We need these times too. We need to steal away from the busyness of life and get alone with God on our "mountain." The mountains were Christ's secret place, and we also need a secret place (see chapter 2):

When we live in the secret place it becomes impossible for us to doubt God, we become more sure of Him than of anything else. Your Father, Jesus says, is in secret and nowhere else. . . . Get into the habit of dealing with God about everything. Unless in the first waking moment of the day you learn to fling the door wide back and let God in, you will work on a wrong level all day; but swing the door wide open and pray to your Father in secret, and every public thing will be stamped with the presence of God.[6]

A friend of mine told me about a conversation she recently had with a busy young woman. Had you questioned this businesswoman about whether she loved God, I'm sure she would have said yes. But when my friend asked her if she prayed, the young woman very flippantly replied, "Ask me if I have time!"

Friends, you'd *better* have time to get alone with God. Jesus took the time and—I'll say it again—if it's good enough for the Son of God, it's good enough for you and me. Jesus prayed because He wanted to spend time with the Father He loved.

But He also prayed because He believed that His Father would *actually answer*. He was firmly persuaded that "the effectual fervent prayer of a righteous man availeth much" (James 5:16 KJV). He came to God *expecting* results.

How many times do we come to God in prayer, and before our knees ever hit the carpet, we *already doubt* that God will answer us? Or worse, *expecting* the worst, we don't pray at all. Don't even ask. This is nothing more than a lack of faith in God, and whatever is not faith is *sin* (Rom. 14:23). But when we come to God in faith, as Jesus did, fully believing that we will receive what we are asking for, make no mistake: *it is worship*, because it shows the Almighty that we have confidence enough in Him, His love, and His *name* to ask Him for the things we need.

Jesus Worshipped Through Heartfelt Praise

"I praise you, Father, Lord of heaven and earth," Jesus exclaimed one day as He was preaching (Matt. 11:25 NCV). A later passage says that "Jesus rejoiced in the Spirit and said, 'I thank You, Father, Lord of heaven and earth'" (Luke 10:21 NKJV). No doubt, Jesus often burst into spontaneous expressions of gratitude and worship. This is poles apart from the "Praise the Lord!" that the self-righteous saint uses almost as a talisman. There's nothing wrong with saying, "Praise the Lord!" or "Hallelujah!" But when either becomes so mechanical that everyone you know can predict when it will come out of your mouth, is it worship? Or has it become a byword? Jesus didn't use bywords. Instead, He was *spontaneously* overcome with awe for God, and He worshipped. We need to follow His example.

Jesus Worshipped Through Song

And finally, Jesus worshipped with singing. We don't know what He sang, but as we noted earlier, it was his "custom" (Luke 4:15 KJV) to attend synagogue, and songs were part of traditional Jewish worship. Bass, baritone, or tenor, I don't know, but I do know that Jesus and His disciples "s[a]ng a hymn" after the meal we know today as the Last Supper (Matt. 28:30; Mark 14:26 NKJV). So the next time you stand grumpily in your pew, mouth clamped tight, because you think songs are silly, picture Jesus, the Son of God, with His mouth wide-open—singing songs of praise to God.

Jesus worshipped the Father in so many ways and in everything He did. He was the perfect example of *lifestyle worship*. But He didn't stop at teaching by example. Jesus had some very pointed things to say about worship both right and wrong.

WHAT DID JESUS TEACH ABOUT WORSHIP?

In the last chapter we witnessed God's disgust with His people during the prophetic age. They were participating in hypocritical worship—that is, efforts heavy on ritualism, but empty of ethics—and heart. Even as they were deeply engaged in all things ritual, both Israel and Judah were just as busy fostering social injustice. They were guilty of bigotry, duplicity, lechery, usury—even murder, no doubt in the "name of God." While filling God's house with animal sacrifices, they wouldn't share a crumb with a starving mother and her orphaned children. Instead, they'd exploit her, making her children slaves and taking the cloak right off her back. These pompous worshippers cared for no one, stepping over the dying in their streets and denying warmth to those shivering from cold. Oh, but they wouldn't *think* of failing to perform their *rites* of worship. Yet God, through the prophets, condemned this two-faced "worship" again and again. Jesus did too. In fact, He spent a great deal of time teaching what worship was *not*.

Worship That Stinks

In Matthew 25, as Jesus was revealing the future, He told His listeners of the day when He, the Son of Man, would judge them as King. "[I] will separate them into two groups," He said, "as a shepherd separates the sheep from the goats"—some for everlasting reward, on [My] right; some for eternal punishment, on [My] left (v. 32 NCV).

Sheep and goats . . . but what would determine the fate of each?

> The King will say to those on his left, "Go away from me. You will be punished. Go into the fire that burns forever . . . I was hungry, and you gave me nothing to eat. I was thirsty, and you gave me nothing to drink. I was alone and away from home, and you did not invite me into your house. I was without clothes, and you gave me nothing to wear. I was sick and in prison, and you did not care for me." Then those people will answer, "Lord, when did we see you hungry or thirsty or alone and away from home or without clothes or sick or in prison? When did we see these things and not help you?" Then the King will answer, ". . . Anything you refused to do for even the least of my people here, you refused to do for me." (vv. 41–45 NCV)

What was Jesus saying? The same thing His Father said through the prophets. To quote chapter 15, "*True* worship . . . embraces protection of the needy and marginalized." It's more than mere ritual. In fact, ritual alone doesn't cut it.

But the Jews loved their ritual. What's more, they loved to be seen "doing" their ritual. Jesus hated that too.

Jewish worship, you may recall, included various festivals, fasts, and offerings. But often, when they fasted or prayed or gave, some—the religious leaders, in particular—would go to great lengths to put their "worship" on display. Jesus called them "hypocrites." "They blow trumpets . . . so that people will see them and honor them. . . . They love to stand in the synagogues and on the street corners and pray so people will see them . . . They make their faces look sad to show people they are giving up eating" (Matt. 6:2, 5, 16 NCV). Jesus rebuked their exhibition, accusing them of making worship "a theatrical production. Do you think God sits in a box seat?" He asked (v. 5 MSG). He also condemned their somber disposition while fasting, warning, "Don't make a production out of it. It might turn you into a small-time celebrity but it won't make you a saint" (vv. 16–17 MSG). Instead, He told them, they should fast in private, and when they must face the public, they were to wash their faces and comb their hair, to avoid flaunting their worship (v. 18).

But the Jews of Jesus' day were big on flaunting. They were also big on rules. In fact, the religious leaders—the Pharisees, Sadducees, and Essenes—imposed *hundreds* of rules upon weary worshippers and were put out with Jesus because His disciples didn't comply with them. "Why don't your followers obey the unwritten laws which have been handed down to us?" they nagged (Matt. 15:2 NCV). "They do not [even] practice [ceremonially] washing their hands before they eat" (v. 2 AMP).

Jesus denounced their hypocrisy: "You [rejected] what God said for the sake of your own rules. You are hypocrites! Isaiah was right when he said about you: 'These people show honor to me with words, but their hearts are far from me. Their worship of me is worthless. The things they teach are nothing but human rules'" (Matt. 15:9 NCV).

Their worship of me is worthless . . . What an indictment. The Son of God incriminated the most "religious" people of their day for their duplicitous worship. In a later chapter, He said of these teachers: "They make strict rules and try to force people to obey them, but they are unwilling to help those who struggle under the weight of their rules" (23:4 NCV). All of these manmade laws were a heavy yoke to the sincere worshipper. No one could keep them. And it made Jesus mad. He intended that man's yoke be easy, his burden light (Matt 11:30 NKJV). Whirling upon these holier-than-thous,

He roared, "You are hypocrites! You close the door for people to enter the kingdom of heaven. You yourselves don't enter" (23:13 NCV).

Poor old Pharisees. They weren't doing *everything* wrong, were they? After all, weren't they at least worshipping God with their substance by faithfully giving the tithe? Indubitably. And yet, Jesus charged them with having double standards: "Hypocrites! You give to God one-tenth of every-thing you earn—even your mint, dill, and cumin. But you don't obey the really important teachings of the law—justice, mercy . . . These are the things you should do, as well as those other things" (v. 23 NCV). But instead of showing mercy to those in need and meting out justice to the oppressed, these charlatans "devour[ed] widows' houses" (v. 14; Luke 20:47 KJV), even as they "for a pretence made long prayers" (Mark 12:40 KJV). Jesus called these leaders "double-damned": "You go halfway around the world to make a convert," He said, "but once you get him you make him into a replica of yourselves" (Matt. 23:15 MSG). And Jesus was exactly right. They were grooming their devotees to be *just like them*: smug, self-satisfied people whose word meant nothing. "You're hopeless!" Jesus spat. "You say, 'If someone makes a promise with his fingers crossed, that's [OK]; but if he swears with his hand on the Bible, that's serious.' What ignorance! . . . What difference does it make if you make your promise inside or outside a house of worship? A promise is a promise. God is . . . watching and hold-ing you to account regardless (Matt. 23:16, 20–22 MSG).

Though *The Message*'s rendering of this passage represents a very broad interpretation of these verses, I think you get the message. And by now the breed of worship that God does *not* want should be crystal clear.

So what kind of worship *does* He want? We'll look at that in the next chapter.

| 17 |

WORSHIP IN THE GOSPELS, PART II

*All of Jesus' life was an expression of his worship to God his Father as he
served him in thought, word and deed, and ultimately as he set the captives
free from Satan's power through his sacrificial death.*

— NOEL DUE[1]

IN THE LAST CHAPTER, WE INTRODUCED GOD THE SON, YESHUA, whom we call *Jesus*. He—God Himself—came to earth, born from a maiden's womb, and lived in a human body.

Why did He come? Because creation from every age past had failed in their attempts to consistently please God. Because of man's undying compulsion to sin, our relationship with God was broken, and the gulf between Him and humanity was infinitely wide. Worse, no number of bleeding animals could close the gap. "For it is not possible," says Hebrews 10:4, "that the blood of bulls and goats could take away sins" (NKJV). Another sacrifice, a *final* sacrifice, would have to be offered. So God sent Jesus Christ to our world to restore our relationship with God.

God has always wanted a relationship with His people, and from the very beginning of this book, we established that the way to a relationship with God is through *worship*. But worship *how?* In the end, all of the old covenant attempts of man came to naught.

That's why Jesus came. True, He came to save us from our sin. We could never do that for ourselves. So Jesus Christ, the Lamb of God, came and died to atone for the bloodiness, the wretchedness, the vileness of the entire world. Then He was raised again, to life! But before any of that, He walked in human form upon the very planet that we do today, and taught us how to live *in relationship* with God—through worship.

As early as the New Testament's third chapter, we see so-called worshippers of God—*teachers* of worship, no less—being called "snakes" by John the Baptist (Matt. 3:7 NCV), because they were *just like* their ancestors, whom we read about in the Prophets. Steeped in tradition, they had their worship "form" down to a science. God's reaction? *Spare Me.* As far as He was concerned, they were hypocrites and sons of hell (Matt. 23:15 NKJV). He despised their "worship," and Jesus told them so. *This stinks!* He may as well have said, and in the last chapter, we examined together a whole class of worship that *does not* please God.

So what kind of worship *does* please Him? The kind Jesus offered. Rather than a stench in God's nostrils, Jesus' worship was a sweet perfume and a pure delight. But of what does such worship consist? Can *we* offer worship of this stripe? If so, how? What can *we* do to worship God to His *utter delight*?

In the introduction, I listed a variety of Greek and Hebrew words for *worship*, along with their various definitions. But then, if you recall, I boiled them all down to just *one* word. Do you remember what it is? It's *love*. Jesus truly, madly, and deeply *loved* His Father, and He taught us to, as well. When asked what was the greatest commandment, Jesus thrice responded that it was to love the Lord with all our hearts, souls, minds, and strength (Matt. 22:37, Mark 12:30, Luke 10:27). But then . . . He went out and did "good" (Acts 10:38 KJV).

Now, let's follow that thought to conclusion.

Worship Through Service

Why did Jesus go about "doing good"? Because it's an integral part of what He considered the greatest command: loving God with all of our hearts, souls, minds, and strength. The Bible makes it clear that if we can't love those made in God's image, then we don't love Him either (1 John 4:20). But if we do love God, then we will love others and will demonstrate that the same way Jesus did. How? *By serving.* Jesus said, "[I] did not come to be served, but to serve." And Jesus *served* by ministering to the sick, feeding the hungry, raising the dead, and, ultimately, by giving "His life a ransom for many" (Mark 10:45 NKJV).

If we are in love with God, we'll serve too, not to garner attention, as the Pharisees did, but because we *love* God and want to demonstrate it by serving Him *and* those made in His image.

Let's look again at the sheep-and-goats story from the last chapter. In this narrative, Jesus told His listeners that on the day of judgment, He would say to His sheep:

> "Come, you who are blessed by my Father; take your inheritance, the kingdom prepared for you . . . For I was hungry and you gave me something to eat, I was thirsty and you gave me something to drink, I was a stranger and you invited me in, I needed clothes and you clothed me, I was sick and you looked after me, I was in prison and you came to visit me." Then the righteous will answer him, "Lord, when did we see you hungry and feed you, or thirsty and give you something to drink? When did we see you a stranger and invite you in, or needing clothes and clothe you? When did we see you sick or in prison and go to visit you?"
>
> The King will reply, ". . . Whatever you did for one of the least of these brothers of mine, you did for me." (Matt. 25:34–40 NIV)

That is our first and best worship—*showing the Lord our sincere love by obeying Him* and mimicking Him on our planet: loving as He loved, serving as He served, and reaching out to a dying world as He reached out to those made in His likeness. That, friends, is worship. Detached from structure. Disconnected from procedure. Unaffected by time or place. In fact, when we engage in this type of worship, the *place* is not important.

In John 4, we read of a Samaritan woman, whom Jesus met at a well. Perceiving that Jesus was a prophet, she said to Him, "Tell me this: Our ancestors worshiped God at this mountain, but you Jews insist that Jerusalem is the only place for worship, right?"

Jesus responded, "The time is coming when you . . . will worship the Father neither here at this mountain nor there in Jerusalem. . . . The time is coming—it has, in fact, come—when . . . where you go to worship will not matter. It's who you are and the way you live that count before God. Your worship must engage your spirit . . . That's the kind of people the Father is out looking for. . . . Those who worship him must do it out of their very being, their spirits, their true selves, in adoration" (John 4:20–24 MSG).

We are to worship God in the spirit of God Himself, because His Spirit dwells *within* us and as worshippers of the Most High, we must allow His Spirit to work *through* us. This is anytime, anywhere worship that we offer from hearts that love, not only God, but all who look like Him. It is worship we can offer to God

- at the grocery store, as we help the woman who is carrying too many bags
- at the door of those poor kids who dress in the last millennium, as we give them good clothes—with the tags still on
- at our neighbors' home, the one with the empty cupboards, as we bring food because the father has lost his job
- at the table of that MS patient we know, whose eyes light up at the sight of the casserole we brought, because she hasn't had a home-cooked meal in ages
- on the roadside, as we pick up that rain-soaked homeless man and get him out of the bitter cold

This is worship heedless of walls and ceiling, of physical address, of stained glass and steeple. And it is worship that is fragrant to God, because when we feed those hungry bellies; when we transport that soggy soul to a warmer place—when we're *serving*—we are in essence, said Christ, doing these same deeds for God Himself.

Now, before you get too excited and think that your charitable service does away with the need for a specific, set-apart place of worship, remember *all* that we've studied. Jesus Himself, we learned in chapter 16, frequented the house of worship—regularly, not sporadically. We should too. He also had His own secret place, the mountain. Adam and Eve had a secret garden (chapter 2). Moses had the Tent of Meeting (chapter 6). And *we* need such a place, a place to get alone with God. So, worship is *public* observance in the house of God, and *private* adoration, when we are "shut in with God." But it is also those acts of service that we perform because Jesus did, and we love Him. If we really love Jesus, then we will want to "flatter" Him, not as the world does, to serve its own interests, but by being *exactly like Him*.

THE MAN WHO CHANGED WORSHIP FOREVER

Just like Amos, of whom we read in chapter 15, Christ was unappreciated. Amos was ordered to stop preaching, and, centuries later, wicked men would also want to stop the Son of God. They hated the Man who would change worship forever. Here He was, they thought, a mere mortal, yet unabashedly receiving worship. Wise men brought Him gold (Matt. 2:9–12). A leper bowed down to him (Matt. 8:2). Another man worshipped Him (John 9; guess it didn't matter to the Pharisees that Jesus had just opened the man's *blind eyes*!). A woman lavished expensive perfume on Him (Mark 14:3). And still another washed His feet with her tears, dried them with her own hair, and even *kissed* them (Luke 7:36–48)! Not to mention the ardent bunch who waved palm branches in front of Him as He rode on a donkey into the city! (John 12:12–14)

And the Pharisees? They wanted His head.

The religious rulers didn't buy that He was the Son of God. Neither did they believe He was qualified to forgive them. What's to forgive? *They* weren't sinful.

Oh yes, they were. Full of sin and in need of a sacrifice for it. Christ came to be that sacrifice, and after His death, they would never have to slice the flesh of an ox or lamb again to atone for their sins, if they would just believe in Him.

But they didn't understand that. They knew just one thing: *They would not worship this Man!*

And so the murder plot began in their hearts. But what they didn't know was that the plot was hatched in another heart before they were ever born.

EUCHARIST—A LITURGY OF LOVE

Just before Jesus' death on the cross, He made arrangements to celebrate Passover with His disciples. He met with them in an upstairs room in the house where they had prepared the meal. "I wanted very much to eat this Passover meal with you," He told them. "I will not eat another Passover meal until it is given its true meaning in the kingdom of God" (Luke 21:15–16 NCV).

This particular Passover would be the most significant that had ever been, because it was at this feast—traditionally known as the Last Supper—that Jesus presented Himself as our *Passover Lamb*.

Seated at the table, Jesus suddenly announced, "I'm going to die . . . and one of *you* will betray Me." The disciples were, naturally, horrified—all except Judas, of course. But Jesus remained calm. He had a job to do. Before dying, He would initiate a liturgy of love—Communion—to forever remind us of God's unfathomable love *for us*.

But first, Jesus would do something else that would impart a living model for Communion-taking Christians in all ages. He would *cleanse* those He loved.

Sacrifices in the Old Testament were always preceded by a time of sanctifying, or purifying. So Jesus, knowing He was about to be sacrificed for all of mankind, required that the disciples' feet be washed as a symbol of *their* purification.

Jesus stood up and took off his outer clothing. Taking a towel, he wrapped it around his waist. Then he poured water into a bowl and began to wash the followers' feet, drying them with the towel that was wrapped around him.

Jesus came to Simon Peter, who said to him, "Lord, are you going to wash my feet?" Jesus answered, "You don't understand now what I am doing, but you will understand later."

Peter said, "No, you will never wash my feet."

Jesus answered, "If I don't wash your feet, you are not one of my people."

This statement of Christ was momentous, because it foretold of the time when any who chose not to be cleansed by faith in Jesus, would not *be* cleansed, period. Peter must have recognized this, because He hastily blurted out, "Lord, then wash not only my feet, but . . . my hands and . . . head, too!" (John 13:4–8 NCV).

Jesus didn't wash Peter's hands and head, but He did wash his feet. And this emblematic cleansing, offered personally by the Messiah, confirmed His role as the only One who could ever cleanse man again. It also signified the need for a clean heart when participating in the act of worship that Jesus would model next:

> While they were eating, Jesus took some bread and thanked God for it and broke it. Then he gave it to his followers and said, "Take this bread and eat it; this is my body." Then Jesus took a cup and thanked God for it and gave it to his followers. He said, "Every one of you drink this. This is my blood which is the new agreement that God makes with his people. This blood is poured out for many to forgive their sins."

Jesus knew that His body was about to be broken, His blood poured out. But He also knew that His offering would become an *official document* establishing the peace between man and God.[2] So He used red wine to symbolize the shedding of His blood that was necessary to restore man's communion with God. His blood would pay for the sins of all humanity. Never again would it be necessary to slaughter lambs, goats, turtledoves, and bulls for atonement. *One* sacrifice would atone for *all* sins, for all time, and usher in a *new covenant.*

The disciples didn't get it. Not yet. They would, later. For now, though, they were just "very sad" (Matt. 26:22 NCV). But as they ate their last meal with Jesus, He said to them, "Do this in remembrance of Me (Luke 22:19 NKJV).

Today, the Church still observes this Last Supper, in remembrance of Christ's death. We call it Holy Communion, though it goes by other names, as well: the Eucharist, the Body and Blood of Christ, the Sacrament of Communion, the Lord's Supper. But no matter how your fellowship refers to it, Communion is an ordinance of the Church, commanded by our Lord Jesus Christ, and we are to partake of it often to remember our Savior. Paul wrote in 1 Corinthians, "Whenever you eat this bread and drink this cup, you proclaim the Lord's death until he comes" (11:26 NIV). Paul was right, of course. We do proclaim and remember His death. But when we take Communion, we also proclaim so much more. See, many men were crucified. In fact, two others would die alongside Jesus. But only

His death would redeem us, snatch us from the claws of Satan, and reconcile us to God. So today, when we partake of the *elements*, or *emblems*, the bread and the wine (or grape juice), we are proclaiming to the world Christ's work of *redemption*.

The Upper Room experience became a defining moment, the turning point, in what we *do* in our worship as Christians today. In the words of Allen Ross, "Jesus . . . transformed worship for all time by giving believers something greater to remember in their worship—His body and his blood that was poured out for the sins of the world. Jesus the Messiah of Israel was fulfilling the Scriptures. . . . Now, true spiritual worship would be in Christ."[3]

Jesus concluded the meal by singing a hymn with His disciples. Since this was consistent with the normal practice of Passover, it was natural for the disciples to end the meal with spontaneous praise and worship.[4]

After the Passover meal, Jesus continued to dialogue with His disciples (John 14–16), and He made them a promise: He would send a comforter to them, in the person of the Holy Spirit: "When I go away, I will send the Helper" (John 16:7 NCV). This Helper would dwell in them, empower them, and bring to their remembrance the teachings of Christ. He would also be part and parcel of worship to come.

Finally, Jesus prayed for His friends. And then they left to go—together—to fateful Gethsemane. Then Jesus—alone—would go to the cross.

THE CROSS AND THE RESURRECTION

While Jesus was praying in the Garden of Gethsemane, Judas, soldiers, and guards of the religious leaders came for Him. For those who love Christ, this is the most painful of stories to read. Jesus' own *friend*, one with whom He had shared His bread (Ps. 41:9), had betrayed Him into the hands of His killers. In loving obedience to His Father, Jesus allowed them to take Him prisoner. Without resistance, He submitted Himself to the cruelty of sinful men. And as excruciating as this story is for us who love Him, His arrest/execution was not a crisis, but the climax of the ages. Jesus had come to give abundant life (John 10:10), and now He would take the step that would ensure it by providing clemency for you and me, freeing us from sin's slavery and restoring us to God.

We come now to the pinnacle of our study about Jesus and worship. *Jesus established a new covenant* by submitting Himself to death on a cross. He fully endured all of the same agony and humiliation rightly reserved for the worst criminal. He was shamed before the Sanhedrin and slapped in the face. He was pierced with thorns, then beaten mercilessly and beyond recognition. He was forced to carry His heavy cross, then hung publicly, between two thieves, and left to die of asphyxiation. He was scoffed by those who stood below Him and disgraced as they gambled for His clothing. Jesus Christ had done no wrong, yet He was crushed, broken, and punished. *We* were the guilty, the sinful, the ones to blame. Yet God would allow Christ to pay our penalty, taking on all of our sins and all of our afflictions.

"It is finished!"

Jesus breathed His last breath. And the sin that had enslaved us since the garden of Eden was finally justified on Golgotha.

You've read what happened next. A spear was thrust into Christ's side. The sky darkened. The earth quaked. The veil in the temple tore in two. And the dead rose from their graves. But that's not all. There's more to this story . . .

A NEW REASON FOR WORSHIP: THE RESURRECTION

Christians love Easter. And whether or not they quibble over the origin of the holy day's name, it is the day of the year when we celebrate the very heart of Christianity—the Resurrection of Christ. You know how the events transpired.

Three days after His crucifixion, Mary Magdalene and another woman went to Jesus' tomb. Suddenly the earth shook, and an angel appeared. "Don't be afraid," he told the terrified women, "You came looking for Jesus . . . but He is not here. He has risen from the dead, just like He said He would" (my translation).

The women quickly ran to tell His disciples. But then, unexpectedly, they met Jesus Himself. "Greetings," He said to them, and they responded by falling at His feet and worshipping. Later, the Eleven saw Him too—JESUS, whom they so loved!

But, this was not the man they knew. This was the *resurrected Christ*, who had paid for their sins—your sins—and mine. And they worshipped Him (Matt. 28:17). In fact, *everyone* who encountered Christ between His resurrection and His ascension responded with worship—all 515 of them![5]

In 1 Corinthians 15, Paul wrote, "If Christ has not been raised, our preaching is useless and so is your faith" (v. 14 NIV). The resurrection of Christ is critical to our understanding of worship. It gives us a reason for worship that no other religion can embrace. Jesus died—and so did all of the other prophets and "holy men"—but only Jesus *rose from the grave*. And He is alive—really alive—today!

The Temple veil ripped in two when Jesus died. The tearing symbolized for all eternity the complete destruction of the barrier between God and man. No longer was the priest the only one permitted to come before God. Jesus' death made possible—for *all*—that which was impossible for Old Testament worshippers—*direct access to God*. This is the paradox of the ages: *even* those so full of hate and envy that they crucified the Son of God now had access to God and, through their victim, could have eternal relationship with God—if they wanted to. Today, Christ's empty tomb stands as a monument to His conclusive victory over Satan and His derailed plan to end God's redemptive plan. We are redeemed, and nothing stands in our way anymore. Jesus is risen, and He—not a human priest—is our own, personal worship leader. Best of all, with His resurrection, He blazed a trail for us to go right to the throne of God—in worship.

ARE *YOU* ON THE TRAIL?

Since this book's opening pages, I have written with the assumption that all of my readers know Christ.

But do *you*? If you do not, then you are not sharing in the hope that Christ's resurrection brings. I want to help you. Do you want to receive Christ? Do you long to become a worshipper of God and to walk in relationship with Him? The way is simple.

First, *recognize that you are a sinner.* Romans 3:23 says that we *all* are, and it is because of our sin that people from every generation suffer death. "But wait," you may be saying, "*I* didn't eat the forbidden fruit. *I* didn't betray

Christ. *I* didn't nail Him to that cross. And *I* am a good person." Good? The Bible says that even our best "righteousnesses" are like "filthy rags" because we are all "unclean" (Isa. 64:6 NKJV). See, through one man, Adam, "sin entered the world, and death through sin, and thus death spread to all men, because all sinned" (Rom. 5:12 NKJV). We are born with a sin nature, a natural proclivity to sin. Yet even though all humans past were sinners—and we along with them—God loved us so much that He sent His Son to die in our place, paying *our* penalty for *our* sin so that we could become worshippers. And Jesus died willingly, before you and I ever accepted Him, because of that same love (vv. 8–9). We are saved from God's wrath—if we will only take the next two steps.

Second, *repent of your sins*. Recognize the wrong you have done. Feel the regret for it. Then change your ways and live for God instead of for yourself. This is what repentance is. It's not just telling God that you are sorry. Oh, *do* that, please. But beyond saying, "I'm sorry," *turn away* from your sin, and do your best to never return to it. If you slip—and you will, from time to time—what do you do? Apologize again, and redirect—turn your back on that sin. Your apology is accepted.

Third, *receive Christ as your savior*. The Bible says that if we proclaim with our lips that Jesus is our Lord and believe in our hearts that God raised him from the dead, we will be saved. We are justified, that is, "just-as-if-we'd-never-sinned." In other words, we are declared *not guilty*; our debt is canceled. So believe. Believe that He is the Son of God, the one sent to repair the breach between God and humankind. Believe that He died. Believe that He rose again. And believe that, through His blood, your sins are forgiven. Then make your belief known to everyone around you—*He is my Lord!*—and *receive* Him.

Recognize, repent, receive. If you have done this, then you have become a *worshipper* of God, and the relationship you were created to enjoy with God—a relationship that will never disappoint—has begun.

PRINCIPLES OF WORSHIP FROM THE GOSPELS

My fellow worshipper, because of the selfless act of Jesus on an old, rugged cross, we can have a bountiful relationship with the God of the Ages and, in the words of the Westminster catechism, "enjoy him forever." This *is* the story of worship, and in this chapter, I have done my best to convey it. But hopefully, you have learned some other lessons, as well, from our study of worship in the Gospels. If you've forgotten because you got carried away with passion over the resurrection of Christ, described in the past few pages, let me refresh your memory:

1. *We need to worship in the house of God.* Jesus did. Anyone who refuses implies that he or she is better than the sinless, flawless Son of God.

2. *We also need to "move toward the mountaintop."* We've studied this already, in chapters 2 and 6. Like Jesus on His mountain, we, too, need to get away to a place unoccupied by voices and faces that would keep our minds off of God. Jesus was refreshed by His "alone time" with the Father. We will be too.

3. *Worship equals submission.* "We should do all things that are God's will," said Christ (Matt. 3:15 NCV). I won't belabor the point. We've already studied this thoroughly in chapters 4 and 8. If you are not willing to surrender to the will of God—in other words, *obey* Him—then you are not a worshipper.

4. *Worship involves service.* If we really love Jesus and seek to worship Him, we will *flatter* Him—not with words alone (and certainly not with insincere ones, as the Pharisees used), but by imitating Him. Like Jesus' love for the Father, our love and worship should energize us to care for the sick, reach out to the helpless among us, and defend the indefensible. That's what Jesus did, and if you want to *really* win His heart with worship, try acting *just like Him.* Nurture your worship in private, as He did on the mountain, but then *live* your worship in public, by serving.

5. *Worship first, then prayer.* God is not a vending machine, and we are not paying "customers." It is absolute effrontery to barge into the presence of God—long "wish list" in hand—and start yammering about the things we *want* before ever giving thanks that He is there in the first place. The apostle Paul wrote that we are to "with *thanksgiving* let [our] requests be made known unto God" (Phil. 4:6 NKJV, emphasis added), but Jesus knew that way before Paul did. So before we ever begin cranking out those prayer requests, like quarters popped into a candy machine, we should take the

time to praise God, worship Him, and exalt His name, as Jesus did when He cried, "Hallowed by Thy Name."

6. *The prayer of faith is worship.* Can asking for things from God be considered worship? You'd better believe it! In its own way, making requests of God is an act of worship—*when we believe.* If we go before Him doubting, feeling doomed before the prayer even leaves our lips, then we may as well not pray at all. The brother of Christ taught us this. "For he that wavereth," wrote James, "is like a wave of the sea driven with the wind and tossed . . . Let not that man think that he shall receive any thing of the Lord" (1:6–7 KJV). But when we "ask in faith, nothing wavering," we honor God by showing our confidence in Him, His promises, and His love.

7. *Hypocrisy stinks!* Insincerity and pretense—no matter how small—devastates the import of genuine worship. It is hypocrisy of the highest order and cannot be tolerated. If you catch yourself, even for a moment, seeking to put your "worship" on display, stop it! Instead, let your worship be unpretentious. Pray with all your might, sure. Sing clear and strong, by all means. Praise loudly and unabashedly, if that's your style. And do every "charitable deed" you can (Matt. 6:1 NKJV). But make sure when you do that it is never to be seen by men but instead to be enjoyed by God. And finally . . .

8. *Worship changed forever when the veil was torn.* Oh, this is lovely! We have now what no Old Testament worshipper ever had, thanks to Jesus. We can approach God without a lamb. Jesus was the Lamb. We never have to shed blood again. Jesus' own blood paid for our sins and sicknesses. We need not pour out drink and grain offerings anymore. Jesus Himself was the Bread and the Wine. And our worship is forevermore unencumbered by the law. Jesus was the fulfillment of the law, and because of Him, the rift between God and mankind is no more. *Thank You, Jesus!*

How did that affect worship postresurrection? What did it mean to the followers of Christ? And how did it change the way things were done?

You'll see . . . in "Worship in the Early Church."

| 18 |

WORSHIP IN THE EARLY CHURCH

SLOWLY, BUT CONFIDENTLY, SHE WALKED TO THE MICROPHONE. No one could have believed, even weeks before, that she would ever stand in front of a crowd again. In fact, just two years ago, doctors had told this fifteen-year-old beauty queen's parents that their daughter would never even walk again. She would never sing in her high school choir, or even think clearly—ever again. They were unsure she would even live through the night.

Annie's* mom, dad, and brother were together in the car that fateful evening—laughing and enjoying each other's company—when a truck in an oncoming lane crossed the median and hit their vehicle head-on. Drunk driver. Everyone in the car was critically injured, but Annie had the most head trauma. For weeks she lay in the hospital—hanging by a thread between life and death.

Tonight, though, she looked incredible, once-thin hair now grown back and neatly styled.

Speech, previously slurred, returned to normal.

Eyes beaming. Huge smile. Beautiful glow.

Doctors had said she would never—*could* never—be normal again. But here she was, mic in hand and ready to give her testimony.

We watched in silence. The anticipation was palpable, the atmosphere in the building intense.

"Good evening," she began. "I'm here tonight to give you my testimony . . ."

---

* Not her real name

Testimony . . .

Testimony is from a fourteenth-century Anglo-French word, from the Latin *testimonium,* meaning "evidence," or "witness." It is a firsthand authentication of an event, an open acknowledgment of what one has experienced, seen, heard, felt, enjoyed, or endured.

Everyone, good or bad, has a testimony, but yours is unique to *you.* No one can give you your testimony, and no one can take it away. And for believers, like Annie, a testimony is a public profession of faith, and a most powerful means of communication.

For years, the Billy Graham Association's huge crusades included the stirring testimonies of well-known celebrities. I remember, as a child, hearing Johnny Cash give his testimony at a crusade in Nashville. He told of how God delivered him from alcohol and drugs, and changed his life. It was a wonderfully moving story of God's grace, and I was moved to worship as he shared his testimony.

A friend of mine has developed an evangelism method called "Love Your Neighbor, Tell Your Story" (LYNTYS).[1] The idea behind it is to love others by taking *every opportunity* to share what God has personally done in our own lives. It is most effective, for it is when we tell our personal stories, our *testimonies,* of how God transformed us, healed us, and delivered us from sin—that we transcend human reason to a sphere of personal relationship with God that skeptics cannot deny. They may contest the authority of the Bible or dispute the existence of God, but no one can deny a personal experience. And it creates believers.

"Oh, give thanks to the Lord! Call upon His name; make known His deeds among the peoples!" (1 Chron. 16:8). This is the meaning of testimony. And whether written or spoken aloud, when we share our testimonies and proclaim the marvels of God, we give evidence of God's goodness to a heathen planet.

Sing to the LORD and praise his name; every day tell how he saves us. Tell the nations of his glory; tell all peoples the miracles he does, because the LORD is great; he should be praised at all times.

—PSALM 96:2–4 NCV

The Worship of Testimony

When I was a kid, my father, who was a pastor, would often set aside time in our Sunday evening services for testimonies. Influenced by the Youth for Christ movement of the late 1940s and 1950s, he followed their model of asking members of the congregation to tell what the Lord had done in their lives, in other words, to give a *testimony*. I remember seeing former stripteasers stand and testify to the saving grace of Jesus; alcoholics explain how God had rescued them from addiction; a young mother tell how the Lord healed her of sickness; and soldiers tell how God had protected them in war. Sometimes I watched teenagers and college-age students stand to confess Jesus as Lord and then commit themselves to full-time ministry. And once, I even saw an Asian family come to the altar, carrying a box full of idols they had been keeping in their home. They wanted to make a public statement that they were giving up their false gods forever so they could instead worship Jesus Christ, the living Lord.

Sometimes, testimonies such as these were planned ahead of time and presented with the sermon. But most often, folks testified spontaneously. I recall a few occasions, usually during a revival, when a testimony service would develop into more than just one or two persons relating personal experiences. People would begin confessing sin, and soon the power of God would sweep across the sanctuary, and the spirit of revival would move through the congregation. Giving preference to the working of the Holy Spirit, my dad would decide not to preach.

These kinds of services are rare today. But for early Christians, sharing what God had done was not at all unusual. In fact, the book of Acts, for example, is not only a secondhand history, but a series of testimonies—eyewitness accounts—of what God was doing in the early church, and how it affected worship.

Consider these examples of testimony in Acts (emphasis added):

- "So Peter *explained the whole story to them* . . . The believers heard . . . [and] praised God.'" (11:4 NCV)
- "When they arrived in Antioch, Paul and Barnabas gathered the church together. They *told the church all about what God had done with them*." (14:27 NCV)

- "Paul . . . *told them everything God had done* among the other nations through him. When they heard this, they praised God. Then they said . . . 'Many thousands of our people have become believers.'" (21:19–20 NCV)

I wish I could have been a "fly on the wall" during one of these testimony times. What would it have been like to hear firsthand about the coming of the Holy Spirit, when three thousand people became worshippers of Christ in one day (Acts 2)? Or the healing of a man who had never walked (Acts 3:1–10)? Peter being freed from prison chains by an angel (Acts 12:6–17)? Or the conversion of a Christian-killer (Acts 9:1–19)?

You are about to hear the testimonies of the very Christians who experienced these events, told to the best of my ability from their points of view. Their stories will speak to the heart of what we believe about our triune God. You'll also see how God reveals Himself through the person and work of the Holy Spirit and understand the freedom He brings to worship God in all His fullness.

Now, let's listen together as John, the disciple who knew Christ best, begins our testimony service and tells us how it all began:

Testimony #1—John the Beloved

Thank you for the opportunity to share my story. My name is John. Jesus called me His beloved, and I love Him too. He is the only begotten Son of God, and I worship Him. I'm here today to give testimony of the mighty things He has done.

The other disciples and I began meeting regularly almost immediately after Jesus was crucified. He had told us to do this, to celebrate the new covenant provided by His blood—that is, to share the bread and cup. So now, we join together on Sundays to remember His death on the cross and to celebrate His Resurrection. We also come together on the Sabbath.

We believers [pointing at the group seated around him] meet daily in the temple and in each other's homes. When we come together, we break bread, worship, pray for the sick and for one another, and just enjoy fellowship. We also preach and sing praises—in the streets, in caves, on hillsides—and in jail. We are very busy teaching others about Jesus, telling our own stories of salvation, healing the sick, assisting widows, and feeding the poor. Because of our work, there is a great respect for God these days. Thousands have become worshippers of Christ as we share testimonies, perform miracles, and offer our unsaved friends an alternative to idolatry and the other false teachings that are so much a part of this culture. [Acts 2:41–47]

WHY DO MOST CHRISTIANS WORSHIP ON SUNDAY?

"Even though believers continued to meet on Sabbath day and on festival days, they also came together on the first day of the week to break bread together (Acts 20:7). This was inspired by the resurrection and especially the appearance of Jesus at Emmaus in the breaking of the bread. Paul also instructed the Corinthians to lay aside their offerings on the first day of the week (I Cor. 16:2). Now that the new covenant had begun, the Jewish Sabbath had lost its symbolic importance as part of the old covenant, for it was fulfilled in Christ (Col. 2:16, Heb. 4:3–13). Christians no longer were compelled to give merely one day a week to the Lord . . . However, the church found it profitable to have a day for the Christian community to assemble. So as time progressed Sunday, the resurrection day, became devoted to the service of the Lord."[2]

Today, I stand before you and say, God is doing wonderful things among us. He is moving in a very public way. But He is also doing something very personal.

Let me explain by quickly sharing my own experience. I was with Jesus every day as His disciple. I saw Him heal the sick and even raise the dead. But a couple of very specific encounters with Jesus changed me forever.

First, I was never the same after I saw the *resurrected* Christ. I even wrote about it in my book. [John 20–21] See, after Jesus was buried, our friend Mary went to the tomb. She was so sad. We all were. But when she got to the tomb, the stone had been rolled away, and Jesus' body was gone. So right away, Mary ran and told us disciples about it, and Peter and I took off for the tomb.

I run faster than Peter, so I got there first. I bent down and looked into the tomb, and I saw strips of cloth, but no body. I couldn't go in. I just couldn't. But Peter did. He saw the cloth, too, the very one that had been wrapped around Jesus' head. It was folded up, real neat, and was just lying there. Finally, I had to go in too.

Jesus wasn't there.

We were so confused. But what could we do? We went home, but Mary stayed at the tomb. And guess who she saw? Yes, *Jesus!* And here she came—again. "I've seen Jesus! I've seen Jesus!" she hollered. "He's *alive!*"

"Slow down, Mary!" we told her. "Tell us what happened."

"I was standing outside the tomb, bawling," she told us, panting, "and someone spoke to me. 'Why are you crying?' He asked me. "And I said, 'Because someone has taken my Lord.' Then, He spoke my name, and when I turned and looked, it was *Jeeeeeesus!*"

That night, we all got together, and we locked the doors. We were scared that the Pharisees were going to come after us, like they had Jesus.

But then, all of the sudden, *He* was there. Right there! And He showed us His hands, where the nails were, and His side, where that soldier had stuck His spear. It was *really* Jesus!

For forty days, He visited with us. We saw Him several times—Peter, you'll have to tell them about when we saw him at the lake [Peter nods]—and He told us He was going to send us a Helper, the "Spirit of truth," He said. [John 16:7–15 NCV] But the one time none of us will ever forget was when Jesus asked us to meet Him on the mountain. In fact, our fellow minister, Matthew, wrote about it in a book. [28:16–20]

That day, when He came into view on that mountainside, I fell down on my face and worshipped Him. I couldn't help it! There He stood, the

Savior of the world—my *own* Redeemer, who took away my guilt and shame. I was embarrassed because we had all abandoned Him during His time of need. But he forgot all of that.

Anyway, all eleven of us were there—Judas had already committed suicide—but it felt like it was just Jesus and me standing there, all alone. Jesus talked with us about the things to come and spent some time telling us what He wanted us to do. "When the Holy Spirit comes to you," He said, "you will receive power. You will be my witnesses—in Jerusalem, in all of Judea, in Samaria, and in every part of the world." [Acts 1:8 NCV]

Then, all of a sudden, He left us. That's right. Jesus finished talking, and then He was lifted up—in the air, into the clouds—and He was gone.

So there we were, eleven of us, gaping at the sky, when suddenly, two men in white robes appeared. "Why are you standing here, looking so lost?" they asked us. "He'll be back, and He'll come the same way He left." [vv. 9–11, author rendering]

Well, you can imagine how that impacted us. But that wasn't the end.

On the day of Pentecost, we all got together again for prayer and worship. Suddenly, a noisy, blustering wind came from heaven and filled the house. Then something that looked like little flames came and hovered over each of us. And we were filled with the Holy Spirit, the Helper that Jesus said would come. Can you believe that? The Spirit of God Himself came into our hearts. Then we began to speak in other languages.

Since it was Pentecost, people from all over the world were staying in Jerusalem. When they heard all the noise, a crowd gathered. And were they surprised! They heard us speaking in *their* languages.

"Hey!" they said. "You're all from Galilee. How come you're speaking *our* languages?" They were from Parthia, Media, Elam, Mesopotamia—all over, yet we were telling them, in their own tongues, all about God. [Acts 2:2–12]

Peter stood up, then, in front of that crowd and explained the scripture that prophesied of this very day. "Joel the prophet wrote," he told them, "that in the last days, God would pour out His Spirit on all people. Boys and girls will prophesy. Young men will see visions. Old men will dream prophetic dreams. The Lord will show miracles on the earth and in the heavens. And anyone who calls on Him will be saved. *That's* what all of this is about!" [Acts 2:14–21, from Joel 2:28–32]

Then Peter starting talking about Jesus. "You saw the miracles He performed," he told the crowd. "You witnessed His signs and wonders. You should have known who He was. But *you* put Him to death! You nailed Him to the cross!"

But Peter wasn't through with them. "But God raised Jesus from the dead," he told them, "and *we* are witnesses to it. We *saw* Jesus ascend into heaven, and today His Father poured out the Holy Spirit—on us—just as Joel said."

You should have seen the looks on those folks' faces. "What are we going to *do*?" they cried.

"Repent!" Peter told them. "And let us baptize you in the name of Jesus Christ! Then your sins will be forgiven, and you'll receive the Holy Spirit too!" Peter, I was awfully proud of you that day. [Peter grins, turns red]

Well, about three thousand people from that crowd believed Peter, and they were baptized. And every day since, our fellowship grew.

Our worship has never been the same. We still assemble in buildings, but now, our worship begins in our hearts. The Spirit of God lives in our physical bodies, and He constantly draws our attention back to Christ our King. He also gives us power to do the same things Jesus did on the earth, like miracles. Oh, and that reminds me . . .

One day Peter and I went to the temple at about three in the afternoon. When we reached the gate, this beggar was sitting there. He was about forty, and had been crippled all of his life. Well, when he saw Peter here, he asked for some money. Now, you know Peter. He looked him right in the eye and said, "I don't have any money—but I've got something else. By the power of Jesus Christ of Nazareth, get up! Walk!" Then Peter grabbed his hand and lifted him right off the ground—and *that man walked*! People, I was there. I saw it with my own eyes. So right away, that man started jumping around, praising God, and everyone watching knew he was that crippled man who always begged at the gate. Now here he was, on his feet, carrying on about how God had healed him, and everyone was amazed! So, Peter and I, we just praised God right along with him! [Acts 3:1–10; 4:21–22] It was incredible. Plus, we got the opportunity to tell a *whole bunch of people* all about Jesus.

But, you know, not everyone was happy. The Sadducees were really upset, and the oldsters grabbed us and threw us in jail overnight. But—get this—

many who had heard us preaching the day before became believers. Now we Christ-followers number about five thousand.

The next day, we had to stand before Annas, the high priest, and his bunch. "By what power did you heal that lame man?" they asked us.

You would have been amazed by Peter. "I'll tell you who!" he says. *"Jesus Christ,* from Nazareth. *You* killed him, but *God* raised him from the dead. Remember Psalms? 'The stone that you builders rejected has become the cornerstone'? [118:22] Jesus is the only one who can save this world—and He is the only one who can save *you."* [Acts 4]

I have never seen Peter speak with such conviction. He's never had any seminary training, but his boldness left our enemies speechless! On the other hand, the folks who witnessed all of this were praising God out loud! The leaders couldn't do a thing to us. They had to let us go. So we went and met with the other believers, a large group.

All at once, the building shook, and *everyone* was filled with the Holy Spirit. And we were fearless from then on. [Acts 4]

Peter, why don't you tell your story now?

"The Spirit in Acts is the witness to the fact that Jesus lives ... Spirit-inspired preaching about Jesus is the way in which his power and authority are made known and people are enabled to respond to the great saving events of his death, resurrection and ascension. Preaching about Christ must be at the heart of a Christian theology of worship. As in the Old Testament, the word of the Lord is central to a genuine encounter with God. Those who are concerned about God-honoring worship will be concerned about the proclamation of the gospel, in the world and in the church, in public teaching and private dialogue. If worship is an engagement with God on the terms that he proposes . . . , preaching Christ is a key to that engagement. Acts points to the proclamation of the heavenly rule of Christ . . . as the means chosen by God to draw people into relationship with himself, through Christ, in the power of the Holy Spirit."[3]

Testimony #2—Peter

Well, my testimony is very similar. As John mentioned, we saw Jesus several times after He was raised from the dead. One of those times, all of us disciples were together, but I was real agitated. "I'm going fishing," I said. I wanted to be alone, but the boys didn't get that. They all came with me, and we fished all night.

Real early the next morning, we saw someone standing on the shore, but it was so far away, we couldn't tell who it was. The man yelled at us. "Catch anything?" he said. "No," we yelled back. We hadn't caught a thing.

"Why don't you throw your nets on the other side of the boat?" So we did—and hit the mother lode! There were so many fish in that net, we couldn't pull it back into the boat.

About that time, I recognized who it was on the beach: *Jesus!* So I jumped out of the boat and swam ashore. I'm ashamed to say I left the guys holding the bag. They had to drag the net toward shore without me. But I did go back to the boat when they got close and pulled them on in.

Anyway, Jesus had a fire going, and he'd cooked some fish. He had some bread too, and we all ate together. He asked me if I loved Him. "You know I do," I told Him. Then He told me to feed His sheep. And that's what I've been trying to do ever since. [John 21]

Now John and I preach every chance we get. We tell everyone we see about Jesus and what He's done for us, and what we've seen Him do for others. And every sick person we pray for gets healed by the power of Jesus Christ. Oh, we get in trouble for it, like John said. The Sadducees got jealous once and threw us in jail. But in the middle of the night, an angel came and got us out. He told us to go right back to the temple and preach some more. The next day, when the high priest sent soldiers to get us, of *course* they didn't find us. I wish I could have seen them trying to explain *that*: "But, sir, the cell doors were locked, and we had guards standing outside!" [Peter snickers] Then someone says, "Hey! Those guys are in the temple again!"

They came after us, and again we got a chance to preach Jesus to those misguided leaders. *And* we got a beating for it. But when they let us go, we left rejoicing. We didn't suffer a fraction of what our Lord did. We were honored to be able to suffer for His cause.

The leaders warned us to stop teaching about Jesus, but we didn't listen.

Every day we showed up at the temple or at somebody's house, to tell the good news, and the network of worshippers just kept on growing. [Acts 5:12–6:1] Paul, you're up.

Testimony # 3—The Apostle Paul (Acts 26)

My name's Paul. Some of you have known me for a long time. Many of you know I was once a good Pharisee. I obeyed their traditions more carefully than any other religious sect. And I *worshipped* the law. I certainly didn't believe in Jesus. Oh, I knew He was a man that Rome had executed, but I did *not* accept that believing on Him would bring eternal life. In fact, the doctrine was appalling to me. Dangerous, even. So when believers were being executed, I was wholeheartedly in favor. In fact, I decided to help.

The foremost priests gave me the power to harass and imprison the Christians. In every Jerusalem synagogue, I punished them and tried to force them to speak against Jesus. Then I started searching in other cities, too, to find and chastise those who called themselves Christians.

One day, on the way to Damascus—it was about noon—a blinding light flashed suddenly from heaven. It was brighter than the sun, and my companions and I fell to the ground. Then a booming voice spoke to me. "Saul!" it thundered. "Why are you persecuting Me? You think you can fight *Me*? You're only hurting yourself."

"Who *are* you?" I asked. (My knees were knocking by this time, because I couldn't see a thing.)

"I am Jesus!" the voice answered. "The one you dare to persecute. Get up! From now one, you will serve *Me*. I'll show you many things, and you will tell others all that you've seen and heard. You will open their eyes, and they will turn from Satan to the light of God. I will forgive their sins, and they will be part of my kingdom of believers."

Then He was gone—and I was totally blind. But soon, God healed my eyes, and from that moment on I obeyed the voice of Christ—He *is* the Christ, you know—and began telling people to repent, turn to God, and live like they believe He's watching. I told everyone I saw, in Damascus, in Jerusalem, *everywhere*. The Jews didn't like it, so they tried to kill me— right in the temple. But God protected me every time, so here I am.

It has been my joy, ever since that day on the road, to serve Christ. I have been thrown in jail, beaten and left for dead, bitten by poisonous snakes, and forced to stand trial for preaching that Jesus is the Son of God. But it has been worth every moment. The Lord has given me a productive ministry and good friends like Barnabas and Luke—you, too, Peter—to stand beside me on this journey.

What's best to me—and I don't understand it to this day—is that *I* have been forgiven. Me! Paul the Christian-killer. Jesus Christ forgave me of self-righteousness—and murder—and taught me how to worship Him, free of the law and the empty Pharisaical formulas. I don't need the high priest to reach God. Jesus is my high priest now, and because of Him, I can go straight to God and communicate with Him, friend to friend.

But here's the best part for you. At one time, salvation was only for us—the Jews—and not all of you are. But now salvation is available to *all* nations. [28:28] Now, that's something to worship about!

Testimony #4—Silas

My name is Silas. I travel with Paul on his mission trips.

Once, when we were in Philippi, we were on our way to a prayer meeting, and we ran into this demon-possessed slave girl. She was a fortune-teller, and she made a lot of money for her master. This girl started following us and yelling. It was very distracting and made it hard for us to minister.

Finally, Paul had had enough. He turned around and said to the evil spirit, "By the power of Jesus Christ, I command you to come out!" Instantly the devil came out of her.

When her owners saw that, they knew she wouldn't be a moneymaker anymore, so they seized us and dragged us before the Roman rulers. "These Jews are making trouble for us," they said. "They're teaching anti-Roman religion."

The officers were very angry. They ripped our clothes off and beat us half to death with rods. It was awful. Then they threw us in jail and told the warden to watch us like a hawk. So he put us in the deepest part of the jail and pinned our feet down.

We were in a lot of pain. But Paul wasn't about to let that get us down. About midnight, we started singing. We sang and sang, and the other prisoners heard our praise songs. God must have heard us too, because suddenly, there was an earthquake. All the cell doors burst open, and all of the prisoners' chains broke too.

This next part is wonderful. The jailer came dashing in and saw the doors all open. He was sure everyone had escaped, and he knew Rome would have his head. So he took out his sword and was going to kill himself, but Paul yelled, "No! Put down your sword! We're here! We're all here."

The jailer was so overcome that he fell down before us. "What must I do to be saved?" he cried.

"Believe on the Lord Jesus," we told him. "Then you and your whole family will be saved."

That jailer became a believer, right there in front of us. Then he took us home with him and cleaned all of our wounds himself. And just as we told him, his whole family became believers in Christ.

PRINCIPLES OF WORSHIP FROM THIS CHAPTER

Wonderful stories, all—but do they really teach us about worship? Positively.

In the introduction, we presented the term *halal*, one of the many Hebrew words for *worship*. It means "to celebrate God foolishly" and "to boast about His attributes." This is exactly what the Gospel writers— Matthew, Mark, Luke, and John—did when they penned the Synoptic Gospels. They boasted about Jesus. In fact, at the conclusion of John's gospel, he wrote, "There are many other things Jesus did. If every one of them were written down, I suppose the whole world would not be big enough for all the books that would be written" (21:25 NCV). This disciple was in awe of the God-man. He *worshipped* Him, both by writing his testimony and by preaching it day after day, as did Peter, Silas, and Paul. And look what this type of worship accomplished for them: It invoked the fear of God among their hearers. It enlarged the body of Christ. It caused God to move on the testifiers' behalf—even got them out of jail. And it opened doors for evangelism (the Philippian jailer and his household).

Now, I'm not promising that testimonial worship will get anyone out of jail. Through the centuries, millions have died for testifying of Christ. Even today, Christians all over the globe are being persecuted, even murdered, because of their testimony. But our testimonies are important.

What has God done for you? What have you *seen* Him do that you know only He could? Tell someone. Better yet, tell *everyone*. It'll open doors. It will cause God to move in your behalf. And it is worship. When you give your *testimony*, celebrating God foolishly and boasting of His attributes, you are *worshipping* God.

What else have we learned? What are the implications of this chapter's stories for our worship today?

First, with the coming of the Holy Spirit, worship was transformed. Believers began to enjoy "triune" worship. Today, the Spirit Himself teaches us how to please God through our worship, *personally* providing an understanding of what worship ought to be. How does He do this? By residing *in* us. God no longer dwells in a cloud, a fire, in tents, or in a temple. God the Holy Spirit now chooses to dwell in the hearts of those who love Him.

Do you remember what Jesus told the Samaritan woman? "The water I give will become a spring of water gushing up inside [you], giving eternal life" (John 4:14 NCV). That water was "Spirit water." And just as He promised, He sent the Spirit to "gush up" inside of us, emboldening our testimonies and making believers out of those who hear us.

Jesus went on to tell the woman, "The time is coming when the true worshipers will worship the Father in spirit and truth, and that time is here already . . . The Father . . . is actively seeking such people to worship him. God is spirit, and those who worship him must worship in spirit and truth" (vv. 23–24 NCV).

And that's how we worship Him today. No longer is our worship of God restricted by past traditions, the things we *do*, or the location of a building. We don't have to go to a mountain, a temple, or a tent in order to worship. Oh, we need such places. We've emphasized that throughout this book. The New Testament church always met *somewhere* for corporate worship:

- "The believers met together in the Temple every day." (Acts 2:46 NCV)
- "In Iconium, Paul and Barnabas went as usual to the synagogue." (14:1 NCV)
- "Paul went into the synagogue as he always did." (17:2 NCV)

See, early Christians congregated *regularly* in the synagogue and the temple. This reflects something of the deep respect they had for the customs of the people. They also assembled from house to house to, as a collective body, worship through prayer, study, Communion—and serving their community. They finally understood that worship had to embody service to God through service to others. So they worshipped *without*.

"Jesus is the object of devotion in the early churches. Christian life and ministry should be viewed as a way of serving God. Christ is the one who makes possible the forgiveness of sins and the outpouring of the Spirit predicted by the prophets, so that God's people are liberated to serve him in a new way. Such worship finds particular expression when Christians gather to minister to one another in word or deed, to pray, and to sound forth God's praises in teaching or singing, but it is not to be restricted in our thinking to these activities.

Fundamentally, the earliest Christians met to express their relationship together to the Lord and their responsibilities in that relationship . . . There is an awareness of being the community of the End-time, loosed from the stricture of Judaism, focusing on Jesus . . . , having its own distinctive forms of prayer and praise, relating to one another and serving one another in everyday contexts such as the household."[4]

But they also worshipped *within*, savoring the immediate presence of God—*at all times*—in their own hearts and lives, because the Spirit of God dwelled *within* them.

And today, friends, He also dwells in *you*. Thanks to the indwelling Spirit of God, we, too, can worship God *in spirit and in truth*.

| 19 |

WORSHIP IN THE EPISTLES: ROMANS–2 CORINTHIANS

CHRIST'S ONCE-AND-FOREVER, ALL-INCLUSIVE, SACRIFICIAL death was and is good news—*the* good news—for worshippers from His day forward. It meant—for you, me, and all mankind—that we are no longer daily bound to bleeding sacrifices for the atonement of our sins. Jesus' *own* blood paid for them all—*every* trespass, *all* broken fellowship, innovating worship for all eternity. Through Jesus Christ, the object of our worship, we are at peace—at one—with God.

In the last chapter, we looked at the book of Acts, which documented the effect of Christ on the practice of worship in the early church. The perfect Lamb of God died, was buried, then rose on the third day, having defeated death, hell, and the grave. He walked—resurrected—among His disciples, showing Himself alive to them. Finally, He went back to the Father, promising first to send His followers a Helper, a Comforter, to bring supernatural power to their experience.

In Acts 2, we witnessed the beginning of the metamorphosis of worship, as Jesus made good on His promise: men and women alike were filled with the Holy Spirit, and from that point on, we began to see lives transformed through miracles wrought at these believers' hands. Why? Because of the *resident* Spirit of God, who began making His dwelling *in* the believer. He still does today. Now, no longer do we simply *go* to the temple of God; we *are* the temple of God.

But this new revelation wasn't making things easy for the fledgling New

Testament church. Christ had ascended, and now they were trying desperately to learn—often by trial and error—how to worship God within their newfound faith. They knew worship was no longer about *legislation*; it was about *lifestyle*. They were to *live out* their worship. We are too. And thankfully, God gave us the Epistles, this chapter's subject, to clearly tell us how. But as you will see, living out worship isn't always easy. It wasn't for the early church . . .

A CULTURE AT ODDS WITH THE GOSPEL

"Daddy, Daddy, come here! Quick! Something is wrong with my fish!"

I ran into the family room, and there stood my five-year-old son, goldfish bowl in hand. A closer look at the fish inside the bowl confirmed my son's fear. Something was definitely wrong. Both goldfish were upside down. Not a good sign.

"Jeremy," I asked, "have you done anything to your fish today?"

"Oh, no," he replied. "I just cleaned out their bowl."

"Tell me how you did this, son," I responded.

"Well . . ." Long sigh. Then, pointing at two Styrofoam cups, he said, "I put water in these cups. Then I took the fish out of the bowl and put them in the cups too. The water in their bowl was *reeeally* nasty, so I poured it in the sink and then filled the bowl with new water—"

"Um, Jeremy, where'd you get the water?" I asked.

"From the kitchen sink."

"Straight from the sink?"

"Yes, and both fish *really* liked the clean bowl," Jeremy said, as if trying to convince me.

Taking the bowl out of his tiny hands and setting it on the coffee table, I took him in my arms. "Son," I said, "you had a really *good* idea . . . but we can't put fish into water straight from the kitchen sink. The water we drink has chlorine in it. It kills germs and keeps us from getting sick. But it kills little fish. We have to put special pills in their water when we clean their bowls, to get rid of the chlorine. Then we can let the fish swim in their new, clean water. But if we don't do that, the fish are not safe."

Perplexed, Jeremy said, "But they looked so happy . . ."

"They didn't know the water would hurt them," I said. "They're used to a bigger world, a great big sea, with no chlorine in it. When we brought them here, they had to learn how to live in a new home, your little fish bowl. But we have to make their water just right, even in this bowl, or they can't live.

"I've got an idea," I went on. "Let's go to K-Mart and get some new fish."

We put on our coats, went to K-Mart, bought new fish, and brought them home to *safe* water. And my now-happy little boy learned to never again put his beloved fish in unfriendly water.

Like Jeremy's fish, the first-century Christians found themselves in unfriendly water. Their entire culture, in fact, was unfriendly—dangerous, even—to their way of life. The preaching of the gospel brought new and radical concepts of worship to both Jew and Gentile. And the transformation from Old to New Testament worship begat an onslaught of challenges. On one hand, these baby Christians faced constant harassment from Jewish leaders, who were tied to tradition and opposed to everything Christ had espoused. On the other hand, they met with persecution spurred on by the surrounding Gentile cultures: Rome and its myriad of gods and goddesses, the Hellenism/humanism of the Greeks, and pantheism in general. These young believers needed something to neutralize their "chlorine"-filled environment. What did they need? Sound teaching—clean water—lest they suffocate in the poisonous worship culture in which they swam.

The apostle Paul, author of approximately two-thirds of the New Testament, was dedicated to just such a cause. Committed, even in the face of certain death, to teach God's people how to conduct themselves *worshipfully*, he and other apostles wrote the Epistles to help the Christians—little fish in a big sea—live out the day-to-day worship of Christ in church, at home, and in their communities. And while time and space do not permit me to discuss all of the epistles—or letters—the epistles of Paul have much to say about the believer's worshipping lifestyle.

Let's begin with Paul's epistle to the church at Rome.

WORSHIP IN THE BOOK OF ROMANS

Readers can immediately draw two basic worship principles from the book of Romans: (1) there's wrong worship, and (2) there's right worship. The differences between the two are crystal all-too-lucid. But before expanding on the issue of worship fair and foul, Paul first defined what worship meant for *him*: the *preaching of the Word of God*.

The Power of Preaching

"I am not ashamed of the gospel," wrote Paul, "because it is the power of God for the salvation of everyone who believes: first for the Jew, then for the Gentile" (Rom. 1:16 NIV). "The language here," wrote David Peterson, "suggests that gospel preaching is necessary to bring about that obedience of faith through Jesus Christ . . . which is the 'understanding worship' of the eschatological era." He continues:

> Paul's "priestly" ministry was radically different because it was con- ducted out in the world, rather than in some sacred place . . . he clearly gives that ministry a novel significance when he describes [preaching] as the means by which he worships . . . God . . . Missionary preaching and the establishment of churches in the truths of the gospel can be described as fulfilling a God-given "liturgy" or service to the churches. At the same time, these vital activities can be regarded as specific and particular expressions of Christian "worship" or service to God.[1]

This is important to our perception of New Testament worship, as it was critical to Paul's understanding. Heretofore, reading of Scripture, sing- ing of songs, praying, and adoration of God had been the primary expres- sions of worship. But Paul viewed preaching of the good news as equally vital to the worship process (Rom. 1:16; 12:1–8; 15:18; 1:5; 16:19; 15:9). This changed forever the role of the preacher from dutiful exhorter to openmouthed worshipper/worship *leader*.

In some circles, it is fashionable to recurrently allow "the move of the Spirit" to take precedence over preaching. And if, in fact, it is the Spirit's moving, who is anyone to deny it? However, the church must exercise cau- tion in minimizing the importance of the Word of God to the practice of corporate worship. Says Warren Wiersbe, "When preaching is an act of wor- ship, the listener's heart is stirred by the vision of God and the Spirit of God says far more to him than what the minister declares from the pulpit . . . The purpose of preaching is not to inform the congregation of the minister's homiletical gifts; it is to bring the congregation face to face with the living God."[2] And isn't that what we all need in this hour, a face-to-face encounter with God? Wiersbe further states, "Because we have lost this high view of preaching as an act of worship, we are now suffering the consequences both in our worship services and in our preaching. Preaching is not what it ought to be and neither is worship . . . and we are paying for it."[3]

Us and Them

After expanding the definition of worship for all who would read his letter, Paul began to draw a line in the sand between "us" and "them." He denounced "worshippers" who had willfully ignored God's revealed truth in nature and had chosen instead to worship "idols made to look like earthly people, birds, animals, and snakes" (1:23 NCV).

Unthankfulness. This same spirit is active today.

Gen Y-ers (aka "millennials") have more than any generation of young people has ever had. And their parents possessed more than the generation that preceded theirs. The hard work once required at the turn of the twentieth century has been replaced in the new millennium with the ease of automatic—and digital—washers and dryers, GPS-equipped automobiles, remote-controlled *everything*, and more. Where kids once carried base-balls, bats, and Barbies, today they are armed with iPhones and BlackBerrys, fully loaded with multimedia messaging tools. *Everybody* has them, Dad . . . or so I hear. And yet, whole books have been written about the hazards of material advantage on society's youth. It has, in fact, created a generation of unhappy kids.[4] They have much, but are grateful for little. They are, in reality, incredibly bored. According to *LA Times* staff writers Robin Abcarian and John Horn, "the YouTubing, MySpacing, multi-tasking teens and young adults," though "the most entertained generation ever," are "bored with it all."[5] They're *dis*contented, *dis*satisfied, *dis*illusioned, or, put another way, *un*thankful, *un*grateful, *un*fulfilled . . . Think that doesn't affect worship? It certainly does.

How did it influence the people of Rome?

People in Paul's day were enjoying the blessings of God in abundance.

Yet "their thinking," he wrote, "became useless" (v. 21b NCV). Sounds like boredom to me. And what did it lead to? The same thing it sets in motion today, a moral breakdown on *every level*:

> They became full of sexual sin, using their bodies wrongly with each other . . . [In fact,] they are filled with every kind of sin, evil, selfishness, and hatred[,] . . . jealousy, murder, fighting, lying, and thinking the worst about each other. They gossip and say evil things about each other. They hate God. They are rude and conceited and brag about themselves. They invent ways of doing evil. They do not obey their parents. They are foolish, they do not keep their promises, and they show no kindness or mercy to others . . . Even their women exchanged natural relations for unnatural ones. In the same way the men also abandoned natural relations with women and were inflamed with lust for one another. Men committed indecent acts with other men. (vv. 23, 29–31 NCV; vv. 26–27 NIV)

What a (dirty) laundry list! *Whatever* did they do to cause them to degenerate to such a state? The *New Century Version* tells us that they "worshiped and served what had been created instead of the God who created those things" (v. 25). For that reason, "God left them and let them go their sinful way (v. 24). Verse 26 says He "left them and let them do the shameful things they wanted to do." And verse 28 puts a triple cap on their demise: "God left them and allowed them to . . . do things they should not do." Do you think Paul was trying to make a point here? *Three* times he wrote, "God *left* them." Why? Because they weren't grateful to Him, and they didn't worship Him. They worshipped something else.

Now, it could be argued that people in this condition are not so much guilty of worshipping the *wrong* thing as they are not worshipping at all. But make no mistake: we all worship *something*. We will not—cannot—be devoid of worship. It's just that when one abandons the desire to worship God, the result is *false* worship. In the words of Noel Due:

> For a human being there can be no vacuum of non-worship. One is either submitted to God in the doing of his will and the glorifying of his name, or one is submitted to someone, or something else. The error

described in Romans 1:18ff., is not the neglect of worship, but the exchange of worship . . . They sin not by *not* worshiping, but by worshiping wrong. . . . The Biblical reality is that men and women are shaped by their worship.[6]

"Shaped by their worship . . ." What kind of "shape" does misplaced worship produce? When God saw the evil worship of the first-century citizens of whom Paul wrote, He "gave them over to a depraved mind" (v. 28 NIV). Translation: they literally no longer had a conscience. They could do whatever they desired without feeling any *guilt*. And friends, if that doesn't describe today's society, I don't know what does. We live in a culture in which children set dogs on fire; mothers drown their "inconveniences" (children); and men try to kill their babies in the microwave.[7] In a phrase, our world is in miserable *shape*.

Oh, the peril of misdirected worship. When God leaves the scene, anything and everything can result. Humankind's depravity knows no bounds.

What is the solution?

A *Living Sacrifice*

"Sacrifice?" you say. "But I thought sacrifices were over. Wasn't Jesus the last sacrifice ever needed?" Well, yes . . . and no.

Let's review, for a moment, one of the Greek words for worship that we have studied. The word is *proskuneo* (Strong's number 4352), and among its other definitions, it means "to fawn" or "to kiss, as a dog licking his master's hand."

Kiss? Fawn? Who would do such a thing? This is Generation Me, after all, one clearly *not* given to servility. And yet, isn't it precisely the servants among us whose love for the Master beckons them to worship Him in such a way? It certainly requires sacrifice—of ego, especially. Yet so much emphasis is placed in modern times on "who we are in Christ." But that's just it. It is *only* because of Christ that we have not been consigned to eternal hell. Think about it. As wonderful as we are (read "tongue in cheek"), our own righteousness is still filthy in God's eyes. I love the way *The Message* describes us at our best: "We're all sin-infected, sin-contaminated.

Our best efforts are grease-stained rags" (Isa. 64:6). We *need* to be "*prosku-neoing*" before our Maker and the Son who died for us. But how does one put that into practice?

> "I beseech you therefore, brethren, by the mercies of God, that ye present your bodies a living sacrifice, holy, acceptable unto God, which is your reasonable service." (Rom. 12:1 KJV)

Note the word *reasonable*. Paul was literally begging his readers to offer themselves as sacrifices to God because it was not only *acceptable,* but *reasonable.* Let's talk about the ramifications of this verse as it relates to worship.

First, we are to *present our bodies* to God, freely. This puts the scripture "do all to the glory of God" in a whole new light (1 Cor. 10:31 KJV). If our very bodies are offerings—indeed, *sacrifices*—to God, then what does that say of the way we are to care for them? This is not a book about, as one preacher I know of says, a-smokin' and a-drinkin' and a-chewin'. But follow this thought to its logical end. What kind of "living sacrifice" are you offering your Creator? One reeking of whiskey and Winstons? A gluttonous temple with high blood pressure and cholesterol through the roof because of bad food choices? A body begging for one good night's sleep? or a little exercise? or a day off? What does your physician think of your bodily condition? If it doesn't satisfy your doctor, *hmm* . . .

Enough said.

Second, the required sacrifice is *living.* The sacrificial concept was certainly consistent with both Jewish and Roman culture. But their worship, and the idols associated with it, required the shedding of blood—to the death. Paul suggested that the sacrifice that is "acceptable" to God is alive, vibrant, fully aware, and obedient—ready to serve. Never again does this sacrifice include the giving of dead animals. It is a *living* sacrifice that encompasses our ambitions, our motives, our hearts. In fact, *by nature* this type of sacrifice includes the thoughts and intent of the heart. There is *nothing* dead about this kind of sacrifice.

Third, the sacrifice of worship involves *holiness.* It requires a person to separate himself from the evil influences and idolatrous cultures all around. Now that our bodies are the new temple, it is important that God's dwelling place be clean, sanctified, purified—fit for service. This was a foreign concept to Roman society. Hedonism was a way of life in Rome. But for the New Testament worshipper, holiness was to be the norm as well as the evidence of honest, genuine worship.

Fourth, the sacrificial worship that Paul described requires *service*. We've talked about this before. It is not merely meeting the expectations or mandate of a holy God. It is highly personal worship substantiated by service to Him. And the very process of "offering the sacrifice," according to Paul, is a *"spiritual act of worship"* (Rom. 12:1 NIV). David Peterson makes the connection between this personal presentation of sacrifice and that which is public and often *viewed* as sacrifice:

> When Christians become preoccupied with the notion of offering God acceptable worship in a congregational context and thus with the minutiae of church services, they need to be reminded that Paul's focus was on the service of everyday life. . . . Congregational worship in some contexts can be like a *narcotic trip* into another world to escape the ethical responsibilities of living a Christian life in this world.[8]

A living sacrifice, with "ethical responsibilities"—that is the worship that most pleases God. Not simply worship that we *do*, but also worship that we *are*. The death of an animal was something worshippers *did*. But the sacrifice of Christ, the dead-but-*alive* Lamb of God, is a reflection on who He *is*. It is the same with us. A dead sacrifice is the result of what a worshipper has *done*. A living sacrifice is the result of who you *are*, a servant in love with your Master. Remember, "from [God] and through him and *to* him are all things" (11:36 NIV, emphasis added). That includes you, and you were *made* to be a servant-sacrifice. You were even made to *want* to. This verse tells us that God is the author of worship, and *our* worship—all of it—is from Him, a gift to mankind, provided by God so that we can know and experience Him. And we were created with an inner desire for exactly that, to know and experience God—through worship. Our innermost beings *want* to be living sacrifices to God. So why fight it? Our spirits are willing, Jesus said. It's our flesh that is weak. (See Matthew 26:41.) That is precisely why we must strive—daily—to present our bodies as living sacrifices. It's also why Paul wrote "I die daily" (1 Cor. 15:31 KJV).

Can You Say, "Submission"?

The idea of submission to any god as a way of life was foreign to Roman culture. Yet submission to God through Jesus Christ is at the very nucleus of New Testament worship explained by Paul. After telling his readers to present their bodies as living sacrifices, he went on to tell them, "Do not be shaped by this world" (Rom. 12:2 NCV), or as the King James Version renders it, "Be not conformed to this world."

I remember, as a little boy, watching my mother make strawberry gelatin. First she'd mix the powdered Jell-O with water. Then she would pour the mixture into plastic or metal molds and place them in the refrigerator. Soon, the gelatin would *conform* to the shapes of the surrounding environments—the molds. Within hours, that yummy, red Jell-O looked exactly like cars, animals, people—whatever *surrounded* that gelatin. In reality, fresh gelatin is not car-shaped, boat-shaped, or what have you. It simply *takes on* the shape of its surroundings. It *submits*.

But Paul said that is exactly what the Christ-follower must *not* do. We are not to submit ourselves to the images of those around us or try to fit into society's "mold." Why? It is idolatrous, and God's rules about idolatry have never changed. Paul's imperative implies that the influences of the ungodly community around us are not healthy on any level. He is right.

To what, then, do we submit? A makeover. The rest of Romans 12:2 says, "Be transformed by the renewing of your mind" (NIV). The *New Living Translation* takes it a step further, saying, "*Let God* transform you into a new person by changing the way you think" (emphasis mine). In a word, *submission*. Our earthy associations cannot be replaced the "old way"—by obeying laws and rules and carving up lambs and bulls. Transformational thinking can only be accomplished by submitting oneself to God. Only then can we "know God's will for [us], which is good and pleasing and perfect" (v. 2b NLT). And when we do, we have achieved biblical worship, the giving of ourselves as living sacrifices, totally submitted and abandoned to the purpose and plan of God.

Individuality

God has no interest in a community of clones. Believe it or not, God is greatly interested in the uniqueness of the individual worshipper. Paul proved that by following his instructions about sacrificial worship with guidelines for our worship interaction with fellow believers. God has imparted giftedness to *each person*, to be used for His glory. And while we want to be careful here to not equate gifts/ministry/service with worship in a wholesale kind of way, remember that our worship is evidenced by our service to God and to others. Unlike our private worship experience, this kind of worship benefits the entire body of Christ. As such, Paul strongly urged the believers to recognize their individual giftings and use them, but with one caveat: *Don't think you are better than you really are* (v. 3 NLT). Our gifts are treasures from the Lord. "It's important [then]," reads *The Message*, "that you not misinterpret yourselves as people who are bringing this goodness to God. No, God brings it all to you" (vv. 2–3). You have been warned.

Having said that, Paul added, "If a man's gift is prophesying, let him use it . . . If it is serving, let him serve; if it is teaching, let him teach; if it is encouraging, let him encourage; if it is contributing to the needs of others, let him give generously; if it is leadership, let him govern diligently; if it is showing mercy, let him do it cheerfully" (vv. 6–8 NIV). Remember that the context of much of Paul's writing is corporate *worship*, so here Paul encouraged the diversification of worship according to individual gifts—a totally new concept. There was no room for individuality in Old Testament worship. It was bound by explicit ritual. There were only so many ways to kill a turtledove, and only so many ways to convey that turtledove to the awaiting priest. But now, the practice of worship would embrace a much more personal element—giftings, and these would be laid at the feet of Christ, for *His* glory, never for the worshipper's. That was sure a new notion for the people of Rome. You can bet they had trouble with it. Do you?

Let's see if the Christians in Corinth did any better . . .

WORSHIP IN 1 AND 2 CORINTHIANS

There were some powerfully disturbing issues facing the church at Corinth. While it was rather large and financially stable, its members were spiritually immature. They were quarrelsome, exclusivist, deluded about their own spirituality, and plagued with misunderstanding, particularly in relation to a most important liturgy, the Lord's Supper. In brief, these brothers and sisters had turned this once-reverent worship rite, meant for serious reflection and adulation of Christ, into a time of partying and personal indulgence. In his pointed first letter to this congregation, Paul sought to lay the groundwork for the practice of Communion, or the Lord's Supper.

The Sacrament of Communion

Jesus had already set precedent for practicing the Lord's Supper in the Upper Room (see chapter 17). Paul expanded our understanding. "When you come together, you are not really eating the *Lord's* Supper," he accused. "When you eat, each person eats without waiting for the others. Some people do not get enough to eat, while others have too much to drink" (1 Cor. 11:20–21 NCV, emphasis added). The Corinthian family had gotten distracted from the main objective of the Eucharist: *commemorating the atoning work of Christ.* Instead, they were making Communion a celebration of their favoritism and lack of restraint. Not only were they forsaking to include in their "worship circle" those less fortunate (v. 22), and giving preference to the wealthier among them; they were also making the Divine Liturgy all about the feast. Paul meant to get them back on track by warning them that it was time they "clean up their act" and remember what the Lord's Supper is *really* about:

> On the night when the Lord Jesus was handed over to be killed, he took bread and gave thanks for it. Then he broke the bread and said, "This is my body; it is for you. Do this to remember me." In the same way, after they ate, Jesus took the cup. He said, "This cup is the new [covenant] that is sealed with the blood of my death. When you drink this, do it to remember me." Every time you eat this bread and drink this cup you are telling others about the Lord's death until he comes." (vv. 23–26 NCV)

Plain and simple. But wait! There's more: "A person who eats the bread or drinks the cup of the Lord in a way that is not worthy of it will be guilty of sinning against the body and the blood of the Lord," Paul added (v. 27 NCV). Now, why did he have to go and say that?

Because there is always a price to pay for misdirected worship.

If you will look back at chapter 3, "The Worship Wars," you will see a lot about "price" and "penalty." Each of the "players" revealed in that chapter failed, in one way or other, at worship. As a result, each not only paid a *personal* price but also set in motion penalties much farther-reaching. I suggest that you take the time to reread chapter 3 as a reminder of the consequences of worshipping anything other than God, because that's exactly what was happening in Corinth. This Greek church was not in any way worshipping the Almighty in their observance of Communion. They were, instead, worshipping their social circle, their appetites, their *bellies*. And for lack of a better term, it ticked Paul off. "You can eat and drink in your own homes!" he fumed (v. 22 NCV).

Thankfully, Paul didn't stop there. He was, though rough around the edges, a loving pastor who didn't want his flock to suffer the fierce judgment of God, "because all who eat the bread and drink the cup without recognizing the body eat and drink judgment against themselves. That is why many in your group are sick and weak," he told them, and many have died" (vv. 29–39 NCV). Knowing this, Paul gave them instructions, and they are as critical today as they were in AD 55, when theologians believe 1 Corinthians was penned: "Look into your own hearts before you eat the bread and drink the cup" (v. 28 NCV).

Holy Communion is considered a worship rite in churches from the most liturgical to the most "chandelier swinging." And the methods employed are as diverse as the churches themselves. Some worshippers drink real, honest-to-goodness wine. Others will only partake of grape juice. Most congregations use small, unleavened wafers. But many tear off chunks from a large, common loaf. With regard to the various beliefs, some believe the bread and wine literally become the blood and body of Christ, a doctrine known as *transubstantiation*. Others disagree. But *all* participants in the Body and Blood of Christ need to remember this: *Take it worthily*. In fact, in *all* that you do in worship, do so worthily. I can't stress this enough. In chapter after chapter, I have emphasized the importance of bringing *repentant hearts* to the time and place of worship. In chapter 7 we saw that before God would ever accept Israel's worship, they first had to prepare their hearts. They looked within, repented of their sin, and then—only then—were they at liberty to worship God without fear. To do otherwise was to ensure God's displeasure.

Again, the rules haven't changed. Worship the Lord, each and every time you partake of the Lord's Supper. Remember what He did *for you*, and what it means to your eternity. But when you do, do so with reverence, with respect, with repentance, "so that in meeting together you will not bring God's judgment on yourselves" (v. 34 NCV).

The Gifts of the Spirit

Paul's exhortation regarding the Last Supper actually opened the door for him to deal with another broad area related to worship, the gifts of the Spirit. In 1 Corinthians 12, we are given a list of spiritual gifts granted to the body of Christ, to be used for "the common good" (v. 7 NCV): "The Spirit gives one person the ability to speak with wisdom, and . . . another the ability to speak with knowledge . . . faith to one person. And, to another, . . . gifts of healing . . . to another person the power to do miracles, to another the ability to prophesy. And he gives to another the ability to know the difference between good and evil spirits. The Spirit gives one person the ability to speak in different kinds of languages and to another the ability to interpret those languages" (vv. 8–10 NCV).

Today, there is, as with Communion, a diversity of opinion about the gifts of the Spirit. Are they in operation today? Did they die with the last apostle? If not, who can employ them? The questions are many, and the views are varied. It is not my intention to debate whether or not speaking in tongues is for today or the gift of healing can be exercised by the modern saint of God. Those seeking a greater understanding of the spirituals gifts are encouraged to examine other resources.[9] But for purposes of this book, we will simply look at the challenges Paul faced as worshippers sought to use their gifts, and the impact of these challenges on corporate worship.

In the fellowship Paul was addressing, some had begun to exalt certain gifts over others in their worship gatherings. Guess what? Nothing's changed. In churches north and south of the equator, we see this same thing, week in and week out: a tug-of-war between "gifted" parties that often results in a carnival rather than a service dedicated to worshipping God. Unfortunately, people leading "praise and worship" are particularly guilty. Their actions scream, "Worship is all about me." They lord their musical gifts over the administrative types—deacons and ushers. And these lord their authority over the teachers. The teachers think that certainly *their* gift is superior to that of the "nurturers" in the fellowship, those who cook meals and make "care calls" and bestow benevolence on behalf of the body. What results is division in the ranks, when what God wants is unity in the body of Christ. In any worship gathering, if you get various groups of "gifted persons" all battling for attention and each trying to outdo the other, the product can only be *confusion*. Satan is its author, and with it he disrupts the working of the Holy Spirit in our services. Remember, the Spirit directs worship back to Christ. But in this atmosphere, *no one* is worshipping Christ; they're worshipping themselves.

Again, it is not this book's purpose to explain, defend, or in any way define the work of the Holy Spirit through spiritual gifts. It is important, however, to glean the principles from 1 Corinthians that we can apply to our own worship services.

- Everything we do in worship should be without confusion (14:40)

- All of our worship should glorify God and point people to Christ.

- Our worship ministries should not exalt people. Prima donnas should exist in the world, not in the church. And most important:

- "The purpose of all [of the gifts] should be to help the church grow strong" (14:26b NCV).

Worship and the Collection

In 2 Corinthians 8 and 9, the apostle Paul lays a foundation for our worship through *giving*. We've already seen the importance of giving (tithes) in the life of Abraham (Gen. 14). We've read of the incredible and positive impact of King David's faithful giving (1 Chron. 29). And Jesus made His feelings clear as He observed a widow giving all she had (Luke 21:1–4). He

would know about giving: He was the ultimate Gift, gift-\
humanity on a scratchy, wooden cross. In all of these cas
reflection of worship to Yahweh.

The apostle took additional opportunity to instruct the
Corinth in how to *worship through giving*: Such worship sh   ..ot be
offered begrudgingly. Giving should come from hearts that are happy to
share from the bountiful blessings provided by God. The Corinthian
church had historically given faithfully and joyously to Paul's ministry. But
there was some resistance to giving of their wealth to other churches in
need. Paul reminded them that their giving was a service that "not only
helps the needs of God's people, it also brings many more thanks [worship]
to God" (9:12 NCV). If that's not enough, he told them, "it is [also] proof of
your faith. Many people will praise God because you obey the Good News
of Christ . . . and freely share with them and with all others" (v. 13 NCV).

What was Paul saying here? Worship begets worship begets worship. As
God's people unselfishly worship through giving, others are inspired to
worship too. And the gift just keeps on giving.

But that's the key, isn't it? *Giving.* All of worship is giving of one kind or
another.

What kind of giver are *you*?

WORSHIP IN THE EPISTLES: GALATIANS—AND BEYOND

LEFT TO OURSELVES, OUR NATURAL INCLINATION WILL BE TO *not* worship Yahweh. But we *will* worship, as I've pointed out in the last chapter and throughout this book. The ache to do so is inborn. What will we worship? Other things certainly, even other deities,[1] but for most, simply *self*. We want to gratify the self, indulge the self, and in so doing, we lose sight of what God wants for us—an intimate relationship with Him through worship.

GALATIANS

In Romans, the apostle Paul listed some of the products of misplaced worship (see chapter 19). In the book of Galatians, one of this chapter's foci, he added to the list. What are some of the bitter fruits of misappropriated worship and the self-indulgence that spawns it? "Repetitive, loveless, cheap sex," wrote Paul, "a stinking accumulation of mental and emotional garbage; frenzied and joyless grabs for happiness; trinket gods; magic-show religion; paranoid loneliness; cutthroat competition; all-consuming-yet-never-satisfied wants; a brutal temper; an impotence to love or be loved; divided homes and divided lives; small-minded and lopsided pursuits; the vicious habit of depersonalizing everyone into a rival; uncontrolled and uncontrollable addictions; ugly parodies of community. I could go on" (5:16–21 MSG). Now compare these to the fruits that Christ's worshippers bear: "The Spirit produces the fruit of love, joy, peace, patience, kindness, goodness, faithfulness, gentleness, self-control" (v. 22 NCV). What a contrast! This passage makes a meaningful point: our worship—good, bad, or ugly—will produce fruit. We can yield to the Spirit and produce the sweet, or we can surrender to self, which is ultimately a surrender to Satan, and produce fruit that is rotten, corrupt, altogether vile. Paul learned that the Galatians, members of churches he had established in Antioch, Derbe, Lystra, and Iconium, were struggling with the choice between good fruit and bad fruit. They had two major problems.

First, these believers were being pressured by a group called the "Judaizers" to bring their *new* faith under the authority of the *old* law. Judaizers refused to validate Christian worship without conformance to the law of Moses, and circumcision in particular. Even the apostle Peter had a problem with it. Paul meant to set them straight. "If you try to be made right with God through the law," he wrote, "your life with Christ is over—you have left God's grace" (Gal. 5:4 NCV). Paul understood that, thanks to Jesus Christ, legalism was no longer a prerequisite in worship that warms God's heart. It was Paul's job to make sure the early church didn't forget it either. Christ had superseded the Old Testament ceremonial worship system. God's people were no longer bound to annual feasts and fasts, or even the Jewish Sabbath—and yet they were observing them dutifully. Paul chastised his flock very pointedly for allowing themselves to be sucked back into this *un*lawful worship. "Now that you know God . . . how is it that you are turning back to those weak and miserable principles? Do you wish to be enslaved by them all over again? You are observing special days and months and seasons and years! I fear . . . that . . . I have wasted my efforts on you" (4:9–11 NIV).

But worse than their temptation to lean toward the *law* again was a new and dangerous tendency on the believers' part to tilt in the direction of *lawlessness*. With Christ having fulfilled the law, worshippers of God now had freedoms they'd never had before. Freedom regarding the Sabbath. Freedom to eat what was once unclean. "[And] God called you to be free," Paul confirmed, "but do not use your freedom as an excuse to do what pleases your sinful self" (Gal. 5:13 NCV). They were taking their newfound Christian liberty to an excess, to satisfy the *self*.

Paul used his letter to the Galatian Christians to introduce a new concept. Self-crucifixion. Paul and his followers knew the Jewish sacrificial system was obsolete. Collectively, they understood that Christ was the once-for-always sacrifice, and never again would anything—or anyone—have to die for the atonement of man's sins. And yet . . . when Christ died, Paul, too, was "put to death on the cross *with* Christ" (2:20 NCV, with emphasis). "I do not live anymore—it is Christ who lives in me," he continued (v. 20b NCV). If that is true of all Christians (and it is), it certainly calls into question some of the actions that many in the body of Christ—maybe even you and I—find acceptable.

Going back to the introduction of this book, I stated that the ultimate definition of *worship* is simply "love." To worship God is to love him unabashedly, passionately, and *radically*. What does that mean, in human terms? Let's look at the human race—"in love."

Ladies, you know "he" doesn't like Chanel No. 5; it makes him sneeze. So you quit wearing it. He loathes the smell of lamb chops, so you never cook them again, even though to you, nothing tastes better. You break habits, change your hairstyle, give up old pursuits (and old flames!)—all because you "worship the ground he walks on."

Men, you used to hang out with "the boys." You don't do that so much anymore, because "she" doesn't like it; you've "crucified" your ways. You'd jump through hoops, bend over backward, climb mountains, and (like the mail carrier of old) dare rain or snow or sleet or hail to keep you from your beloved.

But your beloved never died for you. He or she did not atone for your sins. And no human being other than the risen Son of God, deserves your worship. It is *Him* with whom we need to be "in love."

"Thou shalt love the LORD thy God with all thine heart, and with all thy soul, and with all thy might" (Deut. 6:5 KJV). Paul did; therefore he wrote, "I am crucified with Christ" (Gal. 2:20 KJV)—in churchspeak, he had *died to self*. That's worship, and the only way we can bear the sweet fruit of Galatians 5:22. "Do not be fooled," Paul wrote one chapter later. "People harvest only what they plant. If they plant to satisfy their sinful selves, [it] will bring them ruin. But if they plant to please the Spirit . . . [they] will receive [a] harvest of eternal life" (6:7–9 NCV). Everyone knows that a seed must first die before it can bear fruit (1 Cor. 15:36). It is the same with us. We must die to self by putting to death our sins.

"Sin," wrote Oswald Chambers, "is red-handed mutiny against God. Either God or sin must die in my life. . . . If sin rules in me, God's life in me will be killed; if God rules in me, sin in me will be killed. There is no ultimate but that."[2]

So what is Paul saying to the Galatian churches? That even while being a "living sacrifice" unto God (Rom. 12:1 KJV; see chapter 19), we are to "kill" our flesh, "die to the world" (Gal. 6:14 NCV), and crucify our desires in favor of brazen love for and worship of Christ. Anything less is spiritual idolatry.

EPHESIANS AND COLOSSIANS

This theme of unrestrained love for God continues in Ephesians and Colossians, where Paul presents Christ as our *eternal object of worship*. After reminding believers that the body of Christ was peculiarly chosen to bring praise to God (Eph. 1:12), Paul then identified Christ as the shining star to whom worship is to be directed—now and forever.

Can you imagine how this must have sounded to Paul's society, the Jews in particular? Old Testament worshippers hadn't known Christ. They had been awaiting a Messiah, but when He came, He was not what the world expected. And in Paul's time, even as he identified man's eternal object of worship as the *divine* Jesus, people who had known the *man* Jesus, the carpenter, that strange young man who had said "blasphemous" things, were still alive. These people would be old now, senior citizens all, but they still remembered that flesh-and-blood man named Jesus—who had been executed.

But now, Paul was claiming that God had put that very man "over all rulers, authorities, powers, and kings, not only in this world but also in the next," making Him, in fact, "the head over everything" (vv. 21–22 NCV). "He ranks higher than everything," Paul wrote. Why? "Because Jesus Christ is exactly like [God]" (1:16, 15 NCV). No graven idol could make that claim. Neither could Mary, though pure and chosen by God to give birth to Divinity. And no "saint," no matter how respected, can purport to be exactly like God. As such, none of these is worthy of praise. And angels were certainly not to be praised. Paul made that patent when he warned the church at Colossae not to be beguiled into the "worship of angels" (Col. 2:18). To whom, then, does humankind owe their worship? Jesus Christ, "the head of the church" (Eph. 5:23 NCV).

That said, it was time for Paul to train the church how to not only *live*, but how to *do* worship. So in Ephesians, Paul began coaching his flock in proper *private* worship, and in Colossians, he provided a model for *public* worship.

Let's look at these books together.

The Ideal for Private Worship

From the very beginning, Jesus Himself made it clear that worship was about more than rites (see chapter 16). It was also about charity, integrity, acts of service, attitudes—in other words, everyday conduct, the kind of conduct that He exemplified. "Try to be like him," Paul now urged the Ephesians. "Live a life of love *just as Christ loved* . . . and gave himself . . . as [an] . . . offering and *sacrifice* to God" (5:1–2 NCV, with emphasis).

There's that word again: *sacrifice*. Jesus offered Himself as a sacrifice, an offering, to God . . . and we are supposed to be *just like Him*. What does that mean? Now, you know the answer to that. Paul's been telling us all along (see chapter 19): "Offer your lives as a living sacrifice to [God]," he wrote to the Romans. "[This] . . . is the spiritual way for you to worship" (Rom. 12:1 NCV). Where the rubber meets the road, this type of worship is tendered by taking "your everyday, ordinary life—your sleeping, eating, going-to-work, and walking-around life—and plac[ing] it before God as an offering" (ibid., MSG).

But how? What does it take to live an "everyday . . . sleeping, eating, going-to-work, and walking-around life" that God deems a suitably "spiritual way . . . to worship" (Rom 12:1 NCV)? Put another way, what does it take to be an offering *just like Jesus*?

It requires being "filled with the Spirit" (Eph. 5:18 NCV), and to be *filled* with one thing means to be *emptied* of all else. "In the past you were *full* of darkness," the apostle wrote, "but now you are *full* of light." As living sacrifices, God's people had abandoned the carnal (darkness) and taken on the spiritual (light). Now, said Paul, they were to "live like children who belong to the light . . . Be very careful how you live," he warned them. "Live wisely" (vv. 8–9, 15). In other words, Paul wrote, "There must be no sexual sin among [you] or any kind of evil or greed" (Eph. 5:3 NCV). In fact, those given to greed, he contended, are nothing less than idol worshippers: "Anyone who is greedy is serving a false god" (v. 5 NCV)—without ever kissing its image. He said the same thing in Colossians 3:6.

To summarize, all of these things—greed, carnality, immorality of *any* flavor—must be laid at the altar in order to live a life just like Christ's, a life filled with the Spirit and emptied of self, a living sacrifice. This teaching provides the most solid of evidence that true worship—that embracing Christlike self-sacrifice—is about one's daily life.

But it is also about methodology, and in Ephesians, Paul gives us some directives with regard to worship methodology. In addition to "giving thanks to God," a critical element in worship, we are to make "music" (NCV), or as the King James Version translates it, "melody" in our hearts to the Lord (5:20, 19b). Put plainly, worship in *song* should play a part in our private devotions.

It should also play an integral part in public worship.

Paul's Model for Public Worship

In Colossians, Paul instructed worshippers to "let the word of Christ dwell in [them] richly, in all wisdom" (3:16 NKJV). In other words, they were to feed on the Word of God so that it would enable them to exercise discernment when dealing with spiritual matters. Today, we must do the same. Reflecting and "chewing on" the Word will help us distinguish between what is good and bad, appropriate and inappropriate, acceptable and unacceptable. This is critical for those involved in the worship ministry.

With respect to music in worship, we read in Ephesians 5:19, "Speak to each other with psalms, hymns, and spiritual songs" (NCV). Colossians echoes this admonition: "Teach and instruct each other by singing psalms, hymns, and spiritual songs" (3:16 NCV). Often, musicians unnecessarily quote these twin passages in an attempt to somehow *justify* their role in worship. Yet the use of song in worship is articulated in *many* strategic passages. If a review of chapters 9 and 12 isn't enough to convince you, then recall that before Jesus and the disciples left the Upper Room, Gethsemane-bound, the Son of God Himself led His followers in a hymn (Matt. 28:30; Mark 14:26). Now Paul, too, was advocating the use of psalms, hymns, and spiritual songs during times of corporate worship.

Do you remember our discussion in chapter 11 of the "cocktail party effect," the ability to focus on a single conversation even as scores of other things (music, other conversations, etc.) are going on at the same time? Another word closely associated with this phenomenon is *audiation*, a term coined by music education researcher Edwin E. Gordon in 1979.[3] Audiation is the process of mentally hearing and comprehending music, even when no physical sound is present. One audiates when he rehearses a melody only in his mind, thinking about it, but not vocalizing it. Musicians do this all the time, internalizing the music before actually singing or playing the song. When Paul told the Ephesian worshippers to sing and make melody in their hearts (5:19), he was teaching a type of spiritual audiation: singing internally, not out loud.

But in Colossians 3:16, the apostle instructed the worshippers to sing in clear, audible voices. The mandate is as personal as in Ephesians; it is just demonstrated in *public*, in the corporate worship setting.

So, what do these three musical terms mean? They certainly do *not* imply a *particular* musical style. Not a single verse mandates that worshippers perform these tunes in a fashion either Baroque, Southern gospel, hard rock, country, or pop. Rather, the inference pertains to *context*. These songs, sung both privately and publicly, should exude God's Word.

Psalms, then, are essentially *scriptures in song*, and while "psalms" certainly include selections from the 150 texts in the book of that name, they can also be songs composed of *any* scripture that invokes worship. Old Testament odes, such as Moses' Song and the Songs of David, are examples. So are New Testament texts, from Revelation, for instance. So no matter what is your preferred style of *delivery*, at the core, psalms convey Holy Writ in song.

There is some disagreement on exactly what *hymns* and *spiritual songs* are supposed to mean to the New Testament believer. In most Greek lexicons, both *hymns* and *spiritual songs* refer to some type of religious ode, placing great value on the lyrics. In Western music, a *hymn* is a musical form that is most often *strophic* in design (different verses, but with a repeated melody). Modern dictionaries define a hymn as "a song of praise to God,"[4] but historically, hymns were defined as "songs with doctrine," that were valuable and essential to the Christian church. Charles Wesley published more than five thousand such songs to spread biblical theology throughout society and the church. Congregations today still sing these hymns.

Spiritual songs are noncarnal odes composed of personal testimony to express what God has done in the lives of those who sing them. Their impact should not be underestimated.

In Paul's day, the influence of Gnosticism was significant. He referred to this cult on numerous occasions. Gnostics often hosted lengthy and well-attended "hymn sings" during which they strategically proclaimed false doctrine through song. In addition to propagating theological error, these hymn sings sometimes incorporated illicit sexual activity. Paul did not want the worship of the true God to be associated with these orgies. So, knowing how powerful a means of communication music could be, he carefully established a clear demarcation between the early church's hymns and those sung by the Gnostics by adding to his Colossians directive, "Everything you do or say should be done to obey Jesus your Lord." Applied to today's culture, our use of music in worship should identify us with Christ, *not* with the sensual, oft-profane world at odds with Christianity.

Now I would like to address an issue often faced by worship leaders. Invariably, someone will ask, "What musical styles are acceptable in worship?" To answer that, let me start by saying that one's stylistic preference is not nearly as important as the intent of the heart. Musical selection is not the ultimate issue in true worship. Partialities for certain melodies and rhythms are based on both cultural acceptance and personal norms—most established by individual life experience, interpretation, and demographic surrounding. Hence, music's style and perceived suitability for use in the church change from age to age and people group to people group. What matters is that God calls us to worship *Him*, not the music or its style and manner of expression.

Certainly there is a time and place to have healthy discussion of appropriate music selection. But this chapter will center on the apostle Paul's simple directive to use music in worship, and while doing so, to please the object of our affection, Jesus Christ.

So, what is the practical application of the term *spiritual songs*? In worship, neither our music nor our lyrics should conform to a culture contrary to the Bible. The words should not encourage sinfulness. The presentation should not draw attention to the performer but instead to the Son of God. Whether we like European classical, R&B, Broadway, big band, alt country, garage, or Gregorian chant, we will meet all expectations for holy worship if we stay focused on the person of Jesus and offer our music from hearts of praise.

We've already quoted the first part of Colossians 3:16, "[Sing] psalms, hymns, and spiritual songs" (NCV). The rest of that verse says that we are to do so "with thankfulness . . ." or "with grace in [our] hearts" to God (NCV; NKJV). This is certainly a different disposition from that demonstrated by the unsaved. Our songs reveal an "attitude of gratitude," not the angst and apathy associated with so much of modern music today.

My point is that all music offered in worship to God, as long as it glorifies God and God alone, is acceptable in His sight. Therefore, learn to genuinely appreciate—not judge and condemn—musical worship as expressed by *all* Christians. Do not presume that your own personal bias dictates to God what is holy and acceptable as worship. Some of His people want to offer full and open expressions of praise. Others will be much more reserved. Many in the body of Christ share a deep appreciation for the structure of liturgical worship. Others have no tolerance for it at all, preferring spontaneity, creativity—not to mention screaming guitars and thunderous drums. Still others have a firm conviction that no musical instruments of any sort belong in God's house. To each his own. Don't judge *any* of these believers. The musical style is not critical to Christ-pleasing worship. What *is* important, to worshipper and worship leader alike, is that the worship itself be committed to Christ, not to the music, the drama, the film, the lights, or the *fans*. To put it most succinctly: "Do all to the glory of God" (1 Cor. 10:31 KJV).

PHILIPPIANS

The church at Philippi was one of the most celebrated and faithful communities Paul ever established. In spite of persecution, they faithfully and fervently supported the ministry, often sending gifts and providing workers for the various ministry tasks.

Paul deeply loved these believers. He told them that he thanked God every time he remembered them and prayed for them frequently. "This is my prayer for you," he wrote from prison, "that you will . . . bring glory and praise to God" (Phil. 1:9–11 NCV). Then, using a hymn[5] to communicate to them, he celebrated the incarnation of Christ, reminding the Philippians that in their own lives, they are to think and act like Him (2:5–11). If we think like Him, Paul seemed to be saying, we will worship like Him. "[So] let this mind be in you," he wrote, "which was also in Christ Jesus" (v. 5 KJV). What kind of "mind"? Let's look at Paul's song:

"[Though] Christ himself was like God in everything . . . he did not think that being equal with God was something to be used for his own benefit. But he gave up his place with God and made himself nothing" (vv. 6–7 NCV). Made Himself *nothing*? How different from the approach and attitude we see today. So many postmodern worshippers clamor to be seen and heard, putting *themselves* at center stage during worship!

But *"He became like a servant"* (v. 7 NCV). In Paul's culture, servants were considered the lowest ranking among the socioeconomic groups. They were the poorest of the poor. A person could not go much lower. Yet if we are to have the mind of Christ, taught the apostle, we must be *servants*. Reread the section titled "Worship Through Service" in chapter 17 and you will see that being a servant is "our first and best worship—*showing the Lord our sincere love by obeying Him* and mimicking Him on our planet: loving as He loved, serving as He served, and reaching out to a dying world as He reached out to those made in His likeness" (p. 252).

Paul was especially fond of the term *servant*. In fact, in Romans 1:1, he described himself as a "bond-servant" (NASB), then taught that Jesus Christ became a servant—even though the Son of God fully understood all that He was giving up. But by surrendering His position and accepting the role of a servant, Jesus demonstrated the ultimate role of a worshipper, a *humble* servant. And speaking of humility . . .

"He humbled himself . . . ," Paul's hymn continues (v. 8 NCV). The word

humble does not typically come to mind when we think of great and talented musicians, artists, and performers. Yet God neither chooses nor anoints a worship leader based on talent. He chooses based on one's willingness to humble him- or herself to a servant level. It's the only way to find God's favor. Humility and servanthood are especially appropriate for worship artists, worship leaders, worship pastors, and worship teams—no matter how skilled they are as musicians.

But humility is such a foreign concept in our look-at-me culture. Sadly, I've even met well-meaning, very influential Christian worship leaders who demonstrated great disdain for other worship team members who sought to direct worship in a spirit of humility. Worse, I've heard pastors and evangelists make fun of worship musicians who sought to be authentic and humble. For some reason, these leaders equate humility with a lack of skill and stage presence and deliberately employ the service of arrogance just to get the musical, artistic, and performance environment that *they* want. Now, who's *that* about? And while it meets their preferences in musical style or ministry application, they are screaming to their congregations—and the world—that humility in the pulpit or on the platform doesn't really matter. I hardly think God is pleased with such an attitude. Can you imagine Jesus' actions saying, *Look at Me! I'm the worship leader*? Never. "He who humbles himself will be exalted," Jesus taught (Luke 14:11 NIV), and "whoever wants to be great must become a servant" (Matt. 20:26 MSG).

Did you catch that? Jesus was saying that humility and servitude were the starting places for worship that He would approve. And not only did He approve of such worship; He lived it—day to day humility and servanthood. We should too. It's what it means to have the mind of Christ. And His "mind," lived out in you and me, is *worship* that delights the heart of God.

HEBREWS

In the past God spoke to our forefathers through the prophets . . . but in these last days he has spoken to us by his Son, whom he appointed heir of all things, and through whom he made the universe. The Son is the radiance of God's glory and the exact representation of his being, sustaining all things by his powerful word. After he had provided purification for sins, he sat down at the right hand of the Majesty in heaven. So he became as much superior to the angels as the name he has inherited is superior to theirs. (Heb. 1:1–4 NIV)

In the Gospels we read of Jesus the Man, flesh and blood, feet of clay. The same skin that we have, prone to bruising. The same hair, often in need of a trim. The same bones, breakable, though His were not broken. In the Gospels this Man said He was the Son of God, yet we read about a man (though *we* know He is the God-man).

But in the wonderful book of Hebrews, we see Jesus seated in the heavens, radiant, superior, and not just to the angels, who worship *Him* (1:6). He is also greater than the prophets (1:1–3); Moses (3:3–6); Joshua (4:8); and Aaron (7:11). Not only is Jesus Christ the Son of God; He *is* God. For that reason, Hebrews completely and irreversibly proclaims, more than any other book, why Jesus is worthy of *all* worship.

In Hebrews we find the Bible's most complete biblical presentation of Christ's fulfillment of all the law: the priesthood, every sacrifice, even the sanctuary. Not only that, but as the writer[6] describes the old Mosaic law, now *obsolete* (8:13), he unambiguously shows the reader that all of life is *so much better* under Christ.

Under Moses' law, worshippers and their sacrifices could not go straight to God. There was always a middleman: the priest, and *only* the priest could enter the Holy of Holies and offer sacrifices to atone for the sins of the people.

But in this new and "better covenant" (7:22; 8:6 NKJV), Jesus Himself has become our high priest—*forever* (6:19). No longer does there stand between us and God an *impersonal* human priest. Our new high priest, Christ, is not "a high priest who is unable to sympathize with our weaknesses . . . [He is instead a priest] who has been tempted in every way, just as we are—yet was without sin" (4:15 NIV). Chapter 2 tells us "He [was] made like His brethren, that He might be a merciful and faithful High Priest . . . to make propitiation for the sins of the people. [Since] He Himself has [been] tempted, He is able to aid those who are tempted"

(v. 17 NKJV).

DID YOU KNOW . . .

. . . that Jesus is our *true* worship leader?

[Christ says to the Father,]

"I will declare your name to my brothers;

in the presence of the congregation I will sing your praises."

(Heb. 2:12 NIV)

As followers of Christ, we don't have to worship by our own power. Jesus Christ Himself, our Mediator, faithfully *leads* us in God-pleasing worship. See, when we come before the Father, God views our worship as coming from *His own Son*, with whom He is well pleased. Our efforts may seem bumbling to us, but when we are submitted to our divine Worship Leader, God is also well pleased with *us*. Our worship is fragrant to God.

The fact that our worship is not by our own might, but Christ's, does away with all human pride about "doing worship right." We never will. Worship wasn't our idea. But Jesus knows how to worship God. He is Worship Perfected, and only through our attachment to Him can our worship satisfy God—and it does.

In our next chapter, we'll talk about this some more, but for now, let me recommend an excellent book on this very topic, titled *Proclamation and Praise: Hebrews 2:12 and the Christology of Worship* by Ron Man (Eugene, OR: Wipf & Stock Publishers, 2007).

[Jesus] says, I will declare Your [the Father's] name to My brethren; in the midst of the [worshiping] congregation I will sing hymns of praise to You. (Heb. 2:12 AMP)

Is this confusing to you? Perhaps you wonder, "But isn't there *still* a middleman, a mediator, between us and God? If so, what's the difference?"

Hebrews gives us the answer: "[Christ our] High Priest . . . does not need *daily*, as [the Old Testament] high priests, to offer up sacrifices, first for His own sins and then for the people's . . . This He did *once for all* when He offered up Himself" (7:26–27 NKJV, emphasis added).

God hates sin. He cannot tolerate it in His presence. That is why the Levites were compelled to offer sacrifices on behalf of sinful man, not just every year (9:7), but *every day*, all the while never bringing the sinner *any closer* to his God.

But Jesus, the Lamb without blemish, offered Himself *once*—one time, for all mankind, forever. And because of His blood sacrifice, He is the "Mediator of a better covenant" (8:6 NKJV). Why is it better? His sacrifice was *eternal*, and it purchased for us *eternal* life, *eternal* cleansing, *eternal* covering, and *eternal* forgiveness. Though we are sinners, and God still has no tolerance for sin, He now looks at us through Christ's finished work on the cross. That's what Christ's "mediation" means to you and me. He not only presented the offering; He *was* the offering, forever bridging the gap between God and humanity. Now, unlike all saints BC, we can "come boldly"—and *directly*—"to the throne of grace" (4:16 NKJV), worshipping God *face-to-face*, without the intervention of an old covenant priest who is *just as guilty* as we are. Whereas "the law made nothing perfect . . . [the death of Christ brought] a better hope, through which we [now can] draw near to God (7:19 NKJV). Thanks to our great high priest, we can worship at God's feet and enjoy Him *personally* through Jesus Christ, who is Himself God. This is that "better covenant," the one "established on better promises" (8:6 NKJV). We, unlike Mosaic Israel, don't serve a "copy and shadow" anymore. Jesus Christ and the Messianic system of worship He instituted are the "real deal"!!

So why have I included Hebrews in our study of worship? For the sake of your *appreciation*—and mine. So that you will share with me a copious understanding and remembrance of what we have "lost" in worship. And what have we lost? Cold ritual. Ceaseless sacrifices. Continually flowing animal blood. Insoluble guilt and impenetrable imperfection. What a loss. I won't shed a tear over it.

And what have we gained? Thanks to Christ, we have been [cleansed]

nscience" (10:22 NIV). For that cause, we have "confidence
ost Holy Place by the blood of Jesus" (v. 19 NIV)! Today—and
—we are privileged to "draw near to God with . . . full assur-
. NIV).

If you .e a shouting worshipper, *that's* something to shout about!

*Therefore by Him let us continually offer the sacrifice of praise to God, that
is, the fruit of our lips, giving thanks to His name.*

(HEB. 13:15 NKJV)

PRINCIPLES OF WORSHIP FROM THE EPISTLES

With a book this size, it's difficult to say something new in every chapter
without, at least once, repeating a point (though some principles bear
repeating). So forgive me if I have repeated myself. But at the risk of doing
so, allow me to present some overarching principles seen in the Epistles,
principles that you can use as you seek to worship God in a way that moves
Him to rapture.

1. *Jesus Christ is our eternal object of worship.* He is the HEAD OF THE
CHURCH and our WORSHIP LEADER forever. He is our GREAT HIGH PRIEST, and
because of Him, we no longer have to strain at worship. Our worship is
presented, through Him, the beloved Son, to His Father. The Father
always accepts His Son, and if we are faithfully loving and serving His
Son, then His Son accepts *us*. So what does that mean, in the end? That
the Father, too, accepts us—Jew and Gentile alike—*and* our worship. But
remember, it's all about Jesus. God will receive your praise when you recognize that your object of worship—for always—is Christ.

2. *The Holy Spirit "supersizes" our worship.* Ever since Acts 2, we have
had something in the body of Christ that *no one* in the Old Testament
could enjoy: the indwelling Spirit of God. Yes, today, God the Spirit *dwells*
in the believer, adding "meat" to our worship. When we don't know exactly
how to worship "right," the Spirit is there, *inside* us, to help us acceptably
worship God. *He knows how.* That's why Jesus called Him the "Helper." His
indwelling presence makes our worship better. Praise God for your Helper

today. Abraham, Moses, and Joshua were not so blessed as we.

3. *Preaching is an act of worship.*[7] Pastor, even if you can't sing your way out of a paper bag, you are worshipping your Master *every time* you bring forth, with Godlike intent, the Word of God. God wants *relationship* with people—people who will worship Him. And anytime—every time—your delivery of God's Word reaps the results that His own heart desires—relationship and worship—then *you* have worshipped! Singers and worship leaders, even your songs are "sermons" when they are true to the Word of God. And each time they are . . . you're a music-making *preacher*—and a worshipper too!

4. *Sing, sing, sing, because singing is worship.* God loves to hear you sing. It blesses Him. But it blesses others too. How many times has someone, resistant to every sermon he ever heard, been broken when the Word of God was presented in song? That's why Paul was so emphatic about music being part of worship, both public and private. "Speak to each other with psalms, hymns, and spiritual songs," he wrote (Eph. 5:19 NCV). And if that didn't say enough: "Teach and instruct each other by singing psalms, hymns, and spiritual songs" (Col. 3:16 NCV). He also said that we are to make "music" or "melody" in our own hearts to God. Think music is frivolous? Think again. God loves it. And it is worship.

5. *Worship with Communion—but worship worthily.* Communion is a beautiful act of worship. Think about the salvation Christ's broken body purchased for you. Ponder the healing that His bleeding stripes paid for. It makes me cry, every time. Maybe it does the same for you. But before you take that cup or bite into that symbolic bread, look within. Is there sin there? Are you eating and drinking unworthily? Don't do it! Take the time to repent before God, before you partake of the emblems, so that you needn't fear that you are eating and drinking damnation to yourself.

6. *Worship requires a living sacrifice.* Hey, no more dead animals. God's through with that. Now He wants us to *live out* worship, day by day by day, as a *sacrifice* to Him, substantiated by *service*. It is, as Paul put it, only "reasonable." It is also a "spiritual act of worship" (Rom. 12:1 NIV), because it requires *self-crucifixion*. Real worshippers "kill" their sins, "die daily" to selfishness, and instead commit—indeed, *submit*—to serving God through serving others.

7. *Worship must be done corporately too.* I know. I've already said that elsewhere. We won't beat any dead horses here. But for those who still contend that one does *not* need to be a church attender in order to be a worshipper, let me pose a question: How come so much of the New Testament (*all* of the Epistles) are addressed to *churches*? Paul said so much about it, writing verse after verse about how *congregations* were to conduct themselves during corporate worship, and how the *church* (read "collective") was to respond to those in need. Seems like an awful waste of time, the Epistles, if God doesn't want us to be part of a church body, doesn't it? For the record, God doesn't waste words. If you are not part of a corporate body of believers, find one. Don't wait until you find the "perfect church." You and I would only spoil it—*we're not perfect.* But do find a church, and be faithful to it. Remember, Christ promised to be in the midst of any genuine group that gathers in His name—to worship.

8. *Corporate worship, though collective, is still deeply personal.* Whereas Old Testament worship offered no room for individuality in style and presentation, worshippers under the new covenant are endowed with individual gifts from the Holy Spirit that add to the corporate worship experience. What are your giftings? Seek God about it, and use them. They are from the Holy Spirit, and they proceed from the very throne of God!!

What's next in our study? Can it get any better than this? Oh, yes. We have saved the best for *last.* In our final chapter, on the book of Revelation, we will learn how you and I—and all mankind—will worship Christ, in the new earth . . . for *eternity.*

PART III

Worship in Heaven

Great and marvelous are your deeds, Lord God Almighty.

Just and true are your ways, King of the ages.

Who will not fear you, O Lord, and bring glory to your name?

For you alone are holy.

All nations will come and worship before you,

for your righteous acts have been revealed.

—REVELATION 15:3–4 NIV

| 21 |

WORSHIP IN ETERNITY

THIS IS THE FINAL CHAPTER IN OUR JOURNEY TO DISCOVERY. And what have we discovered? That the entire Bible, Genesis through Revelation, testifies of God's yearning, not only to show Himself to humankind, but to *dwell* with us. The book of Revelation, this chapter's topic and the crowning of Scripture, not only unveils God the Son as no other biblical book can, but broadcasts for all who read it the arrangements Christ is making to dwell *perpetually* with those He loves, in a place made especially for us—the New Jerusalem—where we will worship Him forever.

In the Revelation of Saint John, as many translations render the book's title, the Holy Spirit pulls back the curtain and gives us a sneak preview of a future that culminates in the eternal reign of our *glorified Savior*. You see, the book, no matter its title, is *not* about John the apostle; neither is it about his vision. It's not about the seven congregations in Asia Minor, whom Christ addressed in chapters 2 and 3. Revelation is not about the Antichrist, and it's not about the Tribulation. In John's own words, the final installment of Holy Writ is "the Revelation of Jesus Christ" (1:1 KJV), the very Star of heaven, and in it we see Jesus as Alpha and Omega, judge, King, Bridegroom—but mostly as the singularly worthy Lamb of God. In fact, at least twenty-six times in this book, Jesus is seen as the "sacrificial Lamb"— the Lamb to be *worshipped*.[1]

But worshipped *how*? In the book of Revelation, we will see in living color what our worship in heaven will be like—and what kind of worship Christ already receives there.

But before we begin detailing the glorious worship that will take place in eternity, as recorded in Revelation, it is important to understand the context in which the book was written. Roman emperor Titus Flavius Domitian had issued an edict demanding that he be worshipped as sovereign lord and God.[2] Christians refused, and as a result, severe persecution of believers—most often ending in death—became the rule of the day. John himself, beloved disciple of Jesus, felt the sting of the emperor's edict: he was sent to a penal colony on the island of Patmos. It was there that John penned the book we know as Revelation.

REVELATION: A BOOK OF WORSHIP

Though the end-times theme that characterizes the book of Revelation is certainly important, it will not be our focus. Details regarding eschatological events, especially the battle between Satan and Christ, will be left to those specializing in prophetic scholarship. We already know who wins, anyway—Jesus Christ, the Son of God. He won the battle the day He rose victorious over death.

For purposes of our study, then, we will focus on Revelation as God's *worship manual*, itemizing for His people perfect worship as offered in heaven. But first, let's take a look at how it all began.

On the Lord's day I was in the Spirit, and I heard a loud voice behind me that sounded like a trumpet. [It] said, "Write what you see in a book" . . . I turned to see who was talking to me [and] I saw . . . someone . . . who was "like a Son of Man" . . . He looked like the sun shining at its brightest time. When I saw him, I fell down at his feet like a dead man. [But] he put his right hand on me and said, "Do not be afraid. I am the First and the Last . . . I was dead, but look, I am alive forever and ever! . . . Write the things you see, what is now and what will happen later." (1:10, 12–13, 16–19 NCV)

The future! All that Revelation has become famous for—and the fodder for countless popular apocalyptic books and movies—was about to be revealed to a banished prophet, by Christ Himself! But before the Son of God would open the curtain for John to see things to come, He first singled out seven churches scattered throughout strategic cities in Asia Minor, and instructed John to write letters—from Christ Himself—to each of them. These were real congregations, made up of real people with real problems. Some of them, like John, dealt with persecution on a day-to-day basis. I wonder how the issues they faced will apply to our understanding and practice of worship . . .

Same Old, Same Old

One would think that those serving Christ in this apostolic age would be resistant to the culture around them. After all, they were witnesses of all that the early church had experienced—the gifts of the Spirit, miracles, and widespread reception of the gospel message. And yet . . . the temptation to bow to idols was as strong for these early believers as it was for their Jewish ancestors—for Jeremiah, for Josiah—and for us today. Though the gospel was spreading throughout the world, with the advancement of the kingdom came all of the challenges associated with living in a heathen community. A blurring of the lines, as it were, was seen between God's revealed truth and the cultural influences of the day. The young Christians to whom John wrote were being influenced by tradition, intellectualism, false doctrines of every kind, dishonest teachers, and the consistent lure of idol worship. And all of these factors shaped the way they worshipped Jesus Christ. What did He think of it?

Report Card Time

In the academic community, strong emphasis is placed on *evaluation*. Teachers and administrators establish cognitive/educational objectives, then, based on these objectives, shape a binding agreement between teacher and student: the syllabus. The syllabus lists for the student the sum of the course assignments. Sometimes it also lists the examination schedule. But with or without warning, students know that an evaluation—an exam—is coming.

It was exam time for the seven churches in Revelation. Each congregation was evaluated by the Teacher, and each was given a report card, so to speak, a pass/fail grade on their performance. "These messages from Christ belong to our day as well as to the first century," wrote American pastor

Warren Wiersbe. "Churches are people, and human nature has not changed. So . . . we must not look on these letters as ancient relics. On the contrary, they are mirrors in which we see ourselves."[3] Well said. And to put it even more bluntly, from their feats to their foibles, we can learn from them.

Two churches were commended for their faithfulness, worship, and love for the Lord. Five were rebuked for their shortcomings. But in the end, *every* church, including those applauded by Christ, was given a recipe that would help them "make the grade" and walk in right relationship with God.

Let's see what we can apply to our own worship experience . . .

The Seven Churches

Smyrna and Philadelphia The two churches receiving commendation from the Lord were those in Smyrna and Philadelphia. Because they refused to acknowledge Caesar as Lord, both flocks had endured suffering. But "the church of Christ persecuted [is] the church of Christ pure. The church of Christ patronized has always been the church of Christ impure,"[4] wrote G. Campbell Morgan. These persecuted parishioners received not *one negative* comment from the Lord. Instead they were encouraged to remain faithful (2:11; 3:11) and were given precious promises to sustain them. To the Smyrnans, Christ pledged "a crown of life" (2:10 NCV); to the Philadelphians, a place as "victory pillars" in God's temple. "They will never have to leave it," Jesus told them. And what's more, they would forever bear *divine inscription*: "I will write on them the name of my God . . . I will also write on them my new name" (3:12 NCV).

Can you imagine Christ being so pleased with our twenty-first-century church as to make us His "victory pillars"? That's what He promised these first-century believers—*if* they would stay on task. Any suffering they would endure would be only for a season, and those who stood against them would one day bow at their feet (3:9). "They will know that I have loved you," He said.

My friend, it will be the same for you—if you will remain faithful.

"Faithful?" you may be saying. "What does faithfulness have to do with worship?" Faithfulness has to do with *everything*. Church attendance, for instance: how much good will it do you or anyone else if your commitment is on-again, off-again? And prayer? If you haven't cultivated a *faithful* prayer life, but instead turn to God only when your life is upended . . . You get the message. It is the same with worship. It takes a real commitment,— *faithfulness*—pressing in, with diligence, to be an A+ worshipper. Sometimes you won't feel like it. When everything in life has gone haywire, worship may be the last thing on your mind. (Perhaps that's why the Bible speaks of a *sacrifice* of praise.) But press in. Make the effort. Remain *faithful*.

For a moment here, allow me to address the worship leaders among you. Servants of God, stay *faithful* to your task. Sure, there are days when it seems you're the *only* one on staff with clear vision for how worship should be. The loneliness of the rehearsal room is almost too much to bear. While those under your leadership are getting "pats on the back," your own labor is seemingly ignored. And trying to find songs that meet the needs of *everyone* in your congregation? A waste of time, you're convinced. The old-timers want songs from yesteryear's hymnals; the younger set want their choruses, products of contemporary musicians, projected on the wall. While one group claps enthusiastically, another "claps" their hands over their ears. *It's useless!* your heart sighs. But friend, it's not. Remember, your worship is *unto the Lord*. After all, our worship here is just a rehearsal for our worship in eternity. Meanwhile, just remain faithful, and God will reward your efforts. He—not the church membership—is the righteous Judge. Meanwhile, look at *every* opportunity to promote God's kingdom through worship as *God's* opportunity. Lost men and women, boys and girls, grandparents, friends, and neighbors will be impacted by the worship—and faithfulness—that you demonstrate.

Ephesus, Pergamum, Thyatira, Sardis, Laodicea The remaining five churches whom Christ addressed received reprimands. Oh, they had *some* strengths, at least most of them. But for a couple, their sins outweighed their good. Take Ephesus: they had plenty of zeal for God, but not much *love* for Him. "You have left your first love," Christ told them sadly (2:4 NKJV). And how could they worship adequately Him whom they had forgotten how to love? Their *works*? They had plenty. The Bible says they "work[ed] hard" (v. 2 NCV). And spiritual purity? These Ephesians simply would not tolerate *any* tainted teachings in their midst (2:2). But again quoting Wiersbe, "labor is no substitute for love; neither is purity a substitute for passion."[5] Passion is essential to worship that pleases God. In fact, you simply can't do it unless you "love Christ fervently."[6] But the church of Ephesus no longer did, and so they were just going through the motions. Many of us do too.

The congregation at Pergamum had a different problem. Even though they were true to God and would even go to their deaths for Him, they were also *tolerant*.

Ah, tolerance. In our postmodern era, it seems to have become the word of the day. Schoolchildren are encouraged to be "tolerant" of others' differences, and good advice that is. But how "tolerant" was Christ as buyers and sellers defiled the house of God? *Not*. Yet the Pergamum congregation was allowing their church to become defiled by members who embraced philosophies totally at odds with the gospel of Christ. Ask me if it affected their worship. Better yet, ask Jesus. "Change your hearts," He told them, and He didn't sugarcoat His warning.

Thyatira was even worse. Knowing fully that one of their leaders was engaging in both sexual sin and idol worship—and leading the congregation to do the same—they still tolerated her leadership.

I once knew of a pastor who, like the Thyatirans, was fully aware of the sexual sin of his worship leader. This young man was sleeping around, going to bars, making a mockery of the pulpit from which he led the church in worship—and making a mockery of Christ.

But, oh, did he have talent. And he was *so* well liked—by the pastor anyway. His angelic voice and clever song selection was sure to cheerlead the congregation into a worshipful fury week after week, even as he himself continued to slink into dark taverns and motel rooms weekend after weekend.

Worship leader, if that's you, *stop it*—or get off of the platform! Pastor, if this is going on in your church, remove that worship leader—immediately. If the pastor won't—then, deacons, do it for him. Worshippers, refuse to sit under the ministry of *anyone* who is sinning blatantly and "does not want to change" (2:21 NCV). Don't *tolerate* it. Jesus didn't. He warned the church at Thyatira that if they did not remove the wicked worship leader in their assembly, she—*and they*—would die. Worship is serious to God. He doesn't take it lightly. Neither should you.

Then there was Sardis. Theirs was a congregation marked by formalism, spiritual death, and immobility. Maybe they were so content with their ceremony and liturgy that they had lulled themselves to sleep. "Wake up!" Christ told them, ". . . before what you have left dies completely" (v. 2 NCV). Sadly, folks *thought* this church was really "on fire."

The church in Laodicea certainly couldn't be accused of being "on fire." But neither could they be accused of being stone cold. "I wish you *were* hot or cold!" Jesus spat in disgust. But they were neither; they were lukewarm, and they made Jesus sick (see 3:16).

Perhaps the Laodiceans were like so many congregations today, resting on their laurels while still singing the praises of their *past* achievements. How many worship programs still revel in the successes of bygone Christmas or Easter pageants? Maybe God really did bless those past endeavors. But we cannot be satisfied to *remain* in the past. We must move on to new and exciting venues for proclaiming the wonders of God.

What about those worship ministries that are addicted to the ever-popular *annual worship conference*? Excitedly they bring in worship "experts" and celebrities to help lead and teach worship. All the while, their own worship segments are lifeless, stale, unprepared, dated. All of us have certainly seen ministries like this, each having a wonderful portfolio, but dead and empty on the inside. These once-vibrant and innovative praise teams, whose worship at one time entertained God's favor, are stuck in the past, rejoicing in *historical* achievements, *former* leadership, and *long-ago* revivals, while incapable (or fearful) *today* of attempting to lead their congregations into new worship experiences. In a word, *stagnant*—and happy to be that way. Just like the Laodiceans (see verse 16 MSG).

But the Laodiceans were also rich. "[We] do not need a thing," they said (3:17 NIV). Yes, they did. They needed fresh fire. They just couldn't see it. I've seen churches today just like them. "Our choir lofts are full," they brag. "We have all the money and resources any church could ever want. We've got paid staff, complete with sound engineers, rhythm players, arrangers, lighting personnel . . ." But their *love* for God has gone tepid, as has any passionate commitment to know Him—and lead others to know Him—through worship. As a result, their worship "presentations" wax routine, and their ministry becomes powerless. How does God feel about them? "You make me want to vomit" (v. 16 MSG).

Sadly, there is no record of any one of the five reprimanded churches repenting. And one by one, they drifted off the pages of history, to be forgotten. They should have judged themselves—their ministry, their worship, and their personal relationships with God—long before God had to judge them and remove them from their place.

Dear worship leader, why don't you take a moment now to judge, or evaluate, your own worship ministry? I'll do the same. Are we in danger of the same indictment that Christ pronounced against Ephesus? Does our worship leadership—not to mention our *personal* worship—reveal that we have "lost our first love"?

"How can I know *that?*" you wonder? Well, let's examine what happens during the corporate worship that you lead. Obviously, we worship leaders want to "make worship happen just right." Yet too often, the spotlight is on the presentation—lights, sound, EQ, visuals, great instrumentals performed by phenomenal instrumentalists, tight vocals—with little time spent with God before leading worship. Many of today's ministers of music spend just minutes—if even that long—seeking God and asking for His anointing and manifestation in the worship service. Instead they are seeking to please man. Have to look good, sound good—all selfish motives. Meanwhile, the very One to whom the "sound" is being offered is left out of the picture. No wonder our worship has no power. It's just noise.

You've been there. So have I. And if we're not careful, we will go back to staging those loveless, mechanical worship sets all over again, instead of heeding Christ's counsel to Ephesus: "Remember where you were before you fell" (2:5 NCV). Where *were* we before we fell? We were in love with Jesus.

Let's talk about your sacrifices of praise. Are they being compromised by your desire to be accepted? Do you hungrily seek the approval of an ungodly music/entertainment industry primarily interested in making a quick buck? Be careful. Their favorable reception is often a trap set by the deceiver himself.

And what about your motives for being in the ministry of worship? Are they driven by greed? a commercial opportunity? a desire for recognition?

a craving for professional acclaim? Beware.

Who is in charge of your "praise and worship," really? The Holy Spirit, or a *carnal* spirit that leads you to choose grandstanding over connecting with God?

And how's the content of your worship sets these days? Do your choruses suddenly say less and less about the blood of Jesus? the Cross? repentance? Have these sacred themes been replaced by the latest "worship speak," cool drum loops, or lyrics from dynamic (but shallow), new recordings that reduce the time of worship to a happy-go-lucky sing-along?

It's easy to do. It's easy to substitute "bubble gum" lyrics for those that maximize the Creator and minimize the creature. But worship leader, we *must* keep the main thing, the main thing. As *The Message* says it, "GOD is God, and God, GOD. He made us" (Ps. 100). For what? To worship Him.

So worship Him. Make your worship pure. And lead others in pure worship too. Jesus Christ is your "first love." Don't lose Him, as did Ephesus, in the midst of your "worship." Don't let your worship become a sham, as did those in Thyatira and Sardis. Don't mix the authentic with the carnal, the way worshippers in Pergamum did. And above all, don't *nauseate* the Lord, as did Laodicea, with musty, dusty worship from hearts that have long become lukewarm and numb to His majesty.

Our study in worship could easily stop here with Jesus' messages to the seven churches. But there is so much more. And we really do need to see "the rest of the story." We know what worship is like here on earth. But what will it be like where God Himself lives? How will we worship in "time without end"?

WORSHIP IN ETERNITY

I saw a new heaven and a new earth, for the first heaven and the first earth had passed away . . . Then I, John, saw the holy city, New Jerusalem, coming down out of heaven from God, prepared as a bride adorned for her husband. And I heard a loud voice from heaven saying, "Behold, the tabernacle of God is with men, and He will dwell with them . . . God Himself will be with them." (Rev. 21:1–3 NKJV)

Revelation 21 is proof positive of how deeply God loves you and me. Read the rest of that chapter, why don't you. You'll see how much He cares. He plans to take away all our tears, all our pain, all sorrow, all death, and to cap it all, He is preparing a place—right now—where we will *forever* make our home with Him. Jesus promised this Himself when He told His disciples, "I am going . . . to prepare a place for you. After [that] . . . I will come back and take you to be with me so that you may be where I am" (John 14:2–3 NCV). Jesus wants us to be *with* Him, and someday we will be. For all eternity we will live with Him, walk with Him, talk with Him.

And we will worship Him. Remember, it's what we were created for. Inside each of us is an innate need to worship something. In eternity future, that hunger will be satisfied—by God Himself. No other object of worship has brought satisfaction to humanity, through all their ages-long searching, but in eternity, our thirst will finally be quenched, because *He* will be there, the perfect Object of worship—*with us*. For all time.

It is more than a coincidence that the New Testament word for worship, *proskuneo*, appears more times in Revelation than any other book. It is what we will do in the new heaven and new earth: worship. But what will our worship be like? Forever is a long time. Will we just be singing "Hallelujah" for a million years? And then a million more after that? Or will there be an "order of service"?

A Vision of Worship

> After [my] vision . . . I looked, and there before me was an open door in heaven. And the same voice that spoke to me before, that sounded like a trumpet, said, "Come up here" . . . Before me was a throne in heaven, and someone was sitting on it. The One who sat on the throne looked like precious stones . . . Around the throne there were . . . twenty-four elders . . . dressed in white . . . Around the throne were four living creatures. (4:1–4, 6 NCV)

So often, I hear well-meaning worship leaders talk about "letting the worship flow out of us." But in so doing, some actually refuse to set down an order of worship or establish any kind of liturgy for their presentations of praise. So deeply committed to spontaneity are they, that they will even say, "Look, I want to be genuine in my worship. I'll just let the Spirit move me to choose the right songs."

I'm sure this argument could give one pause, and maybe even spark a debate. We certainly don't want to hinder the working of the Spirit in our worship services or squelch the spontaneous move that He can bring. However, we do need to answer this question: Does God also expect an *order* of worship? Revelation 4 and 5 certainly suggest that God values the organization of praise and worship in heaven. In fact, author Allen Ross, in *Recalling the Hope of Glory*, has identified a sevenfold pattern for worship, based on these very chapters, and encourages today's worshipper to adopt this heavenly pattern in their weekly worship.[7] But whether or not we agree with Ross's suggested order of service, we can still get a bird's-eye view of *worship in heaven* from these scriptures. We can also capture a glimpse of what *our own* worship of God will be like in eternity.

So what does John the Revelator allow us to see in his text? What happened in the heavenly worship service that he witnessed in Revelation 4 and 5?

Corporate Worship

First, there was corporate praise, day and night, initiated by the "worship team," who "give glory, honor, and thanks" to the One seated on the throne (4:9 NCV): "Holy, holy, holy is the Lord God Almighty," they cried. "He was, he is, and he is coming" (v. 8 NCV). Unable to contain their rapture, a congregation of elders joined in, bowing down before God, placing their crowns before His throne, and worshipping Him (v. 10). "You are worthy, our Lord and God, to receive glory and honor and power, because you made all things. Everything existed and was made, because you wanted it" (v. 11 NCV). Then "thousands and thousands of angels" added their voices to the praise, "saying with a loud voice, 'The Lamb who was killed is worthy to receive power, wealth, wisdom, and strength, honor, glory, and praise!'" Finally, "all creatures in heaven and on earth and under the earth and in the sea" cried, "To the One who sits on the throne and to the Lamb be praise and honor and glory and power forever and ever." Then the people "bowed down and worshiped" (5:11–14 NCV).

Notice that no one in these passages seems to be under *compulsion* to worship God. No one is standing there, cracking the whip and demanding veneration. The whole of heaven is rejoicing voluntarily and *from the heart*. Why? Because they know that Jesus Christ is no longer that baby in a manger, represented by so many cracked and peeling images in Nativity sets the world over. Neither is He the bleeding and broken "criminal," humbled and half-naked on a cross, the victim of those who thought they were bigger than Him. And He's not the cold and mangled corpse that once lay in a borrowed tomb either. Those whose praises fill the heavens know that Jesus Christ is exalted. He is *all in all*, and heaven's inhabitants never tire of worshipping Him. Neither will we. You and I will never run out of things to thank Him for, and praising Him will never become boring.

Congregational Singing

A New Song

And they sang a new song: "You are worthy to take the scroll and to open its seals, because you were slain, and with your blood you purchased men for God from every tribe and language and people and nation. You have made them to be a kingdom and priests to serve our God, and they will reign on the earth." (5:9–10 NIV)

And I heard a sound from heaven like the noise of flooding water and like the sound of loud thunder. The sound I heard was like people playing harps. And they sang a new song before the throne. (14:2–3 NCV)

Oh, the music John heard in heaven! And friends, we will make music too, when we join the great company before the throne. You say you don't like to sing? Well, the Greek word used here, *adō*, indicates that what John heard was literally "a lyrical emotion [from] . . . devout, grateful soul[s]." In other words . . . *they couldn't help themselves*! And when we stand before the perfect Lamb of God, we won't be able to contain ourselves either. Filled with emotion, and without reserve, we will sing to Jesus, our hearts full of love and gratitude—not bored resignation. We won't have to "muster up" the energy to open our mouths. Instead, willingly, freely, and enthusiastically we will sing the song of the redeemed:

A Song of Redemption
You are worthy . . .
For You were slain,
And have redeemed us to God by Your blood
Out of every tribe and tongue and people and nation,
And have made us kings and priests to our God;
And we shall reign on the earth. (5:9–10 NKJV)

Even the angels will sit up and take notice as we sing this redemption song. It's a song that they *cannot* sing. Only those who have been purchased by the precious blood of Christ can sing this melody. That's you, my friend, and me, and as we recall in eternity how Jesus bought us with His own blood, "while we were yet sinners" (Rom. 5:8 KJV), you'd better believe we'll sing it, and the angels can only listen!

There is singing up in Heaven such as we have never known,
Where the angels sing the praises of the Lamb upon the
    throne,
Their sweet harps are ever tuneful, and their voices always
    clear,
Oh, that we might be more like them while we serve the
    Master here!

Refrain:
Holy, holy, is what the angels sing,
And I expect to help them make the courts of heaven ring;
But when I sing redemption's story, they will fold their wings,
For angels never felt the joys that our salvation brings.

Then the angels stand and listen, for they cannot join the
    song,
Like the sound of many waters, by that happy, blood-washed
    throng,

For they sing about great trials, battles fought and vict'ries won,
And they praise their great Redeemer, who hath said to them,
  "Well done."

WORDS BY JOHNSON OATMAN JR.
MUSIC BY JOHN R. SWENEY
PUBLIC DOMAIN. WRITTEN IN 1894

A *Victory Song*

Great and marvelous are your deeds, Lord God Almighty. Just and true
are your ways, King of the ages. Who will not fear you, O Lord, and
bring glory to your name? For you alone are holy. All nations will come
and worship before you, for your righteous acts have been revealed.
(Rev. 15:3–4 NIV)

This will be our victory song! When we know that we have seen the
last of our enemy, Satan, our voices will resonate with worship to the
One who defeated him. And our worship will be *perfect*. That which was
intended by God in Eden will now be fulfilled in the new heaven and
the new earth. *Perfect worship in a perfect place!* Free of the commotion
of our day, unhindered by any foe. And brimming with the presence of
the Messiah! It's enough to make even the quietest among us shout,
"Hallelujah!"

The "Hallelujah Chorus"

Then I heard what sounded like a great multitude, like the roar of rush-
ing waters and like loud peals of thunder, shouting: "Hallelujah! For
our Lord God Almighty reigns. Let us rejoice and be glad and give him
glory! For the wedding of the Lamb has come, and his bride has made
herself ready" . . . "Blessed are those who are invited to the wedding
supper of the Lamb!" (19:6–9 NIV)

One day, worshipper, you and I will be a part of that great multitude, that *choir from all the nations.* No one really knows what kind of choir it will be—contemporary, classical, traditional, or gospel—but it won't matter. And even if you couldn't carry a tune on earth, or didn't have a lick of musical talent, it *won't matter.* You and I and all who love Christ will be *qualified* to join the eternal chorus, and together our voices will sound across the universe, in one unified statement: *"We love Jesus; He is worthy to be praised!"* Then, with Him, we will celebrate the consummation of the plan of the ages—Christ's eternal plan to *dwell with those He loves.*

> And he who sits on the throne will spread his tent over them. Never again will they hunger; never again will they thirst. The sun will not beat upon them, nor any scorching heat. For the Lamb at the center of the throne will be their shepherd; he will lead them to springs of living water. And God will wipe away every tear from their eyes. (Rev. 7:15–17 NIV)

HE WANTS TO BRING US *HOME*!

My dear friend Jonathan Thigpen once told me the story of an old missionary who was returning to New York City from Africa—on the same ship that would carry President Teddy Roosevelt to shore. After years of service on the mission field, this missionary and his wife were retiring—physically broken, financially insecure, and emotionally defeated.

As the great ship docked at the New York harbor, thousands of people celebrated the return of the president. The band played. People shouted. And the mayor himself greeted President Roosevelt with great fanfare and glee.

But the missionary couple stood on the dock alone. No one was there to greet them. Nobody even knew they were back in the States. And worse, they had no place to go. The missionary began to despair.

But suddenly he had a vision of heaven—as if he were actually there! Before him were the pearly gates, streets of gold, walls of jasper, and in his mind's eye he could see loved ones who had gone on before him, lined up to welcome him to heaven. Oh, he had missed them, and how he'd longed to see them since they left the earth!

But then someone tapped him on the shoulder. Turning, the missionary looked into the eyes of the One he had *really* longed to see: Jesus! "Welcome home, My son," said the Son of God to the aged missionary, "welcome home." Then that tired but faithful missionary was embraced—by God.

My friend Jonathan has also been embraced by God. Early on a Sunday morning in 2001, after a long battle with Lou Gehrig's disease, Jonathan entered the presence of the Lord. And he is already worshipping before the throne—because he is home. When we get to heaven, we'll be home too, and there, with Jonathan and the old missionary, we will worship in a cloud of glory, for all eternity, with all of the saints that have gone on before us.

But we don't have to wait until we get to heaven to enjoy God. We can enjoy Him in the present. Do you want to? Then go ahead and cultivate a heart for worship *right now*. Yes, I know we "see through a glass, darkly" (1 Cor. 11:11 KJV). "We're squinting in a fog, peering through a mist. But it won't be long before the weather clears and the sun shines bright! We'll see it all then . . . as clearly as God sees us, knowing him directly just as he knows us! But for right now, until that completeness, we have three things to do to lead us toward that consummation: Trust steadily in God, hope unswervingly, love extravagantly" (vv. 11–13 MSG).

Yes, friends, love God *extravagantly*. Thank Him *profusely*. Worship Him *lavishly*. Do your efforts frustrate you? It'll get better; trust me. The worship we do our level best to offer now will be *perfect* someday. But for now, remember . . .

We are not home yet. The best is yet to come.

He who testifies to these things [Jesus] says, "Yes, I am coming soon."
Amen. Come, Lord Jesus.
The grace of the Lord Jesus be with God's people. Amen.

(REV. 22:20–21 NIV)

SUMMARY

It was nearly forty-six years ago that my brother, Rodney, and I stood and watched our husky give birth to her puppies. Rodney was only eleven at the time. Since that day, we have grown up, married, reared children of our own, and pursued careers in education, music, military, and ministry.

But, my brother's love for Siberian huskies remained firm. He had started running sled dogs as a youth—first, in the fifth grade, in the junior races; next, in high school, in the junior North American. Some kids dream of becoming a football hero, baseball legend, or entertainment icon. But Rodney? He dreamed of the day when he could be known as a professional musher, running the big races.

At fifty-six, my brother ran in the "Last Great Race"[1]—the Iditarod Trail Sled Dog Race. This 1,150-mile trail from Anchorage to Nome, Alaska, is one of the most grueling and intense races in the world. Only ninety-five teams qualified to enter, by running in at least three previous competitions totaling 1,000 miles. If nothing else, the qualifying runs are a statement of endurance.

On March 1, 2008, Rodney left Fourth Avenue in downtown Anchorage with sixteen strong, fast, and eager dogs lined up in front of him. See, God had placed something in his heart, at a very young age, that could only be satisfied by running the race—behind a team of dogs across the Alaskan snow.

But God also placed *another* desire in Rodney's heart—and in yours and mine: the desire to know *Him*—and respond to Him in worship.

In *Called to Worship*, we have studied God's Story. And as we watched history (that is, "His story") unfold, we have also witnessed the unfolding of *redemption*—and God's plan to *dwell with man*.

In chapters 1 and 2, we were witnesses of God's first revelation: His desire for *relationship* with man, which would be achieved through *worship*. In the book of Genesis, God revealed Himself to us as the Creator of a perfect universe—and perfect humankind, with whom he chose to dwell.

In chapter 3, we further studied in Genesis the three great worship wars and observed the outcome of those conflicts upon all humanity. Sin. Disgrace. Death. Yet even so, God still seeks to dwell with man. And in chapters 4–6, He made that desire known by revealing Himself to the patriarchs Abraham and Moses.[2] What was the response of these choice servants, each time, to God's revelation?

Worship.

The books of history, which we viewed in chapters 7–11[3] further taught us about man's response to God. And again, man worshipped, teaching us along the way worship both naughty and nice. Chapter 9 focused on worship as defined by three successive kings. One wanted to worship above the law. One chose to worship as a servant. And one, even if for a few years, was a most sincere worshipper. But from the lives of *all three*, valuable lessons in worship are there for the mining.

The books of Poetry and Wisdom, which we looked at in chapters 12–14, taught us about building relationship with God through song—and integrity. The Prophets in chapter 15 gave us counsel for overcoming idolatry. In a phrase: *Come home*. But most men didn't.

So . . . four hundred years of silence, with no official record of God's voice moving in the hearts of men.

But early one Sabbath morning, a priest offered incense—and the silence was broken as God once again chose to reveal Himself. First to Zechariah. Later, to Mary. And then . . . God revealed Himself in human form—in the birth of a baby. How did man respond? Worship in the field. Worship by three sages. Worship from the multitudes. And in chapters 16 and 17, we witnessed the worship of fishermen, prostitutes, soldiers—and the Son of God. Jesus Christ became the ultimate example of worship. He worshipped in the sanctuary; He worshipped by serving; He worshipped in song—and He worshipped by submitting—to death on a cross. As horrific as it was, it was the will of God, and by submission to God's will, Jesus exemplified *perfect worship* as no one else could. Better yet, His provided the once-for-all sacrifice for sin—*our* sin—changing worship forever. And best of all, He rose triumphantly from the grave and stands today at the right hand of the Father in heaven, ever interceding on our behalf and serving as our high priest.

In chapters 18–20, John, Peter, Silas, and Paul drew our attention to the worship of the early church, and again, we saw God revealed—in the indwelling person of the Holy Spirit. From that point on, men and women, with the resident Spirit of God *inside* them, became true catalysts of change. God sent them, empowered, out into a world in need of salvation. Now all of humanity—Jew and Gentile alike—were wholeheartedly welcomed into the fold.

Finally, we beheld the culmination of the plan begun in Genesis—in the book of Revelation. Chapter 21 unveiled both history past *and* the future to come. First, from history, we learned of seven no-longer-existent churches who, even in their absence today, teach us for all time what worship should and should not be.

Then, at last . . . we witnessed the Desire of the Ages, Jesus Christ, the exalted Bridegroom, join His bride and dwell with His worshippers *forever*.

Who is this Jesus, our eternal object of worship?

In Genesis . . .	He is the Creator and the Seed of Woman
In Exodus . . .	He is our Passover Lamb
In Leviticus . . .	He is our High Priest and the Sacrifice for Sins
In Numbers . . .	He is the Cloud, the Fire, and the One High and Lifted Up
In Deuteronomy . . .	He is the One True Prophet
In Joshua . . .	He is the Captain of the Lord's Army
In Judges . . .	He is the Lawmaker, Judge, and Jury
In Ruth . . .	He is our Kinsman Redeemer
In 1 and 2 Samuel . . .	He is the Prophet of the Lord
In Kings and Chronicles . . .	He is our only King
In Ezra . . .	He is our Inerrant Scribe

In Nehemiah . . .	He is the Repairer of the Breach
In Esther . . .	He is our Advocate
In Job . . .	He is our Dayspring and Living Redeemer
In Psalms . . .	He is our Shepherd and Song
In Proverbs . . .	He is Wisdom Personified
In Ecclesiastes . . .	He is the End of All Things
In the Song of Solomon . . .	He is the Shepherd-Lover of our Souls
In Isaiah . . .	He is the Coming Messiah and Prince of Peace
In Jeremiah . . .	He is the Righteous Branch
In Lamentations . . .	He is the Weeping Prophet and the God of Faithfulness
In Ezekiel . . .	He is the Son of Man and the Wheel Within a Wheel
In Daniel . . .	He is the Striking Stone and the Fourth Man
In Hosea . . .	He is the Husband and Healer of the Backslider
In Joel . . .	He is the Baptizer in the Holy Ghost
In Amos . . .	He is the Heavenly Husbandman and Burden Bearer
In Obadiah . . .	He is Our Savior
In Jonah . . .	He is the Resurrection and the One Who Forgives
In Micah . . .	He is the Messenger with beautiful feet
In Nahum . . .	He is the Avenger of God's elect, the Stronghold in the day of trouble
In Habakkuk . . .	He is the Great Evangelist, and the God of our salvation
In Zephaniah . . .	He is the One Who Restores Lost Heritage
In Haggai . . .	He is the Desire of All Nations and the Cleansing Fountain
In Zechariah . . .	He is the Fountain of Life and the Son Who Was Pierced
In Malachi . . .	He is the Sun of Righteousness
In Matthew . . .	He is the Promised Messiah
In Mark . . .	He is the Wonder-working Servant
In Luke . . .	He is the Son of Man

In John . . .	He is the Word Made Flesh and the Son of God
In Acts . . .	He is the Ascended Lord and the Voice from the Heavens
In Romans . . .	He is the One Who Justifies
In 1 and 2 Corinthians . . .	He is our Sufficient Lord
In Galatians . . .	He is the One Who Brings Liberty
In Ephesians . . .	He is the Christ of Great Riches, and our All in All
In Philippians . . .	He is our Joy and the Meeter of All our Needs
In Colossians . . .	He is the Fullness of the Godhead, Bodily Head, Our life
In 1 and 2 Thessalonians . . .	He is our Blessed Hope and Coming King
In 1 and 2 Timothy . . .	He is our Mentor and Mediator
In Titus . . .	He is our Example and Devoted Pastor
In Philemon . . .	He is our Friend and brother
In Hebrews . . .	He is the High Priest, Intercessor, and New Covenant
In James . . .	He is the Great Physician and our Pattern for Daily Living
In 1 and 2 Peter . . .	He is the Chief Shepherd and Cornerstone of our faith
In 1, 2, and 3 John . . .	He is Love Everlasting
In Jude . . .	He is the Lord, coming with ten thousand of His saints
In Revelation . . .	He is the Lamb That Was Slain the Triumphant King the Bridegroom, and the Lord of Lords . . .[4]

and we worship Him!

Now, at the end of all things, what do we need to remember about worship?

Worship is what we were made for. God created man because He wanted relationship. It's what He's about, and by now it must be clear that the way—the only way—to an intimate relationship with God is through *worship*. As we worship, we must be reminded to stay focused on the God of wonder. Worship is NOT the music, the methods, or the messenger. Worship is our expression of *love* to the Father, Son, and Holy Spirit, lived out in our daily lives.

But never forget that there's an enemy to worship. Every worship war past was lost when men and women succumbed to his evil schemes. He is Satan the thief, and he will do everything in his power to rob God of the worship that belongs only to Him. He will also rob you. He will distract you during your times of worship. He will cause you to get your priorities out of order. He will keep you busy and harried so you neglect your time alone with God. And he'll rob you of your companionship with God.

But only if you let him.

You can win the battle for worship, but only to the extent that you know One you worship. So . . .

We must read the Word of God. Worship is our response to God's revelation, and God reveals Himself in His Word. Your successful, meaningful worship, then, will be in direct proportion to your commitment to God's Word. It is impossible to worship the God of truth without spending quality time learning about Him through His written Word. His Word is a shining light. It will reveal God as He really is: powerful, supreme—yet kind and forever loving. It will also reveal us as we really are: shameful, sinful, and rebellious. We will see our sin. And it will leave us broken, and that's a good thing.

Brokenness is a prerequisite for genuine worship. We must be broken in spirit, broken of self, broken . . . and surrendered. The world certainly has done enough to break us. We live in a world of broken lives, broken marriages, broken homes, and broken hearts. But God is in the business of mending hearts, repairing relationships, and putting families back together. But before He can restore us to beauty, we must be broken before Him. We must come to him, with open hands, and surrender our wills as things unclean to a holy God. It is then, during our moment of total surrender, that He will reveal Himself at His best—as Repairer, Restorer, and Lover of our broken souls. And we will worship Him for it!

But, oh, how we like to resist. Our hearts are made of many rooms—and we isolate God to just a few of them. Friends, resistance to the authority of God in our lives, no matter how small the area we seek to control, will disrupt and disengage communication with God. And it will derail our worship.

But if we will stay *broken*—surrendered to God—He will have free control of *every* room in our hearts, and our worship will be vibrant, fulfilling—and precious. *He'll* be there.

Obedience is the very nucleus of worship. If you forget everything else, remember this. We can be broken all we want to. We can be demonstrative until the cows come home. But if we are unwilling to *obey*—if we refuse to do what God *wants* us to—then He will never pick up our broken pieces, and He will reject all of our demonstration. Valid worship begins and ends with obedience—that is, *submission*—to the will of almighty God. And what does He "will" for us?

Holiness. It goes hand in hand with submission. It can never simply be one or the other. Obedience *and* holiness are required of God's bona fide worshippers. But once we do truly submit to God, unreservedly, then our obedience to Him will *drive* us to holiness. We will hunger for it. And we need to. We fool ourselves if we think that our worship will be accepted by God while mixed with hidden sin, anger, malice, jealousy, greed, lust, or hatred. God is holy, and He does not dwell in the presence of sin.

Real worshippers demonstrate personal integrity. In other words, *honest* worship means honesty in *all things*. Public worship is a powerful thing, but it is not enough. We must worship God privately too, and part of that worship is embodied in our *ethics*—toward one another. Sincerity in relationships. Honesty in business. And integrity in conduct toward our families, friends, and neighbors. This is day-to-day, lived-out, private worship, and it bears fruit. A lost generation will only respond to those who are genuine in spirit, presentation, and application. When you worship God *genuinely*, through a lifestyle of integrity, you will impact those around you and attract them to your *God of worship*.

True worship embraces love for the people of God—demonstrated through service. Without a doubt, when God's people turn their hearts to biblical worship, there will be social change. And with that change comes ethical and moral accountability. Our worship of God cannot be isolated from the real world or trapped inside the walls of our "secret place." It must impact us to reach out to and at times confront the culture around us. Remember how Israel neglected the marginalized and abused the widows—and were condemned by the prophets? And remember the religious leaders whom Jesus rebuked for the very same sin? These all were *hypocritical worshippers.* They served no one but themselves. But when we have been truly captured by the glory of God, our worship will play out in service to those in need—believer and unbeliever alike.

Our multifaceted God loves multifaceted worship. There's more than one way to worship: singing, praying, giving, serving, preaching, evangelizing, testifying, drum-beating, guitar-playing . . . and the list goes on. Worship of our many-faceted God can and should include *all* of these expressions. Balanced worship (corporate and private) provides time for them all. We ought to sing. We need to pray. We should testify to everyone we know about Christ. And we *must* feed on His word. But anytime, dear pastor or worship leader, we place emphasis on just one or two areas (such as music or evangelism), our worship gets out of balance, we lose focus, and we give in to the temptation to be controlled by the very elements that should facilitate our worship. Out-of-balance results in compartmentalized worship, that is, worship grouped into a series of activities, events, or strategic marketing moments. Then we will draw worship *boundaries*, determining for ourselves—and others—what is "acceptable" based on cultural pressure, ecclesiastical norms, and our own personal preferences—to the exclusion of anyone else's. Don't do it. Personal preferences will change over time, as will norms, styles, and all that is associated with this world. But . . .

Genuine worship transcends time and culture. Music expressions in worship naturally change with each passing generation. Handel is not quite so popular anymore. Most of us march to the beat of a different drum now. Forms of communication, too, continue to be refined and updated. Once, the gospel was communicated by circuit-riding preachers on horseback. Now we communicate live via satellite, on HDTV and over the Internet. But these methods of communication are *only* facilitators of worship. As technology advances, music become more international, and our information venues continue to develop, the facilitators will change.

But God will not. He is the same yesterday, today, and forever. And the formula for biblical worship will also remain the same: *Love the LORD your God with all your heart, with all your soul, and with all your strength"* (Deut. 6:5 NKJV). That's worship that transcends time and culture. And it's our calling.

Are you answering that *call to worship?*

ACKNOWLEDGMENTS

SCORES OF PEOPLE HAVE HELPED SHAPE THIS BOOK, NONE more important than Beth, my precious wife of more than thirty-five years; our two children, Laurie and Jeremy; and their spouses. Not only have these family members supported me through this endeavor, but they have also taught me. I value the insight they have given me throughout the various stages of crafting this manuscript.

God has also allowed me to learn from the people we served at various churches and the wonderful colleagues with whom I have been privileged to labor over the years—pastors, fellow ministers, musicians, and staff members. Thank you.

Thank-yous also go to hundreds of worship students who have sat under my teaching these past years. They give me energy to stay fresh, pursue the study of worship as a scholarly discipline, and preach/teach worship with authority and conviction. Thank you, too, to my colleagues at the Center for Worship and the administration at Liberty University. These fine folks have stood beside me, supported our ministry, and given much-needed encouragement along the way.

Writing this book has been a journey of faith, inquiry, and at times determination. And, alongside my efforts has been the incredible and professional work of freelance editor Reneé Chavez, and Michael Stephens of Thomas Nelson Publishers. This book would have never seen the light of day without their labor of love, direction, guidance, kind words, firm cautions, editing, more editing, encouragement, more editing, insight, and . . . did I say editing? I am eternally grateful. I love these choice servants.

Finally, the greatest and most important thank-You goes to the Lord, God Himself —the author and finisher of our faith. He is Yahweh, King of the Ages, who in the fullness of time sent His only Son, JESUS, to come to this world to redeem us so that we could become His *worshippers*. I love the Lord with all my heart. I trust that this book tells His story well. After all, it *is His* story.

NOTES

Introduction

1. James Strong, *The New Strong's Exhaustive Concordance of the Bible* (Nashville: Thomas Nelson, 1997). See Hebrew word numbers 7812 and 5457 (*worship*); and 8426, 8416, 7623, 3034, 2167, and 1984 (*praise*); and Greek word numbers 4576, 4352, 3000, 2151, and 1799 (*worship*); and 133, 134, 136, 1867, 1868, and 5214 (*praise*).

Chapter 1

1. Anne Graham Lotz, *God's Story*, 2ⁿᵈ ed. (Nashville: Thomas Nelson, 1999), xii.

2. Etymology: Middle English *revelacioun*, from Anglo-French, from Late Latin *revelation-*, *revelatio*, from Latin *revelare* to reveal; an act of revealing or communicating divine truth. It is something revealed by God to humans; an act of revealing to view or making known; something that is revealed; *especially*: an enlightening or astonishing disclosure.

3. According to Harold Best in *Music Through the Eyes of Faith* (New York: HarperOne, 1993), what God "richly imagines" He also carefully structures (13).

4. Creation is "the act of creating; *especially*: the act of bringing the world into ordered existence." Further, it is "the act of making, inventing, or producing" and is also "something that is created: as . . . an original work of art." (*Merriam-Webster's Online Dictionary*, s.v. "creation," http://mw1.merriam-webster.com/dictionary/creation [accessed October 12, 2007]).

5. According to the *Handbook of Christian Apologetics*, by Peter Kreeft and Ronald K. Tacelli (Downers Grove, IL: InterVarsity Press, 1994), the Greek philosophers thought the notion that God created the world "out of nothing" *(ex nihilo)* was irrational. But, the authors argue, God creating out of nothing is consistent with His character. God is infinite and is not limited by the rules of the finite. Thus, the writers conclude, "the idea of God creating out of nothing is not irrational because it does not claim that anything ever popped into existence without an adequate cause. God did not pop into existence, and nature did have an adequate cause: God" (104–5).

6. *Elohim* is the Hebrew word for God. It is the plural of *El,* meaning "the Strong One." God is the all-powerful Creator of the universe. He knows all, and is everywhere at all times (Nathan Stone, *Names of God* [Chicago: Moody, 1944], 11–17).

7. See Genesis 1:1–3; 18:25; Deuteronomy 10:17; Psalm 7:9–12; 57:2; 68; Mark 13:19; Joshua 2:11; 24:19.

8. The etymology of *create:* Middle English, from Latin *creatus,* past participle of *creare;* akin to Latin *crescere* to grow—a *transitive verb* meaning to bring into existence—Genesis 1:1; to produce or bring about by a course of action or behavior; to produce through imaginative skill; to design. As an *intransitive verb* it means to make or bring into existence something new. (*Merriam-Webster's Online Dictionary*)

9. In John 1:1–5, Jesus was introduced as "the Word."

10. Nathan Stone provides twelve names in *Names of God:* Elohim, Jehovah, El-Shaddai, Adonai, Jehovah-jireh, Jehovah-rophe, Jehovah-nissi, Jeshovah-M'Kaddesh, Jehovah-shalom, Jehovah-tsidkenu, Jehovah-rohi, and Jehovah-shammah.

11. A. W. Tozer, *Whatever Happened to Worship?: A Call to True Worship* (Camp Hill, PA: WingSpread Publishers, 2006), 53.

12. According to Blackaby in Henry Blackaby and Ron Owen, *Worship: Believers Experiencing God* (Nashville: LifeWay Press, 2001), "breathed" describes the intimacy of a face-to-face relationship (3).

13. Gen. 2:20. The NKJV uses the word *comparable.* The NCV uses "right for him."

14. Tozer, *Whatever Happened to Worship?,* 37.

Chapter 2

1. A. W. Tozer, *Worship: Missing Jewel Evangelism* (Camp Hill, PA: Christian Publications, 1996), 3.

2. Leonard Sweet, *Out of the Question . . . Into the Mystery: Getting Lost in the GodLife Relationship* (Colorado Springs: WaterBrook Press, 2004), 10. The premise of Sweet's book is that worship is built on a GodLife relationship. He contends that faith itself is a relationship. He supports this thesis by investigating the truth of relationships with God, God's story, other people of faith, those outside of faith, God's creation, the spiritual world, and more.

3. Allen P. Ross. *Recalling the Hope of Glory: Biblical Worship from the Garden to the New Creation* (Grand Rapids: Kregel Academic, 2006), 90.

4. A. W. Tozer and Gerald B. Smith, *Men Who Met God* (Camp Hill, PA: WingSpread, 2007), 23.

5. "Westminster Shorter Catechism," http://www.reformed.org/documents/WSC. html.

6. C. S. Lewis, *Reflections on the Psalms* (San Diego: Harvest, 1964), 94.

7. Tozer and Smith, *Men Who Met God*, 23.

8. Sweet, *Out of the Question*, 3, 10.

Chapter 3

1. "Who Is the Devil, Part I" (Harvest Online: Harvest Christian Fellowship), http://www.harvest.org/church/index.php/8/20/56.htm.

2. Charles C. Ryrie, *Basic Theology* (Chicago: Victor Books, 1995), 144.

3. Donald Grey Barnhouse, *The Invisible War* (Grand Rapids: Zondervan, 1965), 26–27.

4. See, for example, Numbers 21:6–9; 2 Kings 18:4; Psalm 91:13, 58:4; Isaiah 14:29; 59:5; 2 Corinthians 11:3; Revelation 9:19, 12:9, 20:2.

5. Noel Due, *Created for Worship* (Fearn, Ross-shire, Scotland: Christian Focus Publications, Ltd., 2005), 51.

6. Martin Luther, "Lectures on Genesis 1–5," *Luther's Works* (Concordia), 259, quoted in ibid., 50.

7. Due, *Created for Worship*, 51.

8. http://en.wikipedia.org/wiki/World_War_II_casualties.

9. Ibid.

10. Ibid.

Chapter 4

1. Beth Moore, *The Patriarchs* (Nashville: Lifeway, 2005), 12.

2. For a comparison of the worship of the gods of Abram's home region with the worship of Yahweh, see Ross, *Recalling the Hope of Glory*, 128–30.

3. http://www.searchgodsword.org/enc/isb/view.cgi?number=T9007.

4. *Lord* always means covenant God. The word is a translation of the Hebrew word YHWH. The Hebrews would not speak His name, so they used this word to describe "the Lord" (Ross, *Recalling the Hope of Glory*, 142–44).

5. The English rendering of the Hebrew *YHWH*, the name of the God of Israel. From this word we get the English word *Jehovah*, the name we use for God. *Yahweh* is synonymous with *Elohim*, "the God of all of you."

6. For interesting reading on this encounter, see Moore, *The Patriarchs*, 15–18.

7. Though born of Hagar, according to Mesopotamian law, Ishmael was credited to Sarah.

8. Both Jewish and Islamic traditions consider Ishmael the ancestor of the Arab people. *Ishmael* translates as "God will hear" (*Strong's Dictionary*).

9. *WebBible Encyclopedia*, s.v., "Abraham," http://www.christian.answers.net/dictionary/abraham.html (accessed October 25, 2007).

10. Per Wikipedia, the name *Abraham* is "often glossed as *av hamon (goyim)* 'father of many (nations)' per Genesis 17:5, although it does not have any literal meaning in Hebrew" (http://en.wikipedia.org/wiki/Abraham#_note-0, accessed October 25, 2007). Wikipedia cites JewishEncyclopedia.com, which says, "The form 'Abraham' yields no sense in Hebrew."

11. *Isaac* means "laughter."

12. Blackaby and Owen, *Worship*.

Chapter 5

1. http://lexicorient.com/e.o/maat.htm.

2. *Pharaoh* was the ancient Egyptian name for the office of kingship. The term began as a reference to the king's palace, but the meaning loosened over the course of Egyptian history until in the late period it was interchangeable with the Egyptian word for *king*. Such rulers were believed to be the incarnation of Horus, the god of light (http://en.wikipedia.org/wiki/pharaoh.htm).

3. http://lexicorient.com/e.o/horus.htm.

4. http://lexicorient.com/e.o/pharaoh.htm.

5. http://lexicorient.com/e.o/maat.htm.

6. Ibid.

7. Due, *Created for Worship*, 72–74.

8. Some translators say that these may have been fleas or lice, instead of gnats (http://en.wikipedia.org/wiki/Plagues_of_Egypt). The Hebrew meaning of this word is unclear. But whatever the correct translation, the insect in question was most certainly an annoyance.

9. http://www.everything2.com/index.pl?node_id=1012896.

10. http://www.crystalinks.com/egyptgods6.html.

11. http://www.seedofabraham.com/10_Plagues.html.

12. Ibid.

13. http://www.enduringword.com/commentaries/0209.htm.

14. http://www.bartleby.com/81/745.html.

15. http://www.bible.org/page.php?page_id=138.

16. en.wikipedia.org/wiki/Ptah.

17. www.egyptian-gods.net/imhotep.php.

18. http://www.padfield.com/2002/egypt_2.html.

Chapter 6

1. Willie Morris, *Parade*, available at http://www.sermonillustrations.com/a-z/f/ friendship.htm.

2. Will L. Thompson, "Jesus Is All the World to Me," *New Century Hymnal* (East Liverpool, OH: Will L. Thompson Co., 1904), vv. 1 and 4. Available at http:// www.cyberhymnal.org/htm/j/a/jallworl.htm.

3. Joseph C. Ludgate, "A Friend in Jesus," in the Salvation Army's *The Young Soldier* (1898), available at http://www.cyberhymnal.org/htm/f/r/friendwj.htm.

4. John Trent, *Men of Action* (Winter 1993), 5, on http://www.sermonillustrations. com/a-z/a/affirmation.htm.

5. "When Moses came down from Mount Sinai . . . , he didn't know that the skin of his face glowed because he had been speaking with GOD" (Ex. 34:29 MSG).

Chapter 7

1. *Matthew Henry's Concise Commentary of the Bible*, http://mhc.biblecommenter.com/joshua/5.htm.

2. *John Wesley's Notes on the Bible*, http://wes.biblecommenter.com/joshua/5.htm.

3. Ibid.

4. http://www.answersingenesis.org/creation/v21/i2/jericho.asp#f4.

5. Oswald Chambers, *My Utmost for His Highest*, July 7 and 8.

Chapter 8

1. http://www.jesuswalk.com/joshua/canaanite-religion.htm.

2. Baal-Berith was identical to Baal-zebub (the ba'al of flies), images of whom the Jewish worshippers would often carry in their pockets, so they could retrieve them and from time to time kiss the images. (*JewishEncyclopedia.com*, s.v. "Baal-Berith," http://www.jewishencyclopedia.com/view.jsp?artid=4&letter=B. Accessed November 9, 2007.)

3. Richard J. Foster et al., *The Renovaré Spiritual Formation Bible* (San Francisco: Harper San Francisco, 2006), 405–6.

4. David S. Broder, quoted in Rudolph W. Giuliani, *Leadership Through the Ages: A Collection of Favorite Quotations* (New York: Miramax Books, 2003), 29.

Chapter 9

1. Henrietta C. Mears, *What the Bible Is All About* (Colorado Springs: Regal Books, 1998), 131.

2. Richard J. Foster et al., *The Renovaré Spiritual Formation Bible* (San Francisco: Harper San Francisco, 2006), 797.

3. John C. Maxwell, *The 21 Irrefutable Laws of Leadership*, with a foreword by Zig Ziglar (Nashville: Thomas Nelson, 1998), 215–20.

Chapter 10

1. http://www.gotquestions.org/kings-Israel-Judah.html.

2. *WebBible Encyclopedia*, s.v., "Ahaziah," http://www.christiananswers.net/dictionary/ (accessed November 16, 2007).

3. http://www.bible-history.com/isbe/A/ATHALIAH/

4. *WebBible Encyclopedia*, s.vv., "Jehoram," http://www.christiananswers.net/dictionary/ (accessed November 16, 2007).

5. A. W. Tozer, *The Root of the Righteous* (Camp Hill, PA: Christian Publications, Inc., 1997) 84–85.

6. Wikipedia, s.vv., "U.S. Army War College," http://en.wikipedia.org/wiki/U.S._Army_War_College, accessed November 15, 2007.

7. Joyce Meyer, *The Battle Belongs to the Lord: Overcoming Life's Struggles Through Worship* (Nashville: FaithWords, 2002), 13.

Chapter 11

1. Genser Smith, "Sweeter as the Days Go By," 1961.

Chapter 12

1. Adapted from a sermon outline by Melvin L. Worthington, ThD, EdD.

2. For more on the names of God, visit http://www.allaboutgod.com/names-of-god.htm.

Chapter 13

1. http://en.wikipedia.org/wiki/I-35W_Mississippi_River_Bridge   (accessed December 3, 2007).

2. Elmer L. Towns, *Praying the Book of Job* (Shippensburg, PA: Destiny Image, 2006), 125.

3. Mears, *What the Bible Is All About*, 194.

4. *Merriam-Webster's 11th Collegiate Dictionary*, s.v., "fear."

5. Steven K. Scott, *The Richest Man Who Ever Lived* (Colorado Springs: Water Brook Press, 2007), 248.

6. http://cf.blueletterbible.org/lang/lexicon/lexicon.cfm?strongs=H3374.

7. http://thesaurus.reference.com, s.v., "worship."

8. Cathy Lynn Grossman, "The Gospel of Billy Graham: Inclusion," *USA Today*, May 15, 2005, http://www.usatoday.com/news/religion/2005-05-15-graham-cover_x.htm.

9. Steven K. Scott, author of *The Richest Man Who Ever Lived* (see note 5 of this chapter) has been reading a Proverb a day for more than thirty-five years. He has used its principles to build multimillion-dollar businesses, and continues to use them to promote good business ethics.

Chapter 14

1. Tremper Longman III, in Foster, *Renovaré Spiritual Formation Bible*, 945.

2. Those wishing to delve deeper into the authorship of the book of Ecclesiastes can visit the Quartz Hill School of Theology Web site at http://www.theology.edu/biblesurvey/eccles.htm. There you will find an excellent outline of the book, as well as arguments both in favor of and against Solomonic authorship.

3. Mick Jagger and Keith Richards, "(I Can't Get No) Satisfaction" (UK: London Records, 1965).

4. http://www.jewishvirtuallibrary.org/jsource/biography/Solomon.html.

5. Paul Frances Webster, "Love Is a Many-Splendored Thing," music by Sammy Fain.

6. William Smith, *Smith's Bible Dictionary*, s.v. "Molech," http://www.studylight.org/dic/sbd/view.cgi?number=T3046.

7. Tremper Longman III, in Foster, *Renovaré Spiritual Formation Bible*, 943.

8. Michael Gerson, "Teen Sex Trends Worry Evangelicals," *Reporter News* (Abilene), July 29, 2007, http://www.reporternews.com/news/2007/jul/29/teen-sex-trends-worry-evangelicals/.

9. Dirk Johnson and Hilary Shenfield, "Preachers and Porn," *Newsweek*, April 2004.

10. Kenneth Woodward, "Sex, Morality and the Protestant Minister," *Newsweek*, July 28, 1997, 62.

11. Catholic News Service, "Clergy Abuse Statistics at a Glance," February 27, 2004, http://www.catholicnews.com/data/abuse/abuse12.htm.

12. Information in this paragraph is from Douglas Winnail, "The Return of Epidemic Disease," *Tomorrow's World* 3, no. 5, http://www.tomorrowsworld.org/cgi-bin/tw/tw-mag.cgi?category=Magazine14&item=1104085088.

Chapter 15

1. Ross, Recalling the Hope of Glory, 329–31.

2. David Kinnaman, *Unchristian* (Grand Rapids: Baker Books, 2007), 47.

3. A. W. Tozer, *The Attributes of God*, 194.

4. Ibid.

5. Miller Cunningham, Lecture—Ten Things Every Worshipper Should Know, Liberty University Center for Worship, February 7, 2008.

6. Tozer, *The Attributes of God*, 195.

7. http://cf.blueletterbible.org/lang/lexicon/lexicon.cfm?strongs=05162.

8. http://cf.blueletterbible.org/lang/lexicon/lexicon.cfm?strongs=3340.

9. F. F. Bruce, *The Acts of the Apostles* [Greek Text Commentary] (London: Tyndale, 1952), 97.

10. Melancthon Williams Jacobus, *Notes on the Gospels, Critical and Explanatory* (Edinburgh: William Oliphant and Co., 1863) 158, note 12.

Introduction to Part II

1. http://en.wikipedia.org/wiki/Timeline_of_Jerusalem.

2. http://en.wikipedia.org/wiki/Jewish_Temple.

3. Ervin N. Hershberger, *Seeing Christ in the Tabernacle* (Fairfax, VA: Choice Books, 1995), 10. Tabernacle scriptures include: thirteen chapters in Exodus, eighteen passages in Leviticus, thirteen chapters in Numbers, two references in Deuteronomy, and four segments in Hebrews.

4. Ibid., 15–46. This is an excellent book for those who wish to study the parallels between Christ and the Old Testament tabernacle. I highly recommend this work.

5. Robert Vaughn, *God's Big Picture* (Downers Grove, IL: InterVarsity Press, 2002), 118.

Chapter 16

1. Written by a Jewish Holocaust victim, http://lifestudentoutreach.wordpress.com/2008/01/16/jamfest-recap/.

2. See Luke 1:46–56 for Mary's song of praise to God following Gabriel's announcement.

3. http://cf.blueletterbible.org/lang/lexicon/lexicon.cfm?strongs=4352&t=KJV.

4. Here mankind got its first glimpse of the Trinity: God the Father speaking, God the Holy Spirit descending, and God the Son being divinely and publicly endorsed.

5. Noel Due, *Created for Worship*, 19.

6. Oswald Chambers, *My Utmost for His Highest*, August 23.

Chapter 17

1. Noel Due, *Created for Worship*, 19.

2. Ross, *Recalling the Hope of Glory*, 396–97. According to Ross, the wine brought together three significant Old Testament passages: Exodus 24:8, Moses and the old covenant at Sinai; Jeremiah 31:31–34, the prophecy of a new covenant to be instituted at the end of the age; and, Isaiah 52:13–53:12, He was wounded for our transgressions, etc.

3. Ibid., 405.

4. The song was probably taken from Psalm 118. According to Ross (403), "Christians who use 'Hosannah' and 'Blessed is he who comes in the name of the Lord' in their worship liturgy are celebrating the fulfillment of the divinely inspired hymns used in Passover."

5. Laura Sheahen, "The Resurrection of Jesus: An Interview with Lee Strobel," http://www.beliefnet.com/story/166/story_16690_1.html.

Chapter 18

1. LYNTYS.net©2006 by Dr. Troy Bush, Pace, Florida.

2. Ross, *Recalling the Hope of Glory*, 415.

3. David Peterson, *Engaging with God: A Biblical Theology of Worship* (Downers Grove, IL: InterVarsity Press, 1992), 143–44.

4. Ibid., 159–60.

Chapter 19

1. Peterson, *Engaging with God*, 180–82.

2. Warren Wiersbe, *Real Worship* (Nashville: Thomas Nelson, 1986), 124–25.

3. Ibid., 123.

4. See, for example, Madeline Levine, *The Price of Privilege: How Parental Pressure and Material Advantage Are Creating a Generation of Disconnected and Unhappy Kids* (New York: HarperCollins, 2006).

5. Robin Abcarian and John Horn, "Underwhelmed by It All: For the 12-to-24 Set, Boredom Is a Recreational Hazard," *Los Angeles Times*, 7 Aug 2006. http://www.latimes.com/entertainment/news/la-et-pollmain7aug07,0,1745679.story?coll=la-home-headlines.

6. Noel Due, *Created for Worship*, 27.

7. http://www.wsmv.com/news/13583844/detail.html; http://en.wikipedia.org/wiki/Susan_Smith; http://www.msnbc.msn.com/id/18807327/.

8. Peterson, *Engaging with God*, 187–88.

9. An excellent resource for studying the gifts of the Spirit is *God's Plan for Man*, by Finis Jennings Dake (Lawrenceville, GA: Dake Bible Sales, 1949), Lesson 26, "The Gifts and Fruit of the Holy Spirit," 455–74. Whether or not you personally subscribe to Dake's views on the gifts, this book presents a most comprehensive explanation of the gifts and their individual and collective purposes.

Chapter 20

1. If you don't believe it, take a look at Wikipedia's "List of Religions and Spiritual Traditions" (http://en.wikipedia.org/wiki/List_of_religions) and see for yourself the number of faiths that honor deities other than the Judeo-Christian God.

2. Chambers, *My Utmost for His Highest*, June 23.

3. http://en.wikipedia.org/wiki/Audiation.

4. *Merriam-Webster's 11th Collegiate Dictionary*, s.v., "hymn."

5. Many scholars believe that Philippians 2:5–11 was a song. Songs of this type were sung often both in the worship and in the day-to-day lives of first-century Christians.

6. The authorship of Hebrews is contested. While most believe that Paul authored Hebrews, Apollos, Barnabas, and others have also been suggested as possible authors.

7. Wiersbe, *Real Worship*, 124–25.

Chapter 21

1. Mears, *What the Bible Is All About*, 659.

2. Warren Wiersbe, *The Bible Expositional Commentary*, 566.

3. Ibid., 576.

4. Quoted in ibid., 571.

5. Ibid., 572.

6. Ibid.

7. Ross, *Recalling the Hope of Glory*, 481. Ross's pattern includes: (1) an invitation to worship [4:1]; (2) singing [4:8]; (3) an acknowledgment of God's greatness [4:11]; (4) the bringing forth of the Word [5:1–7]; (5) prayers intermingled with psalms of praise [5:8–10]; (6) a congregational response with versicles devoted to God's worthiness of praise [5:12]; and (7) a closing doxology, ending with a final "amen" [5:13–14]. "Worship would be greatly enhanced if more churches followed this heavenly pattern," wrote Ross.

Summary

1. http://www.iditarod.com.

2. The Patriarchs are generally thought to be Abraham, Isaac, and Jacob, but Moses and Joseph are also known as patriarchs, and in the New Testament, the twelve sons of Jacob, as well as King David, are referred to as patriarchs.

3. As mentioned in chapter 8, the book of Joshua is also considered among the books of history, though our chapter covering Joshua (chapter 7) is not part of the collection of chapters titled "Worship in the Books of History."

4. Taken in part from Mears, *What the Bible Is All About*; and from Jesus Plus Nothing: Christ Centered Bible Study, "Jesus in All the Books of the Bible," http://www.jesusplusnothing.com/jesus66books.htm

SELECT BIBLIOGRAPHY

Allen, Ronald and Gordon Borror. *Worship: Rediscovering the Missing Jewel*. Portland, OR: Multnomah, 1987.

Arn, Charles. *How to Start a New Service*. Grand Rapids: Baker, 1997.

Arthur, Kay, ed. *The New Inductive Study Bible*. Eugene, OR: Harvest House, 2000.

Best, Harold. *Music Through the Eyes of Faith*. New York: Harper, 1993.

____. *Unceasing Worship: Biblical Perspectives on Worship and the Arts*. Downers Grove, IL: InterVarsity Press, 2003.

Blackaby, Henry and Ron Owen, *Worship: Believers Experiencing God*. Nashville: LifeWay, 2001.

Bloesch, Donald G. *The Church: Sacraments, Worship, Ministry, Mission*. Downers Grove: InterVarsity Press, 2002.

Boschman, Lamar. *Future Worship: How a Changing World Can Enter God's Presence in the New Millennium*. Ventura: Renew, 1999.

Bounds, E. M. *The Complete Works of E. M. Bounds on Prayer*. Grand Rapids: Baker, 1990.

Bruce, F. F. *The Acts of the Apostles*. [Greek Text Commentary] London: Tyndale, 1952.

Calvin, John. "The Epistle of Paul the Apostle to the Hebrews." Calvin's New Testament Commentaries Volume 12. Translated by William B. Johnston. Grand Rapids: Eerdmans, 1963.

Carson, D. A. *For the Love of God, Vol. 1*. Wheaton, IL: Crossway Books, 1998.

____. *For the Love of God, Vol. 2*. Wheaton, IL: Crossway Books, 1999.

352 CALLED TO WORSHIP

_____. *The Cross and Christian Ministry*. Grand Rapids: Baker, 1993.

_____. ed. *Worship: Adoration and Action*. Grand Rapids: Baker, 1993.

_____. ed. *Worship By the Book*. Grand Rapids: Zondervan: 2002.

Chambers, Oswald, J. *My Utmost for His Highest*. London: Oswald Chambers Publications Association, Ltd., 1963.

Chan, Simon. *Liturgical Theology: The Church as Worshiping Community*. Downers Grove: InterVarsity Press, 2006.

Cornwall, Judson. *Let Us Worship*. South Plainfield, NJ: Bridge Publishing, 1983.

Dake, Finis Jennings. *God's Plan for Man*, Lawrenceville, GA: Dake Bible Sales, 1949.

Davidson, Robert. *The Vitality of Worship: A Commentary on the Book of Psalms*. Grand Rapids: Eerdmans, 2000.

Dawn, Marva J. *Reaching Out Without Dumbing Down: A Theology of Worship for the Turn-of-the-Century Culture*. Grand Rapids: Eerdmans, 1995.

Dearborn, Tim A. and Scott Coil, Editors. *Worship at the Next Level: Insight from Contemporary Voices*. Grand Rapids: Baker Books, 2004.

DePree, Max. *Leadership Jazz*. New York: Dell, 1992.

Due, Noel. *Created for Worship*. Fearn, Ross-shire, Scotland: Christian Focus Publications, Ltd., 2005.

Edwards, David M. *Worship Three Sixty Five: The Power of a Worshiping Life*. Nashville: Broadman and Holman, 2006.

Foster, Richard J. ed. *The Renovaré Spiritual Formation Bible*. San Francisco: Harper San Francisco, 2006.

Frame, John M. *Contemporary Worship Music: A Biblical Defense*. Phillipsberg, NJ: P and R Publishing, 1997.

_____. *The Doctrine of God: A Theology of Lordship*. Phillipsburg, NJ: P and R Publishing, 2002.

_____. *Worship in Spirit and Truth*. Phillipsburg, NJ: P and R Publishing, 1996.

Giuliani, Rudolph W. *Leadership Through the Ages: A Collection of Favorite Quotations*. New York: Miramax Books, 2003.

Goossen, Gareth J. *Worship Walk: Where Worship and Life Intersect*. Kitchener, Ontario, Canada, 2004.

Hawn, Michael. *One Bread, One Body: Exploring Cultural Diversity in Worship*. Bethesda: The Alban Institute, 2003.

Hayford, Jack. *Worship His Majesty: How Praising the King of Kings Will Change Your Life*. Ventura: Regal Books, 2000.

Hershberger, Ervin N. *Seeing Christ in the Tabernacle*. Fairfax, VA: Choice Books, 1995.

Hill, Andrew E. *Enter His Courts with Praise: Old Testament Worship for the New Testament Church*. Grand Rapids: Baker, 1993.

Hustad, Donald P. *Jubilate II: Church Music in Worship and Renewal*. Carol Stream, IL: Hope, 1993.

Johansson, Calvin. *Music and Ministry: A Biblical Counterpoint*. Peabody: Hendrickson, 1998.

Kauflin, Bob. *Worship Matters: Leading Others to Encounter the Greatness of God*. Wheaton: Crossway, 2008.

Kendrick, Graham. *Learning to Worship as a Way of Life*. Minneapolis: Bethany House, 1984.

Kidd, Reggie M. *With One Voice: Discovering Christ's Song in Our Worship*. Grand Rapids: Baker, 2005.

Kimball, Dan. *Emerging Worship: Creating Worship Gatherings for New Generations*. Grand Rapids: Zondervan, 2004.

Kinnaman, David. *Unchristian*. Grand Rapids: Baker, 2007.

Kreeft, Peter and Ronald K. Tacelli. *Handbook of Christian Apologetics*. Downers Grove, IL: InterVarsity Press, 1994.

Lane, William L. *Hebrews 9–13*. Word Bible Commentary, 48. Dallas: WORD, 1991.

Lathrop, Gordon W. *Holy Things: A Liturgical Theology*. Minneapolis: Fortress Press, 1993.

Lewis, C. S. *Reflections on the Psalms*. San Diego: Harvest, 1964.

Lewis, C. S. *Christian Reflections*. Grand Rapids: Eerdmans, 1967.

Lotz, Anne Graham. *God's Story*, 2nd ed. Nashville: Thomas Nelson, 1992.

Liesch, Barry. *The New Worship: Straight Talk on Music and the Church*. Grand Rapids: Baker Books, 2001.

Martoia, Ron. *Morph!* Loveland, CO: Group Publishing, 2003.

Martin, Ralph P. *The Worship of God*. Grand Rapids: Eerdmans, 1982.

Man, Ron. *Proclamation and Praise: Hebrews 2:12 and the Christology of Worship*. Eugene, Oregon: Wipf and Stock Publishers, 2007.

Maxwell, John C. *The 21 Irrefutable Laws of Leadership*. Nashville: Thomas Nelson, 1998.

McDonald, James. *Ancient Wisdom*. Nashville: Broadman and Holman, 2006.

McNeal, Reggie. *A Work of Heart*. San Francisco, CA: Jossey-Bass Publishing, 2000.

Mears, Henrietta C. *What the Bible Is All About*. Colorado Springs: Regal Books, 1998.

Meyer, Joyce. *The Battle Belongs to the Lord: Overcoming Life's Struggles Through Worship*. Nashville: FaithWords, 2002.

Miller, Kim, and the Ginghamsburg Church Worship Team. *Handbook for Multi-Sensory Worship, Vol. I*. Nashville: Abingdon, 1999.

Moore, Beth. *The Patriarchs*. Nashville: Lifeway, 2005.

Morgan, Robert J. *On This Day*. Nashville: Thomas Nelson, 1998.

____. *The Red Sea Rules*. Nashville: Thomas Nelson, 2001.

____. *Then Sings My Soul*. Nashville: Thomas Nelson, 2002.

____. *Then Sings My Soul, Book 2*. Nashville: Thomas Nelson, 2003.

Morgenthaler, Sally. Worship Evangelism: Inviting Unbelievers into the Presence of God. Grand Rapids: Zondervan, 1995.

Myers, Kenneth A. *All God's Children and Blue Suede Shoes: Christians and Popular Culture*. Westchester, IL: Crossway, 1989.

Navarro, Kevin J. *The Complete Worship Leader*. Grand Rapids: Baker, 2001.

Ortlund, Anne. *Up with Worship: How to Quit Playing Church*. Nashville: Broadman and Holman, 2001.

Packer, J. I. *Concise Theology*. Wheaton, IL: Tyndale House, 1993.

____. *Knowing God*. Downers Grove, IL: InterVarsity Press, 1993.

Park, Andy. *To Know You More: Cultivating the Heart of the Worship Leader*. Downers Grove: InterVarsity Press, 2002.

Pelikan, Jaroslav, ed., "Lectures on Genesis 1–5" by Martin Luther. St. Louis: Concordia, 1958.

Peterson, David. *Engaging with God: A Biblical Theology of Worship*. Downers Grove, IL: InterVarsity Press, 1992.

Piper, John. *Desiring God*. Sisters, Oregon: Multnomah, 1986.

____. *The Pleasures of God*. Sisters, OR: Multnomah, 1992.

____. *When I Don't Desire God*. Wheaton, IL: Crossway, 2004.

Redman, Matt. *The Heart of Worship Files*. Ventura, California: Regal, 2003.

____. *The Unquenchable Worshipper: Coming Back to the Heart of Worship*. Ventura, CA: Regal, 2001.

Roberts, Vaughan. *God's Big Picture: Tracing the Storyline of the Bible*. Downers Grove, IL: InterVarsity Press, 2002.

____. *True Worship*. Berkshire, UK: Authentic Lifestyle, 2002.

Ross, Allen P. *Recalling the Hope of Glory: Biblical Worship from the Garden to the New Creation*. Grand Rapids: Kregel Academic, 2006.

Ryrie, Charles C. *Basic Theology*. Chicago: Victor Books, 1995.

Scott, Steven K. *The Richest Man Who Ever Lived*. Colorado Springs: Water Brook Press, 2007.

Spanger, Ann. *Praying the Names of God*. Grand Rapids: Zondervan, 2004.

Stone, Nathan. *Names of God*. Chicago: Moody 1944.

Sweet, Leonard. *Out of the Question . . . Into the Mystery: Getting Lost in the God-Life Relationship*. Colorado Springs: WaterBrook Press, 2004.

____. *Post-Modern Pilgrims: First Century Passion for the Twenty-first Century Church*. Nashville: Broadman and Holman Publishing, 2000.

Swindoll, Charles R. *Swindoll's Ultimate Book of Illustrations and Quotes*. Nashville: Thomas Nelson, 1998.

Taylor, Jack R. *The Hallelujah Factor*. Nashville: Broadman, 1983.

Thiessen, Donald. *Psalms, Hymns and Spiritual Songs: What the Bible Says about Music*. Chicago: Cornerstone Press, 1994.

Torrance, James B. "The Place of Jesus Christ in Worship." *Theological Foundations for Ministry*, edited by Ray S. Anderson. Grand Rapids: Eerdmans, 1979.

____. *Worship, Community and the Triune God of Grace*. Downers Grove, IL: InterVarsity Press, 1966.

Torrance, Thomas F. *The Mediation of Christ*. Grand Rapids: Eerdmans, 1983.

____. *Royal Priesthood*, Edinburg: Tweeddale Court, 1955.

Towns, Elmer L. *Praying the Book of Job*. Shippensburg, PA: Destiny Image, 2001.

____. *Praying the Book of Psalms*. Shippensburg, PA: Destiny In a_e, 2001.

____. *Praying the Book of Revelation*. Shippensburg, PA: Destiny Image, 2007.

Tozer, A. W. *The Knowledge of the Holy*. New York: Harper San Francisco, 1978.

____. *The Root of the Righteous*. Camp Hill, PA: Christian Publications, Inc., 1997.

____. *The Pursuit of God*. Camp Hill, PA: Christian Publications, Inc., 1948.

____. *Whatever Happened to Worship? A Call to True Worship*. Camp Hill, PA: WingSpread Publishers, 2006.

____. *Worship: Missing Jewel Evangelism*. Camp Hill, PA: Christian Publications, 1996.

Tozer, A. W. and Gerald B. Smith, *Men Who Met God*. Camp Hill, PA: Wingspread, 2007.

Trent, John. *Men of Action*. Winter, Publication of Today's Family. 1993.

Vander Zee, Leonard J. *Christ, Baptism and the Lord's Supper*. Downers Grove: InterVarsity Press, 2004.

Vaughn, Robert. *God's Big Picture*. Downers Grove, IL: InterVarsity Press, 2002.

Webber, Robert E. *Blended Worship: Achieving Substance and Relevance in Worship*. Peabody, MA: Hendrickson, 1996.

____. *Worship Is a Verb: A Biblical, Historical and Practical Introduction*. Waco, TX: WORD, 1985.

____. *Worship Old and New: A Biblical, Historical, and Practical Introduction*. Revised edition. Grand Rapids: Zondervan Publishing, 1994.

Whaley, Vernon M. *The Dynamics of Corporate Worship*. Grand Rapids: Baker, 2001.

____. *Understanding Music and Worship in the Local Church*. Wheaton: Evangelical Training Association, 2004.

White, James F. *A Brief History of Christian Worship*. Nashville: Abingdon, 1980.

Wiersbe, Warren W. *Real Worship*. Nashville: Thomas Nelson, 1986.

____. *The Bible Expositional Commentary, Vol 1*. Wheaton: Victor Books, 1989.

____. *The Bible Expositional Commentary, Vol 2*. Wheaton: Victor Books, 1989.

Willard, Dallas. *The Spirit of the Disciples: Understanding How God Changes Lives*. San Francisco: Harper and Row, 1988.

Woodward, Kenneth. "Sex, Morality and the Protestant Minister," *Newsweek*, July 28, 1997.

Worthington, Melvin L. *An Analysis of the Addresses to the Asian Assemblies — Revelation 2–3*, A Th. D. Dissertation at Luther Rice Seminary, Jacksonville, FL, 1974.

Wyrtzen, Don. *A Musician Looks at the Psalms*. Nashville: Broadman and Holman, 2004.

WEBSITE, INTERNET AND EMAIL RESOURCES

Commentaries, dictionaries, and reference books

http://www.biblegateway.com

Online, searchable Bible in over 100 versions and 50 languages.

http://www.bible-history.com

Study tool that includes: Collection of Bible maps, study resources, quotes, archaeology, Biblical customs, illustrations, ancient images, museum art, and historical time line of the Bible.

http://cf.blueletterbible.org
Excellent resource for Bible translations and paraphrases. Over 4,000,000 links onsite to over 165,000 pages of concordances, lexicons, dictionaries, commentaries, images, and Bible versions!

http://www.christiananswers.net
A mega-site providing biblical answers to contemporary questions for all ages and nationalities with over 45-thousand files

http://www.crosswalk.com
Bible study tools for spiritual life, preaching, youth ministry, devotionals, children and worship ministry.

http://www.studylight.org
William Smith, *Smith's Bible Dictionary*

http://wes.biblecommenter.com/joshua/5.htm.
John Wesley's Notes on the Bible, Joshua

http://mhc.biblecommenter.com
Matthew Henry's Concise Commentary of the Bible

http://www.christiananswers.net/dictionary
WebBible Encyclopedia and other research resources for worship

http://www.reformed.org/documents/WSC.html.
Westminster Shorter Catechism and other historical documents on worship

http://www.harvest.org
On-line resource from Harvest Christian Fellowship Ministries. Includes spiritual resources, on-line book store, church blog, and a variety of information about Harvest.

Resources for Worship
http://www.1christian.net
A dynamic and comprehensive worship planner based on the web, including: church and team songbooks, event calender, stage planner, song usage tracking, service flow chart, and worship team communication center.

http://www.etaworld.org
Evangelical Training Association is a comprehensive organization dedicated to helping churches equip and build strong disciples, leaders and teachers.

www.messengerfellowship.org
Dedicated to seeing local church ministry teams trained, mobilized and linked together for
the purpose of outreach and evangelism.

http://www.lionshare.org/
The *Lionshare Leadership Group* is a non-profit organization that aims to shape leaders in
the ways of God so they are equipped to live and lead with character, perspective and wisdom within the domains of culture where they have been appointed by God to serve.

http://www.worshipministryu.com
Free on-line worship ministry training by leading teachers.

http://www.worshipteleseminar.com/
Revolutionary online worship training conference designed to equip, empower, and refresh
worship leaders, church personnel, and worship ministry!

http://www.prayerfoundation.org
Prayer Teaching & Global Evangelistic Resources for Global ministry. Thoroughly Evangelical
in content.

http://www.sermonillustrations.com
Thousands of *professionally published* sermons, illustrations, children's sermons, worship
aids, archaeological articles, PowerPoint slides, and dramas by over a hundred different professional writers. Contributors to eSermons are the most recognized names in preaching.

http://www.heartstogod.com/websites.html
Designed for contemporary churches, these websites provide convenient and affordable
resources to help busy worship leaders plan their weekly services.

http://www.worshipideas.com
Free website and email newsletter with practical tips for contemporary worship leaders and
teams. Over 80,000 readers since 2003.

http://www.freeworshipbackgrounds.com
Free, still background images you can download and use with PowerPoint or any worship
projection software like EasyWorship, MediaShout, SundayPlus, etc.

http://www.hymncharts.com
Blended worship on a budget - blend praise and worship songs with these contemporary
hymn arrangements. Instrumental and vocal sheet music, praise band charts.

http://www.worshipmax.com
Research service that finds worship links, resources, freebies and discounts on the Internet. The must-have website for every 21st century worship leader.

http://www.worshipflow.com
Download key changes and underscores for your keyboardist and praise band that will help you to transition smoothly from one praise song to another.

http://www.praisesongstore.com
Download free MP3s of new worship songs and order sheet music and charts.

http://www.nationalworshipleaderconference.com
Annual conference of pastors, worship leaders and teachers from within the Church across the nation and around the world.

http://christianmusic.suite101.com/article.cfm/christian_sheet_music_websites
Suite recommends websites as good resources for the worship leaders and musicians looking for sheet music, or guitar and piano tabs for Christian music.

http://www.worshipdirector.org
Song and schedule management for worship leading.

http://www.makeusholy.org
Established for the purpose of bringing continued spiritual renewal into the church through worship, discipleship and prayer ministry.

www.worshipmusic.com
Their mission is to increase worship on the earth! This is an on-line story for worship & praise music by Vineyard, Integrity Music, Maranatha, Worship Together, Hosanna!, Kingsway, Passion/sixsteps, Hillsongs, Brentwood Benson and quality independent & import worship music.

www.maranathamusic.com
Born out of the local ministry of Calvary Chapel in Costa Mesa, California, Maranatha! Music serves churches globally by training worship leaders.

http://www.worshipleader.com
Highly respected, popular and effective magazine for worship leaders, including: song story; worship leader profile; tech trends; feature reviews of books, magazines, and recordings.

http://www.268generation.com/2.0/splash5.htm
The official website of Passion Conferences.

http://www.calvin.edu/worship
Practical resources for congregational leaders and scholarly works on the history, theology, and practice of worship worldwide. Makes available tools and materials for worship planning, preparation, and pastor/lay leadership training. Encourages the development of creativity in liturgical expression, including dance and drama; language arts, music, technology, visual arts, and media arts.

http://www.worshiptogether.com
Worship songs, music and resources. Includes on line community, blog, new song café and devotionals.

http://www.theooze.com
Dedicated to the emerging Church culture, providing a place for open communication on issues of community, culture, faith and ministry.

http://www.willowcreek.com/servicebuilder/
Resources worship leadership, worship arts, students, children, group life, evangelism and stewardship.

http://www.ccli.com/usa/default.aspx
Christian Copyright Licensing International (CCLI) was established in 1988 to provide churches with simple, affordable solutions to complex copyright issues. CCLI helps churches maintain their integrity and avoid costly lawsuits, while also giving churches the freedom to worship expressively and spontaneously.

Schools and Institutes of Worship

Calvin Institute of Christian Worship (CICW)
(www.calvin.edu/worship)
The Calvin Institute of Christian Worship promotes the scholarly study of the theology, history, and practice of Christian worship and the renewal of worship in worshiping communities across North America and beyond. The CICW is an interdisciplinary study and ministry center dedicated to both understanding and revitalizing the practice of Christian worship. CICW partners with congregations, denominations, parachurch organizations, professional organizations, and publishers to further advance their mission. Works with Calvin College to provide undergraduate and graduate degrees in worship studies.

The Center for Worship—Liberty University
(www.liberty.edu/academics/arts-sciences/worship)
Dedicated to training and equipping the next generation of worship leaders for the evangelical church. Provides undergraduate, graduate and post graduate degrees in worship studies. Resident and distant learning education available.

The Robbert Webber Institute of Worship Studies
(http://www.iwsfla.org/)
Offers graduate education in worship studies through distant education leading to the Doctor of Worship Studies (D.W.S.) or the Master of Worship Studies (M.W.S) degrees. Primarily focuses on adult, professional education.

The Taize Community
- international prayer community in France that focuses on prayer and meditation

The Iona Community
- international community in Scotland

CPSIA information can be obtained at www.ICGtesting.com
Printed in the USA
LVOW06s2343190914

404831LV00005B/18/P